P9-DHS-476

SPACE AND PLACE
Focused Inquiry I & II

2018–2019 Edition

VCU Department of Focused Inquiry
University College

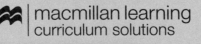
macmillan learning
curriculum solutions

Copyright © 2018 by the Department of Focused Inquiry, University College, Virginia Commonwealth University

Focused Inquiry Textbook Committee, eds.

Photos provided by Hayden-McNeil, LLC are owned or used under license

Cover design by Mohammed Ullah. Mohammed Ullah is currently a second-year student at VCU, majoring in Business Administration. His hobbies include drawing, painting, and creating things.

All rights reserved.

Permission in writing must be obtained from the publisher before any part of this work may be reproduced or transmitted in any form or by any means, electronic or mechanical, including photocopying and recording, or by any information storage or retrieval system.

Printed in the United States of America

10 9 8 7 6 5 4 3 2 1

ISBN 978-1-5339-0794-3

Macmillan Learning Curriculum Solutions
14903 Pilot Drive
Plymouth, MI 48170
www.macmillanlearning.com

Pallo 0794-3 F18

Acknowledgments

Rabih Alameddine—"Hope and Home." *Freeman's Home: The Best New Writing on Home*, ed. John Freeman, New York: Grove Press, 2017, pp. 79–88. Reprinted with permission from the author and Aragi, Inc.

Acknowledgments and copyrights are continued at the back of the book on pages 384–388, which constitute an extension of the copyright page.

macmillan learning
curriculum solutions

Sustainability
Hayden-McNeil's standard paper stock uses a minimum of 30% post-consumer waste. We offer higher % options by request, including a 100% recycled stock. Additionally, Hayden-McNeil Custom Digital provides authors with the opportunity to convert print products to a digital format. Hayden-McNeil is part of a larger sustainability initiative through Macmillan Learning. Visit http://sustainability.macmillan.com to learn more.

bedford/st. martin's • hayden-mcneil
w.h. freeman • worth publishers

EXPLORING *SPACE AND PLACE* IN FOCUSED INQUIRY I & II

As you look at this page, where are you right now? How does that location make it easier or harder to focus on this text, or make the experience of reading more or less meaningful? The question of how place and space matter will be a central one in Focused Inquiry, and the readings in this book consider different ways to reflect on and learn from the concepts of *space and place.* They offer various responses to questions such as:

How do we distinguish between space and place? How does place shape who we were, are, or may become? How do we, in turn, shape places for our own ends? How do different individuals, cultures, and communities perceive, construct, and utilize space? What are the ethical implications of who has access to and uses a space?

Through an investigation of the theme of *space and place* in these readings, we will reflect on familiar places and spaces in unfamiliar ways. We will question how spaces inform our experiences of politics, economics, and understandings of self and other. While all locations are fertile ground for study, possible sites to begin our work could include the local, global, virtual, or hypothetical; spaces either human or nonhuman or both; places that are natural, rural, or urban; and places that are in transition from one thing or way of being to another. Finally, we'll see our study of space and place as rooted in the specific places of Virginia Commonwealth University and the Department of Focused Inquiry, locations that will impact you as you engage with them every day.

TABLE OF CONTENTS

THEMATIC TABLE OF CONTENTS

To aid in the exploration of this reader, we have provided the following arrangement of texts based on the dominant themes found within. In many cases, selections are cross-listed. While the possibilities for cross-listing are potentially limitless—and we certainly encourage you to discover other ways of thinking about these texts—our hope is that this list will serve as a point of entry for understanding the readings that follow.

The City

Defining Space & Place

History & Memory

Home

Humans Meet the Nonhuman World

Identity

Outer Space

Travel, Border-Crossing, Migration, and Colonization

The United States

The University

PREFACE

Welcome

By Melissa Johnson

"Those persons, whom nature has endowed with genius and virtue, should be rendered by liberal education worthy to receive, and able to guard the sacred deposit of the rights and liberties of their fellow citizens; and…they should be called to that charge without regard to wealth, birth or other accidental condition or circumstance."

—Thomas Jefferson, 1779

"Education is by far the biggest and the most hopeful of the Nation's enterprises. Long ago our people recognized that education for all is not only democracy's obligation but its necessity. Education is the foundation of democratic liberties. Without an educated citizenry alert to preserve and extend freedom, it would not long endure."

—Truman Commission on Higher Education, 1947

"The teacher is of course an artist, but being an artist does not mean that he or she can make the profile, can shape the students. What the educator does in teaching is to make it possible for the students to become themselves."

— Paulo Freire, *We Make the Road by Walking: Conversations on Education and Social Change*, 1990

Welcome to Focused Inquiry, VCU's unique, interdisciplinary, first-year academic seminar! This year will be the twelfth year UNIV 111 (Focused Inquiry 1) and UNIV 112 (Focused Inquiry 2) have been required courses at Virginia Commonwealth University. In 2006, a small group of first-year students took UNIV 111 and UNIV 112 rather than ENGL 101 as a pilot. The following year, the two courses were required for all students as the foundation of the new core curriculum. In the time since, first-year retention and the number of students in good academic standing have improved dramatically—over ten percent—and five-year graduation rates of students who take these courses and UNIV 200 is almost ten percent better than those of students who do not. These improvements and achievements are due in part to the type of work you will do in this course this semester and in part to the relationships you will form with your classmates and instructor, with your University and your community as a result of that work.

These courses will help you lay the foundation for a successful academic and professional career, but most importantly, they will help prepare you to take your place as a citizen in a democracy—the highest aim of liberal and democratic education throughout history as can be seen in the first two epigraphs above.

The University College and Department of Focused Inquiry were founded and operate on the principles of liberal education. According to the American Association of Universities and Colleges:

> Liberal Education is an approach to learning that empowers individuals and prepares them to deal with complexity, diversity, and change. It provides students with broad knowledge of the wider world (e.g., science, culture, and society) as well as in-depth study in a specific area of interest. A liberal education helps students develop a sense of social responsibility, as well as strong and transferable intellectual and practical skills such as communication, analytical and problem-solving skills, and a demonstrated ability to apply knowledge and skills in real-world settings.

UNIV 111 and UNIV 112, which are taken early in a student's University studies—before most courses in the major—focus on "broad knowledge of the wider world" (sometimes referred to as general education) as well as "transferable intellectual and practical skills." The courses' theme, Space and Place, gives us a broad focus for exploring questions and ideas through a variety of disciplinary and interdisciplinary perspectives in order to practice and develop an array of important academic and life skills. These skills are: written and oral communication, critical thinking, information fluency, ethical reasoning, collaboration, and quantitative reasoning.

In your Focused Inquiry class this year, you will engage with your own experience and the experiences and ideas of others. You will ask big important questions about real issues and you will seek out and consider a variety of responses to those questions. You will think, write, revise, present, re-think, revise, compose, and grow in understanding with a small group of fellow learners and an instructor whose primary responsibility is teaching and learning. You will do these things because your learning and your success as a student and as a person matter to your instructor and to VCU. Both have invested in you. Your instructor has studied, trained, and continually strives to be an effective teacher, an "artist" of teaching as Freire describes it in the epigraph above. VCU has invested in you by putting you in a small class with this highly trained and learning-centered instructor for one or two semesters. I hope you will make the most of those investments.

As the Chair of the Department of Focused Inquiry and an instructor of Focused Inquiry courses since 2007, I can offer some brief advice for students who wish to make the most of their experience in Focused Inquiry.

Show Up

This one seems obvious, but it is the most common reason that students do not succeed in Focused Inquiry and in college. It is also the reason we have a Department attendance policy (see your syllabus). UNIV 111 and UNIV 112 are process-based courses and students have to be present and engaged to keep up with the processes of thinking, writing, presenting, and composing that the courses include as well as to collaborate effectively with their classmates. Most students will get sick at least once in a semester and most will have transportation

or family or relationship problems at least once. That is why we allow a certain number of absences and that is why you should reserve your absences for those occasions. Otherwise, you will certainly miss out on some great discussion, challenging activity, or useful resource that will make your thinking and writing stronger and better.

Talk and Listen

As important as showing up is, it is not enough just to show up. Successful students show up prepared and ready to talk and listen to others talk about the reading, the assignment, the class activity, or the project they are working on. They show up thoughtful, curious, and ready to exchange ideas. They make the most of the investment they are making in an education and the investment VCU is making in them by helping to create a space where students can speak freely, be heard, and listen to and learn from other students.

Be Open—Delay Judgment

Successful students are curious and open. They are eager and willing to entertain other perspectives because they want to arrive at the *best* answer, proposal, solution, or argument—not just the first or most common answer. Many of you will have to re-discover your curiosity and openness after twelve or more years of standardized testing which often calls for on-the-spot certainty, for argument without questioning and exploration. Your focused inquiry classroom will give you a place to do that—to re-discover wonder, to ask why? And what if? And what is the right thing to do?

Dig Deep—Go Beyond First Thoughts

Openness and the willingness to delay judgment—to "idle in uncertainty" as it was described by the English poet John Keats—will allow you to dig deep and to take your thinking to unfamiliar and hopefully compelling and surprising places. Spending time with a question or topic or problem by seeking out and grappling with other perspectives will allow you to ask better questions and to arrive at more informed and better supported conclusions.

Take Risks

Here—at the beginning of your college education—is the ideal place to take risks in your thinking and learning. The beauty of the Focused Inquiry curriculum is that it rewards discovery and risk-taking because it asks you to make meaning through a process of inquiry rather than to learn an existing body of knowledge. Making meaning is a joyfully messy adventure with many side-trips and detours. Embrace the bumps and even the dead-ends because true success can only be built on a series of failures.

Believe in Yourself

You have earned a place at VCU and VCU is a great place for all students to succeed. We believe in your ability to be successful, but you can only achieve your potential if you believe in yourself. This is often difficult to do if you feel that you don't fit in or that college is not the right place for you or that you are falling behind. These feelings are common among students who are the first in their families to attend college or who encounter setbacks in their studies, but there are many resources on campus to help you overcome these feelings and move forward.

Use Your Resources

Your Focused Inquiry instructor, the Counseling Center, the Well, the Writing Center, the Campus Learning Center, and your academic advisor are all part of your team. Take advantage of their office hours and services to ensure your success. ■

Wishing you a wonder-filled semester in UNIV 111 or UNIV 112,
Melissa Johnson, Ph.D.
Chair and Associate Professor
Department of Focused Inquiry

AUTHOR PROFILE

Dr. Melissa Johnson began teaching Focused Inquiry as an Assistant Professor in the University College in 2007, served as Curriculum Coordinator for University 111/112 from 2009–2014, and was promoted to Associate Professor and elected Chair of the Department of Focused Inquiry in 2014. She teaches UNIV 111, 112, 200, 211, ENGL 215, and ENGL/WMNS 384. Previously, Dr. Johnson was Writing Center Director and Assistant Professor of English at Newberry College in Newberry, SC, where she taught composition, literature, and creative writing courses. She earned an M.F.A. in Creative Writing (poetry) and a Ph.D. in twentieth-century British Literature and Women's Studies from the University of South Carolina. Her research interests include the scholarship of teaching and learning, cultural studies, gender and Modernism, postcolonial literature, and poetry.

A Message from the Writing Center Director

By Brian McTague

Welcome to VCU and the beginning of an exciting new chapter in your life! VCU has a ton of wonderful resources, including the Writing Center, to help you develop the tools you need to succeed in college and your professional life. Writing is one of the most important of these tools, but it is often undervalued and misunderstood. At the Writing Center, we can help you think about your writing in more meaningful and exciting ways. By having conversations about your ideas and how to best articulate them, we will help you to see the potential you have to make a difference in your life and learning through your writing. As scholar R.D. Walshe says in the article, "The Learning Power of Writing," "I am about to use humanity's second greatest invention, writing, with which I will take language from the invisible mind and make it visible on paper where I can work on it with full attention until it becomes the best thinking, the best learning, of which I am capable" (22). At the Writing Center, we will help you reach new levels of capability.

Writing is special in that it is both a transformative learning experience for you, as well as a way to share your thoughts and ideas with others. It has limitless potential to profoundly influence both the writer and reader. Emily Dickinson, the American poet, famously said, "I know nothing in the world that has as much power as a word." Yet, many people still say they do not enjoy writing. This is understandable—after all, writing is hard work. There are various reasons why this might be true: not knowing how to get started on a piece, exploring the unknown alone, or memories of stressful essay exams. Regardless of the source of any writing anxiety you have, or even if you love to write and have been succeeding at it for years, the Writing Center is here to help you make the transition to successful academic writing. Along the way, we may help debunk some myths about writing: that it has to be done in isolation, that it's only about surface correctness, and that using a resource like the Center means you cannot manage on your own. Overall, we strive to make more confident writers who are able to best articulate their ideas. That's something *everyone* can benefit from.

As you become a more confident writer, you will see that writing is so much more than many people realize. Especially at the university level, writing becomes more than just a way to show what you have learned. It is about thinking critically, discovering new things, making meaning out of what you find, and guiding your reader to understand and value that meaning. In the best writing, you continue to think and learn *as you write* and as you get feedback from others. That might all sound challenging, and it is, but in the best way possible. Your collegiate experience will be that much more profound if you fully engage on all levels, discovering new things about yourself and the world you live in. Writing is one of the best ways you can do this, and the Writing Center is here to help you accomplish it.

Our consultants are going to ask you a lot of questions—to get to know about you and your interests, to understand your ideas as they pertain to your assignment, and to help you figure out how you can best articulate those ideas. We're going to ask you to read your work aloud. This is not meant to embarrass you or make you feel self-conscious, but to get you to fully engage with your work. Reading your written words out loud is a powerful way for you to truly gain ownership over your work. You will also be surprised how much proofreading and editing you can get done while reading out loud ("Oh, that comma shouldn't be there!" "That's not the word I meant to use!"), so we can then concentrate on the bigger picture with you. Students are often surprised to find out we do not just read and "correct" papers. It is not that editing and proofreading are not important—they are—but they do not represent the meaningful learning opportunities that, as a learning support service, the Writing Center is dedicated to.

It is this "bigger picture" we are dedicated to helping you understand and learn from. What does this mean? Well, again, it is your ideas and how you are articulating them. As writers, we usually know what we want to say, but finding the best, most academic way of saying it can be more difficult. This is especially true when writing is viewed as an isolated activity, which is something most of us have been taught through our elementary and high school experiences. Through research and experience, however, we have found that dialogue with others is an integral part of the writing process. What better way to figure out how to best represent your ideas than by sharing them with someone else—someone who is not your professor. You never want your instructor to be the first person to read your work. By meeting with a consultant at the Writing Center *before* you turn in a paper, you're sharing and talking about your work with another person—someone who will give you honest feedback to help you revise and strengthen your work.

As I mentioned, we are here to help you evolve into a more self-assured writer who can best articulate the complicated ideas we engage with in college. The more you talk to us, the more confidence you will gain about your work. It makes sense, because you need to talk and think things through in order to make sense of them and figure out what you want to say—and *how* to say it. Academic writing is often different from the school writing you've done in the past. Professors expect a more nuanced, higher level of engagement and critical thinking. Consultants at the Writing Center are all experienced in excelling at that type of writing. We also participate in ongoing training and development so we can best help all students with all types of writing. We are not just here for you while you are in Focused Inquiry, but also for all other classes you are taking, be it Biology, Psychology, Business, or English. We are also here for other writing projects you may have, such as creative work or personal statements. We will continue to be here for your entire time at VCU. Join us and start your journey to becoming the most confident and capable writer you can be! ■

Works Cited

Walshe, R.D. "The Learning Power of Writing." *The English Journal* 76.6 (1987): 22–27. Print.

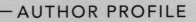

AUTHOR PROFILE

Brian McTague is the Director of the campus Writing Center, which is part of the Student Success learning support services offered to VCU students. He manages a staff of over forty Writing Center consultants who work with a wide variety of students from across the entire university.

Brian received his Master's degree in literature from the VCU English department in 2011. During his time as a grad student, he worked as a consultant in the Writing Center and moved into the Center's Coordinator position after graduation. He was promoted to Assistant Director in 2012 and became the Director in 2013. Since 2010, he has also taught writing and literature classes, including ENGL 491, ENGL 367, ENGL 215, and UNIV 200.

One of Brian's ongoing initiatives is to ensure Writing Center services reach as many VCU students as possible, including First Generation students, English language learners, students with learning differences, and those from the STEM fields. Making the Writing Center a safe, inclusive place for all students to engage in dialogue about their writing is Brian's personal passion and primary professional goal.

Brian is a board member of the Southeastern Writing Center Association (SWCA) and its state group, VA-SWCA, which brings together writing center staff from across the region. Brian was chair and host of the 2018 SWCA conference here at VCU, which brought together over 300 writing professionals and student tutors from around the country.

Brian's presentations and publications include work on personal statements, reflective writing, training and developing writing consultants, scientific writing in writing centers, and writing centers as safe zones. He is currently working with a colleague, Joe Essid, on the anthology, *At the Center of Change*, which aims to offer solutions for writing centers adapting to transitions in the larger academic world.

What Is Focused Inquiry?

by Ruth Walston

1ST PLACE

As I signed up for classes at VCU for the first time, it seemed I had already missed some sort of memo. I read through the usual list of required subjects (math, science, history, etc.) and then there was something called Focused Inquiry. What on earth was Focused Inquiry? By design, this would be only the first question this class would have me asking.

It seems the soundtrack of life today is just a chorus of arguments—a chorus that feels near impossible to tune out. Everywhere I look, cases are being made: any opinion is subject to scrutiny, and each issue lives at the center of some massive, never-ending debate. I was never a fan of debate class, so this chorus always felt a bit like a cacophony before Focused Inquiry. I had always preferred to keep my ideas and feelings inside of myself. Asking and answering questions only within my own headspace, I figured that, as long as I could justify my opinions to myself, that was enough. However, as everyone finds out during the transition into adult life, this lone wolf mentality is not sustainable, especially as the influence of mass communication broadens. FI became my opportunity to learn how to be a better participant in the Information Age.

Whether we are conscious of it or not, we are constantly taking in information from the world around us. It is easy to let our surroundings rush around us and influence our lives without our noticing, but FI encourages us to confront them—through research, analysis, and reason.

In an FI classroom, we dissect historical and current events; nothing is outside the scope of this course. Discussions can address anything from the dynamics of the opiate crisis and the ethics of capital punishment to pop culture trends. Very often, the most satisfying class discussions are the ones marked by unforeseen tangents, which, of course, only lead to more questions than answers. I've come to appreciate that no topic is too big or too small—every observable happening in the world around us warrants thorough investigation by pure virtue of the fact that it is happening.

Never stop asking questions. This is a maxim I feel not only guided me through FI, but has begun to transform my own life. I've come to realize that, while it takes confidence to respond to a question, it takes even more confidence to ask an unprecedented question. I've realized my problem was not that I didn't like arguments; I just did not have the tools to effectively express my opinions. Life and careers are a collaborative process that depends on effective communication. I've experienced how getting to the heart of opposing views leads to a deeper understanding of myself.

Yet now that I've come so far from the first time I saw Focused Inquiry on my class list, I still find it hard to sum up my experience in order to answer the simple question, "What is Focused Inquiry?" How do you summarize semesters-long exercises of research, analysis, and synthesis? Sure, you develop these skills, but above all what crucial theme ties it all together? Curiosity. It's a class that fosters curiosity, outfits us to pursue knowledge, and urges us to evolve our thinking and ourselves. ■

STUDENT PROFILE

Ruth Walston is in her second year as a Communication Arts major at VCU. She composed the letter to future students titled "What is Focused Inquiry?" for this publication. Her interests include fiction writing, pop culture analysis, and taking long drives to new places.

READINGS

Hope and Home

By Rabih Alameddine

When I was in grad school, I went to a classmate's apartment for lunch one afternoon, nothing elaborate, just sandwiches and sodas. As I sat at her particle-board dinette table, unfolded for the occasion, I realized that she was the first in our cohort to begin nesting. She had invited me to lunch—the rest of us just dropped in on each other when we didn't want to get drunk or high publicly. More telling, on the coffee table she had placed a glass vase resplendent with poppies and wildflowers she'd picked herself. She was creating home.

I tried the flower trick to make my place feel homier, but it didn't seem to work. In those days, where I lived always felt transitory, like a cheap hotel room. The fact that I had rented a furnished apartment didn't help. I upgraded a couple of times, but the units I lived in still didn't feel homey. They all felt beige.

I was a late bloomer. It took me years and years, till my early forties, before I was finally able to admit that I wasn't leaving my rent-controlled apartment in San Francisco. I wasn't going to live in Paris, Rome, or Kuala Lumpur; I wasn't going to write verse in the Canary Islands, dance flamenco in Seville, or ride a gaucho in Patagonia. My nesting was gradual. I replaced the avocado carpeting with hardwood floors, painted the walls all kinds of bright colors, organized my books alphabetically in more than a dozen bookshelves. I put up paintings. I threw fabulous dinner parties.

One day I bought a small glass vase that could barely hold a single flower. I thought it exquisite. It reminded me of the delightful things I'd seen in Murano on my first trip to Europe, with my mother and sister when I was thirteen. I placed the vase next to where I sit in the den. No one notices it but me.

A few years ago I was in Beirut visiting family—to be more precise, family visiting me. I stay at my mother's apartment, my second home in a manner of speaking, and I rarely leave it. I become a teenager again: I don't have to cook, clean, or do dishes, which I don't do in San Francisco either, but there's something more comforting about my mother taking care of me.

I was lounging about doing nothing when my friend Anissa Helou, author of many excellent cookbooks, mentioned that she was writing an article on the changes in diet and cooking among the Syrian refugees now that they were in Lebanon, away from home. I thought this was a chance to do something useful. Since I was going to write about the World Cup for a magazine blog, I could tag along, take pictures of some of the children, ask them who they were rooting for and how they were going to watch the games, and publish their responses.

I was unprepared.

That first day, we went to the office of the United Nations High Commissioner for Refugees (UNHCR) in the Jnah neighborhood of Beirut. It was raining, atypical for Beirut in May. Some two hundred refugees sat on molded plastic chairs waiting to officially register with the organization. Anissa, more socially adept than I could ever hope to be, chatted with a few women, asking where they came from and why they had left. I listened, dumbfounded, as they related tales of woe, cities destroyed, relatives killed or tortured, losing everything, losing history.

And I had thought that asking about soccer might be a good idea. I returned to my mother's lovely apartment and hid under the duvet.

Lebanon is home to the largest number of Syrian refugees, and to the largest refugee population per capita in the world. In a country of four million, there are more than a million registered refugees, though the actual number is closer to a million and a half. The operative word here is *registered*, meaning with UNHCR. The official count doesn't include those who choose not to register or who have slipped through the many cracks. Jordan and Turkey have set up camps that allow them to monitor the refugee population as well as control it. Lebanon has no such thing; the country doesn't do control very well. Since their inception, Lebanon and Syria have always had a porous border. Syrians have been living and working here, both legally and not, for as long as anyone can remember. Today the refugees live everywhere, in unofficial tent settlements where they rent a patch of land, in abandoned buildings, storefronts, and warehouses, and in apartments or rooms that only a small percentage of them can afford. Every part of Lebanon has had to deal with the issues arising from the influx. Some Lebanese have been welcoming, others not.

A number of villages and municipalities have put up signs that say, "We ask our Syrian brothers to refrain from any movement in public spaces."

In other words, stay in the homes you don't have.

Americans are up in arms because the United States has promised to admit ten thousand Syrian refugees in 2016.

Terrorists, you know.

After I crawled out from under the duvet, I felt guilty, and guilt is my primary motivator. Not doing anything seemed selfish, maybe even solipsistic. I decided I would talk to refugees, listen to their stories, maybe write something. If nothing else, I could be a witness.

I went south of Beirut first, to a never-finished university building in Sidon where 177 families lived, more than nine hundred people. They had taken over the place, made homes out of classrooms. The building was bald concrete on a mild hill overlooking the Mediterranean. To get to it, l had exited the relatively new seaside highway that connected Beirut to Sidon and South Lebanon, and driven up an unmarked dirt road until I arrived at the end of the line. Laundry and satellite dishes adorned the front of the structure, and children, lots of children, were running around everywhere. The very air smelled of human spoor and a kind of resigned permanency.

Every nook of the five floors was being used, every space peopled. All the families invited me into their homes for tea and a chat—kettles always boiling, always on the ready, doors always open. Noticeable was the higher number of women; it seemed to me that they outnumbered men about four to one. Some husbands and adult sons, afraid of being arrested at the border, had stayed behind in Syria to fend for themselves. Some were out working or looking for work. Most of this compound's refugees were from the rural areas surrounding Hama, from farming and riparian villages.

The rooms I visited were impeccably clean. Colorful mats of woven palm leaves carpeted the floor, intricately patterned textiles covered the walls, both as decoration and to hide the graffiti. For furniture there were one or two cushions and a television, the most important possession—every home had one and it was always turned on. No beds, no chairs, no tables. Rooms with barely enough space for a single person were occupied by families of eight or ten or twelve, sleeping on the ground. Stacks of blankets everywhere.

The Syrian families told their stories, with a cup of tea, of course. All talked about how they left Syria, the routes they took, the journeys lasting days. All told their tales of why they fled, from bombing campaigns and sniper fire to marauding gangs and arbitrary arrests. A common admonishment to misbehaving children was, "Bashar will come take you."

I had the chance to kick around a soccer ball with some kids on the balcony corridor of the third floor. Below us, on the ground floor, the main soccer game was on. More than forty kids moved as one giant amoeba upon the concrete terrace.

I visited a group of women and sat on the floor next to a tall makeshift closet: plywood stacks holding thin mattresses, blankets and clothes, all covered in fake pink shantung below a red tasseled tablecloth that reached only two-thirds of the way down—a closet and Murphy bed in one. The women told me how they hid when fighting was nearby, leaving their villages, running for cover, ducking into any nearby copse or wooded area.

I said that during the Lebanese civil war we used to rush down to the underground garage for safety. For the seventeen years of the civil war, these garages became more than shelter; they became the hearth of the building, where families congregated for comfort, for entertainment, and, most important, for solace.

One woman said that they had no garages. They'd lived in a poor village with few if any cars. Another said that it would have made no difference even if they did have garages, since the MiGs dropped barrel bombs. "We hid from RPGs," they said, "not from MiGs, which were nothing if not quick death, no hiding, no hope."

Two of the women were pregnant.

"We have to replenish what they took from us," one said.

"Let me bring out my sister's boy," another said.

She returned with the parents and a boy of no more than seven months, wide blue eyes and a scrunched brow that made him look like a young philosopher puzzled by our intellectual infirmities—why oh why did we not understand him? His birth name was Ahmad, but that was not what everyone called him. His mother had experienced complications while pregnant and had given birth prematurely. A Lebanese charity was able to pay for the operation but not for the postnatal care in an incubator. The mother was flown to Turkey, where a second charity was able to keep the baby in an incubator for a month. Upon his return to the compound, everyone, and I mean everyone, called him Erdogan.

A

The second compound I visited was also in Sidon, in an abandoned underground Pepsi-Cola storage facility that had fallen into disrepair before the Syrians moved in. A long tunnel with rooms on either side and exits at each end reminded me of the hackneyed expression "moving toward the light." Three women were sweeping the cement outside their rooms, and the usual gaggle of kids was playing all over the place, but what differentiated these children from others I'd seen was that a number of them sported kohl around their eyes. I had heard of the long-ago practice of putting kohl around a newborn's eyes to keep away the evil eye, to keep Satan and his jinn at bay, but when l asked the mothers, they said that what kohl kept away was conjunctivitis.

Big sheets of plywood divided each storage space into three or four rooms, and each room, decorated to the hilt, had a minimum of ten people living and sleeping in it. Every room had at least two vases overfilled with fake flowers. Some group, probably UNHCR, had helped clean the place up and drain the sewage when the refugees moved in. The owner of the building now collected $100 monthly rent per room, a new source of income.

"At the beginning of the month," a woman said, "he arrives in his Range Rover, collects the rent from each family, and leaves. He accepts no excuses. You don't pay, you're out."

A young girl wanted me to meet the new bride.

The new bride?

"You must," the girl said. "You must."

She led us along to a dark drawn-back curtain that functioned as a door. The new bride looked a bit startled to see all of us: a stranger, a group of fifteen children and some of their mothers. She refused to be photographed; her right hand, like a stalking cat, lay upon the savannah above her bosom ready to pounce and cover her face if the camera lens so much as tilted in her direction. A bit tentative, somewhat shy, she stood beneath a large sheet of translucent plastic with metal shutters. She seemed more concerned than afraid. She simply did not wish to risk having her picture taken. Her parents were still in Syria.

The modesty of her dress served to highlight her beauty. Many people from that part of Syria had striking light eyes, yet hers were a remarkable griseous blue that grabbed your attention by its lapel. She was seventeen, she said; when she was fourteen, her parents had sent her to Lebanon with her uncles because the army and the shabiha were raping girls as they went through villages. Two days before my visit, she had married her first cousin. There would be no honeymoon.

She called her aunt to come talk to me. A firebrand, the aunt stormed out of her room. I could hear her approach, stomping on the cement, even though she wore soft slippers.

"Why should I talk to him?" she yelled. "Why? I've talked to journalists, to do-gooders, to everyone. Over and over. Told our stories many times. Does anyone do anything? No." With a dismissive wave of her hand and a flick of her left eyebrow, she glared at me. "If I talk to you will anything change?"

"No," I said, "I'm sorry. Nothing will change."

She regarded me askance for a brief moment and told her story.

I have set up my life in such a way that I rarely have to leave my home. It's where I feel most comfortable. I don't handle being around people too well these days, and I avoid them until I get lonely, at which time I either go out on some excursion or invite friends over for dinner. Did I mention that I have fabulous dinner parties?

Home is where I can be most myself.

Talking to refugees drains me, and then I berate myself for being so fearful and weak. What is my discomfort compared to their suffering? I have what I call tennis match conversations in my head. I keep telling myself that someone with my temperament is not meant for this. I'm meant for sitting at my computer and cuddling with my cats, I'm meant for bubble baths and mud baths—oh, and massages, don't forget massages. I'm a spoiled princess by nature. My traumas involve nothing more than a bad pedicure. I end up interviewing refugees because even though I'm useless, even though there's nothing I can do, doing nothing is a crime.

After spending a week with refugees in Lebanon, I needed time off. I took a trip to Botswana all by myself and happened to join a group of Americans for dinner, thinking that some company might he healthy. They were East Coasters, and they wanted to know whether I liked San Francisco. Of course, I said, I'd been living in the city for over thirty years. I should have stopped there, but I'd had a couple of glasses of lovely wine, the night sky was gloriously decked in stars, the fire ablaze in its pit. I didn't think. I was having an outdoor meal in the vast expanse of the Kalahari, for crying out loud. How could I be guarded? I told my interrogators that I was surprised I'd lasted so long because it never felt like home to me—not the city, not America.

One of the men, dressed in high-end Hemingway, dropped his knife. What did I mean? I should have noted his tone, definitely his flushing face, but neither starlight nor firelight is good for color discernment. Okay, okay. I might have had three glasses of wine. I rambled on. I quoted from one of my books, auto-plagiarized so to speak. "In America, I fit but I do not belong. In Lebanon, I belong but I do not fit." Nothing controversial or confrontational.

I was triple-barreled. Three men began to explain to me that America was a great home, the best home ever in the history of humankind. Their wives nodded in concert. Americans were the kindest, warmest people, the most convivial, the most welcoming people. I would have backtracked if I'd been allowed a word. I did not wish to argue, and, most important, I didn't want to lose my most welcome buzz.

Luckily, the only other non-American at the table was a local woman. In a high Brit accent, she asked the men where home was. One of them said he lived in New York and Florida but had to declare New York his home. If he lived in his Upper East Side apartment for less than six months of the year, he would lose his rent control, so he was unable to take advantage of Florida's lack of income tax. He made sure to insist that the unfairness of his situation caused him no little anguish.

A

In the Bekaa Valley of Lebanon, near Zahlé, I visited a medium-size Syrian settlement. About eighty back-to-back tents ran in a straight line between two agricultural fields—onions, I believe. Almost everyone who lived in that settlement is from the same village near Aleppo or is related to someone in that village. Ahmad M., the man who began the settlement, told me that three-quarters of them are interrelated. A concrete mason, he used to come from Aleppo to Zahlé for a few months each year to work construction jobs in the area. When the bombing of Aleppo began, he brought his family to his small tent in the fields, soon to be followed by his and his wife's relatives. The UNHCR helped make the tents bigger, sturdier, and—though not always successfully—rainproof.

Living on the land was not free. The women had to work the fields for the owner. The deal was this: they worked six hours a day, got paid for five, and the extra hours went toward rent. They were paid 5,000 Lebanese pounds per day, which translates into $3.33 or 55 cents an hour.

The men were paid better if they were lucky enough to find work. One young man had a job as a delivery-truck driver; he left his tent at 4:00 a.m. to deliver yoghurt to Beirut, returning at 6:00 p.m. For fourteen hours a day, he earned $300 a month.

Ahmad M. probably earned a bit more since he had contacts already established, but because of the extra competition, he had less work and his hourly wage had been drastically reduced. He had five children, and one in "the house of fire," a term I had never heard before, meaning a gun chamber—his wife was pregnant with the sixth. Three were in private schools ($600 per child for the year) because he and his wife considered the UN schools not up to par. His wife made sure to mention that her eldest daughter was second in her class, as good as if not better than the local Lebanese.

We sat in their tent drinking sweet tea—unreasonably sweet. Their dwelling consisted of white plastic sheets imprinted with the UNHCR logo, sheets of plywood on the roof, cement floors, one window that was no more than a glassless opening, yet the care and effort that went into making it feel homey was impressive. Knickknacks and tchotchkes all about, violet textiles draped from the ceiling, matching the ones surrounding the television on a hand-built stand, matching the throw blankets covering cushions and futon mattresses. Violet was the main theme in the mother's headscarf as well as the young daughter's dress.

I mentioned that it was wonderful to see such effort going into decorating. I had visited a tent where a young woman had painted the plastic sheeting bright crimson. Another woman had covered a wall with textile embroidered with mirrors (another ward against the evil eye), only to be outdone by a woman who studded her entire pantry with sequins, with results Liberace would have envied.

"We live here," Ahmad M. said.

I last saw the woman with the besequined pantry in 2014, but I think of her often. What would make someone spend so much time gluing sparkles onto sheets of wood that would become a pantry to store nonperishables? Intricate and delicate, no space left uncovered, so over-the-top that many a drag queen would kill for it.

She looked to be in her mid-twenties, if that, and seemed slightly embarrassed, admitting that it took her a long time to finish it, longer than she'd anticipated, what with caring for her four children, cooking, cleaning, and tending to her husband and in-laws.

"It's good to have something beautiful to come home to," she said. "The children love it."

"I do too," I said. "It's magnificent."

She beamed. "I had so many sequins."

To whoever thought it was a good idea to donate thousands of sequins to Syrian refugees who had nothing left, whose entire lives had been extirpated: Bless your heart.

The tents the Syrians live in are nothing like the flimsy ones used by the homeless in San Francisco. UNHCR donates the wood, the sheets of plastic, everything imprinted with the UN logo, and the refugees build the structure. Some organization donates tents to the homeless of San Francisco, but they are meant for camping. A good gust of wind might send them kite-flying. Tent stakes don't go into concrete.

A few days ago, I walked by a serried group of thirty tents on Folsom Street around 18th Street. None of the homeless talked to me or made eye contact. It seemed to me that they considered it bad form to panhandle where one sleeps.

I should have asked one of them if that was so, but I was frightened.

Years ago while riding the 24 northward, I noticed a homeless woman sitting on an old, bulging Samsonite on the corner of Haight and Divisadero, under the faded green awning of Phuket, a Thai restaurant. The sun was shining. Even though I was in a bus and she was a few feet away, the human aromas emanating from her were stupefying. She had a long blond pigtail that looked like a single dreadlock. Glasses on the tip of her nose, she was reading a hardcover of Alice Munro's *The Love of a Good Woman*.

The World Food Programme had given each registered refugee family in Lebanon a debit MasterCard that they can use to buy food at a number of supermarkets all over the country. In 2014, each account received $30 per family member at the beginning of the month. The amount is quite a bit less now; money is running out. Food in Lebanon is by no means cheap. Every woman I talked to complained that she could not afford any meat or fresh fruit. One used an expression I had never heard before: one piece of coal instead of meat (it rhymes in Levantine Arabic). She explained that she would cook rice and vegetables in a pot, then place a hot coal on a small plate with a layer of olive oil, put that in the pot, and cover it. The meal would end up having a "grilled meat" flavor.

What did the refugees buy most? Not rice or bread, not lentils or olive oil. More than twice as much as anything else, they bought sugar and tea, a specific brand called Horse Head, what they drank back home. The tradition of hospitality must be maintained.

I was surprised the first time I was invited into the makeshift homes of refugees. If someone noticed me passing by, the invitation was instantaneous. In Sidon, in the onion fields, they asked me in for tea.

But there were places where I wasn't invited in.

North of Beirut, in the hills above Tripoli, refugees living in an olive grove did not invite me. Their situation seemed more desperate. Their jerry-rigged tents looked like they wouldn't last the first snowstorm. The ground was nothing more than mud because of the rains. There were no decorations, no tapestries, no tchotchkes, no televisions.

Another camp about half an hour's drive from the onion fields in the Bekaa Valley was in worse shape. Though the tents were of the same materials donated by UNHCR, they were shoddily erected. Smells of sewage everywhere. All the adults were in tatters, all had sagging features. The children looked so miserable, so grimy, that they seemed to be made of clay yet to be fired and glazed.

No one invited me into the tent, but everyone assured me that as soon as the situation was settled in Syria, they were moving back.

I have visited Ahmad M. a number of times, and will probably do so again next time I'm in Lebanon, though I have yet to convince him or his wife that if I drink one more cup of their tea I'll develop type 2 diabetes. On my last visit, there had been a major renovation of the tent. They now had two bedrooms, a kitchen (no sequins on their pantry), and a living room where the family ate all their meals. They had two flat screens.

"Hope?" Ahmad said. "I knew we couldn't return the minute the war started."

"We lost everything," his wife said.

Their latest project, which I have yet to see, is to cover the cement floors with Lebanese stone tiles.

I asked what if the impossible happened and the situation calmed down in Syria and everything went back to normal. Would they return?

"It will never happen," he said.

In January 2016, I was on a small hill in the middle of the Moria refugee camp on the island of Lesbos, Greece. The camp is a military facility and looks like nothing if not a prison, with high concrete walls and razor wire. Ironically, there isn't much space inside Moria. Refugees who are lucky sleep in the barracks, the rest in flimsy tents in the olive groves outside the prison.

I was miserable, the thousands of refugees far more so. It was drizzling. I was not yet soaked. I was supposed to be an interpreter, but I couldn't seem to move from my spot next to the NGO offices. I felt so out of place, so wrong. I wished I were smoking again. I would have been able to do something if I had a cigarette. There was a smell of lard and dampness in the air. The view from the hill made me feel anxious, apprehensive, a much stronger feeling than I'd had in any refugee camp before. At the bottom of the hill, the large squadron of Greek riot police in high butch did not help.

So many people, so many. Families, single men, children. Syrians, Iraqis, Afghanis, Iranians, and more, more. North Africans from Algeria, from Morocco, sub-Saharan Africans from Mali, from Congo. They were running away from so much, the Syrian regime, Daesh, the Taliban, terrorist groups with even sillier monikers. Lines everywhere, for registration, for food, for clothes, for donations. And white people directing pedestrian traffic.

19

The sun came out. Newly arrived families trudged up the hill carrying their belongings, pulling rolling suitcases, their voices submerged in the hullabaloo of conversations among the volunteers, the *tap-tap* of hard soles on harder concrete, the bustle of movement. A Syrian family walked up the hill toward me, mother, father, three kids, including a boy of perhaps twelve, his face a picture of glacial determination. A large group of young volunteers in neon orange vests walked next to them, more boisterous, less self-conscious. One of them, a blond in her early twenties, screamed. Everyone stopped. She screamed again, pointing at the sky. "Oh my God, oh my God." She screamed once more before she was able to form an actual sentence. "Look, it's a rainbow," she yelled. She tried to engage a little girl, kept pointing at the far sky, spoke louder in English to make herself understood, but the little girl wanted nothing to do with her. The Syrian family reached me before I was able to hear what they were talking about.

"She's excited because she saw a rainbow," the father said.

The mother shook her head. The twelve-year-old boy said in a quiet voice, not realizing that I spoke his language, "She should shove that rainbow up her ass."

The father snickered. The mother smacked the back of his head, not violently, for they were both carrying heavy loads. ■

AUTHOR PROFILE

Rabih Alameddine (b. 1959) was born in Jordan and grew up in Kuwait and his family's native Lebanon. He moved to the United States when he was 17 and studied engineering and business at UCLA. Alameddine is now a painter and author who lives between San Francisco and Beirut. He is the author of *Koolaids* (1998), *The Perv* (1999), *I, the Divine* (2001), *The Hakawati* (2008), *An Unnecessary Woman* (2014; National Book Critics Circle Award Finalist), *The Angel of History* (2016; winner, the Arab American Book Award and the Lambda Literary Award for Gay Fiction). His works have most often explored gender and sexuality, the traumas of the Lebanese Civil War and the AIDS crisis, and cross-cultural existence. "Hope and Home" first appeared in the third issue of Freeman's literary anthology, *The Best New Writing on Home* (2017).

'Who Shared It?': How Americans Decide What News to Trust on Social Media

By American Press Institute

A

Introduction

When Americans encounter news on social media, how much they trust the content is determined less by who creates the news than by who shares it, according to a new experimental study from the Media Insight Project, a collaboration between the American Press Institute and The Associated Press-NORC Center for Public Affairs Research.

Whether readers trust the sharer, indeed, matters more than who produces the article—or even whether the article is produced by a real news organization or a fictional one, the study finds.

As social platforms such as Facebook or Twitter become major thoroughfares for news, the news organization that does the original reporting still matters. But the study demonstrates that who shares an article on a social media site like Facebook has an even bigger influence on whether people trust what they see.

The experimental results show that people who see an article from a trusted sharer, but one written by an unknown media source, have much more trust in the information than people who see the same article that appears to come from a reputable media source shared by a person they do not trust.

The identity of the sharer even has an impact on consumers' impressions of the news brand. The study demonstrates that when people see a post from a trusted person rather than an untrusted person, they feel more likely to recommend the news source to friends, follow the source on social media, and sign up for news alerts from the source.

All of this suggests that a news organization's credibility both as a brand and for individual stories is significantly affected by what kinds of people are sharing it on social media sites such as Facebook. The sharers act as unofficial ambassadors for the brand, and the sharers' credibility can influence readers' opinions about the reporting source.

This new research by the Media Insight Project is part of an effort to study the elements of trust in news at a time of turbulence in the media. The results offer important new insights to publishers whose digital content increasingly is reaching people outside the domain of their own websites and apps. Indeed, the findings suggest that publishers increasingly need to think of their consumers as ambassadors for their brand. The findings also carry implications for people concerned about so-called fake news and for advocates of "news literacy," the spread of consumer critical thinking skills. The findings also have implications for social networks that might be able to alter the presentation of content to give consumers more information about the source of the news.

The new findings come from an experiment in which 1,489 Americans were presented with a news feed item closely resembling Facebook. Everyone saw the same content, but the person who shared it and the original reporting source varied. After reading the post and short story, respondents answered questions about the story and their trust in the content, providing evidence about which variables had the greatest effect on attitudes.

Using an Experimental Design to Explore Trust in News on Social Media

In an earlier era, the platform by which people got their news and the news brand were the same thing. As a consumer, you watched the evening news from a particular network or read a particular newspaper. Trust was simply determined by the news outlet's own credibility.

Today, as people increasingly get news on social platforms, news often comes via other people.

In a 2016 Media Insight Project national survey about trust and news, people reported that in social media the news organization brand that originally reported the story influenced whether they trusted the content, more so than who shared it. For example, 66 percent of Americans who received news from Facebook said their trust in the original news source had a lot of effect on their trust in the content, while only 48 percent said the same when it comes to the effect of trusting the person sharing the news.

We wanted to test whether that was really true, or whether people just believed that was the case.

To do so, we designed an online survey experiment. We created a simulated Facebook post about health news and presented it to an online sample of 1,489 U.S. adults who are part of AmeriSpeak, NORC's nationally representative survey panel.

Each person saw a health news post from one of eight public figures who often share information about health, a list that ranged from Oprah and Dr. Oz to the Surgeon General of the United States. Half the people were randomly assigned a sharer they had earlier identified as a person they trusted. The other half were randomly shown a sharer they had earlier said they didn't trust.

Screenshot of social media post used in the experiment

After viewing the post, everyone saw the accompanying health article head-lined: "Don't let the scale fool you: Why you could still be at risk for diabetes." This article was originally a piece written by a professor that appeared on The Associated Press (AP) website through an AP partnership. For half the sample, the article was labeled as coming from The AP. For the other half, the article was labeled as coming from a fictional source, something called the DailyNewsReview.com.

Screenshot of article used in experiment

This experimental design tests how different factors affect people's perceptions of news in social media and is an alternative to simply asking people in a survey about what impacts their views.

Who Shared the Article has a Major Impact on Various Trust Indicators

The experiment shows that who shares the article has a major impact on what people think of it.

When people see news from a person they trust, they are more likely to think it got the facts right, contains diverse points of view, and is well reported than if the same article is shared by someone they are skeptical of.

Those who see a social media post from someone they trust evaluate the article more positively than those who see one from someone they do not trust across a range of metrics.

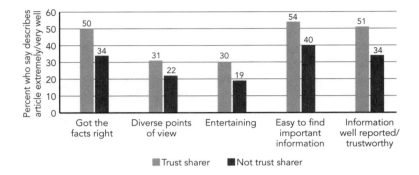

Question: How well does each of the following statements describe the article shared in this social media post?

Source: Media Insight Project poll conducted Nov. 9–Dec. 6, 2016, with 1,489 adults nationwide.

For instance, 51 percent of people say the health article on diabetes is well reported when it is shared by a public figure they trust. Just a third (34 percent) feel that way when the same article is shared by someone they don't trust.

The numbers are nearly identical for whether the story got the facts right. Fifty percent of readers think the health article got the facts right when the person who shared it happens to be someone they trust. Just 34 percent say the same when they are skeptical of the sharer.

The sharer even influences whether people think the article, which presents two perspectives, contains diverse points of view. More people are likely to say an article contains multiple points of view when it comes from a trusted source (31 percent) than when it comes from a less-trusted public figure (22 percent).

Who shared the article also influences, but to a lesser extent, whether people are likely to pass on the article to their own friends. If the article was shared by a trusted source, 38 percent of people say they are likely to share it. If shared by a public figure they don't trust, 24 percent of people still say they are likely to re-share the content anyway.

The sharer tends to have a greater significance on attitudes than the news organization that reported the article in the first place. The reporting source still matters, according to the experiment, just not as much as who shared the article.

For instance, when the story is passed on by a trusted figure and the article is attributed to The AP, 52 percent of people think the article got the facts right. When the article is still attributed to The AP but the person passing it on is less trusted, only 32 percent say the facts were right.

Indeed, more people think the story is accurate if the sharer is trusted but the article is attributed to a fictional news source (49 percent), than do if it is attributed to The AP but they are skeptical of the sharer (32 percent).

Trust in the person who posts a story on social media also impacts engagement with the news source. When people see a post from a trusted figure, they are more likely to say they would share the article and follow the person who shared the article. They are also more likely when they see a post from a trusted person to report they would engage with the *news source* of the article, saying they would recommend the source to friends, follow the source on social media, and sign up for news alerts from the source.

Those who see an article on social media from a person they trust are more likely to engage with it in a variety of ways, not just with the person who shared the article, but also with the news source.

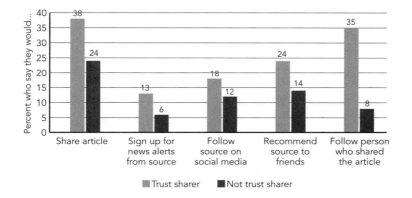

Question: Now that you have read the article shared in this social media post, do you think you would do any of the following, or do you think you would not do these things?

Source: Media Insight Project poll conducted Nov. 9–Dec. 6, 2016, with 1,489 adults nationwide.

About half of the people in our experiment could recall who had shared the post, but only about 2 in 10 could remember the source of the article. The fact that people are fundamentally more aware of who shared the article than who wrote it may be a significant foundation for this effect.

Although People Say They Place More Importance on the Original Reporting Source, the Experiment Shows They Are More Influenced by the Sharer

About half of Americans (51 percent) say they get news from social media, according to our 2016 Media Insight study[1]. Among those who get news on social media, Facebook is by far the most used platform, and other popular platforms for news include YouTube, Twitter, and Instagram.

Despite the popularity of Facebook, few say they trust the news they get there. Just 12 percent say they trust what they see on Facebook a great deal or a lot, while 48 percent say they trust it somewhat and 20 percent trust it very little or not at all. The public has similar skepticism in news on other social media platforms.

---

[1] http://mediainsight.org/Pages/a-new-understanding-what-makes-people-trust-and-rely-on-news.aspx

Most people who use social media to get news do not have a lot of trust in the content.

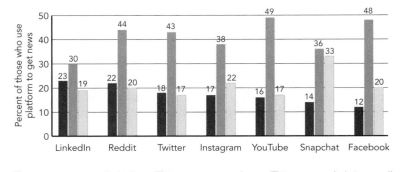

Question: In general, how much do you trust the news and information you see on [SELECTED SOCIAL MEDIA PLATFORM]?

Source: A New Understanding: What Makes People Trust and Rely on News. 2016.

When evaluating news on Facebook, 66 percent said in the survey that whether they trust the original reporting source highly affects whether they trust a piece of news or reporting. Nearly half (48 percent) say whether they trust the person who posted the article influences whether they trust that piece of information. Sixteen percent say whether or not a lot of people have liked it or shared it affects them a lot. The trends are similar for Twitter and YouTube.

But our new experiment tells a different story. These results show that, in fact, a highly trusted or distrusted sharer has a greater effect on reader trust. The discrepancy suggests that people are often not aware of how much they are influenced by the identity of the sharer.

As detailed earlier, the experiment shows that when people see a post from a trusted person rather than a distrusted person, they are more likely to say it was easy to find important information, the information was well reported and trustworthy, and it got the facts right. Trust in the sharer also makes it more likely that people will believe the article provided diverse points of view and was entertaining.

The results from the experiment are consistent with the beliefs of several participants who took part in focus groups that were conducted in 2016 during the first phase of the research into trust in news. When discussing news on Facebook, one participant said that who shares the post is critical. "I look who shared it. If I have a friend that's a creep I might not believe it. If a friend is in a certain field, then I might believe what they post."

Likewise, people acknowledge the importance of who shares the article when asked directly about it during the survey experiments. Of those who saw news from a trusted person, 51 percent said they are more likely to trust the information because of who shared it.

A

The Identity of the Media Outlet Can Impact How People Evaluate a Story on Social Media if They Have a Negative Opinion of the Source

The identity of the media outlet reporting a story can impact how people view the article if people have an explicit mistrust of that media outlet. The results of the experiment indicate that people's assessment of an article does not change much when they see the content branded as a known and trusted media outlet such as The AP or when they see if from an unknown, made-up news organization. However, when someone holds a particularly negative view of the reporting source, it has a similar effect to seeing the article shared by a distrusted person.

There is little difference in overall attitudes toward an article branded to be from The AP (one of the largest media organizations in the world) and the same article from DailyNewsReview.com (a made-up and unknown site). However, the survey experiment included an earlier question asking about trust in The AP, and people's views about The AP are related to their beliefs about the article.

People who report trusting The AP and who saw the story branded to be from that source have similar assessments of the article as do those who saw the article from the unknown news source. However, people who report not trusting The AP have significantly more negative beliefs about the article when it was presented as from The AP than do either those who saw the article from the unknown news source or those who trust The AP.

There is little difference between an unknown and a trusted reporting source on how people assess an article on social media, but a lack of trust in a source has a significant effect.

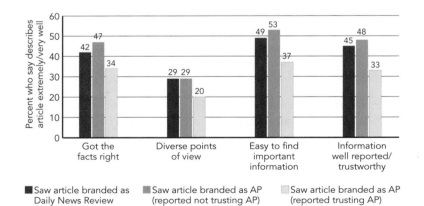

Question: How well does each of the following statements describe the article shared in this social media post?

Source: Media Insight Project poll conducted Nov. 9–Dec. 6, 2016, with 1,489 adults nationwide.

As you would expect, people who do not trust The AP are also much less likely to say they would follow the source on social media or recommend the source to friends.

A lack of trust in a source reduces the likelihood of engaging with the source on social media.

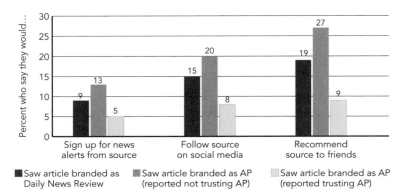

Question: Now that you have read the article shared in this social media post, do you think you would do any of the following, or do you think you would not do these things?

Source: Media Insight Project poll conducted Nov. 9- Dec. 6, 2016, with 1,489 adults nationwide.

During the earlier focus groups, some participants talked about how the news source affected their perception of stories on social media. "When it comes to putting something on my Facebook page, I will only post things that come from a source I trust," said one participant.

But these experimental results indicate something slightly different: that people will have reservations about an article when they decidedly know and distrust the source, but not when they just don't know about the source.

The Bottom Line: A Trusted Sharer Has More Significant Effects on Beliefs about News than a Reputable Media Source

While both the person posting a story and the media outlet can impact how people perceive news on social media, the experiments show that the person posting the article has the greatest effect on opinions toward the article.

In the experiment, there are four possible sharer and news source combinations: 1) trusted sharer and reputable source, 2) trusted sharer and unknown source, 3) untrusted sharer and reputable source, and 4) untrusted sharer and unknown source.

As you would expect, a trusted person sharing an article from a reputable news source leads to the most positive beliefs about an article. And an untrusted person sharing something from an unknown news source leads to generally low credibility.

A

But in the more complicated combinations, you can see whether the person posting the article or the original reporting source most affects attitudes toward an article.

The results illustrate that people who saw the article from a trusted sharer and unknown media source have much more positive opinions of the article than those who saw the story from a distrusted sharer and reputable news source.

A trusted sharer has a more positive impact on beliefs about news than a reputable news source.

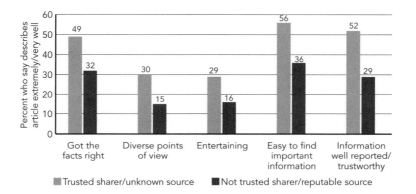

Question: How well does each of the following statements describe the article shared in this social media post?

Source: Media Insight Project poll conducted Nov. 9–Dec. 6, 2016, with 1,489 adults nationwide.

When looking at how respondents might engage with the news outlet, the sharer has even more positive effects than the news outlet itself. Those who trusted the sharer but saw the unknown outlet were more likely than those who did not trust the sharer and saw the reputable outlet to share the article, follow the sharer, sign up for news alerts from the source, and recommend the source to friends.

A trusted sharer has a greater impact on engagement with news than a reputable source.

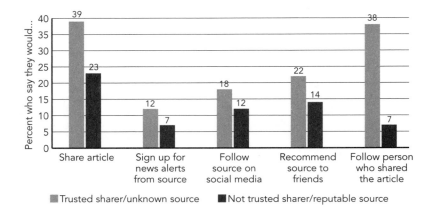

Question: Now that you have read the article shared in this social media post, do you think you would do any of the following, or do you think you would not do these things?

Source: Media Insight Project poll conducted Nov. 9–Dec. 6, 2016, with 1489 adults nationwide.

Implications

These findings shed new light on how journalists and news organizations should think about credibility, and how news is perceived on social networks. Among the interesting implications and inferences we offer are these:

- **To publishers and journalists:** Your readers and followers are not just consumers to monetize, instead they may be social ambassadors whose own credibility with their friends affects your brand's reputation. It is the sharer's credibility, more than your own, which determines other people's willingness to believe you and engage with you. This underscores the importance of news organizations creating strong communities of followers who evangelize the organization to others.

- **To news-literacy advocates:** In light of growing concerns about "fake news" spreading on social media, this experiment confirms that people make little distinction between known and unknown (even made-up) sources when it comes to trusting and sharing news. Even 19 percent of people who saw our fictional news source would have been willing to recommend it to a friend.

- **To Facebook and other social networks:** Facebook and other social networks could do more to emphasize and provide information about the original sources for news articles. The fact that only 2 in 10 people in our experiment could recall the news reporting source accurately after seeing a Facebook-style post suggests that basic brand awareness has a long way to go. We found that sharers affect perceptions more than the original news reporting source—but might that change if Facebook made the reporting source label more prominent?

About the Study

Experiment Methodology

This survey experiment was conducted by the Media Insight Project, an initiative of the American Press Institute (API) and The Associated Press-NORC Center for Public Affairs Research. The survey was conducted from November 9 through December 6, 2016. The survey was funded by API. Staff from API, NORC at the University of Chicago, and AP collaborated on all aspects of the study.

Data were collected using the AmeriSpeak Panel, which is NORC's probability-based panel designed to be representative of the U.S. household population. During the initial recruitment phase of the panel, randomly selected U.S. households were sampled with a known, nonzero probability of selection from the NORC National Sample Frame and then contacted by U.S. mail, email, telephone, and field interviewers (face-to-face). The panel provides sample coverage of approximately 97 percent of the U.S. household population. Those excluded from the sample include people with P.O. Box only addresses, some addresses not listed in the USPS Delivery Sequence File, and some newly constructed dwellings.

Interviews for this survey were conducted, with adults age 18 and over representing the 50 states and the District of Columbia. Panel members were randomly drawn from the AmeriSpeak Panel, and 1,489 completed the survey, all via the web. The final stage completion rate is 34.8 percent, the weighted household panel response rate is 32.4 percent, and the weighted household panel retention rate is 95.5 percent, for a cumulative response rate of 10.8 percent.

The overall margin of sampling error is +/– 3.5 percentage points at the 95 percent confidence level, including the design effect. The margin of sampling error may be higher for subgroups.

Respondents were offered a small monetary incentive for completing the survey ($2 or $4 depending on their initial panel recruitment). All interviews were conducted in English by professional interviewers who were carefully trained on the specific survey for this study.

Once the sample was selected and fielded, and all the study data had been collected and made final, a poststratification process was used to adjust for any survey nonresponse as well as any noncoverage or under-and over-sampling resulting from the study-specific sample design. Poststratification variables included age, gender, Census region, race/ethnicity, and education. The weighted data, which reflect the U.S. population of adults age 18 and over, were used for all analyses.

All analyses were conducted using STATA (version 14), which allows for adjustment of standard errors for complex sample designs. All differences reported between subgroups of the U.S. population are at the 95 percent level of statistical significance, meaning that there is only a 5 percent (or less) probability that the observed differences could be attributed to chance variation in sampling. Additionally, bivariate differences between subgroups are only reported when they also remain robust in a multivariate model controlling for other demographic, political, and socioeconomic covariates. A comprehensive listing of all study questions, complete with tabulations of top-level results for each question, is available on the Media Insight Project's website: www.mediainsight.org. ■

──────────────────────────────── AUTHOR PROFILE

The American Press Institute, founded in 1946, is a nonprofit educational organization that conducts research, training, and advocacy for American news media. They focus on topics such as the news habits of the American public, fact-checking and accountability in journalism, and best business practices for the American news media as they negotiate the shifting media landscape. "'Who Shared It?': How Americans Decide What News To Trust on Social Media," was published on March 20, 2017. This report draws on research done by the Media Insight Project, a collaboration of the American Press Institute and the AP-NORC Center for Public Affairs Research focused on trends in American media.

Story of Cities #future: What Will Our Growing Megacities Really Look Like?

A

By Darran Anderson

Will we live in buildings made out of waste, heavily surveilled smart cities, or maybe floating communities designed to cope with rising sea levels?

Amid the much-mythologised graffiti that appeared around Sorbonne University during the French civil unrest in May 1968, one line still stands out as intriguing and ambiguous: "The future will only contain what we put into it now."

What appears at first utopian has more than a hint of the ominous. While augmented reality creates a city individualised for every occupant, and developments in modular architecture and nanotechnology might result in rooms that change form and function at a whim, the problem lies in the unforeseen. The smart city will also be the surveillance city.

For the moment, we remain largely wedded to superficial visual futures. The likelihood is that the prevailing chrome and chlorophyll vision of architects and urbanists will become as much an enticing, but outdated, fashion as the Raygun Gothic of *The Jetsons* or the cyberpunk of *Blade Runner*. Rather than a sudden leap into dazzling space age-style cityscapes, innovations will unfold in real-time—and so too will catastrophes. The very enormity of what cities face seems beyond the realms of believability, and encourages postponement and denial.

"Survivability" should be added to urban buzzwords like connectivity and sustainability. Three quarters of all major metropolises lie on the coastline. In China alone, 20 million people per year move to cities, with the flood-prone Pearl River Delta now the world's largest urbanised area, according to the World Bank.

A recent report by Christian Aid places more than a billion people in coastal cities vulnerable to severe flooding and extreme weather due to climate change by 2070, with Kolkata, Mumbai and Dhaka topping the list. Many more people face the knock-on effects of severe flooding such as fresh water shortages, refugee crises and political instability.

The question remains whether large-scale adaptation will be possible in the face of short electoral cycles, the abiding influence of commercial interests, and a sense of inertia beneficial to the status quo. Since Kenzō Tange's Tokyo Bay Plan (1960), one tendency has been towards proposing intriguing but as yet ephemeral "floating" cities. For real cities facing sea-level rise, Seth McDowell from Mcdowellespinosa architects identifies three strategies: "Defence, retreat and adaptation."

"Cities and populations with generous resources and engineering capacity will likely simply take the defence strategy and build mega engineering structures to keep the water away—similar to the Delta Works in the Netherlands. For those

with less cultural and economic investments in the water's edge, we will likely see retreat as a strategy. However, I see retreat as both a horizontal and vertical operation. So, retreating does not just mean packing up and moving inland, but could also mean elevating above the water."

Venice is the commonly quoted model for this process, but a more recent example (though considerably less aesthetically appealing) is the platform oil city of Neft Daşhlari in Azerbaijan. "Water becomes a new datum—not so much a habitable space, but rather a fluctuating ground," McDowell explains. "Cities would be designed or reconfigured to accept rising water levels and adapt…to allow for a co-existence between water and civic activities. You can see this strategy in projects like De Urbanisten's Water Square Benthemplein in Rotterdam, where a public square doubles as a water storage basin."

Architecture group Terreform One adopts a similarly counter-intuitive but practical approach in its Governors Hook project, where "instead of keeping the water out, the design allows the water in". The relationship between the urban and rural must be reconsidered, co-founder Mitchell Joachim suggests, to prevent cities adopting a siege mentality and fighting a losing battle with the elements.

"We need to find these much larger soft buffer zones that are accepting of these two worlds of nature and city. Before Hurricane Sandy, we were using these ghost fleets, old military vessels as artificial reefs that would be embedded into the edges of our city and allow sediment and life-forms to build up on top of them over time and create these middle zones between land and sea." The devastation wrought by Hurricane Sandy made these plans seem particularly pertinent, if not prophetic.

Dealing with Waste

The population explosion and advances of the industrial age have produced unprecedented levels of waste into landfill, the sea and the sky. Countering measures, such as developing nanotechnology that would see buildings alleviate pollution at a molecular level, are still in their infancy.

In the meantime, waste is as much a testament to civilisation as our urban skylines. Mcdowellespinosa proposes a shift in thinking: "Waste is just a material state," McDowell says. "Since it tends to be unwanted, it is cheap.

"The main issue to overcome in viewing waste as raw material is the energy required to transform the material from a state of refuse to a state of sophistication. There is also the perceptual challenge—how can waste be transformed to acceptable visual and performance standards? We've explored this idea in projects such as City of Blubber, which imagines converting Hong Kong's food waste into a productive bioplastic material."

What we might see as absurd is already happening through necessity in settings like Manshiyat Naser in Egypt, where a "Garbage City" functions on the refuse of Cairo. Mitchell Joachim agrees that our current approach is a problem. "There is no such thing as waste. Waste is supposed to go away but there is no 'away'. We look at fully 'upcyclable' cities where projects, products, concepts that we make are always intended to be cycled upwards again and again."

This is reflected in Terreform One's Rapid Re(f)use project—a "future city [that] makes no distinction between waste and supply".

A

Engaged in projects from the shifting pods of Peristaltic City to the transformed-Arctic Ecotarium of Future North, Joachim suggests a radical change in our economic and political systems to match our technological ingenuity. "They say we're in the age of the Anthropocene but really it's more accurate to say we're in the Capitalocene. Everyone has to grow and show proof of growth. And we know that is impossible. Nothing grows to infinity. There will always be stresses whether on the market or the environment that will cause it to feedback.

"At Terreform One, we're anticipating, not an endless growth system, but a state where waste doesn't exist—a steady state or closed, stable economy that cycles back and recognises the limits of the earth's metabolism and what we can take out. This would be done with footprint calculations and life-cycle analyses on anything we produce."

Rather than view the city architecturally, Joachim encourages us to see it also as a series of interconnected metabolic systems, akin to a biological organism. "In a culture of biology, you just don't design something for a single purpose. A cherry tree is servicing thousands of other forms of life. It produces thousands of cherries that get absorbed into the soil and feed all different types of flora and fauna. It's connected into a web of life."

Terreform One's ideas and designs might seem wildly visionary on first glance but looking closer, they go beyond speculative concepts into proposing functioning models. "What we do is create very detailed fictive scenarios that don't promise the future will end up this way, but rather we think about what the inherent issues are and bring these to the foreground and talk in a logical way how cities might respond."

The obstacle in adapting cities is the same obstacle in tackling fossil fuel emissions; what Joachim identifies as "predatory drag". "If you're an oil company, you're going to say 'Yes, solar panels are great, we'll invest in that. We think in 2050, we'll all be using solar panels.' Until then, every single day they are in business, there are such enormous profits for them that the point is to delay."

Given how embedded these interests are in political circles, change from within needs an unlikely synthesis of the community-orientated philosophy of Jane Jacobs and the force, connections and leverage of Robert Moses. It will likely take a disastrous jolt ("an environmental Pearl Harbour") to alter the calculus of negligence economics, provide a rousing symbol and focus the issue, by which stage it might be too late.

One day, cities may be forced to follow their inhabitants in becoming mobile. Ron Herron's Walking City for Archigram may still suggest the outer reaches of science fiction, but the idea of moving a city has already happened: the Swedish town of Kiruna was relocated two miles away.

And with developments in the assembling of buildings through drones, nanotechnology-enhanced materials and industrial 3D printing, dissembling and deploying them elsewhere could be much easier than at present.

Changing Cities

Perhaps the likeliest outcome is that cities will simply continue as they are, or be deserted. The costs of change may result in inundated areas simply being abandoned (in the model of Detroit or New Orleans) while more privileged areas will be protected. Sacrifice zones and ruins may form in coastal cities as the authorities and the rich move up or out.

Containing a critique of the present, as every prophesy does, Clouds Architecture Office's Aqualta envisages a partially submerged metropolis where life nevertheless carries on. "The city would in effect lift its skirt allowing water to flow beneath its feet," explains partner Ostap Rudakevych.

"Thinking through the ramifications—flooded subway tunnels, submerged roads and sidewalks, street level retail underwater—allows for new conditions to emerge, such as transport by boat or dirigible, suspended walkways, oyster beds, and a generally slower and quieter lifestyle. Perhaps fossil fuels would be gone by then, yielding a quieter city without the sounds of engines or motors.

"Rather than devising ever more complex technologies in an escalating battle against nature, we adapt and invite the water in."

Beyond the initial surprise, there are sound ideas and a scathing perceptiveness underlying the project: "Aqualta was guided by the observation that people are resistant to change, especially if it means sacrificing comfort or convenience. Needed lifestyle adjustments have been gradual or non-existent. Aqualta was intended as a kind of slow-burn wake-up call, a seductive portrayal of where we're headed, like it or not."

To go beyond the superficial aspects of future cities requires seeing past the architectural shell and the marketing to the systems, relationships and people within—the citizens rather than the citadels.

"A city is more than a place in space," Patrick Geddes pointed out, "it is a drama in time." Change will be continuous, because "designing a city is like painting a watercolour in a stream", says Joachim.

In order to be preserved, the city must become adaptable. So too must its designers and its inhabitants—but they must do so together. We are endlessly, fancifully predicting the future partly in order to distract ourselves from the fact that we're already creating it, for good and ill.■

AUTHOR PROFILE

Darran Anderson is from Derry, Northern Ireland. He is the author of *Imaginary Cities*, a 2015 book that explores the connections between real and imagined cities, and regularly writes on urbanism, technology, and the arts for numerous publications. He is also author of a study of French songwriter Serge Gainsbourg's 1971 album *Histoire de Melody Nelson* and has published several collections of poetry. "Story of Cities #future: What Will Our Growing Megacities Really Look Like?" appeared in *The Guardian* on May 26, 2016 as part of their "The Story of Cities" project.

What It Means When a Man Falls from the Sky

A

By Lesley Nneka Arimah

It means twenty-four-hour news coverage. It means politicians doing damage control, activists egging on protests. It means Francisco Furcal's granddaughter at a press conference defending her family's legacy.

"My grandfather's formula is sound. Math is constant and absolute. Any problems that arise are the fault of those who miscalculate it."

Bad move, lady. This could only put everyone on the defensive, compelling them to trot out their transcripts and test results and every other thing that proved their genius. Nneoma tried to think of where she'd put her own documents after the move, but that led to thinking of where she'd moved from, which led to thinking of whom she'd left behind.

Best not to venture there. Best instead to concentrate on the shaky footage captured by a security camera. The motion-activated device had caught the last fifty feet of the man's fall, the windmill panic of flailing arms, the spread of his body on the ground. When the formula for flight had been revealed short months before, the ceremony had started unimpressively enough, with a man levitating like a monk for fifteen boring minutes before shooting into the air. The scientific community was agog. What did it mean that the human body could now defy things humanity had never thought to question, like gravity? It had seemed like the start of a new era.

Now the newscast jumped to the Mathematicians who'd discovered the equation for flight. They were being ambushed by gleeful reporters at parties, while picking up their children in their sleek black cars, on their vacations, giving a glimpse of luxury that was foreign to the majority of the viewing public, who must have enjoyed the embarrassed faces and defensive outbursts from well-fed mouths.

By blaming the Mathematicians instead of the Formula, Martina Furcal and the Center created a maelstrom around the supposedly infallible scientists while protecting her family's legacy. And their money. Maybe not such a bad move after all.

Nneoma flipped through the channels, listening closely. If the rumor that Furcal's Formula was beginning to unravel around the edges gained any traction, it would eventually trickle down to the twenty-four hundred Mathematicians like her, who worked around the globe, making their living calculating and subtracting emotions, drawing them from living bodies like poison from a wound.

She was one of the fifty-seven registered Mathematicians who specialized in calculating grief, down from the fifty-nine of last year. Alvin Claspell, the Australian, had committed suicide after, if the stories were to be believed, going mad and trying to eat himself. This work wasn't for everyone. And of course Kioni Mutahi had simply disappeared, leaving New Kenya with only one grief worker.

There were six grief workers in the Biafra-Britannia Alliance, where Nneoma now lived, the largest concentration of grief workers in any province to serve the largest concentration of the grieving. Well, the largest concentration that could pay.

It was the same footage over and over. Nneoma offed the unit. The brouhaha would last only as long as it took the flight guys to wise up and blame the fallen man for miscalculating. "Cover your ass," as the North American saying went, though there wasn't much of that continent left to speak it.

A message dinged on the phone console and Nneoma hurried to press it, eager, then embarrassed at her eagerness, then further embarrassed when it wasn't even Kioni, just her assistant reminding her of the lecture she was to give at the school. She deleted the message—of course she remembered—and became annoyed. She thought, again, of getting rid of the young woman. But sometimes you need an assistant, such as when your girlfriend ends your relationship with the same polite coolness that she initiated it, leaving you to pack and relocate three years' worth of shit in one week. Assistants come in handy then. But that was eight weeks ago and Nneoma was over it. Really, she was.

She gathered her papers and rang for the car, which pulled up to the glass doors almost immediately. Amadi was timely like that. Her mother used to say that she could call him on her way down the stairs and open the door to find him waiting. Mama was gone now, and Nneoma's father, who'd become undone, never left the house. Amadi had run his errands for him until Nneoma moved back from New Kenya, when her father gifted him to her, like a basket of fine cheese. She'd accepted the driver as what she knew he was, a peace offering. And though it would never be the same between them, she called her father every other Sunday.

She directed Amadi to go to the store first. They drove through the wide streets of Enugu and passed a playground full of sweaty egg-white children. It wasn't that Nneoma had a problem with the Britons per se, but some of her father had rubbed off on her. At his harshest Papa would call them refugees rather than allies. He'd long been unwelcome in polite company.

"They come here with no country of their own and try to take over everything and don't contribute anything," he often said.

That wasn't entirely true.

When the floods started swallowing the British Isles, they'd reached out to Biafra, a plea for help that was answered. Terms were drawn, equitable exchanges of services contracted. But while one hand reached out for help, the other wielded a knife. Once here, the Britons had insisted on having their own lands and their own separate government. A compromise, aided by the British threat to deploy biological weapons, resulted in the Biafra-Britannia Alliance. Shared lands, shared government, shared grievances. Her father was only a boy when it happened but still held bitterly to the idea of Biafran independence, an independence his parents had died for in the late 2030s. He wasn't alone, but most people knew to keep their opinions to themselves, especially if their daughter was a Mathematician, a profession that came with its own set of troubles. And better a mutually beneficial, if unwanted, alliance than what the French had done in Senegal, the Americans in Mexico.

A

As Amadi drove, he kept the rearview mirror partially trained on her, looking for an opening to start a chat that would no doubt lead to his suggesting they swing by her father's place later, just for a moment, just to say hello. Nneoma avoided eye contact. She couldn't see her father, not for a quick hello, not today, not ever.

They pulled up to ShopRite and Nneoma hopped out. Her stomach grumbling, she loaded more fruit in her basket than she could eat in a week and cut the bread queue, to the chagrin of the waiting customers. The man at the counter recognized her and handed over the usual selection of rolls and the crusty baguette she would eat with a twinge of guilt. The French didn't get money directly, yet she couldn't stop feeling like she was funding the idea of them. Ignoring the people staring at her, wondering who she might be (a diplomat? a minister's girlfriend?), she walked the edges of the store, looping toward the checkout lane.

Then she felt him.

Nneoma slowed and picked up a small box of detergent, feigning interest in the instructions to track him from the corner of her eye. He was well dressed, but not overly so. He looked at her, confused, not sure why he was so drawn to her. Nneoma could feel the sadness rolling off him and she knew if she focused she'd be able to see his grief, clear as a splinter. She would see the source of it, its architecture, and the way it anchored to him. And she would be able to remove it.

It started when she was fourteen, in math class. She'd always been good at math but had no designs on being a Mathematician. No one did. It wasn't a profession you chose or aspired to; either you could do it or you couldn't. That day, the teacher had shown them a long string of Furcal's Formula, purchased from the Center like a strain of virus. To most of the other students, it was an impenetrable series of numbers and symbols, but to Nneoma it was as simple as the alphabet. Seeing the Formula unlocked something in her. From then on she could see a person's sadness as plainly as the clothes he wore.

The Center paid for the rest of her schooling, paid off the little debt her family owed, and bought them a new house. They trained her to hone her talents, to go beyond merely seeing a person's grief to mastering how to remove it. She'd been doing it for so long she could exorcise the deepest of traumas for even the most resistant of patients. Then her mother died.

The man in the store stood there looking at her and Nneoma took advantage of his confusion to walk away. The grieving were often drawn to her, an inadvertent magnetic thing. It made her sheltered life blessed and necessary. The Center was very understanding and helped contracted Mathematicians screen their clients. None of them were ever forced to work with a client or provide a service they didn't want to. Nneoma worked almost exclusively with parents who'd lost a child, wealthy couples who'd thought death couldn't touch them, till it did. When the Center partnered with governments to work with their distressed populations, the job was voluntary and most Mathematicians donated a few hours a week. There were exceptions, like Kioni, who worked with such people full-time, and Nneoma, who didn't work with them at all. Mother Kioni, Nneoma had called her, first with affection, then with increasing malice as things between them turned ugly. This man, in the tidy suit and good shoes, was more along the lines of her preferred clientele. He could very well become a client of hers in the future, but not today, not like this.

At checkout, the boy who scanned and bagged her groceries was wearing a name tag that read "Martin," which may or may not have been his name. The Britons preferred their service workers with names they could pronounce, and most companies obliged them. The tattoo on his wrist indicated his citizenship—an original Biafran—and his class, third. No doubt he lived outside of the city and was tracked from the minute he crossed the electronic threshold till the minute he finished his shift and left. He was luckier than most.

At the car, she checked her personal phone, the number only her father, her assistant, and Kioni knew. Still no message. She hadn't heard from Kioni since she'd moved out. She had to know Nneoma worried, in spite of how they'd left things. None of their mutual New Kenyan contacts knew where to find her, and Kioni's phone went unanswered. Maybe this was what it took for Kioni to exorcise her.

On the way to the school, Nneoma finished off two apples and a roll and flipped through her notes. She had done many such presentations, which were less about presenting and more about identifying potential Mathematicians, who had a way of feeling each other out. She ran a finger along the Formula, still mesmerized by it after all this time. She'd brought fifty-seven lines of it, though she would only need a few to test the students.

When things began to fall apart, the world cracked open by earthquakes and long-dormant volcanoes stretched, yawned, and bellowed, the churches (mosques, temples) fell—not just the physical buildings shaken to dust by tremors, but the institutions as well. Into the vacuum stepped Francisco Furcal, a Chilean mathematician who discovered a formula that explained the universe. It, like the universe, was infinite, and the idea that the formula had no end and, perhaps, by extension, humanity had no end was exactly what the world needed.

Over decades, people began to experiment with this infinite formula and, in the process, discovered equations that coincided with the anatomy of the human body, making work like hers possible. A computer at the Center ran the Formula 24/7, testing its infiniteness. There were thousands and thousands of lines. People used to be able to tour the South African branch and watch the endless symbols race ticker-style across a screen. Then the Center closed to the public, and the rumors started that Furcal's Formula was wrong, that the logic of it faltered millions and millions of permutations down the line, past anything a human could calculate in her lifetime. That it was not infinite.

They were just that, rumors, but then a man fell from the sky.

As they neared the school, they could see a few protesters with gleaming electronic placards. The angry red of angry men. Amadi slowed.

"Madam?"

"Keep going, there are only ten."

But the number could triple by the time she was ready to leave. How did they always know where she'd be?

The car was waved through the school's outer gate, then the inner gate, where Amadi's ID was checked, then double-checked. When the guard decided that

Amadi wasn't credentialed enough to wait within the inner gate, Nneoma stepped in. Her driver, her rules. The guard conceded as she'd known he would, and Amadi parked the car under a covered spot out of the sun. Nneoma was greeted by Nkem Ozechi, the headmaster, a small, neat woman whose hands reminded her of Kioni's. She had a smug air about her and walked with a gait that was entirely too pleased with itself. She spoke to Nneoma as though they'd known each other for years. On a different day, Nneoma might have been charmed, interested, but today she just wanted the session to be over with so she could go home.

The class was filled with bored faces, most around thirteen or fourteen (had she ever looked so young?), few caring or understanding what she did, too untouched by tragedy to understand her necessity. But schools like these, which gathered the best and brightest that several nations had to offer (according to Nkem Ozechi), paid the Center handsomely to have people like her speak, and it was the easiest money she earned.

"How many of you can look at someone and know that they are sad?"

The whole class raised their hands.

"How many of you can tell if someone is sad even if they are not crying?"

Most hands stayed up.

"How many of you can look at a person who is sad, know why they are sad, and fix it?"

All hands lowered. She had their attention now.

The talk lasted fifteen minutes before she brought it to a close.

"Some Mathematicians remove pain, some of us deal in negative emotions, but we all fix the equation of a person. The bravest"—she winked—"have tried their head at using the Formula to make the human body defy gravity, for physical endeavors like flight."

The class giggled, the fallen man fresh in their minds.

"Furcal's Formula means that one day the smartest people can access the very fabric of the universe." For many the Formula was God, misunderstood for so long. They believed that it was only a matter of time before someone discovered the formula to create life, rather than to just manipulate it. But this was beyond the concerns of the teenagers, who applauded politely.

The headmaster stepped from the corner to moderate questions. The first were predictable and stupid. "Can you make people fall in love?" No. "Can you make someone become invisible?" No. Nkem Ozechi might have been embarrassed to know that their questions were no different from those posed by students in the lower schools. Then (again predictably) someone posed a nonquestion.

"What you are doing is wrong." From a reed-thin boy with large teeth. Despite his thinness there was a softness to him, a pampered look.

Nneoma put her hand up to stop Nkem Ozechi from interrupting. She could handle this. "Explain."

"Well, my dad says what you people do is wrong, that you shouldn't be stopping a person from feeling natural hardships. That's what it means to be human."

Someone in the back started to clap until Nneoma again raised her hand for silence. She studied the boy. He was close enough for her to note his father's occupation on his wrist (lawyer) and his class (first). She'd argued down many a person

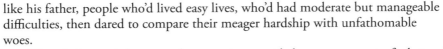

like his father, people who'd lived easy lives, who'd had moderate but manageable difficulties, then dared to compare their meager hardship with unfathomable woes.

"Your father and those people protesting outside have no concept of what real pain is. As far as I'm concerned, their feelings on this matter are invalid. I would never ask a person who hasn't tasted a dish whether it needs more salt."

The boy sat with his arms crossed, pouting. She hadn't changed his mind, you never could with people like that, but she'd shut him up.

In the quiet that followed, another hand raised. *Not her*, Nneoma thought, *not her*. She'd successfully ignored the girl since walking into the classroom. She didn't need to look at her wrist to know that the girl was Senegalese and had been affected by the Elimination. It was etched all over her, this sorrow.

"So you can make it go away?" They could have been the only two people in the room.

"Yes, I can." And to kill her dawning hope, "But it is a highly regulated and very expensive process. Most of my clients are heavily subsidized by their governments, but even then"—in case any hope remained—"you have to be a citizen."

The girl lowered her eyes to her lap, fighting tears. As though to mock her, she was flanked by a map on the wall, the entire globe splayed out as it had been seventy years ago and as it was now. Most of what had been North America was covered in water and a sea had replaced Europe. Russia was a soaked grave. The only continents unclaimed in whole or in part by the sea were Australia and the United Countries—what had once been Africa. The Elimination began after a moment of relative peace, after the French had won the trust of their hosts. The Senegalese newspapers that issued warnings were dismissed as conspiracy rags, rabble-rousers inventing trouble. But then came the camps, the raids, and the mysterious illness that wiped out millions. Then the cabinet members murdered in their beds. And the girl had survived it. To be here, at a school like this, on one of the rare scholarships offered to displaced children, the girl must have lived through the unthinkable. The weight of her mourning was too much. Nneoma left the room, followed by Nkem Ozechi, who clicked hurriedly behind her.

"Maybe some of them will be Mathematicians, like you."

Nneoma needed to gather herself. She saw the sign for the ladies' room and stepped inside, swinging the door in Nkem Ozechi's face. None of those children would ever be Mathematicians; the room was as bare of genius as a pool of fish.

She checked the stalls to make sure she was alone and bent forward to take deep breaths. She rarely worked with refugees, *true* refugees, for this reason. The complexity of their suffering always took something from her. The only time she'd felt anything as strongly was after her mother had passed and her father was in full lament, listing to the side of ruin. How could Nneoma tell him that she couldn't even look at him without being broken by it? He would never understand. The day she'd tried to work on him, to eat her father's grief, she finally understood why it was forbidden to work on close family members. Their grief was your own and you could never get out of your head long enough to calculate it. The attempt had ended with them both sobbing, holding each other in comfort and worry, till her father became so angry at the futility of it, the uselessness of her talents in this one crucial moment, that he'd said words he could not take back.

A

The bathroom door creaked open. Nneoma knew who it was. The girl couldn't help but seek her out. They stared at each other awhile, the girl uncertain, till Nneoma held out her arms and the girl walked into them. Nneoma saw the sadness in her eyes and began to plot the results of it on an axis. At one point the girl's mother shredded by gunfire. Her brother taken in the night by a gang of thugs. Her father falling to the synthesized virus that attacked all the melanin in his skin till his body was an open sore. And other, smaller hurts: Hunger so deep she'd swallowed fistfuls of mud. Hiding from the men who'd turned on her after her father died. Sneaking into her old neighborhood to see new houses filled with the more fortunate of the French evacuees, those who hadn't been left behind to drown, their children chasing her away with rocks like she was a dog. Nneoma looked at every last suffering, traced the edges, weighed the mass. And then she took it.

No one had ever really been able to explain what happened then, why one person could take another person's grief. Mathematical theories abounded based on how humans were, in the plainest sense, a bulk of atoms held together by positives and negatives, a type of cellular math. An equation all their own. A theologian might have called it a miracle, a kiss of grace from God's own mouth. Philosophers opined that it was actually the patients who gave up their sadness. But in that room it simply meant that a girl had an unbearable burden and then she did not.

· · · · · · · · · · · · ·

The ride home was silent. Amadi, sensing her disquiet, resisted the casual detour he usually made past the junction that led to her father's house, whenever they ventured to this side of town. At home, Nneoma went straight to bed, taking two of the pills that would let her sleep for twelve hours. After that she would be as close to normal as she could be. The rawness of the girl's memories would diminish, becoming more like a story in a book she'd once read. The girl would feel the same way. Sleep came, deep and black, a dreamless thing with no light.

The next morning, she turned on the unit to see much the same coverage as the day before, except now the fallen man's widow had jumped into the fray, calling for a full audit of the Center's records and of Furcal's Formula. Nneoma snorted. It was the sort of demand that would win public support, but the truth was the only experts who knew enough to audit anything all worked for the Center, and it would take them decades to pore over every line of the Formula. More likely this was a ploy for a payoff, which the woman would get. The Furcals could afford it.

Nneoma told herself she wouldn't check her messages again for at least another hour and prepared for her daily run. A quick peek revealed that no messages were waiting anyway. She keyed the code into the gate to lock it behind her, stretched, and launched.

The run cleared the last vestiges of yesterday's ghosts. She would call Claudine today to see how serious this whole falling thing was. There'd be only so much the PR rep could legally say, but dinner and a few drinks might loosen her tongue.

Nneoma lengthened her stride the last mile home, taking care to ease into it. The last time she'd burst into a sprint she pulled a muscle, and the pain eater assigned to her was a grim man with a nonexistent bedside manner. She'd felt his disapproval as he worked on her. No doubt he thought his talents wasted in her cozy sector and was tolerating this rotation till he could get back to the camps. Nneoma disliked Mathematicians like him and they disliked ones like her. It was a miracle she and Kioni had lasted as long as they did.

As she cleared the corner around her compound, she saw a small crowd gathered at her gate. *Protesters?* she wondered in shock before she registered the familiar faces of her neighbors. When she neared, a man she recognized but could not name caught her by the shoulders.

"We called medical right away. She was banging on your gate and screaming. She is your friend, no? I've seen her with you before." He looked very concerned, and suddenly Nneoma didn't want to know who was there to see her and why.

It was just a beggar. The woman wore no shoes and her toes were wounds. How on earth had she been able to bypass city security? Nneoma scrambled back when the woman reached out for her, but froze when she saw her fingers, delicate and spindly, like insect legs.

Those hands had once stroked her body. She had once kissed those palms and drawn those fingers into her mouth. She would have recognized them anywhere.

"Kioni?"

"Nneoma, we have to go, we have to go now." Kioni was frantic and kept looking behind her. Every bare inch of her skin was scratched or bitten or cut in some way. Her usually neat coif of dreadlocks was half missing, her scalp raw and puckered as if someone had yanked them out. The smell that rolled from her was all sewage.

"Oh my God, Kioni, oh my God."

Kioni grabbed her wrists and wouldn't surrender them. "We have to go!"

Nneoma tried to talk around the horrified pit in her stomach. "Who did this to you? Where do we have to go?"

Kioni shook her head and sank to her knees. Nneoma tried to free one of her hands and when she couldn't, pressed and held the metal insert under her palm that would alert security at the Center. They would know what to do.

From her current angle, Nneoma could see more of the damage on the other woman, the scratches and bites concentrated below the elbow. Something nagged and nagged at her. And then she remembered the Australian, and the stories of him trying to eat himself.

"Kioni, who did this?" Nneoma repeated, though her suspicion was beginning to clot into certainty and she feared the answer.

Kioni continued shaking her head and pressed her lips together like a child refusing to confess a lie.

Their falling-out had started when Nneoma did the unthinkable. In violation of every boundary of their relationship (and a handful of Center rules), she'd asked Kioni to work on her father. Kioni, who volunteered herself to the displaced Senegalese and Algerians and Burkinababes and even the evacuees, anyone in dire need of a grief worker, was the last person she should have asked for such a thing,

A

and told her so. Nneoma had called her sanctimonious, and Kioni had called her a spoiled rich girl who thought her pain was more important than it actually was. And then Kioni had asked her to leave.

Now she needed to get Kioni to the Center. Whatever was happening had to be fixed.

"They just come and they come and they come."

Nneoma crouched down to hear Kioni better. Most of her neighbors had moved beyond hearing distance, chased away by the smell. "Who comes?" she asked, trying to keep Kioni with her.

"All of them, can't you see?"

She began to understand what was happening to her former girlfriend.

How many people had Kioni worked with over the last decade? Five thousand? Ten? Ten thousand traumas in her psyche, squeezing past each other, vying for the attention of their host. What would happen if you couldn't forget, if every emotion from every person whose grief you'd eaten came back up? It could happen, if something went wrong with the formula millions and millions of permutations down the line. A thousand falling men landing on you.

Nneoma tried to retreat, to close her eyes and unsee, but she couldn't. Instinct took over and she raced to calculate it all. The breadth of it was so vast. Too vast.

The last clear thought she would ever have was of her father, how crimson his burden had been when she'd tried to shoulder it, and how very pale it all seemed now.■

AUTHOR PROFILE

Lesley Nneka Arimah (b. 1984) was born in the United Kingdom and raised in both the UK and Nigeria. She currently lives, teaches, and writes in Minneapolis. She won the 2015 Commonwealth Short Story Prize for Africa for "Light." Her debut short story collection, *What It Means When a Man Falls from the Sky*, appeared in 2017 and won the Kirkus Prize. The same year, she was named one of the National Book Foundation's 5 Best Writers Under 35. The story "What It Means When a Man Falls from the Sky" first appeared in *Catapult* in 2015 and then again in the short story collection that shares its name.

When Universities Swallow Cities

By Davarian L. Baldwin

In March 2016, as New Haven struggled to balance its shrinking budget, Mayor Toni Harp joined alders and local unions calling for a State Senate bill to help fine-tune Yale University's property-tax-exempt status. Universities and their medical centers are registered with the Internal Revenue Service as 501(c)(3) charitable nonprofit groups. Because of the public services that higher-education institutions provide to surrounding communities, their property holdings are exempt from taxation in all 50 states. The Connecticut bill, SB 414, would allow the state to tax university properties that generate $6,000 or more in annual income. Another bill, SB 413, which died in committee, sought to tax unspent returns on Yale's endowment.

Over the past 40 years, Yale had become the single largest commercial power in New Haven, as part of a national urban economy largely driven by universities and hospitals. Harp celebrated Yale's central role "in the city's transformation," but she warned that while cities rely "more and more on eds and meds," New Haven leaders must "be clear as a policy matter about the fiscal impact of this transition." New Haven felt the need to adjust its relationship with Yale University, which had gone from an influential urban stakeholder to a tax-exempt municipal powerhouse.

SB 414 did not pass, however, and New Haven continues to struggle with Connecticut's multibillion-dollar budget deficit while its largest local economic entity remains tax-exempt. (Yale does pay tax on some properties deemed "clearly commercial," such as stores on campus, and offers "payment in lieu of taxes," voluntary contributions that make up a small fraction of the estimated taxes it would pay based on the assessed value of its properties.)

Municipalities across the country face a similar tension: They attempt to patch budget holes while watching the endowments and urban footprints of tax-exempt colleges and universities grow. These problems necessitate a sober look at the inflated role of higher-education institutions in shaping urban policy, planning, and economic development—at the rise of what I call "UniverCities." The quaint notion of the ivory tower is dead, as city schools take on a baron-like stewardship over surrounding neighborhoods to help shore up their fiscal stability in times of economic change. Collectively, these institutions have taken a leading role in shaping the future of urban America. Indeed, urban universities and their attendant medical centers ("meds and eds") stand as perhaps the most central, and yet profoundly underexamined, social force in today's cities. The presumption that higher education is implicitly a public good has for too long distracted critics and scholars from getting to the heart of the matter: What makes universities good for our cities?

The enlarged influence of "meds and eds" over city life dates at least to the end of World War II. We are familiar with universities that supplied academic research for military application during the Cold War. The Massachusetts Institute of Technology has generally been the biggest university defense contractor in the

B

country. Stanford used the defense-contract system to propel itself from a regional school into a science-and-technology powerhouse. Research for the Manhattan Project was conducted at the University of Chicago's Met Lab. But in 1959 a group of city universities lobbied for the "Section 112 credits program" in federal housing legislation that helped make higher education the friendly face of urban-renewal projects across the country. These efforts demolished black neighborhoods and established white residential islands around urban campuses. In 1967 the University of Pennsylvania used the credits program to start displacing approximately 600 low-income and African-American families to build its University City Science Center, the nation's first inner-city urban research park.

Today, higher education's tides of influence have spread far beyond the campus. Universities are now the dominant employers, real-estate holders, policing agents, and education and health-care providers in many major cities. The University of Southern California, for instance, is the largest private-sector employer in Los Angeles. Columbia University and New York University are two of the largest private landowners in New York City. The University of Chicago fields one of the largest private security forces in the country, with jurisdiction over 65,000 nonstudent residents on Chicago's South Side. What happened?

In the middle of the 20th century, there was large-scale economic divestment from urban areas, followed by the flight of largely white urbanites. But starting in the 1990s, municipal leaders began competing to create an attractive "urban experience" to capture the consumer dollars of young professionals and empty nesters venturing back inside their borders. With the decline in manufacturing, the "bell towers" of higher education have become the new "smokestacks"—the signals of a thriving urban economy. In the process, city colleges and universities have recast themselves as institutions that can parcel and repackage "blighted" areas into "destinations" for a safe and profitable urban experience.

After Columbia announced its plans to build a new campus in West Harlem in 2003, President Lee Bollinger acknowledged the university's fraught history with the neighborhood. He proclaimed, "Columbia is a different neighbor now," publicly emphasizing the themes of partnership and collaboration. However, students and residents discovered that, starting in 2004, Columbia began working with the city's Economic Development Corporation, an environmental-consulting firm, and the Empire State Development Corporation to manufacture a "neighborhood conditions" report. This report labeled the West Harlem/Manhattanville area "blighted," which justified the use of eminent domain to take over and demolish properties on 17 acres of the neighborhood for a $6-billion research campus. In 2009 a court found the use of eminent domain unconstitutional and characterized the evidence for blight as "preposterous" and "egregious." But the following year, New York State's highest court upheld Columbia's use of eminent domain and its plans forge ahead.

The university has gone from one small, noble part of the city to serving as a model for the city itself. It is precisely the commercial amenities historically associated with "university life"—concerts, coffee shops, foot-traffic congestion, fully wired networking, high-tech research—that are being sold as a desirable urban experience. Residents have flocked back into cities looking for these university-styled urban experiences at the same time that rapidly shrinking state budgets have led universities to seek new ways to generate capital in the for-profit realms of labor, health care, and land control.

It may be the case that urban universities have been saved by gentrification, or are even the drivers of gentrification. Readers can draw their own conclusions. But what we can say with certainty is that at the same time universities were looking for new revenue, municipal leaders were seeking to remake their cities in the high-tech and high-density model of the university. UniverCities emerged when the interests of higher-education administrators, government officials, business leaders, and young professionals converged in the new service-and-information economy.

In the past, urban-renewal schemes attempted to push poor and nonwhite residents away from campus neighborhoods through primarily residential development. The irony, today, is that colleges and universities are left with few amenities to sell and little commercial development—a problem when it came to attracting what a University of Chicago student called higher education's most "precious set of imported individuals," its students. Now the urban development of impoverished neighborhoods has been handed over to the for-profit arm of higher education. This convergence between money-hungry colleges and the attractiveness of "university life" for new urbanites has given rise to UniverCities.

The urban-planning model of UniverCities provides needed capital to institutions of higher education. University-based urban planning is also celebrated for creating a vibrant kind of public life that attracts wealth-creating entrepreneurs and the workers they employ. In 2009 promotional material in an airline magazine championing economic development in Ithaca, N.Y., went so far as to tout colleges and universities as key weapons for counteracting what it called, with no racial irony, the "bright flight" of the creative class from America's biggest cities. Everyone wants to build a UniverCity.

In 2006, Phoenix passed a $223-million bond to build Arizona State University a downtown campus, with the hopes of converting undergraduates into a ready-made consumer base to energize urban retail and nightlife. Cornell University collaborated with Technion-Israel Institute of Technology and won a 2011 international competition to build a campus in New York City, hoping to spark a boom in the local high-tech sector. Furthermore, the growing faith in higher education as an urban growth engine has gone global. Consider the audaciously named Education City, in Doha, Qatar, or the controversies surrounding NYU's franchising of its university brand in Shanghai and Abu Dhabi.

Many, like the "prosperity expert" Richard Florida, celebrate colleges' and universities' capacity to spark neighborhood vitality by providing museums, lectures, and public-safety protections while also creating new economic opportunities. The University of Pittsburgh, Carnegie Mellon University, and the city government came together to transform an abandoned steel mill into the Pittsburgh Technology Center, a site for advanced academic and corporate research. Saint Louis University instituted the Hometown SLU mortgage-loan-forgiveness program for employees and opened the boutique Hotel Ignacio in the newly revitalized Midtown Alley district. Even during the Great Recession, urban leaders all over the country rushed to pay Richard Florida's consulting firm up to $250,000 for tactics hoping to transform their location into a potentially lucrative "Creative City."

Despite all the triumphalist rhetoric surrounding higher education's expansive reach across American cities, black and Latino communities that surround campuses are left especially vulnerable. These neighboring communities of color frequently sit in zones of relatively cheap and sometimes abandoned land, and hold little political influence. Richard Florida, for instance, has since pulled back on his grand claims, after facing vigorous critiques that an increased creative class can, in fact, increase inequalities.

To be sure, higher-education institutions can deliver positive urban outcomes, but a central question remains: What are the costs when colleges and universities exercise significant power over a city's financial resources, policing, employment, and real estate?

Higher education's noneducational investments in real estate, policing, and labor can carry negative consequences for neighborhoods of color. Urban schools have become islands of wealth amid a sea of poverty. And this uneven geography rapidly gives way to an extension of the campus as a planning model for larger swaths of the city. The result? Poorer neighbors are pushed to the periphery of "meds and eds" prosperity. Large-scale university acquisitions of prime real estate (such as in New Haven, Philadelphia, New York City, and Chicago) lead to housing and land values that skyrocket beyond the reach of community members. The University of Southern California pushes ahead to replace the ancient University Village shopping center with a $900-million complex of stores and dormitories. As related changes quickly follow, including a nearby Expo train line, residents watch landlords convert family-friendly dwellings into student-oriented rentals with rates increased by almost 50 percent.

Many of these same residents may be shunted into the low-wage sectors of higher-education labor: janitors, cooks, groundskeepers, and other kinds of support staff. Harvard wields its $38-billion endowment to continue rapid campus growth into the Allston-Brighton neighborhood, while its food-service workers recently went on strike to protest low wages and rising health-care costs. South Side Chicago residents championed the extension of campus-police jurisdictions into their embattled neighborhoods, but "security," it turned out, largely meant protecting white students amid increased complaints of racial profiling and harassment. Black students at USC have alleged excessive force and racial profiling by the LAPD.

UniverCities are taking over, and yet we fail to examine the consequences of their embracing an increasingly for-profit approach to their urban surroundings. A growing body of work, including Derek Bok's Universities in the Marketplace (Princeton University Press, 2003), Henry A. Giroux's University in Chains (Routledge, 2007), and Jeffrey J. Selingo's College (Un)Bound (New Harvest, 2013) has examined the state of universities today. Soaring tuition costs, staggering student debt, and the inroads of business interests and the defense industries seem to confirm fears of a "corporate university." While insightful, few of these works turn their eyes beyond the campus walls to scrutinize higher education's nationwide expansion across our cities. Our blind spot to the rise of UniverCities comes largely from the assumption that higher education, while hypnotized by corporate power, is still an inherent public good, most clearly marked by its tax-exempt status for providing services that would otherwise come from the government.

B

A public-good paradox arises: Nonprofit status is precisely what allows for an easier transfer of public dollars into higher education's urban developments with little public oversight or scrutiny. Colleges and universities pay virtually no taxes on their increasingly prominent downtown footprints. They also reap the benefits of police and fire protections, snow and trash removal, road maintenance, and other municipal services while shouldering little financial burden. Homeowners and small-business owners ultimately carry the weight of inflated property taxes caused by urban campuses, and the cost of rental properties skyrockets.

Such unfair taxing rates caused residents in the historically black neighborhood of Witherspoon-Jackson to sue and win an $18-million settlement from Princeton University in 2016. Residents argued that while local property taxes increased, the university maintained its exemption for buildings where research had generated millions of dollars in commercial royalties. The public-good paradox creates a lucrative higher-education "shelter economy," in which tax-exempt status helps generate significant private profits with little public benefit. Donors' gifts to endowments are tax-deductible, the investment income earned by endowments is tax-free, and so higher education has a competitive edge over businesses that pay taxes in, say, biotech or property management.

One plaintiff in the Princeton case described the university as "a hedge fund that conducts classes." We must no longer evaluate colleges and universities simply by their stated aim of knowledge production and dissemination. They have become rapacious pro-growth behemoths that discuss students as consumers, alumni as shareholders, and the world beyond the campus walls as either prime real estate or a dangerous threat to their brand.

They also oversee a vast payroll of white-collar and low-wage contingent workers. They maintain cheap workshops where exploited graduate students secure lucrative patents for corporate research. Campuses expand across cities, often choosing to bank land, awaiting its appreciation, rather than invest in services and infrastructure that would aid the local community. Higher education is a key growth machine in today's cities because it has been given the keys to drive the urban economy forward by reorganizing urban space to serve its institutional desires as much as or more than its educational interests.

Caricatures of colleges as ivory-tower bastions of tenured radicals and young "snowflakes," out of touch with reality, abound. But higher education's footprint across the nation's cities tells a different story. How are flourishing colleges acting in the public good when that public is paying for their economic competitive advantage? Has the very notion of the public good been perverted when it is used to justify multimillion-dollar tax-exempt endowments, an enormous contingent and low-wage labor force, the elimination of affordable housing in campus neighborhoods, and increased racial profiling?

Colleges and universities are where we should be able to pose and begin to answer those tough questions. Yet while universities set themselves the task of solving humanity's most difficult problems, they have failed to question their own impact right outside their gates.

There is reason to hope for a better ending to this story. Activism against higher education's urban expansion goes back at least to the 1960s, when residents and students in New York City led protests with the shout "Gym Crow!"

B

after they learned that Columbia University planned to build a gymnasium in Morningside Park that would serve as a physical barrier between the campus and Harlem. More recently, students, workers, neighborhood residents, and even municipal leaders have found innovative ways to rally against higher education's growing hunger for control over today's cities. In 2012 the college-heavy city of Boston asked nonprofit groups with more than $15 million in tax-exempt property to volunteer 25 percent of the property taxes they would owe if not exempt (though many of the institutions involved, including Harvard, have fallen short in their contributions).

At the University of North Carolina at Chapel Hill, the University of California, and many places in between, students have joined forces with campus workers to demand union recognition, living wages, and better health care. Since 2013 the Campaign for Equitable Policing has been fighting to ensure just treatment and end racial profiling in the expanding jurisdiction of the University of Chicago Police Department. Students continue to fight alongside residents against Columbia's use of eminent domain and NYU's rewriting of zoning laws to control large sections of West Harlem and Greenwich Village, respectively.

A new city is emerging before our eyes. City campuses sit at a critical crossroads between their educational mandate and their economic footprint. If colleges and universities are going to be the new company in our "company towns," then campus stakeholders, neighborhood residents, and city leaders must be at the table, in an equal way, for transparent discussions about how higher-education institutions can best serve as a public good. ■

AUTHOR PROFILE

Davarian L. Baldwin received his Ph.D. in American studies from New York University in 2001. He has received numerous fellowships and awards, including the Distinguished Visiting Chair at Marquette University (2013–2014) and Distinguished Lectureship from the Organization of American Historians (2015–2018). His work examines the landscape of global cities through the lens of the African diasporic experience. Currently, he is the Paul E. Raether Distinguished Professor of American Studies at Trinity College in Hartford, CT. He is a frequent speaker at academic and public institutions, and his books include *Chicago's New Negroes: Modernity, the Great Migration*, and *Black Urban Life* (2007) and the edited collection *Escape from New York: The New Negro Renaissance beyond Harlem* (co-editor, 2013), and has also published numerous essays on related subjects. "When Universities Swallow Cities" appeared in *The Chronicle of Higher Education* on August 4, 2017.

Stupid Rich Bastards

By Laurel Johnson Black

Sunday morning, six o'clock. Dad knocks on my door and in a stage whisper tells me to get up and get going. Trying not to wake up my sister, I crawl out of bed into the chilly Massachusetts air and pull on jeans, a T-shirt, a sweatshirt, and sneakers. Nothing that can't get dirty. This isn't church, but it might as well be, an education full of rituals, its own language, its mystery and rewards, its punishments for falling away.

Every Sunday, each child in turn went with Dad to the flea markets, the yard sales, the junk yards, the little stores with names like "Bob's Salvage," "Junk n Stuff," or "The Treasure House." Even in winter, when the outdoor flea markets closed down and leaves spun with litter in circles in the yards, the salvage stores stood waiting for us, bleak and weathered, paint hanging in little flaps from the concrete-block walls, and our breath hanging in the still, frigid air surrounding the old desks and radio tubes, the file cabinets and chandeliers. In each place the man behind the counter would grab the lapels of his old wool coat and pull them tighter around him, saying how one day he'd like to heat the joint. Dad would tell him about the great buy we just saw at the last place but had to pass up this time and then ask him what was new. And each time the answer was, "In heayah? Nothin's evah new! But I got some stuff I didn't have befoah!" They'd laugh with one another, and I would trace my initials next to someone else's in the dust on the display cabinet.

In summer, we passed by the vendors who hawked T-shirts, socks, perfume, or cheap jewelry and walked to the tables covered with stuff from home, tables full of things that someone had wanted and needed for a long time until they needed money more, to pay their rent, fix their car, or feed the next child. Wall hangings, little plaques, beverage glasses with superheroes on them, ashtrays, bedspreads, tricycles, lawn mowers, table lamps, kitchen pots and pans, picture frames, shoes, a spice rack. Always behind one of these tables stood an older man, deeply tanned and showing muscles from long years of hard work, gray-haired and with a cigarette and a hopeful smile, always willing to come down a little on an item, even though it meant a lot to him. Sometimes his wife would also be there, heavy, quiet, holding a styrofoam cup of coffee, sitting in a webbed lawn chair set back a little from the table, judging those who would judge the things she had loved and used for so long.

We touched these items carefully, with respect, because we were that child who needed to be fed, because we knew what it felt like to have your things laid on such a table, touched by many hands and turned over and over while the dew burned off and the pavement heated up and people began to move as though through water, their legs lost in the shimmering heat that slipped sticky arms around buyers, sellers, lookers, and dreamers. And the language of these people behind the tables, and those who respected them and understood why they were there, filled the air like the smell of French fries from the dirty little restaurant next door and hung in my mind and sifted down into my heart.

B

This is not an essay. This is a story. My life is not an essay. We don't live essays or tell them to each other on the front steps on hot nights with beer or iced coffee and pretzels or pass them on to our children or dream them. This is a story, one about love and fear. It's about every child's nightmare of losing her family and the ways in which the world I now tentatively live in tries to make that nightmare come true, to make it not a nightmare but a dream, a goal.

There are a lot of holes in this story that get filled in, as with all stories, differently depending upon who's listening, depending on how I need to fill them in. There's a plot, a very simple one: a young woman goes from poverty to the middle class using education to move closer and closer to the stupid rich bastards she has heard about all her life. She finds ever larger contexts into which she can place everything, can get perspective. ("Perspective"—a word her father used to describe why he kept driving away, a word her mother told her meant to make things seem small and unimportant.) Until someone says "Fuck you!" and it all collapses. Then she pulls it back together like a quilt she had as a child, one she hid under rather than take her medicine, one she gasped under in the stifling heat rather than run through her room with the hornet circling in it. This is a story about war and injury, about stuffing the holes blown in hearts and brains and tongues with words, with the batting of anger and desire. It's about language.

Language for me has always been inseparable from what I am, from what and who people are. My house was filled with the language I associate with the working class and the poor, people who haven't the means to physically keep all the "dirty" parts of life at bay and who see no reason to do so with words. Shouting to each other across the yards in the old mill town where I grew up, my mother and her friends Pat and Barbara kept up their friendship and shared gossip and complaints about their lives. They wove their voices into the fabric of words and life I knew. As we played after school in the stand of woods along the river down behind the factory, we heard our names called for supper. The more time we took to get home to the table, the sharper the tone became and the longer the wonderful string of curses stretched out, echoing off the brick walls.

We talked about whatever touched us as we sat down to eat—who had stopped up the upstairs toilet, who had fought in the hallway at school, the girl who was stabbed in the head with a fork in the lunchroom, name calling on the bus, whether the home economics teacher was having an affair with the phys. ed. teacher, what my father saw in the house he'd just put a tub in, who we knew who'd been arrested. Bodily functions, secretions, garbage, crimes and delinquency, who got away with what were as much a part of our language as they were of our lives. They were part of the humor that filled my home. My father rising up from his chair to fart, shouting out in mock seriousness, "'Repoaht from the reah!' the sahgent replied," set us off in hysterics, imitations, and stories of passed gas and the contexts that made them so funny. Swearing was also a part of our lives— among adults, among kids away from their parents, and in the bad kids' homes, everyone swore fluently before they were eighteen or out of school. "Damn" and "shit" were every other word and so became like "and" and "well" to us as we talked with each other.

I lived in a web of narrative, something I've missed in graduate school. My father was a storyteller and a traveler, a man who would go away for a week or

two at a time on "business" of an undetermined nature. When he came back, he didn't bring presents but stories. Only a few years ago did I realize why the tale of Odysseus had seemed so familiar to me in the eighth grade and again as an undergraduate. He was a relative, or a friend, not just a character in an old story. In the tales told by my father and the men he bartered with, the "stupid rich bastards" almost always "got it" in the end, outwitted by the poor little guy. I learned that the stupid rich bastards always underestimated us, always thought we were as dumb as we were poor, always mistook our silence for ignorance, our shabby clothes and rusted cars for lack of ambition or enterprise. And so they got taken, and sharing stories about winning these small battles made us feel better about losing the war.

My father knew all the regular merchants at the flea markets. As we wandered along the aisles he'd yell over to Tony, a heavy man with thinning black hair patted into an ugly, oily arc across his head, "Hey! Ya fat Guinea! Ya still sellin' the same old junk? Huh? I've seen stuff move fasta in the toilets I unplug!" Tony would wave him off, turning a little away from him and throwing back over his shoulder, "What would you know about merchandise, ya stupid Swede? Huh? Shit for brains!" He'd touch his forehead with his middle finger, grin maliciously, and so would my father. As we worked our way closer to Tony, past the booth with old tools, past the book booth, Dad would ask, "So why haven't the cops bustid ya yet for alla this, Tony? What, you got a captain on ya payroll? This stuff is hot enough to burn ya hands off!" He'd blow on his fingers and wave them in the air, grinning. Tony grinned back at the compliment. "Naah, I buy this legit." He'd widen his eyes and look cherubic. "Really." They'd both laugh.

During the week, during my life, my father was a sometimes plumber, sometimes car salesman, sometimes junkman, sometimes something. My mother worked as a cook, a school crossing guard, at a McDonald's counter for a while. It was never enough. I remember one Saturday afternoon in August, my father was melting down old lead pipes. All afternoon he cut the soft pipes into small pieces and fed them into the heat of the kettle, then poured the liquid metal out into the little cupcake-shaped molds he'd set in the dirt of the driveway. Late in the afternoon, the heavy clouds broke and rain began spattering down on his back and shoulders. While I watched from the kitchen he kept working, the rain hissing and turning into steam as it struck the melting lead. Over and over, he reached forward to drop chunks of pipe in to melt, and his arms, then shoulders, then head disappeared in the fog of metal and mist. He became that man to me, the half-man in steam. He was the back I saw sometimes wearily climbing the stairs to sleep for a few hours. He was the chains rattling in the truck as it bounced down the pitted driveway and whined back up late at night as he came home. It wasn't enough. There was a stack of dunnings and notices that covered the end of the old stereo.

I remember when the man from the bank came to repossess our car. I had just broken my foot, and I hung onto the car door handle while my mother stood next to me talking to the man who wanted to take the car. Her voice was high, and with one hand she opened and closed the metal clasp on her purse. Finally she opened the car door, pushing me in and sliding in next to me. The man from the bank stepped back as she started the engine, and she rolled up the window as he leaned over to say something to us. She gunned it, careening wildly backward across the yard out into the street, crying. "So this is what we've got," she said. "This is it."

We were working poor and so we were alternately afraid and ashamed and bold and angry. We prayed to nothing in particular that no one would notice our clothes or that the police wouldn't notice the car didn't have a valid inspection sticker. My mother had to decide between a tank of gas and an insurance payment. She had to decide whether or not we really needed a doctor. We shopped as a group so that if my new dress for the year cost two dollars less than we had thought it would, my sister could get one that cost two dollars more. We didn't say such things out loud, though we thought them all the time. Words are ideas, ways of believing, connected to desire and fear. If I ate seconds, maybe I was eating my sister's dress. If Susan was really sick, then maybe I couldn't get new shoes. But if anyone ever said those things, it would all come crashing in. All of it—the idea that working hard would get you some place better, that we were just as good as anyone else—would crash to the floor like some heirloom dish that would never be the same again, even if we could find all the shards.

At some point in my life, when I was very young, it had been decided that I would be the one who went on to college, who earned a lot of money, who pulled my family away from the edge of the pit, and who gave the stupid rich bastards what they had coming to them. I would speak like them but wouldn't be one of them. I would move among them, would spy on them, learn their ways, and explain them to my own people—a guerrilla fighter for the poor. My father had visions of litigation dancing in his head, his daughter in a suit, verbally slapping the hell out of some rich asshole in a courtroom.

As I was growing up, the most important people I knew, the ones I most respected, were my teachers. I wanted to be like them. They had made the supreme sacrifice, had gone away and succeeded, but had chosen to come back to help us. They drove cars I could imagine appearing occasionally in my father's lot. They wore scuffed shoes and shopped at K-Mart. They didn't belong to a country club, didn't refuse to teach us because we were poor, didn't treat us with pity or condescension. They often worked year round, teaching summer school or even, as with my history teacher, driving a beer truck from June through August.

They were the only people I knew and trusted who might be able to teach me to speak like and understand the stupid rich bastards who held our lives in their hands and squeezed us until we couldn't breathe: doctors who refused to treat us without money up front; lawyers who wrote short, thick, nasty letters for credit companies who, in turn, spoke for someone else; insurance agents who talked in circles and held up payment; loan officers who disappeared into the backs of banks and didn't look at us when they told us we were too much of a risk; police and town selectmen who told us to get rid of our cars and clean up our disgraceful yards and lives—all the people who seemed always to be angry that they had to deal with us in any way. My teachers moved, I thought, with ease between my world and this other world. I hoped they would help me do the same.

My teachers tried to bridge the gap with speech. "In other words," they said, looking from the text to us, "what they're saying is…" They tried to bridge the gap with their bodies, one hand pointing to the board, the other hand stretched

55

out palm up, fingers trying to tug words from mouths contorted with the effort to find the right speech. We were their college-bound students, the ones who might leave, might be them again, might even do better. They were like our parents in their desire to have us succeed, but they had skills and knowledge that counted to the white-shirted men who sat behind the glass windows at the savings and loan, to the woman who handled forms for free butter, cheese, and rice.

I wanted to be like my teachers, but I was afraid of standing up before a classroom filled with students like the ones who laughed in the back of the classroom. The only writing these students did was carving names and sexual slurs or boasts on their desks, and their dreams, I imagined, were of lives like they already knew. I was afraid, too, that when I had become like these teachers I admired so much, I would still drive down the main street of a rotting industrial town and go into the 7-Eleven and somehow I would be no different than I was now. The very ones I admired most I also most suspected: if my teachers were such successes, why were they back here? Why did they make so little money? Drive those cars? I was afraid I would have nothing to say or show to the students who sat in the back, afraid that if they actually asked what I only thought—"So what?"—I would have no answer.

I worked summers at a resort in Maine, making beds and scrubbing toilets, earning tips and room and board. During the school year, I worked as a cook in a nursing home and as a maid for rich women who made me change sheets, crawl out on window ledges to clean glass, and scrub their kitchen floors on my knees. I had saved about five hundred dollars. I sent in cards to request material from any college that would send it to me. Every day, stacks of brochures and catalogues and letters awaited me when I came home from school. One or two that looked good—smiling students on the cover—I brought with me to work at the nursing home, and I read the captions while I ate my supper. The others I looked through at night for the cost to attend and the amount of aid usually awarded. When I filled out the financial aid forms, my father told me to put a zero on every line. I told him that no one would believe it. "Yah? So what? Think they'd believe thirteen dollahs eitha? Put it down." I did.

I decided on three colleges, all small, private ones because I was afraid of the throngs of students in the brochures for the state schools. Some of the schools had said they were "teaching institutions"; I avoided those too, believing that I would have to become a teacher if I went there. I was going to be a lawyer, was going to fulfill my father's vision. I was going to go where the kids of lawyers went. I filled out forms largely on my own, knowing that my parents didn't understand the questions and would be embarrassed at not being able to help me. I took all the standardized tests and did only okay, confused by analogies of bulls and bears (I thought they referred to constellations, not the stock market) and questions about kinds of sailing boats.

When my first-choice college sent me a letter telling me I was on their waiting list, my mother hugged me and told me how proud she was. My father asked me how long I'd have to wait and if I'd work in the meantime. My mother thought that merely making the waiting list was an achievement, something she could brag about to Pat and Barbara and the mailman, while my father thought that there was only a limited number of spaces in colleges all over the country and each student waited in turn to get in. I went upstairs and cried for hours. When I came back down for supper, my mother had fixed a cake in celebration.

I was in my first English class at my second-choice school, never having made it off the waiting list at my first-choice school. I'd never visited this college and knew little about it. I hadn't gone to orientation, begging off because of work. That was only partially true. Actually, I had begun to look at those smiling catalogue faces and bodies and then to look at myself. I had crooked teeth. I wore makeup. I wasn't tanned and lithe from summers of tennis and sailing. I wore old jeans patched at the thighs and ragged around the cuffs. I wore T-shirts and work boots, not clothing from L. L. Bean's. I read statements from the happy students, moving my lips and trying to make the words sound like they could be mine, but I realized that it was wrong, that I was wrong. What could I say to all these people? What could they say to me? And what people did I belong to?

My mother had also seen the pictures. She tried to buy me some clothes that matched theirs, and she watched as I packed, anxious that I not be made fun of. My grandfather, who had completed grade school, told me gruffly, "Now that youah goin' to college, you'll be too good t' talk to us anymoah." I protested but he shook his head; it was the last thing he ever said to me. I felt like my family wanted me so badly to be something other than what I was. And suddenly, all I wanted to be was "Lau-doop," as my father had called me when I was younger. It was enough to have been accepted at a college, to have been a high school valedictorian. That was bragging rights forever for my mother. Why did I need more? What was wrong with what I had and was?

Now I was here, dropped off by my sister and brother, who had turned the car around and headed for home after dumping off my box and bag. My roommate was crying because she couldn't fit all her Pendleton wools in her closet and drawers and had taken over some of mine. Her father, a successful lawyer, sized up the situation, watching me sit in silence in my flannel shirt and unfashionable jeans. "What should we call you?" he asked politely. I thought for a moment. "Johnson." He laughed delightedly. "Johnson? That's great! Sue, this'll be good for you," he chortled as he led his sniffling daughter and perfectly coiffed wife out to get lunch.

Now I was being asked to write editorials, but I didn't know what one was. My family had always bought the newspaper with the big photos in it, and the little local weekly had columns about who'd been arrested and what stores had gone out of business. I didn't understand the articles I had to read in order to write my editorials. I summarized what I'd read in two major paragraphs and turned it in, over and over, week after week. I got a B each time, no comments.

In French government class, students talked excitedly about their travels abroad. I felt the chip on my shoulder getting heavier and heavier. I'd been through all of New England; they'd been to France. Big fucking deal. Lions, Lee-ons, Lyons, it's all the same. Unless someone laughs at you for not knowing how to say what everyone else can not only say but describe from personal experience.

Poetry class. I describe in a long narrative poem what things I see around my neighborhood. The teacher gushes over it. It reminds him of T. S. Eliot, he says, and when I say, "Who's that?" he is astounded. He decides he has a diamond in the rough; he calls me a lump of coal with lots of potential. (Later, he asks me if I want to sleep with him.)

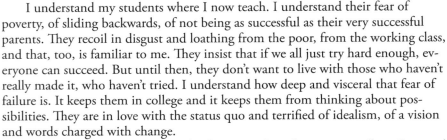

I understand my students where I now teach. I understand their fear of poverty, of sliding backwards, of not being as successful as their very successful parents. They recoil in disgust and loathing from the poor, from the working class, and that, too, is familiar to me. They insist that if we all just try hard enough, everyone can succeed. But until then, they don't want to live with those who haven't really made it, who haven't tried. I understand how deep and visceral that fear of failure is. It keeps them in college and it keeps them from thinking about possibilities. They are in love with the status quo and terrified of idealism, of a vision and words charged with change.

I was terrified of success. By Thanksgiving of my first year in college, I wanted to go home and stay there. What was I doing at this place for rich kids? What was I accomplishing? How was I helping my family? I was a mute, a heavy drinker, a class skipper. My sister was in a nursing program and was paying rent to my mother; another sister was also working and helping out. What was I doing? I was going to college on grants and loans, and while I was not sucking money from my family, I wasn't contributing to it either. I knew I could go home and each day I had stayed in college would count as part of my success. I could have failed by my fellow students' standards and still not have failed by my own. I would have been part of that story where the system beats down the good ones who try to make it out, where you try and try and try and still the stupid rich bastards squish you just when you might succeed. I could have come home and said, "Hey, they were a bunch of rich assholes. What do you want?" No further explanation would have been demanded or necessary.

In the dormitories at night the girls gathered into groups in the lounges or the hallway floors and told stories about their lives. I was silent, stricken dumb with fear. What would I tell them when my turn came? The truth? A lie? But I needn't have worried. My turn never came. I don't know whether it was out of compassion or snobbishness, but no one ever asked me about my family, my home, my friends, even my major or my hoped-for career. And as much as I hated myself for being ashamed of my life, I hated the girls more for knowing it.

In my conferences with teachers I sat mute, nodding weakly when it seemed called for, when their voices rose as if in a question. Whatever they suggested was right. In lectures, I took notes furiously, narrative notes, full sentences, trying to get the exact words spoken by the teacher. I knew if I took down just a word here and there I would have to fill in the gaps with my own words, and those words were horribly wrong. I was horribly wrong.

Maybe my mother knew. She's dead now and I never asked her. But she wrote me letters every now and then, and not once did she say she'd like me back. Not once did she explicitly give me the option of returning. After one letter in which I came close to admitting my despair, she wrote back, "We love you and we're proud of you. Don't show your face in the door until you're supposed to."

I had gotten an F+ on an English paper. On the bottom of the last page, Dr. B. had written, "Come and see me about this." I was now a second-semester sophomore and still had not gotten an A in my major, English; in fact, I had barely survived the drinking and class cutting of my first year. My parents had never seen my grade report, only knew that I was allowed to come back a second year, more reason for pride. I had learned to buy my classmates' thrown-away clothes at the local thrift store, and if I kept my mouth shut I could pass as one of them in most of my classes. I stopped wearing makeup, even stopped sitting in the groups in the dorms. Instead, I worked in the library on Friday nights and Saturday mornings, which gave me an excuse (I imagined one day I would need one) for never going out and spending money with anyone on weekends. Now, though, I had to hide from teachers, the people I had once wanted so much to be like.

I went to Dr. B.'s office about one minute before his office hours were over. I made sure the secretary saw me and that I had a piece of paper to write a note like: "Stopped by to talk about my paper. I'll catch you some other time." I inched my way down the hall toward his door, reading the numbers so I could pretend I had missed him because I had gotten lost.

Dr. B was still in his office. He welcomed me in, appearing surprised. He pulled his chair over next to mine, took my paper, and began to go over it, line by line, word by word. He peered over his little glasses, sometimes giving his head a violent nod so they would drop down on his chest and he could sit back and watch my reactions to his statements. I couldn't breathe. My chest felt like it was full, but I had no air. I didn't dare blink because my eyes were full of tears. I kept my head bent, my chin in my hand, and stared at my paper.

He sighed. Finally, he said something like, "Look. See this paragraph? This is a good one. There's a good idea in here. That's your idea. But it's not phrased well. Listen to it phrased this way." And he reread my idea in words that sounded like all my professors. Words that could have kept a stupid rich bastard listening. My idea. His words. But they were connected then. For the first time, I felt like I might make it through. I choked out a thank you, and he looked up, surprised. The conference wasn't over, but I was standing up. I thanked him again, stuffing the paper into my bookbag, and left before the tears came pouring down my face. I didn't know why I was crying, whether it was because I was so stupid that I got an F+ and had to sit there and make a nice man frustrated or because I felt that I could take that one paragraph and begin again, begin learning how to speak about what I thought and felt to people who weren't like me. Stupidity and relief. They've dogged me ever since.

The phone rang at two in the morning. It was my little sister, sobbing and nearly hysterical. Her boyfriend, drunk or high on something, had leaped from a closet and attacked her. She had beaten him off, clubbing him with a brass statue that my mother had given her. Now, while two friends tried to stop her bleeding—she had a broken nose, broken ribs, a broken foot—she choked out why she had called.

"He said the apahtment was in his name an' I gotta be outta heyah tomorrow mohnin' or he's takin' all the stuff heyah an' sellin' it an' he'll keep the dog too! An' I OWN this stuff, I paid fuh it an' *I* pay the rent but I don't got anywayah to go. You know legal stuff, right? Laurel, ya gotta help me!"

I searched my brain for what little I remembered from my pre-law days at college, a decade earlier. Now in a Ph.D. program in composition and rhetoric, far away from the gritty New England town where my sister lived and near which we grew up, I felt useless. Again. I began to ask her about her lease, to tell her

about the Legal Aid Society; I even began to think out loud through cases from a textbook I remembered. Suddenly she interrupted me, screaming over the line, "Fuck you! Fuck you! Don't talk to me like college, talk to me like a sista!"

I remember clearly the first time I chose to say to a professor, "Really!" instead of the more natural (to me), and what others might think of as more colorful, "Get outta heyah!" I remember when I began to believe that I might go into English and not law. It was a course on realism and naturalism. I began to tremble when I read *McTeague* (which I've been told many times since is not great literature but is useful as a demonstration of certain ideas in limited courses). Here were people I recognized! Here were characters who spoke like I did, who swore and hoped and dreamed for so damn little, for a place to stay that was clean, for respect, for something of their own that would last. Here were novels that showed that the poor weren't poor because they wanted to be, because they were lazy, but because of sweeping faceless economic forces that smashed them down and kept them down, and here were stupid rich bastards shown as they were in my own life. Here were writers who had words that spoke to me, that invited me not to join in some fantasy world but to confront and describe my own *real* world.

My parents (and in some ways, my whole family) never got over my defection from law. I tried to soften the blow by going into archeology; while it paid little, it was at least exotic and held out the hope of discovering some kind of lost treasure—imagine, money without working! But it was reconstructing lives and words, not ancient cultures but my own culture, that I kept being drawn to. I have come through poetry, sales, admissions, and finally composition, where first-year students begin to learn how their words hurt and heal, probe and hide, reshape, connect, embrace, and gag. It is a field that feels like work, where the texts are of a home and life so close to the world that the arguments mean something. They are like "sista," not "college."

Here, on paper, I can be in two worlds and control them both. But on the phone, my father asks me how that "school thing" is going, and what I still need to do, and what kind of salary I expect next year when I finally get a job. And I find it easier to slip into his world than to bring him into mine, to listen to his odysseys and believe in him as my mother did when she first married him. While a brother and sister are now doing well, two others are still living in poverty, and when I speak to my siblings my world slips around until I am dizzy.

l can bring their world into my own only in narratives, only distantly. No one in my family has ever read what I write. No one has visited my office or my classroom, at least not physically. I tell my students about my family, though; I talk to them in my language to show them there are many ways to say things. When we share our writing, I share a letter to home, full of swear words, little jokes, scatological humor, assertions that will be accepted without evidence solely because my sister and I "know" what stupid rich bastards are like and what they will say and do. And then we look at an essay I've written and then a poem, all dealing with my life, with words. They begin to feel their own words working in different ways, different contexts, begin to value the phrases and words that make them one thing and understand that these same words make it hard to be another thing. For most of my students, these exercises are often just an interesting diversion from reading literature. Some of them write in their journals of their relief. They, too, are first-generation college students, working class, afraid and silent. They appear at my door, ready to talk, knowing that I have been there and do not entirely want to leave.

When I work with my colleagues, with "real" faculty, I say little. I rehearse what I will say if I can predict the course of a meeting, and I miss some of what is going on while I hold my speech in my head, waiting for the opening in which I will speak like them long enough to fool them into thinking I *am* one of them. I am and I am not. My father's dream of how I would live and move between two worlds, two ways of speaking and knowing, haunts me.

I used to sit on the school bus on the way home from high school and look around at my classmates and wonder who would still be in my town in twenty years, who would go on, get out, succeed in ways that no one dreamed of. I used to think I would be one of those. Now I sometimes sit in meetings and classrooms and wonder who else would like to cut the shit and say what they feel. I feel suspended, dangling. If I put my toe down at any point, I might root there. I cannot move among the rich, the condescending, the ones who can turn me into an object of study with a glance or word, cannot speak like them, live in a house like them, learn their ways, and share them with my family without being disloyal to someone. I thought learning would make it easier for me to protect and defend my family, myself, but the more I learn the harder it is to passionately defend anything.

I am seeking a way to keep the language of the working class in academia, not just in my office with my working-class office mate, to nurture its own kind of vitality and rawness and directness, its tendency to ask "Why?" even as it says "Ah, what the fuck." I would like my colleagues to listen for the narratives embedded in their own writing, to feel the power of that movement forward just as they feel the power of the turning concept, the academic idea. And I would like my colleagues to turn my language over in their mouths with the same respect that my father and I turned over the items on those flea market tables. ■

AUTHOR PROFILE

Laurel Johnson Black earned her Ph.D. from Miami University of Ohio in 1996 and is currently an Associate Professor of English at Indiana University of Pennsylvania. Her academic interests include sociolinguistics, in addition to composition and creative writing. Her book *Between Talk and Teaching: Reconsidering the Writing Conference* (1998), offers a scholarly, yet personal, investigation of student-teacher conferences. "Stupid Rich Bastards" appeared in the edited collection *This Fine Place So Far From Home* (1995).

In defense of the code-switch or why you talk like that or why you gotta always be cussing

By Roger Bonair-Agard

I'm pretty certain my people
    Yoruba. We speak drum
and dust. We are barefoot.
We are also Mumbai
and the venomed thin blood streaks
of slave masters—France, England,
Spain, Portugal, Germany, America.

but my mother taught me *The Hardy Boys*,
the word *precise* and *Where Babies Come From*
She say read Walter Rodney. She say read Kamau Brathwaite
She say read Baldwin

Long before Chicago taught me borders
    and *Joe*, what loose squares are,
the hieroglyph fist twirl dance
and gang sign

my high school principal, Winston Douglas
said *It is a sin against God*
your parents, and yourself, so to profane
the gift with which you were born

    and so I learned the English
of John Milton, Derek Walcott
and the Mighty Sparrow—

but Brooklyn say *Sun* and *Godbody*
and the streets of Arouca taught
me the brilliant run-on elegance
of the eloquent cuss—*Fock You*
with an O so deep and round
you could tumble into the greeting.

Ruby say *not poncho; rebozo*
    and bit my bottom lip
    and cried when the moon was full
Melana say *ghost-pose* and Nita

B

say *it raining horchata.*
I talk middle-finger, nigger,
son, and espouse
on the theoretical and practical difficulties
of blackness as lived experience,
a metaphysical longing akin
to madness—and Northside say

You're so articulate. Oh my God.
See—Look, even white women love you
and the books say I code-switch,
say I double-tongued, say I adapt/
able. And I say I don't switch
shit. Stop trying to crack
the code and we'll stop (maybe)
inventing new syntaxes for
survive; for making paper,
for stacking cheddar, for getting
our money right. Switch/nothing.
I say I contain several
kinds of niggas—because I know Hindi

words for eggplant, rolling pin, machete,
and several kinds of cloth folded to drape
the oiled body of a woman. I say *Love*

when I talk to a woman, and I say *Love*
when I greet my homies, and *Family*
to address a sweet sister in the street
and *black* when I mean all my people
and *dead presidents* because Rakim,
Biggie, Jay-Z, Nas and the Wu Tang Clan
added vocabularies to the throng
of me. Chicago jails school me

BD, traphouse, swag, pole and bundle;
school me, you could be 10 years old
thrown to the ground arrested
in school, so I talk like *precisely*
greet my gods with the deep O
of a well, of a drum; speak barefoot
and folklorico, speak J'ouvert morning
and Toni Morrison. I recite Winston
Douglas's *never sacrifice principle*
for expediency. I holler at my boys
with a complicated-ass handshake.
I say *Horse.* I say *Blood.* My brothers
answer back. I sing. I lift every

tongue. I speak drum fool. I speak
drum homie. I speak drum dawg. I speak
drum god. I speak drum nigga. I speak
drum

Joe. ■

AUTHOR PROFILE

Roger Bonair-Agard (b. 1968) was born in Trinidad and moved to the United States in 1987. He studied political science at Hunter College in New York City and intended to pursue law, but instead decided to focus on poetry. In 1997, Bonair-Agard was a member of the Nuyorican Poets Café Poetry Slam team, which went on to win the National Poetry Slam Championship in Austin, Texas, which he again won in 1999. Over the past decade he has worked with the youth at Urban Word in New York City, at Volume in Ann Arbor, and with poetry youth organizations in Seattle and San Francisco. He has appeared three times on HBO's *Def Poetry Jam* and is Co-founder and Artistic Director of the LouderARTS Project in New York. Currently, he teaches creative writing with Free Write Jail Arts & Literacy Program at the Cook County Illinois Temporary Juvenile Detention Center in Chicago, Illinois. His other known titles are *Tarnish and Masquerade* (2007), *Gully* (2011), *Bury My Clothes* (2013), and *Where Brooklyn At* (2016). "In defense of the code-switch..." most recently appeared in the edited anthology *The Breakbeat Poets: New American Poetry in the Age of Hip-Hop* (2015).

A Palestinian's Daily Commute through an Israeli Checkpoint

By William Booth and Sufian Taha

BETHLEHEM, West Bank—Under starry skies, a young Palestinian Everyman wakes before dawn to begin his daily commute to work in Israel.

There are thousands like him. They are building Israel. Five or six mornings a week, long before the Muslim morning prayers, before the cocks crow, when packs of dogs still own the dumpsters, his alarm beeps. Today it is 3:30 a.m.

His name is Tarek Al Taweel. He is a Palestinian construction worker, not without skills. He builds modern high-rise apartments in a Jewish settlement in East Jerusalem, where a five-bedroom penthouse sells for $600,000.

The job is okay, he said. He makes 250 shekels, about $68 a day, twice what he would make in the West Bank. He works beside his father, uncles and brothers. They're proud of their craftsmanship. They keep photographs on their mobile phones of their aluminum work, fine carpentry, elaborate tiling.

It's not the work. It's the Israeli checkpoint. "I hate it," Taweel told us. The daily crossing drains him. It makes him feel that life is desperate and ugly.

"Sometimes I wake up in the morning and I don't want to go to the checkpoint. Sometimes I put my head back on the pillow," Taweel said. "My wife will say to me, 'You have to feed our child. Get up. Get up!' And I get up and go."

The Israeli occupation of the Palestinian territories of the West Bank and the Gaza Strip began 50 years ago in June.

Taweel turned 30 last year.

Like Taweel, four of every five Palestinians have never known anything but the occupation—an evolving system by which the Israeli military and intelligence services exert control over 2.6 million Arabs in the West Bank, with one system for Palestinians, another for Israelis.

This summer, the Israelis will celebrate their near-miraculous victory in the 1967 war, when in just six days, they took all of Jerusalem and their armed forces crushed the Arab armies thrown against them.

On the other side, the Palestinians will mark a military occupation going on for so long that many Israelis barely seem to notice anymore, except the young soldiers sent to enforce it.

Prime Minister Benjamin Netanyahu refers to it, when he speaks of it at all, as "the so-called occupation."

Some of his fellow citizens say there is really no occupation, because all the Land of Israel was awarded to the Jews by God. Other Israelis argue that Gaza is no longer occupied, because Israel unilaterally withdrew from the coastal strip a decade ago.

Whatever it is called, it appears to be never-ending. Shelves of books have been written about who is to blame for not making peace. Presidents Bill Clinton, George W. Bush and Barack Obama failed to find a "two-state solution." President Trump says he wants to make "the deal of the century" between Israelis and Palestinians, and just spent two days here.

But what does it feel like? To be "occupied" in 2017, by a country that boasts to be the only democracy in the Middle East?

The first time we saw Taweel he wore dusty jeans and carried a plastic bag with a can of oily tuna fish and a short stack of pita bread. On the spur of the moment he agreed to be a guide of sorts, not only through the chaotic Israeli checkpoint he dreads, but the emotions felt, but not always expressed, at the crossing between his worlds.

His father cautioned him that speaking to two journalists, even for an American newspaper, could jeopardize his permission to enter Israel.

"The permit is life," the father told us.

The Israeli domestic security service, Shin Bet, keeps voluminous files on Palestinians, and it denies and revokes work, travel and medical permits every day, and need give no more reason than "security."

"I don't care," Taweel said. "It's okay."

Embarking in the Dark

It is dark outside his family's three-story home in Hebron when we arrive to follow Taweel on his daily commute.

Although it might take him three or four hours to get to his construction site in East Jerusalem, the entire trip is only 20 miles as the crow flies.

His uncles, brothers and their families live in the kind of extended family compound many Palestinians prefer. A little after 4 a.m., the first lamps appear in the windows, just for a minute, switched on, then off, as if someone is looking for a lost boot and doesn't want to wake everyone inside.

One of his uncles comes out to offer a cup of coffee. "We leave in the dark and return in the dark," he said.

"It's unnatural."

Taweel has a high school diploma and a handsome face that is hard to read. He's got hazel eyes, square shoulders and an athletic build.

He is recently married, and when we see him away from the checkpoint, with his family, he doesn't look anxious, but alive with pleasure. Nine months ago, his wife gave birth to a chubby-cheeked boy they dress in cute little track suits.

Taweel is skilled at stonework, drywall and plaster. His competence got him a job.

But it was his baby that got him his permit.

Israel is closed to Palestinians without travel or work permits, except for residents of East Jerusalem, who have a special status. Palestinian women over 50 and men over 55 may enter for a day without a permit from the West Bank, if the checkpoints are open. All Palestinians living in Gaza need special permission.

Construction workers from the West Bank who seek permits must generally be at least 23 years old, married, and have a child, so Taweel could not get an Israeli work permit until his son was born.

Today there are more than a hundred kinds of permits issued by the Israeli military authority for movement.

A permit to travel or study abroad, pray at the Jerusalem holy sites, visit relatives, attend a wedding or funeral, get medical treatment and work on the other side of the separation barrier.

To get out of Gaza—which is under the control of the Islamist militant movement Hamas, a terrorist organization—is even harder. Israel pulled out of the Gaza Strip in 2005 but still maintains a land, sea and air blockade with restrictions on travel and trade. No Palestinians from Gaza commute to work in Israel.

Taweel's work permit allows him to enter Israel in the early morning, but he must leave by the end of the day.

The Israeli intelligence officers assume that family men like Taweel are not only less likely to carry out terrorist attacks, but less likely to commit any crimes—such as smuggling or spending the night in Israel—for fear of losing their permit.

Around 4:20 a.m., Taweel and six co-workers walk to the end of their street and pile into a van for the ride to Bethlehem. Everyone but the driver immediately nods off.

Taweel said, "More sleep is a blessing."

Heading north on two-lane Highway 60, they pass the Palestinian town of Saer, home to many construction workers and also a dozen of the young stabbers and car-rammers in last year's wave of violence, which left 35 Israelis dead.

Across the highway is Kiryat Arba, the Jewish settlement infamous as the home to the American-born physician Baruch Goldstein, who massacred 29 Muslim worshipers with a machine gun at the Cave of the Patriarchs in 1994.

Taweel's van speeds toward a crossing called Checkpoint 300, or Checkpoint Rachel, because it abuts the Tomb of Rachel, the biblical matriarch, a shrine sacred to Muslims and Christians and considered one of the holiest for Jews.

Checkpoint 300 passes through Israel's high concrete walls, tagged with Palestinian graffiti and Banksy murals, erected during the second intifada, or uprising, in the early 2000s, when Palestinian suicide bombers were targeting Israeli civilians.

The crossing today is the scene of frequent clashes between young Palestinians throwing rocks and burning tires, and young Israeli soldiers who fire tear gas, rubber-coated bullets and live ammunition.

Into the Scrum

It's now almost 5 a.m. Bethlehem is asleep, only the bakeries are bright. But as the convoys of taxis, vans and buses reach the checkpoint, men stir and rush toward Israel's separation barrier, here a 26-foot-tall cement wall with watch towers.

There are already swelling crowds. It's a Sunday, busiest day of the week, with thousands of men shoving forward, squirming under fluorescent bulbs.

Taweel was not ready to risk the crush. He is perched above the entrance to the checkpoint on the Bethlehem side, squatting on his heels, elevated on the rubble of an old stone wall, watching the shoving match below.

"It's too crazy," he said. "Let's wait."

Taweel saw his impatient uncles and brothers shoulder first into the scrum, followed by his father. They pushed on the back of the man in front. His father smiled weakly up at his eldest son through the bars. Father and son looked sad.

Later, Taweel explained that they were ashamed that a foreigner had come to watch such a spectacle.

A few years earlier, Taweel's father suffered cracked ribs, when he was crushed at the checkpoint. An uncle with high blood pressure once fainted and had to be rescued. During our visit to the checkpoint, one man had a heart attack and another with asthma collapsed.

"You never, ever want to fall down," Taweel warned.

There are now 70,000 Palestinians working legally in Israel, most of them in construction, plus an additional 30,000 to 50,000 working without permits, who scramble through drainage pipes and scale walls with grappling hooks and handmade ladders, to enter Israel.

There's no panic this morning. Real panic is rare. But you could see easily how it could happen, like a stampede at a rock concert or a soccer stadium.

It looks a little scary, we said.

"It is scary," Taweel said.

There are 13 major crossings that allow Palestinians with work permits like Taweel's to enter Israel. Palestinians will argue which checkpoint is the slowest, fastest, the most crowded, the easiest, with the rudest or most professional soldiers or private security, and the most vile toilets.

Some crossings have vastly improved. But Palestinians say Checkpoint 300 is still one of the worst.

Thousands of workers from all over the southern West Bank must squeeze through each morning. There are no real alternatives. If you're from Hebron and work in Jerusalem or Tel Aviv, it is the straightest line.

As we watched the crush, the Palestinians we asked conjured fantastical words in Arabic to describe the experience to come.

First the workers say they're funneled into "cages," the long barred passage-ways, then jammed into "chicken pluckers," the clicking turnstiles. Then they pass through the "aquariums," where the bored Israeli soldiers sit behind thick bullet-proof glass, matching green IDs to faces.

It doesn't take a psychologist to see the meanings behind the metaphors. The Palestinians say the words all describe animals in a zoo.

The crowds were thinning a bit. The line was moving.

After about 30 minutes, Taweel said, "Let's go."

'They Do It Deliberately'

The men are wearing work clothes still dirty from the day before. The older ones in coats and the young in hoodies. They are rugged-looking, a lot of them skinny, with hacking coughs. They are carrying table saws and joint knives.

The men move as a kind of wave, back and forth, two steps forward, a step back.

On this side of the separation barrier, there are no Israeli soldiers or security. No Palestinian police either. The movement forward is by remote control of the Israelis watching closed-circuit TV screens. Once into the chute, we stand three shoulders abreast, every part of your body touching someone or something.

The men smoke cigarettes to the filter, even in the lines. Vendors sell paper cups of coffee, which are passed through the bars. The men joke, flash anger, and check their phones.

The later it gets, the more the workers begin to push.

As Taweel gets closer to the turnstiles, Palestinians are climbing over the bars and almost stepping on our heads.

The workers call them "wall crawlers" and "snakes," the young who jump over and slither under the bars to cut the line. Those who did not cut in lines said the crawlers demeaned themselves—and that this was intentional, that the Israelis wanted this to happen. Why else would they let these conditions persist year after year, they asked.

When ordinary Palestinian workers at Checkpoint 300 are asked what it feels like to be "occupied," they use three words, consistently. Frustration. Humiliation. Pressure.

With the word "pressure" they sometimes grabbed their chests, mimicking a heart attack, or held their hands together and squeezed, like it felt in the cages.

"I think they do it deliberately, to put us in our place," said Abu Rafat, 51, a stout barrel of a man with gray hair, a tile worker.

Before we enter the crossing, Abu Rafat points at a scrawny man hovering at the edge of our conversation. The man is growing anxious, keeps looking at his mobile phone, because if he doesn't make it through the crossing by 7 a.m., his ride to Tel Aviv will leave without him and his boss will dock a day's wages.

"Look at his eyes," Abu Rafat said. "Does he want to kill himself? Or somebody else? You can't tell."

We reach the turnstile. Three men crowd into a space for one. It is locked, then opened, then locked. You can't see by whom—a distant security officer or young soldier.

"Watch your hands," someone shouted.

Taweel and others rush toward the aquariums. They rip off their belts. Their things are scanned. They passed through metal detectors. They press their thumbs on fingerprint readers.

If the workers don't make it to their job site, they also lose money because most pay a Palestinian broker (who likely pays a cut to an Israeli contractor) 2,000 shekels, or $550, a month in excess "commissions," charges that both the workers and Israeli government consider a bribe.

The work permit system has been condemned by Israeli human rights groups, as well as the Bank of Israel, as riven by corruption. The Palestinian workers are as likely to blame their own people as the Israelis.

"Permit millionaires," one laborer described the middlemen.

"Scammers," said another. "Thieves."

A worker with a bristly beard and hands like sandpaper, named Abu Omar, 42, said: "We've lost our leaders. Our government doesn't care."

He waves toward the checkpoint. "Look at us," he said. "We're sheep without a shepherd."

On the Israeli side, Taweel runs toward his ride.

He is late for work. ∎

AUTHOR PROFILE

William Booth has worked as *The Washington Post's* London bureau chief since the summer of 2017. His appointment came after almost 30 years of reporting for *The Post* across the world. Before coming to *The Post*, Booth wrote for *Science* magazine. He was a Vannevar Bush Fellow at the Massachusetts Institute of Technology and graduated from the University of Texas in Austin. He was on *The Post's* Pulitzer Prize-finalist team that covered the Fort Hood shootings, and has covered upheaval and transformation in Catalonia, Ukraine, Egypt, Libya, Iraq, Haiti, Honduras, and the Balkans. In Mexico, his work focused on drug trafficking and the state response. In the Middle East, he covered the Israel-Palestinian conflict. "A Palestinian's Daily Commute…" reports this experience and was published in *The Post* on May 25, 2017.

Sufian Taha is a contract correspondent for *The Washington Post* covering the West Bank. Taha studied at City University of New York. Currently, he lives with his wife in his native East Jerusalem, working as a translator. He has reported with award-winning journalists William Booth and Leila Fadel, and his work has led to his arrest on multiple occasions.

Black and Blue

By Garnette Cadogan

"My only sin is my skin. What did I do, to be so black and blue?"

—Fats Waller, "(What Did I Do to Be So) Black and Blue?"

"Manhattan's streets I saunter'd, pondering."

—Walt Whitman, "Manhattan's Streets I Saunter'd, Pondering"

My love for walking started in childhood, out of necessity. No thanks to a stepfather with heavy hands, I found every reason to stay away from home and was usually out—at some friend's house or at a street party where no minor should be—until it was too late to get public transportation. So I walked.

The streets of Kingston, Jamaica, in the 1980s were often terrifying—you could, for instance, get killed if a political henchman thought you came from the wrong neighborhood, or even if you wore the wrong color. Wearing orange showed affiliation with one political party and green with the other, and if you were neutral or traveling far from home you chose your colors well. The wrong color in the wrong neighborhood could mean your last day. No wonder, then, that my friends and the rare nocturnal passerby declared me crazy for my long late-night treks that traversed warring political zones. (And sometimes I did pretend to be crazy, shouting non sequiturs when I passed through especially dangerous spots, such as the place where thieves hid on the banks of a storm drain. Predators would ignore or laugh at the kid in his school uniform speaking nonsense.)

I made friends with strangers and went from being a very shy and awkward kid to being an extroverted, awkward one. The beggar, the vendor, the poor laborer—those were experienced wanderers, and they became my nighttime instructors; they knew the streets and delivered lessons on how to navigate and enjoy them. I imagined myself as a Jamaican Tom Sawyer, one moment saunter-ing down the streets to pick low-hanging mangoes that I could reach from the sidewalk, another moment hanging outside a street party with battling sound systems, each armed with speakers piled to create skyscrapers of heavy bass. These streets weren't frightening. They were full of adventure when they weren't serene. There I'd join forces with a band of merry walkers, who'd miss the last bus by mere minutes, our feet still moving as we put out our thumbs to hitchhike to spots nearer home, making jokes as vehicle after vehicle raced past us. Or I'd get lost in Mittyesque moments, my young mind imagining alternate futures. The streets had their own safety: Unlike at home, there I could be myself without fear of bodily harm. Walking became so regular and familiar that the way home became home.

The streets had their rules, and I loved the challenge of trying to master them. I learned how to be alert to surrounding dangers and nearby delights, and prided myself on recognizing telling details that my peers missed. Kingston was a map

of complex, and often bizarre, cultural and political and social activity, and I appointed myself its nighttime cartographer. I'd know how to navigate away from a predatory pace, and to speed up to chat when the cadence of a gait announced friendliness. It was almost always men I saw. A lone woman walking in the middle of the night was as common a sight as Sasquatch; moonlight pedestrianism was too dangerous for her. Sometimes at night as I made my way down from hills above Kingston, I'd have the impression that the city was set on "pause" or in extreme slow motion, as that as I descended I was cutting across Jamaica's deep social divisions. I'd make my way briskly past the mansions in the hills overlooking the city, now transformed into a carpet of dotted lights under a curtain of stars, saunter by middle-class subdivisions hidden behind high walls crowned with barbed wire, and zigzag through neighborhoods of zinc and wooden shacks crammed together and leaning like a tight-knit group of limbo dancers. With my descent came an increase in the vibrancy of street life—except when it didn't; some poor neighborhoods had both the violent gunfights and the eerily deserted streets of the cinematic Wild West. I knew well enough to avoid those even at high noon.

I'd begun hoofing it after dark when I was ten years old. By thirteen I was rarely home before midnight, and some nights found me racing against dawn. My mother would often complain, "Mek yuh love street suh? Yuh born a hospital; yuh neva born a street." ("Why do you love the streets so much? You were born in a hospital, not in the streets.")

I left Jamaica in 1996 to attend college in New Orleans, a city I'd heard called "the northernmost Caribbean city." I wanted to discover—on foot, of course— what was Caribbean and what was American about it. Stately mansions on oak-lined streets with streetcars clanging by, and brightly colored houses that made entire blocks look festive; people in resplendent costumes dancing to funky brass bands in the middle of the street; cuisine—and aromas—that mashed up culinary traditions from Africa, Europe, Asia, and the American South; and a juxtaposition of worlds old and new, odd and familiar: Who wouldn't want to explore this?

On my first day in the city, I went walking for a few hours to get a feel for the place and to buy supplies to transform my dormitory room from a prison bunker into a welcoming space. When some university staff members found out what I'd been up to, they warned me to restrict my walking to the places recommended as safe to tourists and the parents of freshmen. They trotted out statistics about New Orleans's crime rate. But Kingston's crime rate dwarfed those numbers, and I decided to ignore these well-meant cautions. A city was waiting to be discovered, and I wouldn't let inconvenient facts get in the way. These American criminals are nothing on Kingston's, I thought. They're no real threat to me.

What no one had told me was that I was the one who would be considered a threat.

Within days I noticed that many people on the street seemed apprehensive of me: Some gave me a circumspect glance as they approached, and then crossed the street; others, ahead, would glance behind, register my presence, and then speed up; older white women clutched their bags; young white men nervously greeted me, as if exchanging a salutation for their safety: "What's up, bro?" On one occasion, less than a month after my arrival, I tried to help a man whose wheelchair was stuck in the middle of a crosswalk; he threatened to shoot me in the face, then asked a white pedestrian for help.

I wasn't prepared for any of this. I had come from a majority-black country in which no one was wary of me because of my skin color. Now I wasn't sure who was afraid of me. I was especially unprepared for the cops. They regularly stopped and bullied me, asking questions that took my guilt for granted. I'd never received what many of my African-American friends call "The Talk": No parents had told me how to behave when I was stopped by the police, how to be as polite and cooperative as possible, no matter what they said or did to me. So I had to cobble together my own rules of engagement. Thicken my Jamaican accent. Quickly mention my college. "Accidentally" pull out my college identification card when asked for my driver's license.

My survival tactics began well before I left my dorm. I got out of the shower with the police in my head, assembling a cop-proof wardrobe. Light-colored oxford shirt. V-neck sweater. Khaki pants. Chukkas. Sweatshirt or T-shirt with my university insignia. When I walked I regularly had my identity challenged, but I also found ways to assert it. (So I'd dress Ivy League style, but would, later on, add my Jamaican pedigree by wearing Clarks Desert Boots, the footwear of choice of Jamaican street culture.) Yet the all-American sartorial choice of white T-shirt and jeans, which many police officers see as the uniform of black troublemakers, was off-limits to me—at least, if I wanted to have the freedom of movement I desired.

In this city of exuberant streets, walking became a complex and often oppressive negotiation. I would see a white woman walking toward me at night and cross the street to reassure her that she was safe. I would forget something at home but not immediately turn around if someone was behind me, because I discovered that a sudden backtrack could cause alarm. (I had a cardinal rule: Keep a wide perimeter from people who might consider me a danger. If not, danger might visit me.) New Orleans suddenly felt more dangerous than Jamaica. The sidewalk was a minefield, and every hesitation and self-censored compensation reduced my dignity. Despite my best efforts, the streets never felt comfortably safe. Even a simple salutation was suspect.

One night, returning to the house that, eight years after my arrival, I thought I'd earned the right to call my home, I waved to a cop driving by. Moments later, I was against his car in handcuffs. When I later asked him—sheepishly, of course; any other way would have asked for bruises—why he had detained me, he said my greeting had aroused his suspicion. "No one waves to the police," he explained. When I told friends of his response, it was my behavior, not his, that they saw as absurd. "Now why would you do a dumb thing like that?" said one. "You know better than to make nice with police."

A few days after I left on a visit to Kingston, Hurricane Katrina slashed and pummeled New Orleans. I'd gone not because of the storm but because my adoptive grandmother, Pearl, was dying of cancer. I hadn't wandered those streets in eight years, since my last visit, and I returned to them now mostly at night, the time I found best for thinking, praying, crying. I walked to feel less alienated—from myself, struggling with the pain of seeing my grandmother terminally

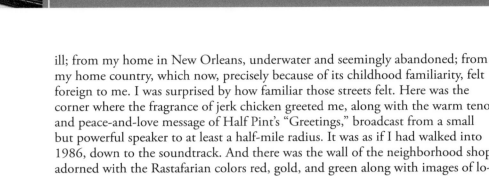

ill; from my home in New Orleans, underwater and seemingly abandoned; from my home country, which now, precisely because of its childhood familiarity, felt foreign to me. I was surprised by how familiar those streets felt. Here was the corner where the fragrance of jerk chicken greeted me, along with the warm tenor and peace-and-love message of Half Pint's "Greetings," broadcast from a small but powerful speaker to at least a half-mile radius. It was as if I had walked into 1986, down to the soundtrack. And there was the wall of the neighborhood shop, adorned with the Rastafarian colors red, gold, and green along with images of local and international heroes Bob Marley, Marcus Garvey, and Haile Selassie. The crew of boys leaning against it and joshing each other were recognizable; different faces, similar stories. I was astonished at how safe the streets felt to me, once again one black body among many, no longer having to anticipate the many ways my presence might instill fear and how to offer some reassuring body language. Passing police cars were once again merely passing police cars. Jamaican police could be pretty brutal, but they didn't notice me the way American police did. I could be invisible in Jamaica in a way I can't be invisible in the United States.

Walking had returned to me a greater set of possibilities. And why walk, if not to create a new set of possibilities? Following serendipity, I added new routes to the mental maps I had made from constant walking in that city from childhood to young adulthood, traced variations on the old pathways. Serendipity, a mentor once told me, is a secular way of speaking of grace; it's unearned favor. Seen theologically, then, walking is an act of faith. Walking is, after all, interrupted falling. We see, we listen, we speak, and we trust that each step we take won't be our last, but will lead us into a richer understanding of the self and the world.

In Jamaica, I felt once again as if the only identity that mattered was my own, not the constricted one that others had constructed for me. I strolled into my better self. I said, along with Kierkegaard, "I have walked myself into my best thoughts."

When I tried to return to New Orleans from Jamaica a month later, there were no flights. I thought about flying to Texas so I could make my way back to my neighborhood as soon as it opened for reoccupancy, but my adoptive aunt, Maxine, who hated the idea of me returning to a hurricane zone before the end of hurricane season, persuaded me to come to stay in New York City instead. (To strengthen her case she sent me an article about Texans who were buying up guns because they were afraid of the influx of black people from New Orleans.)

This wasn't a hard sell: I wanted to be in a place where I could travel by foot and, more crucially, continue to reap the solace of walking at night. And I was eager to follow in the steps of the essayists, poets, and novelists who'd wandered that great city before me—Walt Whitman, Herman Melville, Alfred Kazin, Elizabeth Hardwick. I had visited the city before, but each trip had felt like a tour in a sports car. I welcomed the chance to stroll. I wanted to walk alongside Whitman's ghost and "descend to the pavements, merge with the crowd, and gaze with them." So I left Kingston, the popular Jamaican farewell echoing in my mind: "Walk good!" *Be safe on your journey*, in other words, *and all the best in your endeavors.*

I arrived in New York City, ready to lose myself in Whitman's "Manhattan crowds, with their turbulent musical chorus!" I marveled at what Jane Jacobs praised as "the ballet of the good city sidewalk" in her old neighborhood, the West Village. I walked up past midtown skyscrapers, releasing their energy as lively people onto the streets, and on into the Upper West Side, with its regal Beaux Arts apartment buildings, stylish residents, and buzzing streets. Onward into Washington Heights, the sidewalks spilled over with an ebullient mix of young and old Jewish and Dominican-American residents, past leafy Inwood, with parks whose grades rose to reveal beautiful views of the Hudson River, up to my home in Kingsbridge in the Bronx, with its rows of brick bungalows and apartment buildings nearby Broadway's bustling sidewalks and the peaceful expanse of Van Cortlandt Park. I went to Jackson Heights in Queens to take in people socializing around garden courtyards in Urdu, Korean, Spanish, Russian, and Hindi. And when I wanted a taste of home, I headed to Brooklyn, in Crown Heights, for Jamaican food and music and humor mixed in with the flavor of New York City. The city was my playground.

I explored the city with friends, and then with a woman I'd begun dating. She walked around endlessly with me, taking in New York City's many pleasures. Coffee shops open until predawn; verdant parks with nooks aplenty; food and music from across the globe; quirky neighborhoods with quirkier residents. My impressions of the city took shape during my walks with her.

As with the relationship, those first few months of urban exploration were all romance. The city was beguiling, exhilarating, vibrant. But it wasn't long before reality reminded me I wasn't invulnerable, especially when I walked alone.

One night in the East Village, I was running to dinner when a white man in front of me turned and punched me in the chest with such force that I thought my ribs had braided around my spine. I assumed he was drunk or had mistaken me for an old enemy, but found out soon enough that he'd merely assumed I was a criminal because of my race. When he discovered I wasn't what he imagined, he went on to tell me that his assault was my own fault for running up behind him. I blew off this incident as an aberration, but the mutual distrust between me and the police was impossible to ignore. It felt elemental. They'd enter a subway platform; I'd notice them. (And I'd notice all the other black men registering their presence as well, while just about everyone else remained oblivious to them.) They'd glare. I'd get nervous and glance. They'd observe me steadily. I'd get uneasy. I'd observe them back, worrying that I looked suspicious. Their suspicions would increase. We'd continue the silent, uneasy dialogue until the subway arrived and separated us at last.

I returned to the old rules I'd set for myself in New Orleans, with elaboration. No running, especially at night; no sudden movements; no hoodies; no objects—especially shiny ones—in hand; no waiting for friends on street corners, lest I be mistaken for a drug dealer; no standing near a corner on the cell phone (same reason). As comfort set in, inevitably I began to break some of those rules, until a night encounter sent me zealously back to them, having learned that anything less than vigilance was carelessness.

After a sumptuous Italian dinner and drinks with friends, I was jogging to the subway at Columbus Circle—I was running late to meet another set of friends at a concert downtown. I heard someone shouting and I looked up to see a police officer approaching with his gun trained on me. "Against the car!" In no time, half a dozen cops were upon me, chucking me against the car and tightly hand-cuffing me. "Why were you running?" "Where are you going?" "Where are you coming from?" "I said, why were you running?!" Since I couldn't answer everyone at once, I decided to respond first to the one who looked most likely to hit me. I was surrounded by a swarm and tried to focus on just one without inadvertently aggravating the others.

It didn't work. As I answered that one, the others got frustrated that I wasn't answering them fast enough and barked at me. One of them, digging through my already-emptied pockets, asked if I had any weapons, the question more an accusation. Another badgered me about where I was coming from, as if on the fifteenth round I'd decide to tell him the truth he imagined. Though I kept say-ing—calmly, of course, which meant trying to manage a tone that ignored my racing heart and their spittle-filled shouts in my face—that I had just left friends two blocks down the road, who were yes, sir, yes, officer, of course, officer, all still there and could vouch for me, to meet other friends whose text messages on my phone could verify that, it made no difference.

For a black man, to assert your dignity before the police was to risk assault. In fact, the dignity of black people meant less to them, which was why I always felt safer being stopped in front of white witnesses than black witnesses. The cops had less regard for the witness and entreaties of black onlookers, whereas the concern of white witnesses usually registered on them. A black witness asking a question or politely raising an objection could quickly become a fellow detainee. Deference to the police, then, was sine qua non for a safe encounter.

The cops ignored my explanations and my suggestions and continued to snarl at me. All except one of them, a captain. He put his hand on my back, and said to no one in particular, "If he was running for a long time he would have been sweating." He then instructed that the cuffs be removed. He told me that a black man had stabbed someone earlier two or three blocks away and they were search-ing for him. I noted that I had no blood on me and had told his fellow officers where I'd been and how to check my alibi—unaware that it was even an alibi, as no one had told me why I was being held, and of course, I hadn't dared ask. From what I'd seen, anything beyond passivity would be interpreted as aggression.

The police captain said I could go. None of the cops who detained me thought an apology was necessary. Like the thug who punched me in the East Village, they seemed to think it was my own fault for running.

Humiliated, I tried not to make eye contact with the onlookers on the sidewalk, and I was reluctant to pass them to be on my way. The captain, maybe noticing my shame, offered to give me a ride to the subway station. When he dropped me off and I thanked him for his help, he said, "It's because you were polite that we let you go. If you were acting up it would have been different."

I realized that what I least liked about walking in New York City wasn't merely having to learn new rules of navigation and socialization—every city has its own. It was the arbitrariness of the circumstances that required them, an arbitrariness that made me feel like a child again, that infantilized me. When we first learn to walk, the world around us threatens to crash into us. Every step is risky. We train ourselves to walk without crashing by being attentive to our movements, and extra-attentive to the world around us. As adults we walk without thinking, really. But as a black adult I am often returned to that moment in childhood when I'm just learning to walk. I am once again on high alert, vigilant.

Some days, when I am fed up with being considered a troublemaker upon sight, I joke that the last time a cop was happy to see a black male walking was when that male was a baby taking his first steps. On many walks, I ask white friends to accompany me, just to avoid being treated like a threat. Walks in New York City, that is; in New Orleans, a white woman in my company sometimes attracted more hostility. (And it is not lost on me that my woman friends are those who best understand my plight; they have developed their own vigilance in an environment where they are constantly treated as targets of sexual attention.) Much of my walking is as my friend Rebecca once described it: A pantomime undertaken to avoid the choreography of criminality.

Walking while black restricts the experience of walking, renders inaccessible the classic Romantic experience of walking alone. It forces me to be in constant relationship with others, unable to join the New York flaneurs I had read about and hoped to join. Instead of meandering aimlessly in the footsteps of Whitman, Melville, Kazin, and Vivian Gornick, more often, I felt that I was tiptoeing in Baldwin's—the Baldwin who wrote, way back in 1960, "Rare, indeed, is the Harlem citizen, from the most circumspect church member to the most shiftless adolescent, who does not have a long tale to tell of police incompetence, injustice, or brutality. I myself have witnessed and endured it more than once." Walking as a black man has made me feel simultaneously more removed from the city, in my awareness that I am perceived as suspect, and more closely connected to it, in the full attentiveness demanded by my vigilance. It has made me walk more purposefully in the city, becoming part of its flow, rather than observing, standing apart.

But it also means that I'm still trying to arrive in a city that isn't quite mine. One definition of home is that it's somewhere we can most be ourselves. And when are we more ourselves but when walking, that natural state in which we repeat one of the first actions we learned? Walking—the simple, monotonous act of placing one foot before the other to prevent falling—turns out not to be so simple if you're black. Walking alone has been anything but monotonous for me; monotony is a luxury.

A foot leaves, a foot lands, and our longing gives it momentum from rest to rest. We long to look, to think, to talk, to get away. But more than anything else, we long to be free. We want the freedom and pleasure of walking without fear—without others' fear—wherever we choose. I've lived in New York City for almost a decade and have not stopped walking its fascinating streets. And I have not stopped longing to find the solace that I found as a kid on the streets of Kingston. Much as coming to know New York City's streets has made it closer to home to me, the city also withholds itself from me via those very streets. I walk them, alternately invisible and too prominent. So I walk caught between memory and forgetting, between memory and forgiveness. ◼

AUTHOR PROFILE

Garnette Cadogan is a celebrated essayist who has lectured as a Visiting Scholar at MIT, New York University, and the University of Virginia. His research explores the promise and perils of urban life, the vitality and inequality of cities, and the challenges of pluralism. Named by the literary magazine Freeman's as one of 29 writers from around the world who "represent the future of new writing" in 2017, he writes about culture and the arts for various publications. The editor-at-large of *Non-Stop Metropolis: A New York City Atlas* (co-edited by Rebecca Solnit and Joshua Jelly-Schapiro), he is at work on a book on walking. "Black and Blue" first appeared in the October 2015 publication Freeman's: *The Best New Writing on Arrival.*

Silent Spring

By Rachel Carson

1. A Fable for Tomorrow

There was once a town in the heart of America where all life seemed to live in harmony with its surroundings. The town lay in the midst of a checkerboard of prosperous farms, with fields of grain and hillsides of orchards where, in spring, white clouds of bloom drifted above the green fields. In autumn, oak and maple and birch set up a blaze of color that flamed and flickered across a backdrop of pines. Then foxes barked in the hills and deer silently crossed the fields, half hidden in the mists of the fall mornings.

Along the roads, laurel, viburnum and alder, great ferns and wildflowers delighted the traveler's eye through much of the year. Even in winter the roadsides were place of beauty, where countless birds came to feed on the berries and on the seed heads of the dried weeds rising above the snow. The countryside was, in fact, famous for the abundance and variety of its bird life, and when the flood of migrants was pouring through in spring and fall people traveled from great distances to observe them. Others came to fish the streams, which flowed clear and cold out of the hills and contained shady pools where the trout lay. So it had been from the days many years ago when the first settlers raised their houses, sank their wells, and built their barns.

Then a strange blight crept over the area and everything began to change. Some evil spell had settled on the community: mysterious maladies swept the flocks of chickens; the cattle and sheep sickened and died. Everywhere was a shadow of death. The farmers spoke of much illness among their families. In the town the doctors had become more and more puzzled by new kinds of sickness appearing among their patients. There had been several sudden and unexplained deaths, not only among adults but even among children, who would be stricken suddenly while at play and die within a few hours.

There was a strange stillness. The birds, for example—where had they gone? Many people spoke of them, puzzled and disturbed. The feeding stations in the backyards were deserted. The few birds seen anywhere were moribund; they trembled violently and could not fly. It was a spring without voices. On the mornings that had once throbbed with the dawn chorus of robins, catbirds, doves, jays, wrens, and scores of other bird voices there was now no sound; only silence lay over the fields and woods and marsh.

On the farms the hens brooded, but no chicks hatched. The farmers complained that they were unable to raise any pigs—the litters were small and the young survived only a few days. The apple trees were coming into bloom but no bees droned among the blossoms, so there was no pollination and there would be no fruit.

The roadsides, once so attractive, were now lined with browned and withered vegetation as though swept by fire. These, too, were silent, deserted by all living things. Even the streams were now lifeless. Anglers no longer visited them, for all the fish had died.

In the gutters under the eaves and between the shingles of the roofs, a white granular powder still showed a few patches; some weeks before it had fallen like snow upon the roofs and the lawns, the fields and streams.

No witchcraft, no enemy action had silenced the rebirth of new life in this stricken world. The people had done it themselves.

This town does not actually exist, but it might easily have a thousand counterparts in America or elsewhere in the world. I know of no community that has experienced all the misfortunes I describe. Yet every one of these disasters has actually happened somewhere, and many real communities have already suffered a substantial number of them. A grim specter has crept upon us almost unnoticed, and this imagined tragedy may easily become a stark reality we all shall know.

What has already silenced the voices of spring in countless towns in America? This book is an attempt to explain.

2. The Obligation to Endure

The history of life on earth has been a history of interaction between living things and their surroundings. To a large extent, the physical forms and the habits of the earth's vegetation and its animal life have been molded by the environment. Considering the whole span of earthly time, the opposite effect, in which life actually modifies its surroundings, has been relatively slight. Only within the moment of time represented by the present century has one species—man—acquired significant power to alter the nature of his world.

During the past quarter century this power has not only increased to one of disturbing magnitude but it has changed in character. The most alarming of all man's assaults upon the environment is the contamination of air, earth, rivers, and sea with dangerous and even lethal materials. This pollution is for the most part irrecoverable; the chain of evil it initiates not only in the world that must support life but in the living tissues is for the most part irreversible. In this now universal contamination of the environment, chemicals are the sinister and little-recognized partners of radiation in changing the very nature of the world—the very nature of its life. Strontium 90, released through nuclear explosions into the air, comes to earth in rain or drifts down as fallout, lodges in soil, enters into the grass or corn or wheat grown there, and in time takes up its abode in the bones of a human being, there to remain until his death. Similarly, chemicals sprayed on croplands or forests or gardens lie long in soil, entering into living organisms, passing from one to another in a chain of poisoning and death. Or they pass mysteriously by underground streams until they emerge and, through the alchemy of air and sunlight, combine into new forms that kill vegetation, sicken cattle, and work unknown harm on those who drink from once pure wells. As Albert Schweitzer has said, "Man can hardly even recognize the devils of his own creation."

It took hundreds of millions of years to produce the life that now inhabits the earth—eons of time in which that developing and evolving and diversifying life reached a state of adjustment and balance with its surroundings. The environment, rigorously shaping and directing the life it supported, contained elements that were hostile as well as supporting. Certain rocks gave out dangerous radiation; even within the light of the sun, from which all life draws its energy, there were short-wave radiations with power to injure. Given time—time not in years but in millennia—life adjusts, and a balance has been reached. For time is the essential ingredient; but in the modern world there is no time.

The rapidity of change and the speed with which new situations are created follow the impetuous and heedless pace of man rather than the deliberate pace of nature. Radiation is no longer merely the background radiation of rocks, the bombardment of cosmic rays, the ultraviolet of the sun that have existed before there was any life on earth; radiation is now the unnatural creation of man's tampering with the atom. The chemicals to which life is asked to make its adjustment are no longer merely the calcium and silica and copper and all the rest of the minerals washed out of the rocks and carried in rivers to the sea; they are the synthetic creations of man's inventive mind, brewed in his laboratories, and having no counterparts in nature.

To adjust to these chemicals would require time on the scale that is nature's; it would require not merely the years of a man's life but the life of generations. And even this, were it by some miracle possible, would be futile, for the new chemicals come from our laboratories in an endless stream; almost five hundred annually find their way into actual use in the United States alone. The figure is staggering and its implications are not easily grasped—500 new chemicals to which the bodies of men and animals are required somehow to adapt each year, chemicals totally outside the limits of biologic experience.

Among them are many that are used in man's war against nature. Since the mid-1940's over 200 basic chemicals have been created for use in killing insects, weeds, rodents, and other organisms described in the modern vernacular as "pests"; and they are sold under several thousand different brand names. These sprays, dusts, and aerosols are now applied almost universally to farms, gardens, forests, and homes—nonselective chemicals that have the power to kill every insect, the "good" and the "bad," to still the song of birds and the leaping of fish in the streams, to coat the leaves with a deadly film, and to linger on in soil—all this though the intended target may be only a few weeds or insects. Can anyone believe it is possible to lay down such a barrage of poisons on the surface of the earth without making it unfit for all life? They should not be called "insecticides," but "biocides."

The whole process of spraying seems caught up in an endless spiral. Since DDT was released for civilian use, a process of escalation has been going on in which ever more toxic materials must be found. This has happened because insects, in a triumphant vindication of Darwin's principles of the survival of the fittest, have evolved super races immune to that particular insecticide used, hence a deadlier one has always to be developed—and then a deadlier one than that. It has happened also because, for reasons to be described later, destructive insects often undergo a "flareback," or resurgence, after spraying, in numbers greater than before. Thus the chemical war is never won, and all life is caught in its violent crossfire.

Along with the possibility of the extinction of mankind by nuclear war, the central problem of our age has therefore become the contamination of man's total environment with such substances of incredible potential for harm—substances that accumulate in the tissues of plants and animals and even penetrate the germ

C

cells to shatter or alter the very material of heredity upon which the shape of the future depends.

Some would-be architects of our future look toward a time when it will be possible to alter the human germ plasm by design. But we may easily be doing so now by inadvertence, for many chemicals, like radiation, bring about gene mutations. It is ironic to think that man might determine his own future by something so seemingly trivial as the choice of an insect spray.

All this has been risked—for what? Future historians may well be amazed by our distorted sense of proportion. How could intelligent beings seek to control a few unwanted species by a method that contaminated the entire environment and brought the threat of disease and death even to their own kind? Yet this is precisely what we have done. We have done it, moreover, for reasons that collapse the moment we examine them. We are told that the enormous and expanding use of pesticides is necessary to maintain farm production. Yet is our real problem not one of *overproduction*? Our farms, despite measures to remove acreages from production and to pay farmers *not* to produce, have yielded such a staggering excess of crops that the American taxpayer in 1962 is paying out more than one billion dollars a year as the total carrying cost of the surplus-food storage program. And is the situation helped when one branch of the Agriculture Department tries to reduce production while another states, as it did in 1958, "It is believed generally that reduction of crop acreages under provisions of the Soil Bank will stimulate interest in use of chemicals to obtain maximum production on the land retained in crops."

All this is not to say there is no insect problem and no need of control. I am saying, rather, that control must be geared to realities, not to mythical situations, and that the methods employed must be such that they do not destroy us along with the insects.

The problem whose attempted solution has brought such a train of disaster in its wake is an accompaniment of our modern way of life. Long before the age of man, insects inhabited the earth—a group of extraordinarily varied and adaptable beings. Over the course of time since man's advent, a small percentage of the more than half a million species of insects have come into conflict with human welfare in two principal ways: as competitors for the food supply and as carriers of human disease.

Disease-carrying insects become important where human beings are crowded together, especially under conditions where sanitation is poor, as in time of natural disaster or war or in situations of extreme poverty and deprivation. Then control of some sort becomes necessary. It is a sobering fact, however, as we shall presently see, that the method of massive chemical control has had only limited success, and also threatens to worsen the very conditions it is intended to curb.

Under primitive agriculture conditions the farmer had few insect problems. These arose with the intensification of agriculture—the devotion of immense acreages to a single crop. Such a system set the stage for explosive increases in specific insect populations. Single-crop farming does not take advantage of the principles by which nature works; it is agriculture as an as engineer might conceive it to be. Nature has introduced great variety into the landscape, but man has displayed a passion for simplifying it. Thus he undoes the built-in checks and balances by which nature holds the species within bounds. One important natural check is a limit on the amount of suitable habitat for each species. Obviously then, an insect that lives on wheat can build up its population to much higher levels on a farm devoted to wheat than on one in which wheat is intermingled with other crops to which the insect is not adapted.

The same thing happens in other situations. A generation or more ago, the towns of large areas of the United States lined their streets with the noble elm tree. Now the beauty they hopefully created is threatened with complete destruction as disease sweeps through the elms, carried by a beetle that would have only limited chance to build up large populations and to spread from tree to tree if the elms were only occasional trees in a richly diversified planting.

Another factor in the modern insect problem is one that must be viewed against a background of geologic and human history: the spreading of thousands of different kinds of organisms from their native homes to invade new territories. This worldwide migration has been studied and graphically described by the British ecologist Charles Elton in his recent book *The Ecology of Invasions*. During the Cretaceous Period, some hundred million years ago, flooding seas cut many land bridges between continents and living things found themselves confined in what Elton calls "colossal separate nature reserves." There, isolated from others of their kind, they developed many new species. When some of the land masses were joined again, about 15 million years ago, these species began to move out into new territories—a movement that is not only still in progress but is now receiving considerable assistance from man.

The importation of plants is the primary agent in the modern spread of species, for animals have almost invariably gone along with the plants, quarantine being a comparatively recent and not completely effective innovation. The United States Office of Plant Introduction alone has introduced almost 200,000 species and varieties of plants from all over the world. Nearly half of the 180 or so major insect enemies of plants in the United States are accidental imports from abroad, and most of them have come as hitchhikers on plants.

In new territory, out of reach of the restraining hand of the natural enemies that kept down its numbers in its native land, an invading plant or animal is able to become enormously abundant. Thus it is no accident that our most troublesome insects are introduced species.

These invasions, both the naturally occurring and those dependent on human assistance, are likely to continue indefinitely. Quarantine and massive chemical campaigns are only extremely expensive ways of buying time. We are faced, according to Dr. Elton, "with a life-and-death need not just to find new technological means of suppressing this plant or that animal"; instead we need the basic knowledge of animal populations and their relations to their surroundings that will "promote an even balance and damp down the explosive power of outbreaks and new invasions."

Much of the necessary knowledge is now available but we do not use it. We train ecologists in our universities and even employ them in our governmental agencies but we seldom take their advice. We allow the chemical death rain to fall as though there were no alternative, whereas in fact there are many, and our ingenuity could soon discover many more if given opportunity.

Have we fallen into a mesmerized state that makes us accept as inevitable that which is inferior or detrimental, as though having lost the will or the vision to demand that which is good? Such thinking, in the words of the ecologist Paul Shepard, "idealizes life with only its head out of water, inches above the limits of toleration of the corruption of its own environment…Why should we tolerate a diet of weak poisons, a home in insipid surroundings, a circle of acquaintances who are not quite our enemies, the noise of motors with just enough relief to prevent insanity? Who would want to live in a world which is just not quite fatal?"

Yet such a world is pressed upon us. The crusade to create a chemically sterile, insect-free world seems to have engendered a fanatic zeal on the part of many specialists and most of the so-called control agencies. On every hand there is evidence that those engaged in spraying operations exercise a ruthless power. "The regulatory entomologists…function as prosecutor, judge and jury, tax assessor and collector and sheriff to enforce their own orders," said Connecticut entomologist Neely Turner. The most flagrant abuses go unchecked in both state and federal agencies.

It is not my contention that chemical insecticides must never be used. I do contend that we have put poisonous and biologically potent chemicals indiscriminately into the hands of persons largely or wholly ignorant of their potentials for harm. We have subjected enormous numbers of people to contact with these poisons, without their consent and often without their knowledge. If the Bill of Rights contains no guarantee that a citizen shall be secure against lethal poisons distributed either by private individuals or by public officials, it is surely only because our forefathers, despite their considerable wisdom and foresight, could conceive of no such problem.

I contend, furthermore, that we have allowed these chemicals to be used with little or no advance investigation of their effect on soil, water, wildlife, and man himself. Future generations are unlikely to condone our lack of prudent concern for the integrity of the natural world that supports all life.

There is still very limited awareness of the nature of the threat. This is an era of specialists, each of whom sees his own problem and is unaware of or intolerant of the larger frame into which it fits. It is also an era dominated by industry, in which the right to make a dollar at whatever cost is seldom challenged. When the public protests, confronted with some obvious evidence of damaging results of pesticide applications, it is fed little tranquilizing pills of half truth. We urgently need an end to these false assurances, to the sugar coating of unpalatable facts. It is the public that is being asked to assume the risks that the insect controllers calculate. The public must decide whether it wishes to continue on the present road, and it can do so only when in full possession of the facts. In the words of Jean Rostand, "The obligation to endure gives us the right to know." ■

──────────────────────────── AUTHOR PROFILE

Rachel Carson (1907–1964) was an American author, marine biologist, and conservationist. Carson originally studied English at Chatham University but earned her Bachelor's Degree in Biology. She earned a Master's Degree in Zoology from Johns Hopkins. Carson worked for the U.S. Bureau of Fisheries, first writing for the radio program "Romance Under the Waters," then full time as a junior aquatic biologist. Carson wrote *The Sea Around Us* in 1951 and encountered the pesticide DDT (Dichlorodiphenyltrichloroethane) while working at the Bureau. This led to Carson's most famous work *Silent Spring* (1962), which made the general public aware of the dangers of pesticide and started the grassroots environmental movement that led to the creation of the EPA (Environmental Protection Agency) in 1970. Carson fought for the environment while being treated for breast cancer. She died in 1964 but was awarded the Presidential Medal of Freedom posthumously in 1980.

C

Nashville

By Tiana Clark

is hot chicken on sopping white bread with green pickle
chips—sour to balance prismatic, flame-colored spice
for white people. Or, rather, white people now curate hot
chicken for $16 and two farm-to-table sides, or maybe

they've hungered fried heat and grease from black food
and milk—but didn't want to drive to Jefferson Street or
don't know about the history of Jefferson Street or Hell's
Half Acre, north of downtown. Where freed slaves lived

on the fringe of Union camps, built their own new country.
Where its golden age brought the Silver Streak, a ballroom
bringing Basie, Ellington, and Fitzgerald. First-run movies
at the Ritz and no one had to climb to the balcony. 1968,

they built the interstate. I-40 bisected the black community
like a tourniquet of concrete. There were no highway exits.
120 businesses closed. Ambulance siren driving over
the house that called 911, diminishing howl in the distance,

black bodies going straight to the morgue. At the downtown
library, a continuous loop flashes *SNCC* videos with black
and white kids training for spit and circular cigarette burns
as the video toggles from coaching to counters covered

in pillars of salt and pie and soda—magma of the movement.
On I-65, there is a two-tone Confederate statue I flick off
daily on my morning commute. Walking down Second Avenue,
past neon honky-tonks playing bro-country and Cash

and herds of squealing pink bachelorette parties—someone
yelled *Nigger-lover* at my husband. Again. Walking down
Second Avenue, I thought I heard someone yelling at the back
of my husband. I turned around to find the voice and saw

myself as someone who didn't give a damn. Again. I turned
around to find that it was I who lived inside the lovely word
made flesh by white mouths masticating mashed sweet potatoes
from my mother's mother's mother—Freelove was her name,

a slave from Warrior, North Carolina, with twelve children
with names like Pansy, Viola, Oscar, Stella, and Toy—my
grandmother. There is always a word I'm chasing inside and
outside of my body, a word inside another word, scanning

the O.E.D. for soot-covered roots: 1577, 1584, 1608…Tracing my
finger along the boomerang shape of the Niger River for my blood.
1856, 1866, 1889…*Who said it?* A hyphen—crackles and bites,
burns the body to a spray of white wisps, like when the hot comb,

with its metal teeth, cut close to petroleum jelly edging the scalp—
sizzling. Southern Babel, smoking the hive of epithets hung fat
above bustling crowds like black-and-white lynching photographs,
mute faces, red finger pointing up at my dead, some smiling,

some with hats and ties—all business, as one needlelike lady
is looking at the camera, as if looking through the camera, at me,
in the way I am looking at my lover now—halcyon and constant.
Once my mother-in-law said *Watch your back*, and I knew exactly

what she meant. Again. I turned around to find I am the breath
of Apollo panting at the back of Daphne's wild hair, chasing words
like arrows inside the knotted meat between my shoulder blades—
four violent syllables stabbing my skin, enamored with pain.

I am kissing all the trees—searching the mob, mumbling to myself:
Who said it?
Who said it?
Who said it?■

AUTHOR PROFILE

Tiana Clark grew up in Nashville and southern California. She is a graduate of
Tennessee State University, and has received scholarships to the Bread Loaf
Writers' Conference. She is the author of *Equilibrium*, which was selected
for the 2016 Frost Place Chapbook Competition. She is the winner of the
2017 Furious Flower's Gwendolyn Brooks Centennial Poetry Prize, the 2016
Academy of American Poets University Prize, and the 2015 Rattle Poetry
Prize. Her writing has appeared in the *New Yorker, American Poetry Review,
Kenyon Review*, and the *New England Review* among other prestigious literary journals. Currently, she is the 2017–2018 Jay C. Ruth Halls Poetry Fellow
at the Wisconsin Institute of Creative Writing. Her poem "Nashville" originally
appeared in *The New Yorker* in 2017.

Students' Right to Their Own Language

By Conference on College Composition and Communication

Introduction

American schools and colleges have, in the last decade, been forced to take a stand on a basic educational question: what should the schools do about the language habits of students who come from a wide variety of social, economic, and cultural backgrounds? The question is not new. Differences in language have always existed, and the schools have always wrestled with them, but the social upheavals of the 1960's, and the insistence of submerged minorities on a greater share in American society, have posed the question more insistently and have suggested the need for a shift in emphasis in providing answers. Should the schools try to uphold language variety, or to modify it, or to eradicate it?

The emotional nature of the controversy has obscured the complexities of the problem and hidden some of the assumptions that must be examined before any kind of rational policy can be adopted. The human use of language is not a simple phenomenon: sophisticated research in linguistics and sociology has demonstrated incontrovertibly that many long held and passionately cherished notions about language are misleading at best, and often completely erroneous. On the other hand, linguistic research, advanced as much of it is, has not yet produced any absolute, easily understood, explanation of how people acquire language or how habits acquired so early in life that they defy conscious analysis can be consciously changed. Nor is the linguistic information that is available very widely disseminated. The training of most English teachers has concentrated on the appreciation and analysis of literature, rather than on an understanding of the nature of language, and many teachers are, in consequence, forced to take a position on an aspect of their discipline about which they have little real information.

And if teachers are often uninformed, or misinformed, on the subject of language, the general public is even more ignorant. Lack of reliable information, however, seldom prevents people from discussing language questions with an air of absolute authority. Historians, mathematicians, and nurses all hold decided views on just what English teachers should be requiring. And through their representatives on Boards of Education and Boards of Regents, businessmen, politicians, parents, and the students themselves insist that the values taught by the schools must reflect the prejudices held by the public. The English profession, then, faces a dilemma: until public attitudes can be changed—and it is worth remembering that the past teaching in English classes has been largely responsible for those attitudes—shall we place our emphasis on what the vocal elements of the public think it wants or on what the actual available linguistic evidence indicates we should emphasize? Shall we blame the business world by saying, "Well, we realize that human beings use language in a wide variety of ways, but employers demand a single variety"?

Before these questions can be responsibly answered, English teachers at all levels, from kindergarten through college, must uncover and examine some of the assumptions on which our teaching has rested. Many of us have taught as though there existed somewhere a single American "standard English" which could be isolated, identified, and accurately defined. We need to know whether "standard English" is or is not in some sense a myth. We have ignored, many of us, the distinction between speech and writing and have taught the language as though the talk in any region, even the talk of speakers with prestige and power, were identical to edited *written* English.

We have also taught, many of us, as though the "English of educated speakers," the language used by those in power in the community, had an inherent advantage over other dialects as a means of expressing thought or emotion, conveying information, or analyzing concepts. We need to discover whether our attitudes toward "educated English" are based on some inherent superiority of the dialect itself or on the social prestige of those who use it. We need to ask ourselves whether our rejection of students who do not adopt the dialect most familiar to us is based on any real merit in our dialect or whether we are actually rejecting the students themselves, rejecting them because of their racial, social, and cultural origins.

And many of us have taught as though the function of schools and colleges were to erase differences. Should we, on the one hand, urge creativity and individuality in the arts and the sciences, take pride in the diversity of our historical development, and, on the other hand, try to obliterate all the differences in the way Americans speak and write? Our major emphasis has been on uniformity, in both speech and writing; would we accomplish more, both educationally and ethically, if we shifted that emphasis to precise, effective, and appropriate communication in diverse ways, whatever the dialect?

Students are required by law to attend schools for most of their adolescent years, and are usually required by curriculum makers to take English every one of those years, often including "developmental" or "compensatory" English well into college if their native dialect varies from that of the middle class. The result is that students who come from backgrounds where the prestigious variety of English is the normal medium of communication have built-in advantages that enable them to succeed, often in spite of and not because of, their schoolroom training in "grammar." They sit at the head of the class, are accepted at "exclusive" schools, and are later rewarded with positions in the business and social world. Students whose nurture and experience give them a different dialect are usually denied these rewards. As English teachers, we are responsible for what our teaching does to the self-image and the self-esteem of our students. We must decide what elements of our discipline are really important to us, whether we want to share with our students the richness of all varieties of language, encourage linguistic virtuosity, and say with Langston Hughes:

I play it cool and dig all jive
That's the reason I stay alive
My motto as I live and learn
Is to dig and be dug in return.

It was with these concerns in mind that the Executive Committee of the Conference on College Composition and Communication, in 1972, passed the following resolution:

> We affirm the students' right to their own patterns and varieties of language—the dialects of their nurture or whatever dialects in which they find their own identity and style. Language scholars long ago denied that the myth of a standard American dialect has any validity. The claim that any one dialect is unacceptable amounts to an attempt of one social group to exert its dominance over another. Such a claim leads to false advice for speakers and writers, and immoral advice for humans. A nation proud of its diverse heritage and its cultural and racial variety will preserve its heritage of dialects. We affirm strongly that teachers must have the experiences and training that will enable them to respect diversity and uphold the right of students to their own language.

The members of the Committee realized that the resolution would create controversy and that without a clear explanation of the linguistic and social knowledge on which it rests, many people would find it incomprehensible. The members of the Executive Committee, therefore, requested a background statement which would examine some common misconceptions about language and dialect, define some key terms, and provide some suggestions for sounder, alternate approaches. What follows is not, then, an introductory course in linguistics, nor is it a teaching guide. It is, we hope, an answer to some of the questions the resolution will raise.■

AUTHOR PROFILE

The Conference on College Composition and Communication (CCCC) is an American professional organization representing college and university writing instructors. Established in 1949 within the National Council of Teachers of English, it is the world's largest organization to promote the teaching and study of college composition and communication. "Students' Right to Their Own Language" first appeared in the fall 1974 as a special issue of the College Composition and Communication journal (Volume 25), which publishes research in rhetoric and composition studies.

The Trouble with Wilderness; or, Getting Back to the Wrong Nature

By William Cronon

The time has come to rethink wilderness.

This will seem a heretical claim to many environmentalists, since the idea of wilderness has for decades been a fundamental tenet—indeed, a passion—of the environmental movement, especially in the United States. For many Americans wilderness stands as the last remaining place where civilization, that all too human disease, has not fully infected the earth. It is an island in the polluted sea of urban-industrial modernity, the one place we can turn for escape from our own too-muchness. Seen in this way, wilderness presents itself as the best antidote to our human selves, a refuge we must somehow recover if we hope to save the planet. As Henry David Thoreau once famously declared, "In Wildness is the preservation of the World." (1)

But is it? The more one knows of its peculiar history, the more one realizes that wilderness is not quite what it seems. Far from being the one place on earth that stands apart from humanity, it is quite profoundly a human creation—indeed, the creation of very particular human cultures at very particular moments in human history. It is not a pristine sanctuary where the last remnant of an untouched, endangered, but still transcendent nature can for at least a little while longer be encountered without the contaminating taint of civilization. Instead, it's a product of that civilization, and could hardly be contaminated by the very stuff of which it is made. Wilderness hides its unnaturalness behind a mask that is all the more beguiling because it seems so natural. As we gaze into the mirror it holds up for us, we too easily imagine that what we behold is Nature when in fact we see the reflection of our own unexamined longings and desires. For this reason, we mistake ourselves when we suppose that wilderness can be the solution to our culture's problematic relationships with the nonhuman world, for wilderness is itself no small part of the problem.

To assert the unnaturalness of so natural a place will no doubt seem absurd or even perverse to many readers, so let me hasten to add that the nonhuman world we encounter in wilderness is far from being merely our own invention. I celebrate with others who love wilderness the beauty and power of the things it contains. Each of us who has spent time there can conjure images and sensations that seem all the more hauntingly real for having engraved themselves so indelibly on our memories. Such memories may be uniquely our own, but they are also familiar enough be to be instantly recognizable to others. Remember this? The torrents of mist shoot out from the base of a great waterfall in the depths of a Sierra canyon, the tiny droplets cooling your face as you listen to the roar of the water and gaze up toward the sky through a rainbow that hovers just out of reach.

Remember this too: looking out across a desert canyon in the evening air, the only sound a lone raven calling in the distance, the rock walls dropping away into a chasm so deep that its bottom all but vanishes as you squint into the amber light of the setting sun. And this: the moment beside the trail as you sit on a sandstone ledge, your boots damp with the morning dew while you take in the rich smell of the pines, and the small red fox—or maybe for you it was a raccoon or a coyote or a deer—that suddenly ambles across your path, stopping for a long moment to gaze in your direction with cautious indifference before continuing on its way. Remember the feelings of such moments, and you will know as well as I do that you were in the presence of something irreducibly nonhuman, something profoundly Other than yourself Wilderness is made of that too.

And yet: what brought each of us to the places where such memories became possible is entirely a cultural invention. Go back 250 years in American and European history, and you do not find nearly so many people wandering around remote corners of the planet looking for what today we would call "the wilderness experience." As late as the eighteenth century, the most common usage of the word "wilderness" in the English language referred to landscapes that generally carried adjectives far different from the ones they attract today. To be a wilderness then was to be "deserted," "savage," "desolate," "barren"—in short, a "waste," the word's nearest synonym. Its connotations were anything but positive, and the emotion one was most likely to feel in its presence was "bewilderment" or terror. (2)

Many of the word's strongest associations then were biblical, for it is used over and over again in the King James Version to refer to places on the margins of civilization where it is all too easy to lose oneself in moral confusion and despair. The wilderness was where Moses had wandered with his people for forty years, and where they had nearly abandoned their God to worship a golden idol. (3) "For Pharaoh will say of the Children of Israel," we read in Exodus, "They are entangled in the land, the wilderness hath shut them in." (4) The wilderness was where Christ had struggled with the devil and endured his temptations: "And immediately the Spirit driveth him into the wilderness. And he was there in the wilderness for forty days tempted of Satan; and was with the wild beasts; and the angels ministered unto him." (5) The "delicious Paradise" of John Milton's Eden was surrounded by "a steep wilderness, whose hairy sides /Access denied" to all who sought entry." When Adam and Eve were driven from that garden, the world they entered was a wilderness that only their labor and pain could redeem. Wilderness, in short, was a place to which one came only against one's will, and always in fear and trembling. Whatever value it might have arose solely from the possibility that it might be "reclaimed" and turned toward human ends—planted as a garden, say, or a city upon a hill. (7) In its raw state, it had little or nothing to offer civilized men and women.

But by the end of the nineteenth century, all this had changed. The wastelands that had once seemed worthless had for some people come to seem almost beyond price. That Thoreau in 1862 could declare wildness to be the preservation of the world suggests the sea change that was going on. Wilderness had once been the antithesis of all that was orderly and good—it had been the darkness, one might say, on the far side of the garden wall—and yet now it was frequently likened to Eden itself. When John Muir arrived in the Sierra Nevada in 1869, he would declare, "No description of Heaven that I have ever heard or read of seems half so fine." (8) He was hardly alone in expressing such emotions. One by one, various corners of the American map came to be designated as sites whose wild beauty was so spectacular that a growing number of citizens had to visit and see them for themselves. Niagara Falls was the first to undergo this transformation, but it was soon followed by the Catskills, the Adirondacks, Yosemite, Yellowstone, and others. Yosemite was deeded by the U.S. government to the state of California in 1864 as the nation's first wildland park, and Yellowstone became the first true national park in 1872. (9)

By the first decade of the twentieth century, in the single most famous episode in American conservation history, a national debate had exploded over whether the city of San Francisco should be permitted to augment its water supply by damming the Tuolumne River in Hetch Hetchy valley, well within the boundaries of Yosemite National Park. The dam was eventually built, but what today seems no less significant is that so many people fought to prevent its completion. Even as the fight was being lost, Hetch Hetchy became the battle cry of an emerging movement to preserve wilderness. Fifty years earlier, such opposition would have been unthinkable. Few would have questioned the merits of "reclaiming" a wasteland like this in order to put it to human use. Now the defenders of Hetch Hetchy attracted widespread national attention by portraying such an act not as improvement or progress but as desecration and vandalism. Lest one doubt that the old biblical metaphors had been turned completely on their heads, listen to John Muir attack the dam's defenders. "Their arguments," he wrote, "are curiously like those of the devil, devised for the destruction of the first garden—so much of the very best Eden fruit going to waste; so much of the best Tuolumne water and Tuolumne scenery going to waste." (10) For Muir and the growing number of Americans who shared his views, Satan's home had become God's Own Temple.

The sources of this rather astonishing transformation were many, but for the purposes of this essay they can be gathered under two broad headings: the sublime and the frontier. Of the two, the sublime is the older and more pervasive cultural construct, being one of the most important expressions of that broad transatlantic movement we today label as romanticism; the frontier is more peculiarly American, though it too had its European antecedents and parallels. The two converged to remake wilderness in their own image, freighting it with moral values and cultural symbols that it carries to this day. Indeed, it is not too much to say that the modern environmental movement is itself a grandchild of romanticism and post-frontier ideology, which is why it is no accident that so much environmentalist discourse takes its bearings from the wilderness these intellectual movements helped create. Although wilderness may today seem to be just one environmental concern among many, it in fact serves as the foundation for a long list of other such concerns that on their face seem quite remote from it. That is why its influence is so pervasive and, potentially, so insidious.

To gain such remarkable influence, the concept of wilderness had to become loaded with some of the deepest core values of the culture that created and idealized it: it had to become sacred. This possibility had been present in wilderness

even in the days when it had been a place of spiritual danger and moral temptation. If Satan was there, then so was Christ, who had found angels as well as wild beasts during His sojourn in the desert. In the wilderness the boundaries between human and nonhuman, between natural and supernatural, had always seemed less certain than elsewhere. This was why the early Christian saints and mystics had often emulated Christ's desert retreat as they sought to experience for themselves the visions and spiritual testing He had endured. One might meet devils and run the risk of losing one's soul in such a place, but one might also meet God. For some that possibility was worth almost any price.

By the eighteenth century this sense of the wilderness as a landscape where the supernatural lay just beneath the surface was expressed in the doctrine of the sublime, a word whose modern usage has been so watered down by commercial hype and tourist advertising that it retains only a dim echo of its former power. (11) In the theories of Edmund Burke, Immanuel Kant, William Gilpin, and others, sublime landscapes were those rare places on earth where one had more chance than elsewhere to glimpse the face of God. (12) Romantics had a clear notion of where one could be most sure of having this experience. Although God might, of course, choose to show Himself anywhere, He would most often be found in those vast, powerful landscapes where one could not help feeling insignificant and being reminded of one's own mortality. Where were these sublime places? The eighteenth century catalog of their locations feels very familiar, for we still see and value landscapes as it taught us to do. God was on the mountaintop, in the chasm, in the waterfall, in the thundercloud, in the rainbow, in the sunset. One has only to think of the sites that Americans chose for their first national parks—Yellowstone, Yosemite, Grand Canyon, Rainier, Zion—to realize that virtually all of them fit one or more of these categories. Less sublime landscapes simply did not appear worthy of such protection; not until the 1940s, for instance, would the first swamp be honored, in Everglades National Park, and to this day there is no national park in the grasslands. (13)

Among the best proofs that one had entered a sublime landscape was the emotion it evoked. For the early romantic writers and artists who first began to celebrate it, the sublime was far from being a pleasurable experience. The classic description is that of William Wordsworth as he recounted climbing the Alps and crossing the Simplon Pass in his autobiographical poem "The Prelude." There, surrounded by crags and waterfalls, the poet felt himself literally to be in the presence of the divine—and experienced an emotion remarkably close to terror:

> The immeasurable height
> Of woods decaying, never to be decayed,
> The stationary blasts of waterfalls,
> And in the narrow rent at every turn
> Winds thwarting winds, bewildered and forlorn,
> The torrents shooting from the clear blue sky,
> The rocks that muttered close upon our ears,
> Black drizzling crags that spake by the way-side

As if a voice were in them, the sick sight
And giddy prospect of the raving stream,
The unfettered clouds and region of the Heavens,
Tumult and peace, the darkness and the light
Were all like workings of one mind, the features
Of the same face, blossoms upon one tree;
Characters of the great Apocalypse,
The types and symbols of Eternity,
Of first, and last, and midst, and without end. (14)

This was no casual stroll in the mountains, no simple sojourn in the gentle lap of nonhuman nature. What Wordsworth described was nothing less than a religious experience, akin to that of the Old Testament prophets as they conversed with their wrathful God. The symbols he detected in this wilderness landscape were more supernatural than natural, and they inspired more awe and dismay than joy or pleasure. No mere mortal was meant to linger long in such a place, so it was with considerable relief that Wordsworth and his companion made their way back down from the peaks to the sheltering valleys. Lest you suspect that this view of the sublime was limited to timid Europeans who lacked the American know-how for feeling at home in the wilderness, remember Henry David Thoreau's 1846 climb of Mount Katahdin, in Maine. Although Thoreau is regarded by many today as one of the great American celebrators of wilderness, his emotions about Katahdin were no less ambivalent than Wordsworth's about the Alps.

It was vast, Titanic, and such as man never inhabits. Some part of the beholder, even some vital part, seems to escape through the loose grating of his ribs as he ascends. He is more lone than you can imagine...Vast, Titanic, inhuman Nature has got him at disadvantage, caught him alone, and pilfers him of some of his divine faculty. She does not smile on him as in the plains. She seems to say sternly, why came ye here before your time? This ground is not prepared for you. Is it not enough that I smile in the valleys? I have never made this soil for thy feet, this air for thy breathing, these rocks for thy neighbors. I cannot pity nor fondle thee here, but forever relentlessly drive thee hence to where I am kind. Why seek me where I have not called thee, and then complain because you find me but a stepmother? (15)

This is surely not the way a modern backpacker or nature lover would describe Maine's most famous mountain, but that is because Thoreau's description owes as much to Wordsworth and other romantic contemporaries as to the rocks and clouds of Katahdin itself. His words took the physical mountain on which he stood and transmuted it into an icon of the sublime: a symbol of God's presence on earth. The power and the glory of that icon were such that only a prophet

might gaze on it for long. In effect, romantics like Thoreau joined Moses and the children of Israel in Exodus when "they looked toward the wilderness, and behold, the glory of the Lord appeared in the cloud." (16)

But even as it came to embody the awesome power of the sublime, wilderness was also being tamed—not just by those who were building settlements in its midst but also by those who most celebrated its inhuman beauty. By the second half of the nineteenth century, the terrible awe that Wordsworth and Thoreau regarded as the appropriately pious stance to adopt in the presence of their mountaintop God was giving way to a much more comfortable, almost sentimental demeanor. As more and more tourists sought out the wilderness as a spectacle to be looked at and enjoyed for its great beauty, the sublime in effect became domesticated. The wilderness was still sacred, but the religious sentiments it evoked were more those of a pleasant parish church than those of a grand cathedral or a harsh desert retreat. The writer who best captures this late romantic sense of a domesticated sublime is undoubtedly John Muir, whose descriptions of Yosemite and the Sierra Nevada reflect none of the anxiety or terror one finds in earlier writers. Here he is, for instance, sketching on North Dome in Yosemite Valley:

> No pain here, no dull empty hours, no fear of the past, no fear of the future. These blessed mountains are so compactly filled with God's beauty, no petty personal hope or experience has room to be. Drinking this champagne water is pure pleasure, so is breathing the living air, and every movement of limbs is pleasure, while the body seems to feel beauty when exposed to it as it feels the campfire or sunshine, entering not by the eyes alone, but equally through all one's flesh like radiant heat, making a passionate ecstatic pleasure glow not explainable.

The emotions Muir describes in Yosemite could hardly be more different from Thoreau's on Katahdin or Wordsworth's on the Simplon Pass. Yet all three men are participating in the same cultural tradition and contributing to the same myth—the mountain as cathedral. The three may differ in the way they choose to express their piety—Wordsworth favoring an awe-filled bewilderment, Thoreau a stern loneliness, Muir a welcome ecstasy—but they agree completely about the church in which they prefer to worship. Muir's closing words on North Dome diverge from his older contemporaries only in mood, not in their ultimate content:

> Perched like a fly on this Yosemite dome, I gaze and sketch and bask, oftentimes settling down into dumb admiration without definite hope of ever learning much, yet with the longing, unresting effort that lies at the door of hope, humbly prostrate before the vast display of God's power, and eager to offer self-denial and renunciation with eternal toil to learn any lesson in the divine manuscript. (17)

Muir's "divine manuscript" and Wordsworth's "Characters of the great Apocalypse" are in fact pages from the same holy book. The sublime wilderness had ceased to be place of satanic temptation and become instead a sacred temple, much as it continues to be for those who love it today.

But the romantic sublime was not the only cultural movement that helped transform wilderness into a sacred American icon during the nineteenth century. No less important was the powerful romantic attraction of primitivism, dating back at least to of that the best antidote to the ills of an overly refined and civilized modern world was a return to simpler, more primitive living. In the United States, this was embodied most strikingly in the national myth of the frontier. The historian Frederick Jackson Turner wrote in 1893 the classic academic statement of this myth, but it had been part of American cultural traditions for well over a century. As Turner described the process, easterners and European immigrants, in moving to the wild unsettled lands of the frontier, shed the trappings of civilization, rediscovered their primitive racial energies, reinvented direct democratic institutions, and by reinfused themselves with a vigor, an independence, and a creativity that the source of American democracy and national character. Seen in this way, wild country became a place not just of religious redemption but of national renewal, the quintessential location for experiencing what it meant to be an American.

One of Turner's most provocative claims was that by the 1890s the frontier was passing away. Never again would "such gifts of free land offer themselves" to the American people. "The frontier has gone," he declared, "and with its going has closed the first period of American history." (18) Built into the frontier myth from its very beginning was the notion that this crucible of American identity was temporary and would pass away. Those who have celebrated the frontier have almost always looked backward as they did so, mourning an older, simpler, truer world that is about to disappear, forever. That world and all of its attractions, Turner said, depended on free land—on wilderness. Thus, in the myth of the vanishing frontier lay the seeds of wilderness preservation in the United States, for if wild land had been so crucial in the making of the nation, then surely one must save its last remnants as monuments to the American past—and as an insurance policy to protect its future. It is no accident that the movement to set aside national parks and wilderness areas began to gain real momentum at precisely the time that laments about the passing frontier reached their peak. To protect wilderness was in a very real sense to protect the nation's most sacred myth of origin.

Among the core elements of the frontier myth was the powerful sense among certain groups of Americans that wilderness was the last bastion of rugged individualism. Turner tended to stress communitarian themes when writing frontier history, asserting that Americans in primitive conditions had been forced to band together with their neighbors to form communities and democratic institutions. For other writers, however, frontier democracy for communities was less compelling than frontier freedom for individuals. (19) By fleeing to the outer margins of settled land and society—so the story ran—an individual could escape the confining strictures of civilized life. The mood among writers who celebrated frontier individualism was almost always nostalgic; they lamented not just a lost way of life but the passing of the heroic men who had embodied that life. Thus Owen Wister in the introduction to his classic 1902 novel *The Virginian* could write of

"a vanished world" in which "the horseman, the cow-puncher, the last romantic figure upon our soil" rode only "in his historic yesterday" and would "never come again." For Wister, the cowboy was a man who gave his word and kept it ("Wall Street would have found him behind the times"), who did not talk lewdly to women ("Newport would have thought him old-fashioned"), who worked and played hard, and whose "ungoverned hours did not unman him." (20) Theodore Roosevelt wrote with much the same nostalgic fervor about the "fine, manly qualities" of the "wild rough-rider of the plains." No one could be more heroically masculine, thought Roosevelt, or more at home in the western wilderness:

> There he passes his days, there he does his life-work, there, when he meets death, he faces it as he has faced many other evils, with quiet, uncomplaining fortitude. Brave, hospitable, hardy, and adventurous, he is the grim pioneer of our race; he prepares the way for the civilization from before whose face he must himself disappear. Hard and dangerous though his existence is, it has yet a wild attraction that strongly draws to it his bold, free spirit. (21)

This nostalgia for a passing frontier way of life inevitably implied ambivalence, if not downright hostility, toward modernity and all that it represented. If one saw the wild lands of the frontier as freer, truer, and more natural than other, more modern places, then one was also inclined to see the cities and factories of urban-industrial civilization as confining, false, and artificial. Owen Wister looked at the post-frontier "transition" that had followed "the horseman of the plains," and did not like what he saw: "a shapeless state, a condition of men and manners as unlovely as is that moment in the year when winter is gone and spring not come, and the face of Nature is ugly." (22) In the eyes of writers who shared Wister's distaste for modernity, civilization contaminated its inhabitants and absorbed them into the faceless, collective, contemptible life of the crowd. For all of its troubles and dangers, and despite the fact that it must pass away, the frontier had been a better place. If civilization was to be redeemed, it would be by men like the Virginian who could retain their frontier virtues even as they made the transition to post-frontier life.

The mythic frontier individualist was almost always masculine in gender: here, in the wilderness, a man could be a real man, the rugged individual he was meant to be before civilization sapped his energy and threatened his masculinity. Wister's contemptuous remarks about Wall Street and Newport suggest what he and many others of his generation believed—that the comforts and seductions of civilized life were especially insidious for men, who all too easily became emasculated by the feminizing tendencies of civilization. More often than not, men who felt this way came, like Wister and Roosevelt, from elite class backgrounds. The curious result was that frontier nostalgia became an important vehicle for expressing a peculiarly bourgeois form of antimodernism. The very men who most benefited from urban-industrial capitalism were among those who believed they must escape its debilitating effects. If the frontier was passing, then men who had the means to do so should preserve for themselves some remnant of its wild landscape so that they might enjoy the regeneration and renewal that came from sleeping under the stars, participating in blood sports, and living off the land. The frontier might be gone, but the frontier experience could still be had if only wilderness were preserved.

Thus the decades following the Civil War saw more and more of the nation's wealthiest citizens seeking out wilderness for themselves. The elite passion for wild land took many forms: enormous estates in the Adirondacks and elsewhere (disingenuously called "camps" despite their many servants and amenities), cattle ranches for would-be rough riders on the Great Plains, guided big-game hunting trips in the Rockies, and luxurious resort hotels wherever railroads pushed their way into sublime landscapes. Wilderness suddenly emerged as the landscape of choice for elite tourists, who brought with them strikingly urban ideas of the countryside through which they traveled. For them, wild land was not a site for productive labor and not a permanent home; rather, it was a place of recreation. One went to the wilderness not as a producer but as a consumer, hiring guides and other backcountry residents who could serve as romantic surrogates for the rough riders and hunters of the frontier if one was willing to overlook their new status as employees and servants of the rich. In just this way, wilderness came to embody the national frontier myth, standing for the wild freedom of America's past and seeming to represent a highly attractive natural alternative to the ugly artificiality of modern civilization. The irony, of course, was that in the process wilderness came to reflect the very civilization its devotees sought to escape. Ever since the nineteenth century, celebrating wilderness has been an activity mainly for well-to-do city folks. Country people generally know far too much about working the land to regard unworked land as their ideal. In contrast, elite urban tourists and wealthy sportsmen projected their leisure-time frontier fantasies onto the American landscape and so created wilderness in their own image.

There were other ironies as well. The movement to set aside national parks and wilderness areas followed hard on the heels of the final Indian wars, in which the prior human inhabitants of these areas were rounded up and moved onto reservations. The myth of the wilderness as "virgin " uninhabited land had always been especially cruel when seen from the perspective of the Indians who had once called that land home. Now they were forced to move elsewhere, with the result that tourists could safely enjoy the illusion that they were seeing their nation in its pristine, original state, in the new morning of God's own creation. (23) Among the things that most marked the new national parks as reflecting a post-frontier consciousness was the relative absence of human violence within their boundaries. The actual frontier had often been a place of conflict, in which invaders and invaded fought for control of land and resources. Once set aside within the fixed and carefully policed boundaries of the modern bureaucratic state, the wilderness lost its savage image and became safe: a place more of reverie than of revulsion or fear. Meanwhile, its original inhabitants were kept out by dint of force, their earlier uses of the land redefined as inappropriate or even illegal. To this day, for instance, the Blackfeet continue to be accused of "poaching" on the lands of Glacier National Park that originally belonged to them and that were ceded by treaty only with the proviso that they be permitted to hunt there. (24)

The removal of Indians to create an "uninhabited wilderness"—uninhabited as never before in the human history of the place—reminds us just how invented, just how constructed, the American wilderness really is. To return to my opening argument: there is nothing natural about the concept of wilderness. It is entirely a creation of the culture that holds it dear, a product of the very history it seeks to deny. Indeed, one of the most striking proofs of the cultural invention of wilderness is its thoroughgoing erasure of the history from which it sprang. In virtually all of its manifestations, wilderness represents a flight from history. Seen as the original garden, it is a place outside of time, from which human beings had to be ejected before the fallen world of history could properly begin. Seen as the frontier, it is a savage world at the dawn of civilization, whose transformation represents the very beginning of the national historical epic. Seen as the bold landscape of frontier heroism, it is the place of youth and childhood, into which men escape by abandoning their pasts and entering a world of freedom where the constraints of civilization fade into memory. Seen as the sacred sublime, it is the home of a God who transcends history by standing as the One who remains untouched and unchanged by time's arrow. No matter what the angle from which we regard it, wilderness offers us the illusion that we can escape the cares and troubles of the world in which our past has ensnared us. (25)

This escape from history is one reason why the language we use to talk about wilderness is often permeated with spiritual and religious values that reflect human ideals far more than the material world of physical nature. Wilderness fulfills the old romantic project of secularizing Judeo-Christian values so as to make a new cathedral not in some petty human building but in God's own creation, Nature itself. Many environmentalists who reject traditional notions of the Godhead and who regard themselves as agnostics or even atheists nonetheless express feelings tantamount to religious awe when in the presence of wilderness—a fact that testifies to the success of the romantic project. Those who have no difficulty seeing God as the expression of our human dreams and desires nonetheless have trouble recognizing that in a secular age Nature can offer precisely the same sort of mirror.

Thus it is that wilderness serves as the unexamined foundation on which so many of the quasi-religious values of modern environmentalism rest. The critique of modernity that is one of environmentalism's most important contributions to the moral and political discourse of our time more often than not appeals, explicitly or implicitly, to wilderness as the standard against which to measure the failings of our human world. Wilderness is the natural, unfallen antithesis of an unnatural civilization that has lost its soul. It is a place of freedom in which we can recover the true selves we have lost to the corrupting influences of our artificial lives. Most of all, it is the ultimate landscape of authenticity. Combining the sacred grandeur of the sublime with the primitive simplicity of the frontier, it is the place where we can see the world as it really is, and so know ourselves as we really are—or ought to be.

But the trouble with wilderness is that it quietly expresses and reproduces the very values its devotees seek to reject. The flight from history that is very nearly the core of wilderness represents the false hope of an escape from responsibility, the illusion that we can somehow wipe clean the slate of our past and return to the tabula rasa that supposedly existed before we began to leave our marks on the world. The dream of an unworked natural landscape is very much the fantasy of people who have never themselves had to work the land to make a living— urban folk for whom food comes from a supermarket or a restaurant instead of a field, and for whom the wooden houses in which they live and work apparently have no meaningful connection to the forests in which trees grow and die. Only people whose relation to the land was already alienated could hold up wilderness as a model for human life in nature, for the romantic ideology of wilderness leaves precisely nowhere for human beings actually to make their living from the land.

This, then, is the central paradox: wilderness embodies a dualistic vision in which the human is entirely outside the natural. If we allow ourselves to believe that nature, to be true, must also be wild, then our very presence in nature represents its fall. The place where we are is the place where nature is not. If this is so—if by definition wilderness leaves no place for human beings, save perhaps as contemplative sojourners enjoying their leisurely reverie in God's natural cathedral—then also by definition it can offer no solution to the environmental and other problems that confront us. To the extent that we celebrate wilderness as the measure with which we judge civilization, we reproduce the dualism that sets humanity and nature at opposite poles. We thereby leave ourselves little hope of discovering what an ethical, sustainable, honorable human place in nature might actually look like.

Worse: to the extent that we live in an urban-industrial civilization but at the same time pretend to ourselves that our real home is in the wilderness, to just that extent we give ourselves permission to evade responsibility for the lives we actually lead. We inhabit civilization while holding some part of ourselves—what we imagine to be the most precious part—aloof from its entanglements. We work our nine-to-five jobs in its institutions, we eat its food, we drive its cars (not least to reach the wilderness), we benefit from the intricate and all too invisible networks with which it shelters us, all the while pretending that these things are not an essential part of who we are. By imagining that our true home is in the wilderness, we forgive ourselves the homes we actually inhabit. In its flight from history, in its siren song of escape, in its reproduction of the dangerous dualism that sets human beings outside of nature—in all of these ways, wilderness poses a serious threat to responsible environmentalism at the end of the twentieth century.

By now I hope it is clear that my criticism in this essay is not directed at wild nature per se, or even at efforts to set aside large tracts of wild land, but rather at the specific habits of thinking that flow from this complex cultural construction called wilderness. It is not the things we label as wilderness that are the problem— for nonhuman nature and large tracts of the natural world do deserve protection—but rather what we ourselves mean when we use the label. Lest one doubt how pervasive these habits of thought actually are in contemporary environmentalism, let me list some of the places where wilderness serves as the ideological underpinning for environmental concerns that might otherwise seem quite remote from it. Defenders of biological diversity, for instance, although sometimes appealing to more utilitarian concerns, often point to "untouched" ecosystems as

the best and richest repositories of the undiscovered species we must certainly try to protect. Although at first blush an apparently more "scientific" concept than wilderness, biological diversity in fact invokes many of the same sacred values, which is why organizations like the Nature Conservancy have been so quick to employ it as an alternative to the seemingly fuzzier and more problematic concept of wilderness. There is a paradox here, of course. To the extent that biological diversity (indeed, even wilderness itself) is likely to survive in the future only by the most vigilant and self-conscious management of the ecosystems that sustain it, the ideology of wilderness is potentially in direct conflict with the very thing it encourages us to protect. (26) The most striking instances of this have revolved around "endangered species," which serve as vulnerable symbols of biological diversity while at the same time standing as surrogates for wilderness itself. The terms of the Endangered Species Act in the United States have often meant that those hoping to defend pristine wilderness have had to rely on a single endangered species like the spotted owl to gain legal standing for their case—thereby making the full power of the sacred land inhere in a single numinous organism whose habitat then becomes the object of intense debate about appropriate management and use. (27) The ease with which antienvironmental forces like the wise-use movement have attacked such single-species preservation efforts suggests the vulnerability of strategies like these.

Perhaps partly because our own conflicts over such places and organisms have become so messy, the convergence of wilderness values with concerns about biological diversity and endangered species has helped produce a deep fascination for remote ecosystems, where it is easier to imagine that nature might somehow be "left alone" to flourish by its own pristine devices. The classic example is the tropical rain forest, which since the 1970s has become the most powerful modern icon of unfallen, sacred land—a veritable Garden of Eden—for many Americans and Europeans. And yet protecting the rain forest in the eyes of First World environmentalists all too often means protecting it from the people who live there. Those who seek to preserve such "wilderness" from the activities of native peoples run the risk of reproducing the same tragedy—being forceably removed from an ancient home—that befell American Indians. Third World countries face massive environmental problems and deep social conflicts, but these are not likely to be solved by a cultural myth that encourages us to "preserve" peopleless landscapes that have not existed in such places for millennia. At its worst, as environmentalists are beginning to realize, exporting American notions of wilderness in this way can become an unthinking and self-defeating form of cultural imperialism. (28)

Perhaps the most suggestive example of the way that wilderness thinking can underpin other environmental concerns has emerged in the recent debate about "global change." In 1989 the journalist Bill McKibben published a book entitled *The End of Nature*, in which he argued that the prospect of global climate change as a result of unintentional human manipulation of the atmosphere means that nature as we once knew it no longer exists. (29) Whereas earlier generations inhabited a natural world that remained more or less unaffected by their actions, our own generation is uniquely different. We and our children will henceforth live in a biosphere completely altered by our own activity, a planet in which the human and the natural can no longer be distinguished, because the one has over-whelmed the other. In McKibben's view, nature has died, and we are responsible for killing it. "The planet," he declares, "is utterly different now." (30)

But such a perspective is possible only if we accept the wilderness premise that nature, to be natural, must also be pristine—remote from humanity and un-touched by our common past. In fact, everything we know about environmental history suggests that people have been manipulating the natural world on various scales for as long as we have a record of their passing. Moreover, we have unassail-able evidence that many of the environmental changes we now face also occurred quite apart from human intervention at one time or another in the earth's past. (31) The point is not that our current problems are trivial, or that our devastating effects on the earth's ecosystems should be accepted as inevitable or "natural." It is rather that we seem unlikely to make much progress in solving these problems if we hold up to ourselves as the mirror of nature a wilderness we ourselves cannot inhabit.

To do so is merely to take to a logical extreme the paradox that was built into wilderness from the beginning: if nature dies because we enter it, then the only way to save nature is to kill ourselves. The absurdity of this proposition flows from the underlying dualism it expresses. Not only does it ascribe greater power to hu-manity that we in fact possess—physical and biological nature will surely survive in some form or another long after we ourselves have gone the way of all flesh—but in the end it offers us little more than a self-defeating counsel of despair. The tautology gives us no way out: if wild nature is the only thing worth saving, and if our mere presence destroys it, then the sole solution to our own unnaturalness, the only way to protect sacred wilderness from profane humanity, would seem to be suicide. It is not a proposition that seems likely to produce very positive or practical results.

And yet radical environmentalists and deep ecologists all too frequently come close to accepting this premise as a first principle. When they express, for instance, the popular notion that our environmental problems began with the invention of agriculture, they push the human fall from natural grace so far back into the past that all of civilized history becomes a tale of ecological declension. Earth First! founder Dave Foreman captures the familiar parable succinctly when he writes,

> Before agriculture was midwifed in the Middle East, humans were in the wilderness. We had no concept of "wilderness" because everything was wilderness and we were a part of it. But with irrigation ditches, crop sur-pluses, and permanent villages, we became apart from the natural world… Between the wilderness that created us and the civilization created by us grew an ever-widening rift. (32)

In this view the farm becomes the first and most important battlefield in the long war against wild nature, and all else follows in its wake. From such a start-ing place, it is hard not to reach the conclusion that the only way human beings can hope to live naturally on earth is to follow the hunter-gatherers back into a wilderness Eden and abandon virtually everything that civilization has given us.

It may indeed turn out that civilization will end in ecological collapse or nuclear disaster, whereupon one might expect to find any human survivors returning to a way of life closer to that celebrated by Foreman and his followers. For most of us, though, such a debacle would be cause for regret, a sign that humanity had failed to fulfill its own promise and failed to honor its own highest values—including those of the deep ecologists.

In offering wilderness as the ultimate hunter-gatherer alternative to civilization, Foreman reproduces an extreme but still easily recognizable version of the myth of frontier primitivism. When he writes of his fellow Earth Firsters that "we believe we must return to being animal, to glorying in our sweat, hormones, tears, and blood" and that "we struggle against the modern compulsion to become dull, passionless androids," he is following in the footsteps of Owen Wister. (33) Although his arguments give primacy to defending biodiversity and the autonomy of wild nature, his prose becomes most passionate when he speaks of preserving "the wilderness experience." His own ideal "Big Outside" bears an uncanny resemblance to that of the frontier myth: wide open spaces and virgin land with no trails, no signs, no facilities, no maps, no guides, no rescues, no modern equipment. Tellingly, it is a land where hardy travelers can support themselves by hunting with "primitive weapons (bow and arrow, atlatl, knife, sharp rock)." (34) Foreman claims that "the primary value of wilderness is not as a proving ground for young Huck Finns and Annie Oakleys," but his heart is with Huck and Annie all the same. He admits that "preserving a quality wilderness experience for the human visitor, letting her or him flex Paleolithic muscles or seek visions, remains a tremendously important secondary purpose." (35) Just so does Teddy Roosevelt's rough rider live on in the greener garb of a new age.

However much one may be attracted to such a vision, it entails problematic consequences. For one, it makes wilderness the locus for an epic struggle between malign civilization and benign nature, compared with which all other social, political, and moral concerns seem trivial. Foreman writes, "The preservation of wildness and native diversity is the most important issue. Issues directly affecting only humans pale in comparison." (36) Presumably so do any environmental problems whose victims are mainly people, for such problems usually surface in landscapes that have already "fallen" and are no longer wild. This would seem to exclude from the radical environmentalist agenda problems of occupational health and safety in industrial settings, problems of toxic waste exposure on "unnatural" urban and agricultural sites, problems of poor children poisoned by lead exposure in the inner city, problems of famine and poverty and human suffering in the "overpopulated" places of the earth—problems, in short, of environmental justice. If we set too high a stock on wilderness, too many other corners of the earth become less than natural and too many other people become less than human, thereby giving us permission not to care much about their suffering or their fate.

It is no accident that these supposedly inconsequential environmental problems affect mainly poor people, for the long affiliation between wilderness and wealth means that the only poor people who count when wilderness is the issue are hunter-gatherers, who presumably do not consider themselves to be poor in the first place. The dualism at the heart of wilderness encourages its advocates to conceive of its protection as a crude conflict between the "human" and the "non-human"—or, more often, between those who value the nonhuman and those who do not. This in turn tempts one to ignore crucial differences among humans and the complex cultural and historical reasons why different peoples may feel very differently about the meaning of wilderness.

Why, for instance, is the "wilderness experience" so often conceived as a form of recreation best enjoyed by those whose class privileges give them the time and resources to leave their jobs behind and "get away from it all?" Why does the protection of wilderness so often seem to pit urban recreationists against rural people who actually earn their living from the land (excepting those who sell goods and services to the tourists themselves)? Why in the debates about pristine natural areas are "primitive" peoples idealized, even sentimentalized, until the moment they do something unprimitive, modern, and unnatural, and thereby fall from environmental grace? What are the consequences of a wilderness ideology that devalues productive labor and the very concrete knowledge that comes from working the land with one's own hands? (37) All of these questions imply conflicts among different groups of people, conflicts that are obscured behind the deceptive clarity of "human" vs. "nonhuman." If in answering these knotty questions we resort to so simplistic an opposition, we are almost certain to ignore the very subtleties and complexities we need to understand.

But the most troubling cultural baggage that accompanies the celebration of wilderness has less to do with remote rain forests and peoples than with the ways we think about ourselves—we American environmentalists who quite rightly worry about the future of the earth and the threats we pose to the natural world. Idealizing a distant wilderness too often means not idealizing the environment in which we actually live, the landscape that for better or worse we call home. Most of our most serious environmental problems start right here, at home, and if we are to solve those problems, we need an environmental ethic that will tell us as much about using nature as about not using it. The wilderness dualism tends to cast any use as abuse, and thereby denies us a middle ground in which responsible use and non-use might attain some kind of balanced, sustainable relationship. My own belief is that only by exploring this middle ground will we learn ways of imagining a better world for all of us: humans and nonhumans, rich people and poor, women and men, First Worlders and Third Worlders, white folks and people of color, consumers and producers—a world better for humanity in all of its diversity and for all the rest of nature too. The middle ground is where we actually live. It is where we—all of us, in our different places and ways—make our homes.

That is why, when I think of the times I myself have come closest to experiencing what I might call the sacred in nature, I often find myself remembering wild places much closer to home. I think, for instance, of a small pond near my house where water bubbles up from limestone springs to feed a series of pools that rarely freeze in winter and so play home to waterfowl that stay here for the protective warmth even on the coldest of winter days, gliding silently through streaming mists as the snow falls from gray February skies. I think of a November evening long ago when I found myself on a Wisconsin hilltop in rain and dense fog, only to have the setting sun break through the clouds to cast an otherworldly golden

light on the misty farms and woodlands below, a scene so unexpected and joyous that I lingered past dusk so as not to miss any part of the gift that had come my way. And I think perhaps most especially of the blown-out, bankrupt farm in the sand country of central Wisconsin where Aldo Leopold and his family tried one of the first American experiments in ecological restoration, turning ravaged and infertile soil into carefully tended ground where the human and the nonhuman could exist side by side in relative harmony. What I celebrate about such places is not just their wildness, though that certainly is among their most important qualities; what I celebrate even more is that they remind us of the wildness in our own backyards, of the nature that is all around us if only we have eyes to see it.

Indeed, my principal objection to wilderness is that it may teach us to be dismissive or even contemptuous of such humble places and experiences. Without our quite realizing it, wilderness tends to privilege some parts of nature at the expense of others. Most of us, I suspect, still follow the conventions of the romantic sublime in finding the mountaintop more glorious than the plains, the ancient forest nobler than the grasslands, the mighty canyon more inspiring than the humble marsh. Even John Muir, in arguing against those who sought to dam his beloved Hetch Hetchy valley in the Sierra Nevada, argued for alternative dam sites in the gentler valleys of the foothills—a preference that had nothing to do with nature and everything with the cultural traditions of the sublime. (38) Just as problematically, our frontier traditions have encouraged Americans to define "true" wilderness as requiring very large tracts of roadless land—what Dave Foreman calls "The Big Outside." Leaving aside the legitimate empirical question in conservation biology of how large a tract of land must be before a given species can reproduce on it, the emphasis on big wilderness reflects a romantic frontier belief that one hasn't really gotten away from civilization unless one can go for days at a time without encountering another human being. By teaching us to fetishize sublime places and wide open country, these peculiarly American ways of thinking about wilderness encourage us to adopt too high a standard for what counts as "natural." If it isn't hundreds of square miles big, if it doesn't give us God's eye views or grand vistas, if it doesn't permit us the illusion that we are alone on the planet, then it really isn't natural. It's too small, too plain, or too crowded to be authentically wild.

In critiquing wilderness as I have done in this essay, I'm forced to confront my own deep ambivalence about its meaning for modern environmentalism. On the one hand, one of my own most important environmental ethics is that people should always be conscious that they are part of the natural world, inextricably tied to the ecological systems that sustain their lives. Any way of looking at nature that encourages us to believe we are separate from nature—as wilderness tends to do—is likely to reinforce environmentally irresponsible behavior. On the other band, I also think it no less crucial for us to recognize and honor nonhuman nature as a world we did not create, a world with its own independent, nonhuman reasons for being as it is. The autonomy of nonhuman nature seems to me an indispensable corrective to human arrogance. Any way of looking at nature that helps us remember—as wilderness also tends to do—that the interests of people are not necessarily identical to those of every other creature or of the earth itself is likely to foster responsible behavior. To the extent that wilderness has served as an important vehicle for articulating deep moral values regarding our obligations and responsibilities to the nonhuman world, I would not want to jettison the contributions it has made to our culture's ways of thinking about nature.

If the core problem of wilderness is that it distances us too much from the very things it teaches us to value, then the question we must ask is what it can tell us about home, the place where we actually live. How can we take the positive values we associate with wilderness and bring them closer to home? I think the answer to this question will come by broadening our sense of the otherness that wilderness seeks to define and protect. In reminding us of the world we did not make, wilderness can teach profound feelings of humility and respect as we confront our fellow beings and the earth itself. Feelings like these argue for the importance of self-awareness and self criticism as we exercise our own ability to transform the world around us, helping us set responsible limits to human mastery—which without such limits too easily becomes human hubris.

Wilderness is the place where, symbolically at least, we try to withhold our power to dominate. Wallace Stegner once wrote of

> the special human mark, the special record of human passage, that distinguishes man from all other species. It is rare enough among men, impossible to any other form of life. It is simply the deliberate and chosen refusal to make any marks at all…We are the most dangerous species of life on the planet, and every other species, even the earth itself, has cause to fear our power to exterminate. But we are also the only species which, when it chooses to do so, will go to great effort to save what it might destroy. (39)

The myth of wilderness, which Stegner knowingly reproduces in these remarks, is that we can somehow leave nature untouched by our passage. By now it should be clear that this for the most part is an illusion. But Stegner's deeper message then becomes all the more compelling. If living in history means that we cannot help leaving marks on a fallen world, then the dilemma we face is to decide what kinds of marks we wish to leave. It is just here that our cultural traditions of wilderness remain so important. In the broadest sense, wilderness teaches us to ask whether the Other must always bend to our will, and, if not, under what circumstances it should be allowed to flourish without our intervention. This is surely a question worth asking about everything we do, and not just about the natural world.

When we visit a wilderness area, we find ourselves surrounded by plants and animals and physical landscapes whose otherness compels our attention. In forcing us to acknowledge that they are not of our making, that they have little or no need of our continued existence, they recall for us a creation far greater than our own. In the wilderness, we need no reminder that a tree has its own reasons for being, quite apart from us. The same is less true in the gardens we plant and tend ourselves: there it is far easier to forget the otherness of the tree. (40) Indeed, one could almost measure wilderness by the extent to which our recognition of its otherness requires a conscious, willed act on our part. The romantic legacy

means that wilderness is more a state of mind than a fact of nature, and the state of mind that today most defines wilderness is wonder. The striking power of the wild is that wonder in the face of it requires no act of will, but forces itself upon us—as an expression of the nonhuman world experienced through the lens of our cultural history—as proof that ours is not the only presence in the universe.

Wilderness gets us into trouble only if we imagine that this experience of wonder and otherness is limited to the remote corners of the planet, or that it somehow depends on pristine landscapes we ourselves do not inhabit. Nothing could be more misleading. The tree in the garden is in reality no less other, no less worthy of our wonder and respect, than the tree in an ancient forest that has never known an ax or a saw—even though the tree in the forest reflects a more intricate web of ecological relationships. The tree in the garden could easily have sprung from the same seed as the tree in the forest, and we can claim only its location and perhaps its form as our own. Both trees stand apart from us; both share our common world. The special power of the tree in the wilderness is to remind us of this fact. It can teach us to recognize the wildness we did not see in the tree we planted in our own backyard. By seeing the otherness in that which is most unfamiliar, we can learn to see it too in that which at first seemed merely ordinary. If wilderness can do this—if it can help us perceive and respect a nature we had forgotten to recognize as natural—then it will become part of the solution to our environmental dilemmas rather than part of the problem.

This will only happen, however, if we abandon the dualism that sees the tree in the garden as artificial—completely fallen and unnatural—and the tree in the wilderness as natural—completely pristine and wild. Both trees in some ultimate sense are wild; both in a practical sense now depend on our management and care. We are responsible for both, even though we can claim credit for neither. Our challenge is to stop thinking of such things according to set of bipolar moral scales in which the human and the nonhuman, the unnatural and the natural, the fallen and the unfallen, serve as our conceptual map for understanding and valuing the world. Instead, we need to embrace the full continuum of a natural landscape that is also cultural, in which the city, the suburb, the pastoral, and the wild each has its proper place, which we permit ourselves to celebrate without needlessly denigrating the others. We need to honor the Other within and the Other next door as much as we do the exotic Other that lives far away—a lesson that applies as much to people as it does to (other) natural things. In particular, we need to discover a common middle ground in which all of these things, from the city to the wilderness, can somehow be encompassed in the word "home." Home, after all, is the place where finally we make our living. It is the place for which we take responsibility, the place we try to sustain so we can pass on what is best in it (and in ourselves) to our children. (41)

The task of making a home in nature is what Wendell Berry has called "the forever unfinished lifework of our species." "The only thing we have to preserve nature with" he writes, "is culture; the only thing we have to preserve wildness with is domesticity." (42) Calling a place home inevitably means that we will use the nature we find in it, for there can be no escape from manipulating and working and even killing some parts of nature to make our home. But if we acknowledge the autonomy and otherness of the things and creatures around us—an autonomy our culture has taught us to label with the word "wild"—then we will at least think carefully about the uses to which we put them, and even ask if we should use them at all. just so can we still join Thoreau in declaring that "in Wildness is the preservation of the World," for wildness (as opposed to wilderness) can be found anywhere: in the seemingly tame fields and woodlots of Massachusetts, in the cracks of a Manhattan sidewalk, even in the cells of our own bodies. As Gary Snyder has wisely said, "A person with a clear heart and open mind can experience the wilderness anywhere on earth. It is a quality of one's own consciousness. The planet is a wild place and always will be." (43) To think ourselves capable of causing "the end of nature" is an act of great hubris, for it means forgetting the wildness that dwells everywhere within and around us.

Learning to honor the wild—learning to remember and acknowledge the autonomy of the other—means striving for critical self-consciousness in all of our actions. It means the deep reflection and respect must accompany each act of use, and means too that we must always consider the possibility of non-use. It means looking at the part of nature we intend to turn toward our own ends and asking whether we can use it again and again and again—sustainably—without its being diminished in the process. It means never imagining that we can flee into a mythical wilderness to escape history and the obligation to take responsibility for our own actions that history inescapably entails. Most of all, it means practicing remembrance and gratitude, for thanksgiving is the simplest and most basic of ways for us to recollect the nature, the culture, and the history that have come together to make the world as we know it. If wildness can stop being (just) out there and start being (also) in here, if it can start being as humane as it is natural, then perhaps we can get on with the unending task of struggling to live rightly in the world—not just in the garden, not just in the wilderness, but in the home that encompasses them both. ■

Notes

1. Henry David Thoreau, "Walking," *The Works of Thoreau*, ed. Henry S. Canby (Boston, Massachusetts: Houghton Mifflin, 1937), p. 672.
2. *Oxford English Dictionary*, s.v. "wilderness"; see also Roderick Nash, *Wilderness and the American Mind*, 3rd ed. (New Haven, Connecticut: Yale Univ. Press, 1982), pp. 1–22; and Max Oelsehlaeger, *The Idea of Wilderness: From Prehistory to the Age of Ecology* (New Haven, Connecticut: Yale Univ. Press, 1991).
3. Exodus 32:1–35, KJV.
4. Exodus 14:3, KJV.
5. Mark 1:12–13, KJV; see also Matthew 4:1–11; Luke 4:1–13
6. John Milton, "Paradise Lost," *John Milton: Complete Poems and Major Prose*, ed. Merritt Y. Hughes (New York: Odyssey Press, 1957), pp. 280–81, lines 131–42.
7. I have discussed this theme at length in "Landscapes of Abundance and Scarcity," in Clyde Milner et al., eds., *Oxford History of the American West* (New York: Oxford Univ. Press, 1994), pp. 603–37. The classic work on the Puritan "city on a hill" in colonial New England is Perry Miller, *Errand into the Wilderness* (Cambridge, Massachusetts: Harvard Univ. Press, 1956).

8. John Muir, My First Summer in the Sierra (1911), reprinted in John Muir: *The Eight Wilderness Discovery Books* (London, England: Diadem; Seattle, Washington: Mountaineers, 1992), p. 211.

9. Alfred Route, *National Parks: The American Experience*, 2nd ed. (Lincoln: Univ. of Nebraska Press, 1987).

10. John Muir, The Yosemite (1912), reprinted in *John Muir: Eight Wilderness Discovery Books*, p. 715.

11. Scholarly work on the sublime is extensive. Among the most important studies are Samuel Monk, *The Sublime: A Study of Critical Theories in XVIII Century England* (New York: Modern Language Association, 1935); Basil Willey, *The Eighteenth-Century Background: Studies on the Idea of Nature in the Thought of the Period* (London, England: Chattus and Windus, 1949); Marjorie Hope Nicolson, *Mountain Gloom and Mountain Glory: The Development of the Aesthetics of the Infinite* (Ithaca, New York: Cornell Univ. Press, 1959); Thomas Weiskel, *The Romantic Sublime: Studies in the Structure and Psychology of Transcendence* (Baltimore, Maryland: Johns Hopkins Univ. Press, 1976); Barbara Novak, *Nature and Culture: American Landscape Painting, 1825–1875* (New York: Oxford Univ. Press, 1980).

12. The classic works are Immanuel Kant, *Observations on the Feeling of the Beautiful and Sublime* (1764), trans. John T. Goldthwait (Berkeley: Univ. of California Press, 1960); Edmund Burke, *A Philosophical Enquiry into the Origin of Our Ideas of the Sublime and Beautiful*, ed. James T. Boulton (1958; Notre Dame, Indiana: Univ. of Notre Dame Press, 1968); William Gilpin, *Three Essays: On Picturesque Beauty; on Picturesque Travel; and on Sketching Landscape* (London, England, 1803).

13. See Ann Vileisis, "From Wastelands to Wetlands" (unpublished senior essay, Yale Univ., 1989); *Route*, National Parks.

14. William Wordsworth, "The Prelude," bk. 6, in Thomas Hutchinson, ed., *The Poetical Works of Wordsworth* (London, England: Oxford Univ. Press, 1936), p. 536.

15. Henry David Thoreau, *The Maine Woods* (1864), in Henry David Thoreau (New York: Library of America, 1985), pp. 640–41.

16. Exodus 16:10, KJV.

17. John Muir, *My First Summer in the Sierra*, p. 238. Part of the difference between these descriptions may reflect the landscapes the three authors were describing. In his essay, "Reinventing Common Nature: Yosemite and Mount Rushmore—A Meandering Tale of a Double Nature," Kenneth Olwig notes that early American travelers experienced Yosemite as much through the aesthetic tropes of the pastoral as through those of the sublime. The ease with which Muir celebrated the gentle divinity of the Sierra Nevada had much to do with the pastoral qualities of the landscape he described. See Olwig, "Reinventing Common Nature: Yosemite and Mount Rushmore—A Meandering Tale of a Double Nature," *Uncommon Ground: Toward Reinventing Nature*, ed. William Cronon (New York: W. W. Norton & Co, 1995), pp. 379–408.

18. Frederick Jackson Turner, *The Frontier in American History* (New York: Henry Holt, 1920), pp. 37–38.

19. Richard Slotkin has made this observation the linchpin of his comparison between Turner and Theodore Roosevelt. See Slotkin, *Gunfighter Nation: The Myth of the Frontier in Twentieth-Century America* (New York: Atheneum, 1992), pp. 29–62.

20. Owen Wister, *The Virginian: A Horseman of the Plains* (New York: Macmillan, 1902), pp. viii–ix.

21. Theodore Roosevelt, *Ranch Life and the Hunting Trail* (1888; New York: Century, 1899), p. 100.

22. Wister, Virginian, p. x.

23. On the many problems with this view, see William M. Denevan, "The Pristine Myth: The Landscape of the Americas in 1492," *Annals of the Association of American Geographers* 82 (1992): 369–85.

24. Louis Warren, "The Hunter's Game: Poachers, Conservationists, and Twentieth-Century America" (Ph.D. diss., Yale University, 1994).

25. Wilderness also lies at the foundation of the Clementsian ecological concept of the climax. See Michael Barbour, "Ecological Fragmentation in the Fifties" in Cronon, Uncommon Ground, pp. 233–55, and William Cronon, "Introduction: In Search of Nature," in Cronon, *Uncommon Ground*, pp. 23–56.

26. On the many paradoxes of having to manage wilderness in order to maintain the appearance of an unmanaged landscape, see John C. Hendee et al., *Wilderness Management*, USDA Forest Service Miscellaneous Publication No. 1365 (Washington, D.C.: Government Printing Office, 1978).

27. See James Proctor, "Whose Nature?: The Contested Moral Terrain of Ancient Forests," in Cronon, *Uncommon Ground*, pp. 269–97.

28. See Candace Slater, "Amazonia as Edenic Narrative," in Cronon, *Uncommon Ground*, pp. 114–31. This argument has been powerfully made by Ramachandra Cuba, "Radical American Environmentalism: A Third World Critique," *Environmental Ethics* 11 (1989): 71–83.

29. Bill McKibben, *The End of Nature* (New York: Random House, 1989).

30. McKibben, *The End of Nature*, p. 49.

31. Even comparable extinction rates have occurred before, though we surely would not want to emulate the Cretaceous-Tertiary boundary extinctions as a model for responsible manipulation of the biosphere!

32. Dave Foreman, *Confessions of an Eco-Warrior* (New York: Harmony Books, 1991, p. 69 (italics in original)). For a sampling of other writings by followers of deep ecology and/or Earth First!, see Michael Tobias, ed., *Deep Ecology* (San Diego, California: Avant Books, 1984); Bill Devall and George Sessions, *Deep Ecology: Living as if Nature Mattered* (Salt Lake City, Utah: Gibbs Smith, 1985); Michael Tobias, *After Eden: History, Ecology, and Conscience* (San Diego, California: Avant Books, 1985); Dave Foreman and Bill Haywood, eds., *Ecodefense: A Field Guide to Monkey Wrenching*, 2nd ed. (Tucson, Arizona: Ned Ludd Books, 1987); Bill Devall, *Simple in Means, Rich in Ends: Practicing Deep Ecology* (Salt Lake City, Utah: Gibbs Smith, 1988); Steve Chase, ed., *Defending the Earth: A Dialogue between Murray Bookchin & Dave Foreman* (Boston, Massachusetts: South End Press, 1991);

John Davis, ed., *The Earth First, Reader. Ten Years of Radical Environmentalism* (Salt Lake City, Utah: Gibbs Smith, 1991); Bill Devall, *Living Richly in an Age of Limits: Using Deep Ecology for an Abundant Life* (Salt Lake, City, Utah: Gibbs Smith, 1993); Michael E. Zimmerman et al., eds., E*nvironmental Philosophy: From Animal Rights to Radical Ecology* (Englewood Cliffs, New Jersey: Prentice-Hall, 1993). A useful survey of the different factions of radical environmentalism can be found in Carolyn Merchant, *Radical Ecology: The Search for a Livable World* (New York: Routledge, 1992). For a very interesting critique of this literature (first published in the anarchist newspaper Fifth Estate), see George Bradford, *How Deep is Deep Ecology?* (Ojai, California: Times Change Press, 1989).

33. Foreman, *Confessions of an Eco-Warrior*, p. 34.

34. Foreman, *Confessions of an Eco-Warrior*, p. 65. See also Dave Foreman and Howie Wolke, *The Big Outside: A Descriptive Inventory of the Big Wilderness Areas of the U.S.* (Tucson, Arizona: Ned Ludd Books, 1989).

35. Foreman, *Confessions of an Eco-Warrior*, p. 63.

36. Foreman, *Confessions of an Eco-Warrior*, p. 27.

37. See Richard White, "'Are You an Environmentalist or Do You Work for a Living?': Work and Nature," in Cronon, *Uncommon Ground*, pp. 171–85. Compare its analysis of environmental knowledge through work with Jennifer Price's analysis of environmental knowledge through consumption. It is not much of an exaggeration to say that the wilderness experience is essentially consumerist in its impulses.

38. Compare with Muir, Yosemite, in *John Muir: Eight Wilderness Discovery Books*, p. 714.

39. Wallace Stegner, ed., *This Is Dinosaur: Echo Park Country and Its Magic Rivers* (New York: Knopf, 1955), p. 17 (italics in original).

40. Katherine Hayles helped me see the importance of this argument.

41. Analogous arguments can be found in John Brinckerhoff Jackson, "Beyond Wilderness," *A Sense of Place, a Sense of Time* (New Haven, Connecticut: Yale Univ. Press, 1994), pp. 71–91, and in the wonderful collection of essays by Michael Pollan, *Second Nature: A Gardener's Education* (New York: Atlantic Monthly Press, 1991).

42. Wendell Berry, *Home Economics* (San Francisco, California: North Point, 1987), pp. 138, 143.

43. Gary Snyder, quoted in *New York Times*, "Week in Review," 18 September 1994, p. 6. Excerpted from *Uncommon Ground: Toward Reinventing Nature*, edited by William Cronon. Copyright © 1995 by William Cronon. Reprinted with permission of the publisher, W. W. Norton & Company, Inc.

——————————————————— AUTHOR PROFILE

William Cronon (b. 1954) is an environmental historian who works to understand the relationship between humans and the nonhuman world. In particular, he is interested in how our view of history shapes how we understand the world and the decisions we make about it: better histories, he argues, will lead to better environmentalist practices. Much of Cronon's work focuses on the history of the American West, as seen in *Under an Open Sky: Rethinking America's Western Past* (1992) and *Uncommon Ground: Rethinking the Human Place in Nature* (1995). "The Trouble With Wilderness" generated controversy among traditional environmentalists for attacking highly valued concepts like "wilderness" and "nature." For this many saw Cronon as attacking environmentalism in general and betraying academic environmental studies in particular. Cronon, however, asserts that environmental scholars also have a responsibility to public activism and that environmentalist goals can only be met if all citizens have access to current environmental thought. Currently, Cronon is a Research Professor of History, Geography, and Environmental Studies at the University of Wisconsin–Madison. He is working on a history of Portage, Wisconsin, spanning the end of the last Ice Age to the present. "The Trouble With Wilderness" was originally published in *Uncommon Ground: Rethinking the Human Place in Nature* in 1995 and has been reprinted widely.

C

Principles of Environmental Justice

Delegates to FNPCELS

Delegates to the First National People of Color Environmental Leadership Summit held on October 24–27, 1991, in Washington, D.C., drafted and adopted 17 principles of Environmental Justice. Since then, The Principles have served as a defining document for the growing grassroots movement for environmental justice.

WE, THE PEOPLE OF COLOR, gathered together at this multinational People of Color Environmental Leadership Summit, to begin to build a national and international movement of all peoples of color to fight the destruction and taking of our lands and communities, do hereby re-establish our spiritual interdependence to the sacredness of our Mother Earth; to respect and celebrate each of our cultures, languages and beliefs about the natural world and our roles in healing ourselves; to ensure environmental justice; to promote economic alternatives which would contribute to the development of environmentally safe livelihoods; and, to secure our political, economic and cultural liberation that has been denied for over 500 years of colonization and oppression, resulting in the poisoning of our communities and land and the genocide of our peoples, do affirm and adopt these Principles of Environmental Justice:

1. **Environmental Justice** affirms the sacredness of Mother Earth, ecological unity and the interdependence of all species, and the right to be free from ecological destruction.

2. **Environmental Justice** demands that public policy be based on mutual respect and justice for all peoples, free from any form of discrimination or bias.

3. **Environmental Justice** mandates the right to ethical, balanced and responsible uses of land and renewable resources in the interest of a sustainable planet for humans and other living things.

4. **Environmental Justice** calls for universal protection from nuclear testing, extraction, production and disposal of toxic/hazardous wastes and poisons and nuclear testing that threaten the fundamental right to clean air, land, water, and food.

5. **Environmental Justice** affirms the fundamental right to political, economic, cultural and environmental self-determination of all peoples.

6. **Environmental Justice** demands the cessation of the production of all toxins, hazardous wastes, and radioactive materials, and that all past and current producers be held strictly accountable to the people for detoxification and the containment at the point of production.

7. **Environmental Justice** demands the right to participate as equal partners at every level of decision-making, including needs assessment, planning, implementation, enforcement and evaluation.

8. **Environmental Justice** affirms the right of all workers to a safe and healthy work environment without being forced to choose between an unsafe livelihood and unemployment. It also affirms the right of those who work at home to be free from environmental hazards.

9. **Environmental Justice** protects the right of victims of environmental injustice to receive full compensation and reparations for damages as well as quality health care.

10. **Environmental Justice** considers governmental acts of environmental injustice a violation of international law, the Universal Declaration On Human Rights, and the United Nations Convention on Genocide.

11. **Environmental Justice** must recognize a special legal and natural relationship of Native Peoples to the U.S. government through treaties, agreements, compacts, and covenants affirming sovereignty and self-determination.

12. **Environmental Justice** affirms the need for urban and rural ecological policies to clean up and rebuild our cities and rural areas in balance with nature, honoring the cultural integrity of all our communities, and provided fair access for all to the full range of resources.

13. **Environmental Justice** calls for the strict enforcement of principles of informed consent, and a halt to the testing of experimental reproductive and medical procedures and vaccinations on people of color.

14. **Environmental Justice** opposes the destructive operations of multi-national corporations.

15. **Environmental Justice** opposes military occupation, repression and exploitation of lands, peoples and cultures, and other life forms.

16. **Environmental Justice** calls for the education of present and future generations which emphasizes social and environmental issues, based on our experience and an appreciation of our diverse cultural perspectives.

17. **Environmental Justice** requires that we, as individuals, make personal and consumer choices to consume as little of Mother Earth's resources and to produce as little waste as possible; and make the conscious decision to challenge and reprioritize our lifestyles to ensure the health of the natural world for present and future generations. ▄▌

D

AUTHOR PROFILE

As grassroots organizations began challenging America's largest environmental groups about the racism inherent in their platforms, activists Charles Lee, Benjamin Chavis, Richard Moore, Pat Bryant, Dana Alston, Donna Chavis, and Robert Bullard planned the First National People of Color Environmental Leadership Summit. It was held in Washington, D.C. in October of 1991. The summit sought to address concerns that "mainstream" environmentalist movements failed to recognize historic environmental efforts led by native people and people of color. These movements also overlooked the disproportionate amounts of toxicity, denial of access to land, and other environmental injustices experienced by people of color. 700 activists and observers attended the summit, and the result was an environmental justice platform that recognized that the social and economic experiences of people of color are inseparable from their experiences of the environment. Fair environmental policy, the delegates argued, must necessarily include awareness of race, class, and gender. The "Principles of Environmental Justice" created at this conference were adopted by many grassroots environmental movements as well as by President Bill Clinton's 1994 executive order on the environment, and continue to influence environmental justice thinking today.

The Mapping of Massacres

By Ceridwen Dovey

From New York to Cape Town to Sydney, the bronze body doubles of the white men of empire—Columbus, Rhodes, Cook—have lately been pelted with feces, sprayed with graffiti, had their hands painted red. Some have been toppled. The fate of these statues—and those representing white men of a different era, in Charlottesville and elsewhere—has ignited debate about the political act of publicly memorializing historical figures responsible for atrocities. But when the statues come down, how might the atrocities themselves be publicly commemorated, rather than repressed?

In the course of her long career, the historian Lyndall Ryan has thought about little else. In the late nineties and early aughts, Ryan found herself on the front lines of what came to be known, in Australia, as the History Wars: skirmishes fought with words, source by disputed source, often in the national media. At stake was whether the evidence existed to prove—as Ryan and others had argued, and conservative historians and politicians refused to accept—that Indigenous Australians had been massacred in enormous numbers during colonization, from late in the eighteenth century to the middle of the twentieth. Even among those who grudgingly accepted that there had been widespread killings, there were still bitter, and, in some cases, ongoing, fights over the exact number of Indigenous people killed, the strength of their resistance to British settlement, and the reliability of oral versus written history. A truce has never been reached in what the Indigenous writer Alexis Wright calls Australia's entrenched "storytelling war." (In October, Prime Minister Malcolm Turnbull rejected the core recommendations of the government-appointed Referendum Council, which, after six months of deliberative dialogue across Aboriginal and Torres Strait Islander communities, had called for establishing an Indigenous voice to Parliament, and a process of "truth-telling about our history.")

In 2005, in the midst of the public disputes over Australia's history, Ryan came across the work of the French sociologist Jacques Sémelin. After the Srebrenica massacre, in 1995, there was renewed interest from European scholars in understanding massacre as a phenomenon. Sémelin defined a massacre as the indiscriminate killing of innocent, unarmed people over a limited period of time, and he characterized massacres as being carefully planned—i.e., not done in the heat of the moment or the fog of war—and deliberately shrouded in secrecy by the systematic disposal of bodies and the intimidation of witnesses. Sémelin's typology prompted Ryan to reconsider her own earlier scholarship on the Tasmanian War, which was waged between British colonists and Aboriginal people early in the nineteenth century. This time, Ryan concluded that there were not four massacres of Indigenous people but, in fact, more than forty.

"Most historians of my generation were brought up with the idea that Aboriginal people were killed in ones or twos, similar to how settlers were killed when there'd been a dispute over stock, or women," Ryan told me recently, at an art gallery in Sydney's vibrant neighborhood of Kings Cross, where she was about

to give a talk. Ryan, who is seventy-four, has short-cropped white hair and a slow, deliberate way of speaking that belies a very quick mind. She realized, once she'd started researching massacres, how many of her peers were still deeply in denial about the past. "People would say to me, 'We will never know how many massacres there were, or how many Aboriginal people were killed, so what's the point in trying to find out?' But they would never say that about World War One or Two."

Ryan is based at the Centre for the History of Violence at Newcastle University, up the coast from Sydney. A few years ago, she applied for a research grant to embark on a hugely ambitious undertaking: to map the site of every Australian colonial frontier massacre on an interactive Web site. Ryan defines a massacre, in this context, as the indiscriminate killing of six or more undefended people. Since Aboriginal communities tended to live together in camps of about twenty people, losing six or more people in one killing—a "fractal" massacre— usually led to the whole community collapsing.

Four years of painstaking research later, with the grant depleted, Ryan's map is nowhere near finished. So far, it includes more than a hundred and seventy massacres of Indigenous people in eastern Australia, as well as six recorded massacres of settlers, from the period of 1788 to 1872. She estimates that there were more than five hundred massacres of Indigenous people over all, and that massacres of settlers numbered fewer than ten. (Ryan has not yet researched any massacres of Torres Strait Islander people, who are culturally distinct from mainland Aboriginal groups but share their history of colonization.) In July, Ryan and her tiny team decided it was time to release the partially completed map online. Since its launch, the site has had more than sixty thousand visitors. Contrary to Ryan's fears, it was widely and mostly respectfully covered in the Australian media, and, at least for now, there has been no public response from conservative figures.

At the gallery in Kings Cross, the lights were turned off, and a map appeared, projected onto a large screen, showing Australia's unmistakable outline—the continent declared by the British on their arrival to be *terra nullius*, land considered to belong to nobody, and thus ripe for the taking. Spread across the eastern states were dozens of yellow dots, often clustered together. Each one represented the site of a massacre of Aboriginal people.

The map's data management still needs improvement—a consequence, in part, of limited funding, and also of Ryan's admitted mistake in thinking she should do all the research first, before getting input from the project's digital cartographer, Mark Brown, and digital-humanities specialist, Bill Pascoe. Even so, its power is undeniable. Ryan clicked on the yellow dot representing one of five massacres in the region of Jack Smith Lake, in eastern Victoria. On a fresh page, an aerial snapshot from ArcGIS, the geographic-information system, showed a slice of green and brown farmland and bush bordering a long, thin line of sand beside the ocean. A small square section was shaded yellow, delineating a five-kilometre radius around the site of the killings. The exact coördinates of the massacres are not identified, Ryan explained. "For many Aboriginal communities, the preference is not to pinpoint the actual site, out of respect for what is considered a taboo site of trauma. But also because sites tend to be desecrated if identified very specifically." Some sites are on private land, or mining properties; others are at the bottom of reservoirs, because so many of the massacres happened at campsites close to creeks.

On the left of the screen was a graph, cataloguing the details of this series of massacres carried out in 1843. Aboriginal Language Group: Brataualang. Aboriginal people killed: sixty (at each of the five sites). Colonists killed: zero. Weapons used: Double-barrelled Purdey. Attacker details: twenty horsemen, known as the "Highland Brigade," organized by Angus McMillan. In a box titled "Narrative," these fragments form a horrific tale. McMillan, a local settler, and his group of armed horsemen, all Scots, had, for years, been attacking Aboriginal camps with impunity. In this instance, they attacked five campsites over five days. At one camp, people jumped into the waterhole but were shot as soon as they re-surfaced to breathe. One of the survivors, a young boy who'd been shot in the eye, was captured by the Brigade and forced to lead them to other camps. "Human bones have been found at each of these sites on several occasions," the text notes. "The rampage would fit the criteria of 'genocidal massacre.'"

Bruised by the History Wars, Ryan set herself strict criteria for including a massacre on the map. A key signals the strength of the evidence: three stars means that there is high-quality evidence drawn from disparate sources, while one or two stars indicates that there are only one or two reliable sources, respectively, with more corroboration welcome. Most of the evidence used for the map, she told the gathering, is from contemporaneous "white people's sources"—newspaper articles, official reports—rather than Indigenous sources, such as oral histories or social memory. (Some Aboriginal testimony is captured in those white textual sources, in the rare cases where survivors gave statements to officials or to missionaries. But Aboriginal people were for a long time prohibited from being called as witnesses in legal proceedings.) Many existing place names around the country are them-selves a form of damning evidence, as the historian Ian Clark has noted in his own pioneering work on frontier massacres: Murderers Flat, Massacre Inlet, Murdering Gully, Haunted Creek, Slaughterhouse Gully.

Earlier this year, Ryan presented a draft version of the map at the Australian Institute of Aboriginal and Torres Strait Islander Studies, in Canberra. The feed-back was largely positive, though she was advised to use a different color for the dots than red, which is considered sacred for many communities and shouldn't be associated only with death. As Ryan moves on to more recent massacres, she will increasingly draw on Aboriginal sources. She hopes the map will eventually be expanded to include massacres that aren't represented in written evidence but have been known about and passed down through memory and story by descendants of victims, survivors, and perpetrators. Since the map was released, she's heard from more than five hundred people, black and white, many from rural areas, many with details of massacres not on the map. Pascoe told me that viewers, on first seeing the map, are sometimes so overwhelmed they have to look away, but to him this is the point of *mapping* this kind of trauma. "People whose ancestors were involved already know what happened. But it becomes personal for everyone, because you can see what happened in a place near you, or where you grew up."

Ryan's decision to focus, for now, on archival research rather than community consultations was driven by funding and time constraints, but she also believes that white Australians who are skeptical about widespread frontier massacres need to be confronted with the gruesome truths recorded by their own ancestors—the magistrates and crown-lands commissioners, the settlers who wrote about killing

sprees in their journals or correspondence. In the History Wars, she noted, the denialists figured out ways of discounting all evidence of massacre, no matter its provenance. "They'd say things like, well, you can't trust evidence from a convict, they're born liars. Same with the Native Police. Women don't tell the truth. Soldiers who weren't officers clearly didn't know what was going on." This sort of thinking would leave only sources from the two categories of whites with the most to gain from covering up massacres: the officers who gave the orders, and the male settlers who often carried them out.

Ryan is also working with historians in South Africa, Canada, and the United States to consider massacres from a comparative perspective. The same men who were brutalized by mass warfare in Europe—during the Napoleonic wars, for example—became the brutal colonizers of the new world. (Angus McMillan fled Scotland during the Highland Clearances, when Highlander tenants were forcibly removed from their land.) In the eighteen-twenties, massacres in Tasmania and Victoria were usually carried out at dawn, to give the perpetrators—who used unreliable weapons, such as muskets, which often misfired—the advantage of surprise. When more sophisticated weapons, like the repeating rifles which were first manufactured around the time of the American Civil War, spread across the globe, the nature of frontier violence changed. By the eighteen-seventies, massacres were more often done in broad daylight. The awful intimacy of the violence is another shared feature of massacre, as is the divide-and-conquer strategy of recruiting Indigenous people into Native Police forces commanded by white officers and compelled to carry out killings.

While people milled around after Ryan's talk, I spoke to Aleshia Lonsdale, a young Wiradjuri artist from the country town of Mudgee, who was showing work in the gallery. Lonsdale, who has curly red hair and a gap-toothed smile, had created an assemblage of stone tools tightly bound in cling wrap. She told me about visiting her local museum, where stone tools were massed together, and feeling as if she were in a morgue. "There was nothing saying where the tools had come from, only who had donated them to the collection—you know, 'a stone tool donated by Mrs. Brown,'" she said. Mudgee is now a tourist town, but the massacres and forced removals that occurred there almost destroyed the Aboriginal community. "It's not just something in the history book, or dots on a map, it still impacts on people today," she said. "Even in terms of Aboriginal identity, and people not knowing who they are or where they're from—sometimes that can stem back to the massacres."

I asked her what she thought of Ryan's approach. "When I first heard about the map, I went online and had a look," she said. "I told people in my community about it. Some were taken aback. They wanted to know why *their* massacre wasn't on there. So, for me, it was helpful to hear from Lyndall today. Because there are a lot of massacre places that the community knows about that wouldn't fit those criteria." Lonsdale paused to greet a well-wisher. "Where some of the massacres happened, in my own country, there's still a bad feeling," she said to me. "There's certain roads people won't drive along. It's not just felt by Aboriginal people but by non-Aboriginal people as well. We need a place to go, to mourn or say sorry, but Aboriginal people need to determine what form that recognition takes."

Recently, the Indigenous Australian artist Judy Watson, who lives in Brisbane, débuted a different kind of massacres map. Watson, who is fifty-eight, is a descendant of the Waanyi people, of northwest Queensland; her great-great-grandmother Rosie hid under a windbreak to survive a massacre carried out by the Native Police at Lawn Hill. Watson has been researching and making art about the massacres for decades. Earlier this year, her multimedia, research-based art work "the names of places" was shown in an exhibition at the National Gallery of Australia, in Canberra. Superimposed on the shaky, ever-moving boundaries of a map of Australia is a scrolling, alphabetized list of hundreds of massacre sites and images of other work by Watson on the same theme—such as "pale slaughter," which lists weapons used (bayonets, revolvers), and "the names of men," which lists perpetrators. Next to this video, Watson set up a touch-screen map that people could use to bring up historical documents associated with different massacres. The map is now online for anybody to explore, and visitors can share information—including "hearsay"—about massacres in their own communities.

In many Indigenous communities, art works have long had dual functions as historical sources, as repositories of cultural or spiritual knowledge, and as maps of territory. There is an established tradition of mapping massacre sites through art, as in the acclaimed paintings by the Aboriginal artists Rover Thomas, Queenie McKenzie, and Rusty Peters, among others. Watson wanted viewers of her video to be aware that any map is a slippery, contested artifact, and also to have a bodily response to the work. She told me the story of one of her relatives, who, after viewing the video, turned to her in anguish, saying, "Where *wasn't* there a massacre?"

Jonathan Richards, a historian based at the University of Queensland and an expert on the history of the Native Police, worked on both Watson's and Ryan's maps. The biggest technical challenge, he told me, was matching historical data with actual G.P.S. coördinates. "I am conscious of the fact that we might identify a massacre site that nowadays is somebody's home or backyard, and they have no connection with the violence," he said. "So a little caution was crucial." The online version of Watson's map is somewhat unwieldy—again a function of limited funding, and of the enormous amount of time that both the historical and technical work of mapping requires. (She, too, has a very small team.) But, taken together, the two maps allow for "a welling up of this aspect of our shared history," as Watson put it when I spoke with her over the phone. If the funding allows, she hopes to hire a historian to travel with "the names of places" video as it tours around Australia, and meet with communities at each location to gather massacre stories. Richards told me that his research has permanently changed the way he sees the landscape. "In fact, the drive from Brisbane to Cairns these days is really, for me, just a linked pathway of brutal massacre sites."

There are about twenty, mostly very small, physical memorials to Aboriginal massacre sites across Australia, according to Genevieve Grieves, an Indigenous artist who is writing a Ph.D. on the memorialization of frontier violence. The majority, Grieves says, are community-created and landscape-based: a sculpture trail or a plaque on a single boulder, for instance. Watson and Ryan hope that their maps might act as digital memorials, which can circulate fluidly and are not as vulnerable

to desecration. For, while the statues of white men have been targeted lately, the few public memorials commemorating Aboriginal history have been vandalized repeatedly for years. In Perth, there is a bronze statue of the Noongar resistance fighter Yagan, whose head was sent to England after he was killed by white settlers, in 1833. In 1997, his head was repatriated to Australia; soon after, a vandal used an angle grinder to behead the statue. It was repaired, but later beheaded again. (The 1997 beheading inspired Archie Weller to write a short story, later turned into a film, "Confessions of a Headhunter," in which two Noongar men travel across the country, taking off the heads of every bronze colonial statue they find, and finally melting them down to create a sculpture of an Aboriginal mother and her children looking out to sea at Botany Bay, where Captain Cook landed.)

One of the memorials often held up as exemplary is the Myall Creek Massacre and Memorial Site, at the top of a bluff in northern New South Wales. It was established, in 2000, after years of advocacy work by Sue Blacklock, a descendant of one of the survivors, in collaboration with both Aboriginal and non-Aboriginal members of the local community. In 1838, on the farmland visible below the hill, thirty Wirrayaraay people were massacred, and their bodies burned, in what Ryan calls an "opportunity massacre." It's an extremely unusual case: afterward, some of the white perpetrators were arrested and tried in court, and seven of them were hanged. As the site's heritage listing notes, it was "the first and last attempt by the colonial administration to use the law to control frontier conflict." This memorial, too, has been subject to vandalism: in 2005, the words "murder" and "women and children" were hammered out of the metal plaques.

Each June, a ceremony is held at the site, bringing together the descendants of victims, survivors, and perpetrators. Watson attended this year. When she told me about the experience, her voice broke with emotion. She filmed the descendants' interactions, and Greg Hooper, her technical collaborator and sound designer, put a contact microphone (similar to a stethoscope) "against one of the ancient trees that had stood witness to the events in the valley below, and captured a sound like gurgling water deep within it." School children stood at each of the plaques on the path up the hill, reading aloud. The descendant of a perpetrator got up with his grandson to speak, saying how sorry he was for what had happened. "It was like watching history slowly unravelling," Watson said. "We all take a thread and pull it, and, as it tightens, we start to see what is there." ∎

AUTHOR PROFILE

Ceridwen Dovey grew up in South Africa, received an M.A. in social anthropology from New York University, and now lives in Sydney, Australia. Her debut novel *Blood Kin* (2009) was shortlisted for the Dylan Thomas Award and selected for the U.S. National Book Foundation's "5 Under 35" honors list; her short-story collection *Only the Animals: Stories* won the 2014 Readings New Australian Writing Award. Her latest novel *In the Garden of the Fugitives* was published in March 2018, while her book *Writers on Writers: Ceridwen Dovey on J.M. Coetzee* will be published in October 2018 within the Black Inc.'s Writers on Writers Series. The article "The Mapping of Massacres" appeared in *The New Yorker* on December 6, 2017.

La Ciudad Mágica

By Patricia Engel

You see them walking along the shaded perimeters of parks, dressed like nurses in pressed white uniforms, pushing strollers, talking to the babies in their care. You see them sitting together on benches near the playground, watching the children on the swings, occasionally calling to them not to climb so high on the jungle gym.

You see them walking along the road, carrying the child's backpack on the way home from school, while the child walks a few steps ahead, laughing with a friend. You see these women waiting outside of karate and ballet class, sitting in church pews beside the children on Sundays.

You see these women at the supermarket, pushing the cart down the aisle, the child perched atop the seat, legs dangling between the metal rails, while she pulls food from the shelves to buy and prepare for the family. You see these women sitting at the ends of tables in restaurants, keeping the children entertained with coloring books and video games, cutting their food into small pieces, whisper-begging the child to take another bite, so as not to interrupt the parents' dinner conversation.

You see these women in the morning, as early as sunrise, stepping off the bus from the downtown terminal, walking quickly along the avenue to arrive at the place of their employment in time to wake the children, feed them breakfast, and get them ready for school.

You see these women in the evening, sitting five to a bench beneath the bus stop shelter, shielding themselves from the summer sun or from the winter rain, waiting for the bus to come to take them home.

. . . .

A group of mothers dressed in exercise clothes, adorned with jewelry and painted with makeup, gather for lunch at a café in Coral Gables—where streets lined with ficus and poinciana trees have Spanish names like Valencia, Minorca, and Ponce de León.

You overhear their lunch conversation, comparing nannies by country of origin.

"I prefer the Panamanians and Nicaraguans," says one woman, picking at her salad, "because they know their place. They don't try to get too friendly with me. I *hate* that."

Another woman jumps in. "Oh, you mean when they address you directly? My God, it's like, 'Who gave you permission to open your mouth?'"

"Brazilians are just crazy, and you can't trust Colombians or Ecuadorians. They steal and they'll flirt with your husband," offers another woman. "Don't even bother trying them out. And Guatemalans come with too many problems. They're always crying about something. Like, *hello*? I hired a nanny, not a charity!"

123

The women laugh, then brag to one another how their children are fluent in Spanish, and though it annoys them that now the nannies and their offspring can have private conversations, at least it's still cheaper than hiring an American babysitter or paying an agency commission for a European au pair.

• • • • • • • • • • • • •

Tuesday morning at a bakery in The Roads.

Two men ahead of you on the counter line catch up after not having seen each other in a while.

One man tells the other he and his family plan on moving away soon.

"We're tired of feeling like foreigners around here. You can't go anywhere in this city without hearing Spanish spoken. I don't want my children growing up around that."

He says they're thinking about moving north to Broward or Collier County. "Somewhere *spic-free*."

"But they're everywhere," his friend says, laughing. "You can't escape them."

"We want to get away from the Miami kind. They're the ones taking over."

Then each man takes his turn at the counter, ordering a dozen empanadas to go.

• • • • • • • • • • • • •

After eight days at sea, twenty-four Cuban migrants making their way to Florida shores on a shabby vessel spot the coast guard in their wake. They throw themselves into the water and climb the American Shoal Lighthouse six miles off the coast of Sugarloaf Key, hoping it will amount to having touched dry land. It takes an entire day for officials to coax the Cubans off the red iron lighthouse rails. They are detained for a month until a judge rules that the lighthouse, despite its name, does not count as U.S. soil. The Cubans will be repatriated and will likely serve prison sentences for having fled their island.

The Magic City.

La Puerta de las Américas.

The Capital of Latin America.

• • • • • • • • • • • • •

The rainbowed Brickell Avenue high-rises, made as famous as the flamingos in the opening credits of *Miami Vice,* are now tiny folds in a much taller and more congested panorama of mirrored towers that glisten like machetes; the Miami that cocaine and money laundering built.

Brickell Avenue snakes into Biscayne Boulevard, cutting through downtown, a place everyone but the diamond and drug dealers used to avoid, now lined with new condos and chic restaurants, with a view of the restored waterfront parks, unfolding along the bay into urban pockets where longtime residents have been edged out by developers and hiked rents, christened with catchy names and written about in travel magazines as the trendy new neighborhoods to explore.

. . . .

Far down Biscayne, in a sleepy subdivision built along the Intracoastal, your friends Joe and Nicole live in a small stucco house with a red-shingle Spanish roof. Their next-door neighbors recently moved out so their baby could pursue a career in toddler modeling in Atlanta. A single guy in his forties moved in a few weeks later.

You all assume he's a bachelor because of the different girls coming to the house. Young, beautiful. Some in fancy cars. Others dropped off. There is a girl who arrives on a skateboard. Another, on her own Ducati.

One day while barbecuing in the backyard, Joe decides the neighborly thing is to invite the bachelor over.

The guy arrives and drinks tequilas around the patio table till long after dark.

At one point he leans over to you and says, "I hear you're Colombian. I've got a couple of Colombian girls working for me. They're the best. Second only to the Russians."

You ask what sort of business he's in.

"Film production."

"What kind of films?"

"Well, not really films, per se. More like video production. For the Internet."

Another tequila and the guy admits he's running a porn studio out of his house. Each bedroom outfitted with lights and cameras operated from a central control room. The girls perform for subscription Internet channels. Most have loyal followings and do private shows, sometimes alone, sometimes with each other.

"Where do you find these girls?" is all you think to ask.

"It's easy. One girl tells another. I've got a waitlist thirty girls deep."

He pats your hand as if to assure you.

"Believe me, it's all perfectly legal. I don't hire minors. I leave that to the guys up in Fort Lauderdale."

. . . .

In the mailroom of your apartment building, you say hello to another resident checking her box near yours. She's the type who complains about anything. The weather. The color of the paint on the walls. A speck of lint on the lobby floor. "This country is screwed," she always says, "especially Florida." She kicks herself every day for moving down from Delaware twenty years ago and constantly threatens to go back.

"How's work?" you say.

She's a masseuse and tells you her least favorite clients are the "Latins" because they make her use the service entrance when entering their homes—the same door meant for the maids, cooks, and plumbers.

"Can you imagine?" she says, horror streaked across her face. "They treat me like a servant. They don't even want me to walk in the front door. They act like

they own this city. They're so entitled. They've ruined Miami, turning it into their own colony."

"Now you know how it feels," you say, dropping your junk mail in the garbage.

Your neighbor stares at you, her pale cheeks flushed with anger, but says nothing in response and walks away.

· · · · · · · · · · · · ·

There's a saying locals throw around:
The best thing about Miami is how close it is to the United States.

· · · · · · · · · · · · ·

They come from other cities and from other countries, looking for paradise by the sea; looking to be South Beach models, to marry rich and become queens of Star Island, but instead find themselves in the republic of pills and powders and paid sex.

You see them standing outside of hotel lobbies on Collins Avenue, dressed in designer clothes, balanced on sharp high heels. Legs tanned and shiny. Breasts large and fake. You see tourist men come out of the building to look for a girl to take in to the hotel bar, or up to a room. You see red rented Ferraris pull up to the curb and the women step over to them casually, as if the man were just asking for directions, and then climb into the passenger seat. He doesn't even open the door for her.

You see them walking along Biscayne Boulevard, even in parts the city has worked so hard to clean up. You see them outside of the Wonderland strip club on Seventy-Ninth, ignored by cops patrolling the area, and among the homeless and stray dogs in the concrete yards beneath I-95 that used to hold the Mariel refugee tent city.

You see them standing outside the motels among teenagers smoking cigarettes and working as lookouts for drug dealers. You see them wandering the few vacant lots still left along the bay that haven't yet been bulldozed and flattened to make room for more skyscrapers; the ones where body parts often wash up—a hand, a foot, even a whole leg, that will remain forever unidentified.

You knew one of these girls once. A white Texan named Toni who worked a five-block stretch on lower Biscayne where your boyfriend at the time lived with his bandmates. She was always high and would get in the car of any guy who whistled her way, but always said hello and watched after you when you walked alone to your car late at night.

"This city's not safe for nice girls like you and me," she used to say.

One day her father came from Dallas to collect her. Everyone in the neighborhood heard her shouting that she didn't want to leave. You and your boyfriend watched from the second-floor window as she fell to her knees on the sidewalk and cried. But then her father scooped her up, embraced her long, and she let him take her home.

• • • • • • • • • • • • •

A dozen Cuban migrants land on the beach near your apartment building. They arrive in a motorless wooden boat loaded with broken paddles, empty water jugs, and a torn plastic sheet they used as a sail during their two weeks at sea. They are sunburned and filthy, thin, their faces crusted with sea salt. A mob of beachgoers gather on the sand around them, welcoming them to Miami, offering the migrants their sunglasses, hats, towels, and shirts with which to cover their charred shoulders; water and beers from their coolers, until the police arrive to process them for amnesty, and release them to their relatives.

La Ciudad Mágica.

La Ciudad del Sol.

Cuba con Coca-Cola.

• • • • • • • • • • • • •

Down U.S.-1, past the waterfront mansions of Coco Plum and Gables by the Sea, the sprawling estates and ranches of Pinecrest, a few turns off the highway onto a narrow dusty road, you find people selling fruit out of tin shacks; papayas the size of footballs, guanabana, carambola, and unbruised mangos, perfectly ripe, erupting with nectar.

Here you will drink straight from the coconut while, a few yards down, another vendor offers barbecued iguana—the same ones they sell in pet stores that owners grow bored of and release to the wild, and people in the suburbs pay to have removed from their property—or wild hog, alligator, and diced python, served with hot sauce and rice, freshly hunted down in the Everglades.

Out here, you can pick out a pig from a corral and they'll slaughter it right in front of you, ready to take home, head and all, to roast for all your friends in your caja china; or you can whisper your request to a guy who knows another guy, and in a few minutes find someone to sell you horsemeat.

Out here you can watch a live dogfight, buy a peacock to take home and keep in your backyard to protect you from the evil eye of your enemies, have your illnesses cured by the polvos of a curandero, and a spell cast by a brujo so you'll be lucky in money and in love.

Nobody will ever know you were here.

E

• • • • • • • • • • • • •

The shrine to La Virgen de la Caridad del Cobre sits on Biscayne Bay, with its own replica of the Havana malecón. Elderly people are bussed in daily from retirement communities and senior centers; families come together in pilgrimage from all over the state. Here, people gather to pray to Cuba's patron saint, and to leave sunflowers for her other face, the orisha Ochún.

A year ago, on a day like any other, as the viejitos sat before the altar praying for freedom from Fidel, as they often do, President Obama entered the church unannounced, walked down the aisle, and knelt beside the faithful in the pews.

127

Your friend Alejandro's grandmother was there.

She said it was like seeing Jesucristo himself.

Alejo was born in Cuba and spent three months in a Guantanamo refugee camp before his family received permission to enter the United States. His father worked as a dishwasher in Sweetwater. His mother sold watermelons at the intersection of Eighty-Seventh Avenue and Coral Way. He's a lawyer now and plans on running for a public office.

"Why do you think Obama came that day?" he says. "It's because every politician knows that without the abuelos of Miami in your pocket, you won't make it to the corner."

He says there are other major Latino cities. Los Angeles. Houston, San Diego. Even Chicago and New York. But none like Miami, where a national minority is the ruling majority, with 67 percent of the population, where the money and the political power sit firmly in Latino hands.

"Miami is the city of the future," Alejo says, "and in a few years, the rest of the country will finally catch up."

· · · · · · · · · · · · · ·

Your Miami begins in New Jersey where you were raised far from the ocean in an Anglo suburb near woods and mountains, speaking Spanish among family and close friends, while outside your home, classmates and townspeople mocked the color of your skin and your parents' accents, asking with suspicion how they managed to come to this country, and they'd answer that they came on a jet plane.

Your only community was your family. From the world beyond your tíos and primos, you were made to understand, before you could spell your own name, that even if you were born in this country, even if you speak the language, you will always be an outsider; this country will never belong to you.

Your Miami begins in New York, where you moved to at eighteen, lived in different downtown apartments and tried on different lives for more than a decade before finally deciding to leave.

Your Miami begins in the Andean highlands, across the mountainous cordillera, low in the valleys of the Río Cauca, and deep in the wetlands of the Orinoco; before Bolívar, before the conquest, before Colombia was Colombia, when you were Muisca and spoke Chibcha; and before that, it begins across the Atlantic, on the northern coast of Africa.

Your Miami begins in Puerto Rico, where your older brother was born, and before that, it begins in the other América, where your father worked since age fourteen to support his family of eleven in Medellín; where your parents married in a chilly church in Bogotá; your Miami begins in Colombia, the country your parents loved but left, like so many others, so you, the child they did not yet know they would have, might have a chance at something more.

· · · · · · · · · · · · ·

After they settled in the United States, as soon as they could afford it, your father took your mother on vacation to Miami. There is a photograph of her leaning on a crooked palm tree in the last pink hour before sunset. She stares at your father, who holds the camera. She is barely twenty-two. Her long hair colored a rusty red, still pearl-skinned from the lifelong overcast of Bogotá despite her indigenous blood.

There is a picture of you holding your father's hand a decade later; you, a child of two or three years old. Your mother took the photograph from the beach while your father led you into the shallow and flat edge of the ocean. He stands above you like a tower; you, in your red gingham baby bikini. They tell you that you hated the ocean when you first felt it on your skin. You tried to stomp and slap it away. You cried and reached for firm land. But then something changed and you began to swim on your own before you could speak full sentences. And then they couldn't pull you out of the water.

As you grew older, despite the years you spent in other cities, feeling their claim on you, you knew Miami would one day be your home, at least for a little while.

You are not a refugee, but here in Miami you believe you have found a sort of refuge.

• • • • • • • • • • • • •

You walk along a nature trail in one of the city's spectacular ecological reserves, canopied with thick banyans and mangroves lining a lagoon. As you pass him standing on the edge of the trail, an old man with a thick belly and a T-shirt crescented with pit stains calls you over to him and points out a fat, furry golden weaver, what locals call "lighting spiders," centered on a web shining like glass in the fractured sunlight.

"That is one big spider," you say.

"I used to practice shooting on them when I was a kid. Till I got bitten by one and my hand swelled so much the skin split like a banana peel."

He misses the old Miami, he says, when it was vast and empty, and you could walk for miles from what's now the Palmetto Expressway to Dinner Key and not run into a soul.

"Now it's crazy and crowded and full of foreigners. It's like watching your first love turn into a junkie and finding her begging for pennies under the highway."

You tell him you still think there's a lot of beauty to Miami. Just look around.

"You didn't grow up around here. I can tell."

"That's right. I didn't. But I've lived here for twelve years so far."

"You're real brown. How'd you learn to speak English so good?"

You look back at the spider and then at the man, tell him to have a nice day, continue on your way down the trail, leaving him alone by the trees.

The man calls after you.

"You watch out for those big spiders, girl. Miami is dangerous territory. Remember, there are people like *me* out there." ■

AUTHOR PROFILE

Patricia Engel was born to Colombian parents and raised in New Jersey. A graduate of New York University with an MFA from Florida International University, she is currently a Visiting Professor of Practice in Creative Writing at the University of Miami and the literary editor of the *Miami Rail*. Her works have been translated into many languages, and she is the author of several award-winning books: *Vida* (2010, Notable Book of the Year & Premio Biblioteca de Narrativa Colombiana); *It's Not Love, It's Just Paris* (2014, International Latino Book Award); and *Veins of the Ocean* (2016, *New York Times* Editors' Choice, *San Francisco Chronicle* Best Book of the Year, Dayton Literary Peace Prize). A recipient of the National Endowment for the Arts fellowship and several other awards, she has also received the *Boston Review* fiction prize. Her fiction and nonfiction have appeared in many anthologies, including *The Best American Short Stories*, *The Best American Mystery Stories*, *The Atlantic*, and *Harvard Review*. Her short story "La Ciudad Mágica" appeared in *Tales of Two Americas* in 2017.

The Great Settling Down

By Claude S. Fischer

In 1971, the great Carole King sang: 'So far away/ Doesn't anyone stay in one place anymore?' Thirty years later, the editors of *The New York Times* explained that families in the United States are changing because of 'the ever-growing mobility of Americans'. And in 2010, a psychologist argued that 'an increased rate of residential mobility played a role in the historical shift' toward individualism. It's a common US lament that human bonds are fraying because people are moving around more and more. Americans fear the fracturing of communities that constant moving seems to bring.

Yet when King sang, Americans had been moving around *less and less* for generations. That decline was even more obvious when the *Times* editorial appeared in 2001, and it has continued to decline through the 2010s. The increasingly mobile US is a myth that refuses to move on.

One might imagine that the documented increase in settling down would have relieved Americans of their anxieties about transience and the loss of community. But it has not, because most Americans believe that residential mobility is accelerating and that it is a source of social ills. In truth, neither lament nor celebration of this growing rootedness is in order, because the ramifications of a more settled US are not all to be valued. But first of all we must recognise that the US is in the midst of a great settling down—and not breaking apart by never staying put.

The idea that the US was once made up of stable and tight-knit communities is a false portrait that took root in the 1830s and grew in the decades that followed. Of course, some Americans in the 18th and 19th centuries did indeed stay home: the financially secure. But most people—common farm families and ordinary workers, not to mention slaves, servants and immigrants—lived on thin margins. Uncontrollable events such as drought, pests, accidents, epidemics, depressions, conflicts and more often washed away those margins and swept people onto the open road.

Researchers have found creative ways to measure rates of geographic mobility in past centuries. Some have looked simply at how many Americans in any given year lived outside their states of birth. Coming from out of state was relatively frequent in the mid-19th-century but then became much less so until the 1970s. The rate of leaving one's state of birth then rose again until dropping quite recently. But leaving one's state of birth is a special type of mobility. Counting those moves captures the many one-time relocations Americans made as the population spread west in the 19th century and then to the Sunbelt in the late 20th century—but by counting only these, we miss the vast majority of moves that people make.

A better sense of how common moving was in the past comes from studies that assessed turnover in local communities. Historians have tabulated how many of the people who were listed for one year in a community record (in a census, city directory, tax roster or voting register) were listed again in the next year's or the next decade's record. The answer, from the 18th through the 19th centuries, is almost always relatively few.

F

For example, in Abraham Lincoln's Sangamon County, Illinois, about 80 per cent of the households recorded as living there in 1850 could not be found there in 1860. These studies describe a widespread churning of the population, much greater than in the 20th century. There are technical problems with this method of calculating mobility, but it's most likely an error of *underestimating* the turnover by not counting people who came and went so rapidly that they were never listed in the first place.

The evidence that mobility has declined is more robust for roughly the past 65 years, thanks to annual census-bureau mass surveys. Around 1950, about 20 per cent of Americans changed homes from one year to the next. In the 1980s, under 18 per cent did. By the 2000s, under 15 per cent—and now we are approaching annual moving rates of only 10 per cent. About two-thirds of movers do not go far, relocating within the same county, and the frequency of such local moves has dropped by about half since the Second World War. The proportion of Americans who move across county and state lines is considerably lower, but that rate, too, has dropped substantially, from about 6.5 per cent in the 1950s to under 4 per cent now.

This trend toward staying in place has accelerated since 2001. Why? The geographer Thomas J Cooke at the University of Connecticut largely credits the economic crisis, but he argues that mobility would still have declined in any event because of a general societal trend toward 'increased rootedness'. The economists Raven Molloy, Christopher L Smith and Abigail Wozniak have speculated that perhaps technological changes have made telecommuting easier and therefore moving for job reasons is less necessary. Another explanation offered is that US communities have become so similar in terms of employment that there's no financial point in moving. But, in short, no clear explanation has yet emerged for what many economists, as I discuss later, consider a problem.

The end of the great 19th-century and early 20th-century migrations to and across the US, when millions of Italians, Poles, Germans and other Europeans came here, would *seem* to be part of the explanation for mobility's decline. But the resurgence of large-scale immigration to the US since the 1970s of Mexicans, Chinese and others from around the globe did not bring with it a rise in overall mobility rates. Those rates kept falling. Meanwhile, some scholars point to the rise in homeownership over the 20th century as an explanation for the great settling down, since homeowners move less often than do renters. But the increase in ownership was not as great as the decline in mobility. Moreover, though homeownership rates in the US have dropped by 5 percentage points in the past decade, mobility has continued to decline. Nor can demographic changes, such as a growing aged population, explain the long-term trend.

So what is the cause? My best guess is that the greatest single factor in the great settling down was the increasing physical and economic security of US life.

Thanks to a growing and stabilising economy, spreading affluence, vastly improved public health, the establishment of government institutions from policing to business regulation, and all sorts of 'safety net' programmes over several generations—from Social Security to federal disaster assistance—fewer and fewer Americans have been *forced* to move because of unemployment, floods, the death of a breadwinner, and so on. Greater security also helps account for an apparent shift from the 19th to 20th centuries in *who* was likeliest to move.

Roughly speaking, in the 18th and 19th centuries, poorer Americans moved much more than did better-off Americans. Whether it was, for example, the younger sons of Colonial New England farmers who had to move further into the wilderness to get their own land, freed slaves searching for decent *paying* jobs after the Civil War, or textile workers in the late 1800s laid off in slow periods moving back to their parents' farms, the typical moves of earlier eras were not made by choice. Well-off Americans and their children made fewer, but longer-distance moves, often to pursue yet better opportunities.

Then, in the 20th century, that class gap in moving narrowed as working-class life became more secure. In the same period, the well-off continued or perhaps even accelerated their moving, notably their long-distance moving, as national employment markets developed for professionals. Think of how doctors, lawyers, professors, corporate executives, and people like them, build careers today compared with a century ago—more often by attending colleges far from home and competing for jobs nationally.

New transportation technologies comprise a second part of the explanation for the long-term decline in mobility. The streetcar in its various forms, from trolleys to subways to automobiles, allowed Americans to change jobs without changing homes. In the 19th century, workers generally had to find housing within a couple of miles of where they worked, because employees, unless they boarded with their employers, walked to work. But for 20th-century Americans, fast transportation, together with the telephone, reduced the social pressures for moving. For example, widowed mothers could stay in their own homes longer now that their grown children were a short drive and quick call away.

There are two distinctions to make in order to understand the historical changes in mobility. First, long-distance moves, which are largely driven by career reasons, must be distinguished from local ones, which often result from housing reasons. Second, voluntary moves, which tend to be beneficial, must be kept separate from forced ones, which often are not. Keeping these in mind help us better understand who is likely to move and for what reasons. The consequences of moving depend on the kind of move.

Despite the recent surge in stay-at-home young adults, 20-somethings move more than anyone else, almost one in four of them a year. They move both near and far, as they leave home, go to college, begin new jobs, and start their families. These are, for the most part, life-building moves. Moving rates decline as people age: only about 4 per cent of senior citizens move in a year.

College graduates are much more likely to move across state lines than are Americans with less education, and more than twice as likely as high-school dropouts. But the least-educated are more likely to move locally. These are signs that many of the moves that less-educated Americans make are reactions to problems rather than the grasping of new opportunities. In his book *Evicted* (2016), the sociologist Matthew Desmond documents the residential reality at the next-to-lowest rung of the socioeconomic ladder: poor, single mothers and their children who haven't enough income to afford even the worst housing, and who consequently bounce from dilapidated unit to dilapidated unit. (The lowest rung of the ladder is, of course, occupied by the homeless.) Desmond argues that residential instability itself is a major factor in the perpetuation of poverty.

F

The consequences of moving depend greatly on why people move. In the latest census data, more than half of local movers said that they moved for housing reasons, especially to get a better or cheaper home. Only one in 10 moved because of job reasons, commonly to shorten the commute. Those who crossed county or state lines, in contrast, largely explained the move in terms of work, mainly to start new jobs. So most moves in recent years are voluntary.

For willing movers, the move is typically positive. They face a period of adjustment as they find their way around, try to stay in touch with friends and family, and make new friends. But the net effect is often good—and, for some, positively life-changing. For example, research by the sociologist Rob Sampson at Harvard shows that residents of poor neighbourhoods in Chicago who manage to move out and stay out of their original neighbourhoods fare better than those who stay behind or return to the old community. Other research suggests that members of cultural minorities who move, especially if they move to larger cities, find a wider range of freedom to 'be themselves'.

Forced moves, on the other hand, resulting from foreclosure, divorce, job loss and the like, can leave long-term scars, as Desmond has documented for the evicted. Children are especially vulnerable. They don't decide whether and where to move, and they are especially sensitive to their immediate environments. Children who move repeatedly are at particular risk. In one study of adolescents, new students had fewer friends and were less integrated into their schools than those who had been in the community several years. Other research shows that multiple moves in a short time adversely affect children's mental health. Children who move frequently typically do so because they are in highly unstable families; many live with a single mother and a succession of her boyfriends. While the children's repeated relocations often result from deeper problems, the moving itself seems to weaken children's social ties and wellbeing.

Moving doesn't just affect the movers: there are important consequences for *communities* too. In general, high rates of residential turnover in a neighbourhood or town undercut local solidarity and the ability of neighbours to coordinate action, such as controlling the behaviour of teens, ensuring child safety, and mobilising politically. High turnover also increases residents' anxiety. (The pattern is complex, however: in some very disadvantaged neighbourhoods, residential stability can actually accentuate problems by reinforcing troublesome local norms—e.g., don't talk to the police.)

Given such evidence, the great American settling-down should be building solidarity, sociability, and community-feeling in neighbourhoods across the nation. But that has not happened. If anything, Americans are more likely to ignore their neighbours these days in favour of their relatives and friends outside the neighbourhood than generations ago. One reason is the march of wives and mothers out of the home and into the workplace from the 1950s. Fewer people are home during the day, and more people are focused on their jobs and co-workers. Also, the very transportation and communication advances that allow people to stay in their homes as they change jobs cuts down on neighbourly sentiment. People dine out with friends that live miles away rather than invite a neighbour over for dinner. They gossip by Skype with a friend on the other side of the globe rather than chat over the fence. Today, staying in place can go together with freedom *from* place.

The widespread value Americans place on community continuity is evident in the escalating conflicts over gentrification in booming neighbourhoods such as central San Francisco and Brooklyn. Activists not only complain about the damage done to those who are forced out by rising costs, but also about the loss of a 'traditional' community as newcomers change its culture. For example, the author Michael Henry Adams recently lamented in *The New York Times* that the Harlem of black churches, stores and art—the Harlem of the Harlem Renaissance—was being erased by incoming whites. In rural America, there remains widespread concern about the out-migration of young people and the in-migration of city commuters, as there has been for many generations. Americans value the settled community.

But for some, casting off from home is how they can best realise themselves. And in the wake of the slow recovery from the Great Recession, some economists suggest that we have, in fact, too-settled a society. Unemployment and poverty are concentrated in particular places (the median house price in the Silicon Valley is more than 12 times that in the Youngstown area of Ohio). Americans of working age, they argue, should flee those pockets, be they rural hollows in coal country or inner-city ghettoes. Social insurance and supports that allow people to stay home and stabilise communities might be a social problem.

In the end, most Americans should find the settling down of the nation a positive change. Yet they seem unaware of it. Every time I have written about this trend—the first time was in the 1970s—the reaction I get is of amazement. How could that be so, since everyone 'knows' we live in an ever-more mobile society? Why the surprise, especially given that every year the census bureau releases, and the press reports, the latest data on the drop in mobility?

Perhaps the myth of increasing rootlessness persists because it fits so well into the bigger picture Americans have of 'modern' versus 'traditional' society, fitting comfortably alongside other myths such as rising isolation, moral decay, mental disturbance and alienation. As unintuitive as it might seem to most Americans, it is simply a myth that no one stays in one place anymore. We are staying longer and longer. ■

F

AUTHOR PROFILE

Claude S. Fischer has been teaching at the University of California, Berkeley, since 1972 and is currently Professor of the Graduate School in Sociology at the University of California, Berkeley. Over the years he has authored or co-authored numerous books, including *Made in America: A Social History of American Culture and Character* (2010), a study of cultural change since the colonial era, and *Still Connected: Family and Friends in America Since 1970* (2011), which focuses on personal relationships in more recent times. His latest book is *Lurching Toward Happiness in America* (2014). "The Great Settling Down" was published by the digital magazine *Aeon* on November 17, 2016.

The Dividing of a Continent: Africa's Separatist Problem

By Max Fisher

When the nations of Nigeria and Cameroon went to settle a border dispute in 2002, in which both countries claimed an oil-rich peninsula about the size of El Paso, they didn't cite ancient cultural claims to the land, nor the preferences of its inhabitants, nor even their own national interests. Rather, in taking their case to the International Court of Justice, they cited a pile of century-old European paperwork.

Cameroon was once a German colony and Nigeria had been ruled by the British empire; in 1913, the two European powers had negotiated the border between these West African colonies. Cameroon argued that this agreement put the peninsula within their borders. Nigeria said the same. Cameroon's yellowed maps were apparently more persuasive; it won the case, and will officially absorb the Bekassi Peninsula into its borders next month.

The case, as Reuters once explained, "again highlighted Africa's commitment to colonial borders drawn without consideration for those actually living there." African borders, in this thinking, are whatever Europeans happened to have marked down during the 19th and 20th centuries, which is a surprising way to do things given how little these outsider-drawn borders have to do with actual Africans.

In much of the world, national borders have shifted over time to reflect ethnic, linguistic, and sometimes religious divisions. Spain's borders generally enclose the Spanish-speakers of Europe; Slovenia and Croatia roughly encompass ethnic Slovenes and Croats. Thailand is exactly what its name suggests. Africa is different, its nations largely defined not by its people's heritage but by the follies of European colonialism. But as the continent becomes more democratic and Africans assert desires for national self-determination, the African insistence on maintaining colonial-era borders is facing more popular challenges, further exposing the contradiction engineered into African society half a century ago.

When European colonialism collapsed in the years after World War Two and Africans resumed control of their own continent, sub-Saharan leaders agreed to respect the colonial borders. Not because those borders made any sense—they are widely considered the arbitrary creations of colonial happenstance and European agreements—but because "new rulers in Africa made the decision to keep the borders drawn by former colonizers to avoid disruptive conflict amongst themselves," as a Harvard paper on these "artificial states" put it.

Conflict has decreased in Africa since the turbulent 1960s and '70s, and though the continent still has some deeply troubled hotspots, the broader trend in Africa is one of peace, democracy, and growth. The threats of destabilizing war, of coups and counter-coups, have eased since the first independent African leaders pledged to uphold European-drawn borders. But a contradiction remains in the African system: leaders are committed to maintaining consistent borders, and yet as those governments become more democratic, they have to confront the fact that popular will might conflict.

A Kenyan group called the Mombasa Republican Council is just the latest of Africa's now 20-plus separatist movements, according to the *Guardian*, which has charted them all in an interactive map. The Mombasa group wants the country's coastal region to secede, citing its distinct heritage due to centuries of trade across the Indian Ocean. It's unlikely to happen, but as the *Guardian* notes it's part of a trend of "encouraged" separatist movements as Africans seem to become more willing and interested in pursuing borders that more closely reflect the continent's diverse ethnic, religious, and linguistic lines.

Consider Angola. In 1575, 100 Portuguese families and 400 Portuguese troops landed on the African continent's southwestern coast at what is now the city of Luanda. They expanded from there, stopping only when they reached German, Belgian, or British claims. The Portuguese consolidated the vast, California-sized holdings into a single colony. The only thing that the people who lived there shared in common was that they answered to Portuguese masters, and in 1961 that they rebelled against that rule, which they threw off in 1975. They became the country of Angola, an essentially invented nation meant to represent disparate and ancient cultures as if they had simply materialized out of thin air that very moment. Today, as some Angolans are quick to point out, their country is composed of ten major ethnic groups, who do not necessarily have a history of or an interest in shared nationhood. This may help explain why there are two secessionist groups in Angola today.

Had pre-industrial-era Portuguese colonists not pressed so far up along Africa's western coast so quickly, for example, then Africa's seven million Kikongo-speakers might today have their own country. Instead, they are split among three different countries, including Angola, as minorities. The Bundu dia Kongo separatist group, which operates across the region, wants to establish a country that would more closely resemble the old, pre-colonial Kongo Kingdom, and give the Kikongo-speakers a country.

There's no reason to think that Bundia dia Kongo or the Mombasa Republican Council have any chance at establishing sovereign states; their movements are too weak and the states they challenge are too strong. But, as the 2011 division of Sudan into two countries demonstrated, the world can sometimes find some flexibility in the unofficial rule about maintaining colonial African borders. Sudan was an extreme example, an infamously poorly demarcated state that encompassed some of the widest ethnic and religious gulfs in the world, but as G. Pascal Zachary wrote in TheAtlantic.com at the time, it provided an opportunity to question whether those arbitrary borders hold Africa back. After all, in countries such as Nigeria or the Democratic Republic of Congo, disparate cultural groups have tended to band together, competing with one another for finite power and resources, sometimes disastrously. With tribal identities strong and national identities weak (after all, the latter tends to be ancient and deeply rooted, the latter new and artificial), national cooperation can be tough.

Of course, the actual practice of secession and division would be difficult, if it's even functionally possible; Africa's ethnic groups are many, and they don't tend

to fall along the cleanest possible lines. The debate over whether or not secession is good for Africa, as Zachary explained, is a complicated and sometimes contentious one. But the simple fact of this debate is a reminder of Africa's unique post-colonial borders, a devil's bargain sacrificing the democratic fundamental of national self-determination for the practical pursuits of peace and independence. And it's another indication of the many ways that colonialism's complicated legacy is still with us, still shaping today's world. ■

AUTHOR PROFILE

Max Fisher is the *The Washington Post's* foreign affairs blogger. He graduated from William and Mary with a degree in English Language, and holds an M.A. in Security Studies from Johns Hopkins University. Fisher also writes *The Interpreter*, a news column and newsletter that explore the ideas and context behind major world events for *The New York Times*. Based in Washington, D.C., he uses political science and social science to examine and explain topics from authoritarianism to arms control. In an article for William and Mary in 2008, Fisher said, "I will admit that, for a time after graduation, I wondered whether I should've majored in political science or international relations, since those classes would've provided me with knowledge more directly applicable to the topics I cover. After all, Faulkner doesn't have a lot to say about U.S. strategic objectives in Afghanistan. I don't think that anymore. The skill I learned as an English major has served me best—even better than learning how to write, which is just hugely important in itself—is how to read critically." Fisher is a former writer and editor for *The Atlantic*, which is where "The Dividing of a Continent" appeared on September 10, 2012.

Photograph of My Room

By Carolyn Forché

                    after Walker Evans
Thirty years from now, you might
hold this room in your hands.
So that you will not wonder:
the china cups are from Serbia
where a man filled them with plum
wine and one night talked
of his life with the partisans
and in prison, his life
as a poet, Slavko, his life
as if it could not have been otherwise.
The quilt was Anna's.
There are swatches taken
from her own clothes, curtains
that hung in a kitchen in Prague,
aprons she never took off
in all her years in America.
Since her death, the stitches,
one scrap to another
have come loose.

The bundle of army letters
were sent from Southeast Asia
during '67, kept near a bottle
of vodka drained by a woman
in that same year who wanted
only to sleep; the fatigues
were his, it is she
whom I now least resemble.

In the trunk, the white eyelet
and cheap lace of underthings,
a coat that may have belonged
to a woman who approached me
on a street in April
saying, as it was spring,
would I spare her a smoke?

Under the bed, a pouch of money:
pesetas, dinar, francs, the coins
of no value in any other place.
In the notebooks you will find
those places: the damp inner thighs,
the delicate rash left by kisses,

F

139

fingers on the tongue, a swallow
of brandy, a fire.
It is all there, the lies
told to myself because of Paris,
the stories I believed in Salvador
and Granada, and every so often
simply the words calling back
a basket of lemons and eggs,
a bowl of olives.

Wrapped in a tissue you will find
a bullet, as if from the rifle
on the wall, spooned from the flesh
of a friend who must have thought
it was worth something.
Latched to its shell, a lattice
of muscle. *One regime*
is like another said the face
of a doctor who slid
the bullet from the flat
of his blade to my hands saying
this one won't live to the morning.

In the black cheese crock
are the ashes, flecked
with white slivers of bone,
that should have been scattered
years ago, but the thing
did not seem possible.
The rest of the room remains
a mystery, as it was
in the shutter of memory
that was 1936, when it belonged
to someone already dead, someone
who has no belongings. ■

AUTHOR PROFILE

Carolyn Forché (b. 1950) was born in Detroit, Michigan, and earned her MFA at Bowling Green State University in 1974. She won the Yale Series of Younger Poets Competition in 1976 for her collection *Gathering the Tribes*. *The Country Between Us* (1981) won the Lamont Poetry Selection of the Academy of American Poets and in 2006. That same year she also won the Robert Creeley Award. Currently, she is Director of the Lannan Center for Poetry and Poetics and holds the Lannan Chair in Poetry at Georgetown University in Washington D.C. Some of Forché's other works include the famous poem "The Colonel" (1981) and "The Garden Shukkei-en" (1994). "Photograph of My Room" was originally published in *The Country Between Us.*

Life in the Meta City

By William Gibson

My first city was Conan Doyle's London, in the company of Holmes and Watson. My mother gave me a two-volume omnibus edition when I was 10. London was a vast, cozy, populous mechanism, a comforting clockwork. Foreigners and criminals served as spices, highlighting the assumed orderliness and safety of the Empire's capital (assuming one were sufficiently comfortably placed in society, and in Doyle one tended to be).

I lived in rural southwestern Virginia, the nearest cities several hours away and those were smallish cities. Relatively little of what I saw on television conveyed much sense of urban reality, perhaps because it was still inherently difficult to film in large cities. Except for Los Angeles, and I saw a lot of that, and Los Angeles never did become much a part of my imagination's map of cities.

I reverse-engineered a concept of urban life from Doyle's rich and intriguing (and cozy) construct. I walked through my hometown, imagining it a city. What I was imagining, I now see, was an increase not in size but in number of choices.

Cities afforded more choices than small towns, and constantly, by increasing the number and randomization of potential human and cultural contacts. Cities were vast, multilayered engines of choice, peopled primarily with strangers.

You never know whom you might meet in the city. In a small town, you're less likely to encounter people or things or situations you haven't encountered previously. These people or things or situations may be wonderful or horrible, in either city or town, but cities have the numbers, the turnover. To a writer of fiction, this is extremely handy, a city being able, more or less believably, to mask excessive coincidence, producing, as Doyle taught me, whatever the narrative might require.

Should the populous mechanism of the fictive city fail to produce phenomena of sufficient weirdness, our literature of the fantastic often turns, quite reflexively, to dead cities, our most profoundly and mysteriously haunted artifacts.

Many deserted cities probably never were engines of choice. To stand in the vast plaza of the pre-Columbian Monte Albán, for instance, is to know that Monte Albán was about decreasing choice, narrowing it. Monte Albán was a control machine, an acoustically perfect environment with magnificent lines of sight: a theater of power. We don't know why Monte Albán was as abruptly deserted as it may have been. Perhaps the show failed, finally, to come off, and no other was available, or possible, within that inflexible, unipurposed structure.

That's the danger of choice reduction, of top-down control. And the curse of gated attractions, the ultimate fate of every Disneyland: you can't repurpose a theme park. Cities, to survive, must be capable of extended fugues of retrofitting. Only the most pubescent of cities have never witnessed, to whatever extent, their own ruins. Berlin has, Rome has, London has, Tokyo has, New York has. Relative ruin, relative desertion, is a common stage of complex and necessary urban growth. Successful (which is to say, ongoing) cities are built up in a lacquering of countless layers: of lives, of choices encountered and made.

The most crucial layers are those of various essential technologies, all of which must in some sense be present and functional for a city to endure. We didn't begin to build cities until we could secure adequate supplies of food, which generally meant growing and storing it. Growth beyond a certain size requires mastery of sewage-disposal technologies. The city evolves as a pyramid of technologies, some essential, others incidental.

Cities can be at their experientially richest during periods of relative disjunction. Cities that are somewhat dysfunctional in one sense can be brilliantly functional in others. The city you want, as a young creative person, is partially ruined, marked by areas semimoribund in real estate values. Low rents, minimal policing, casual welding allowed on sidewalks. Manhattan in the 1970s, a place and time people my age now regard with mixed nostalgia, was fraught with ruins, with buildings abandoned, nights lit by insurance fires. On first observing this, in 1979, I suggested, half-seriously, that the Japanese be allowed to sort the place out, given their way with urban real estate. New Yorkers smirked at my bumpkin naïveté, knowing the Bowery would always be the Bowery.

Today the Bowery is nothing like the Bowery. Cities can do that, reversing out of disjunction, throwing themselves into a different gear. Although in doing so, they run the risk of Disneylanding themselves, of building themselves too permanently into a given day's vision of what they should be. Paris feels that way to me, lovely as it is, with New York and London hurrying to catch up.

Meanwhile, though, some of the world's largest human settlements are now not only places where one can weld on the sidewalk but places that have bypassed many of the ways in which Europeans and North Americans have assumed cities necessarily need to grow: Rio, Mumbai, Nairobi, Istanbul, Mexico City…. Vast squatter conurbs, semi-neo-Medieval in their structure and conditions. The future will emerge from such cities as surely as it will emerge from the Disneylanded capitals of an Old World that now includes North America.

The future of cities will consist of two different modalities combined within the ageographical and largely unrecognized meta city that is the Internet.

As a boy, I took myself away to cities as quickly as I could and have lived in them ever since. When I travel now, I travel mainly to cities, and I tend to return to those I know, taking a deepening pleasure in the serial experience. The idea of visiting a fascinating city only once saddens me, and I seldom leave a city I've come to know without wondering if I'll see it again. But in our ageographical existence, I am never entirely not in London, entirely not in Tokyo.

We all inhabit the meta city now, regardless of physical address. ■

—————————————————— AUTHOR PROFILE

William Gibson is a Canadian-American speculative-fiction author best known for establishing the subgenre of cyberpunk with the short story "Burning Chrome" (1982) and the novel *Neuromancer* (1984). Cyberpunk's beginnings in the early days of personal computers led it to explore how our minds, bodies, cultures, and places might change as access to information devices and networks became universal, and his work strongly influenced developing digital culture and language. Aside from his major *Sprawl*, *Bridge*, and *Blue Ant* trilogies, Gibson's work also includes experimental multimodal work that takes advantage of new technology, such as the 1992 collaborative art piece *Agrippa (The Book of the Dead)*, written with Dennis Ashbaugh and Kevin Begos, Jr. This piece consisted of an art book and Gibson's poem text published on a 3.5" floppy disk which was supposedly programmed to display the poem once in its entirety, then encrypt itself, rendering it inaccessible, as a way of exploring the poem's themes of memory loss. Gibson's writing has appeared in television and film as well, including several episodes of the television series *The X-Files* and a film adaptation of his short story "Johnny Mnemonic." His nonfiction essay "Life in the Meta City," which first appeared in *Scientific American* in September 2011, explores the changing nature of cities and their cultures over time, a frequent theme in his speculative work.

G

Should Immigration Require Assimilation?

By Tom Gjelten

The ceremony in which Marta Quintanilla Call became a U.S. citizen was held in a cavernous high-school auditorium in Oakton, Virginia. She and 499 other immigrants stood, put their hands on their hearts, and repeated the oath of allegiance, prompted by a woman on the stage. Next came a videotaped congratulatory message from President Obama and a slideshow of American scenery accompanied by a recording of Lee Greenwood singing "God Bless the U.S.A." The country hit, played incessantly on radio stations after the 9/11 attacks and again after Osama bin Laden was killed, would have struck some of the immigrant Americans as inappropriate if they knew what the songwriter actually thought about foreigners. "If America changes to the point that it is no longer a Christian nation and no longer protects itself from aliens who come and go," Greenwood said in 2010, "then it won't be America anymore." The new citizens nevertheless seemed to feel welcomed. At the end of the ceremony, they cheered and waved the little American flags they received with their naturalization certificate.

Though the ceremony was not personal or intimate (or culturally sensitive), its very size made it impressive, because of the diversity on display. The people who filled the auditorium that morning in August 2014 came from 82 countries (about half with a non-Christian heritage) and represented nearly all the nationalities on the planet. Many of the women wore headscarves, and some of the men wore skullcaps. Three of the top four countries represented—India, Pakistan, and Ethiopia—had prior to 1965 been allocated only a few U.S. visa slots per year.

The fourth country was El Salvador, Call's native land. Along with her, 37 other Salvadorans took the citizenship oath. For Marta, the ceremony was the culmination of a sojourn in America that had begun 22 years earlier at a detention center on the Texas-Mexico border. America to her was the place where imagined futures did not seem hopelessly out of reach, as they would have in the village where she was raised. She wore a new black dress for the occasion and had her hair highlighted with a blond streak. A colleague from her Days Inn cleaning job met her at the high school with a dozen red roses, which Marta held throughout the ceremony. Her husband and their two young children, Kimberly and Carlos, accompanied her to the ceremony, as did Jonis, Marta's son from her first marriage. They celebrated afterward at the International House of Pancakes. Erick and René, the two sons from El Salvador, were still resentful of her and jealous of Jonis, and they skipped the ceremony. Both nevertheless wanted to follow in their mother's footsteps and intended to apply for citizenship themselves as soon as they could. René, the younger, said he wanted to join the Army.

In theory, the decision to become a U.S. citizen separates migrants who want only to take advantage of economic opportunity from those who are ready to acquire a new national identity. It suggests an ideological commitment that goes beyond the intent to live and work in the United States simply for money. As a "legal permanent resident," Call could have stayed in the United States indefinitely while retaining her Salvadoran citizenship, but she was determined to vote in U.S. elections, carry a U.S. passport, and be as much a part of America as her husband and three U.S.-born children. One reason Chinese migrant workers encountered such hostility in the western U.S. in the 19th century was that they were not seen as coming to the country to start new lives. The men often journeyed alone, under labor contracts, and intended eventually to return to their families in China. The idealized immigration story is that people come to America freely, with a willingness to participate fully in the country's life.

A similar criticism was sometimes made of Hispanic immigration. A 2013 study by the Pew Hispanic Center found that people arriving from other parts of the world were almost twice as likely to become U.S. citizens as were those coming from Mexico or Central America. One possible explanation was the proximity of their homelands, which made it easier for these Hispanics to maintain old bonds that might otherwise be broken by the migration experience. Critics of Hispanic immigration also pointed to the prevalence of Spanish-speaking communities in the United States, suggesting that this showed that Hispanics were not assimilating. Samuel Huntington argued in his 2004 book *Who Are We?* that the scale and persistence of immigration from Mexico and the rest of Latin America, along with the widespread and continuing use of Spanish by immigrants from those countries, "could change America into a culturally bifurcated Anglo-Hispanic society with two national languages."

But the delay in Hispanic assimilation was also tied to other factors, notably poverty and low educational attainment, often associated with a lack of self-confidence. A 2000 survey of Salvadoran immigrant parents with children in Fairfax County public schools found that fewer than 30 percent had completed high school, and more than 80 percent reported household incomes of less than $40,000 per year. Call could have applied for U.S. citizenship earlier than she did, but she did not feel ready. To become a citizen, she had to be able to speak, read, write, and understand basic English and demonstrate some knowledge of U.S. government and history. Having reached only the fourth grade in her rural Salvadoran school, she was barely literate in Spanish, much less in English, and the burden of raising children and struggling constantly to make ends meet had left little time for education.

To prepare for the language and civic tests and learn more about the naturalization process, Marta attended nightly citizenship classes sponsored by Catholic Charities. Volunteer instructors tutored her and fellow immigrants on such matters as the number of senators and representatives in Congress and the roles of the legislative, executive, and judicial branches of government. The immigrants needed to learn what led to the Declaration of Independence and what was in the U.S. Constitution. The students could continue in the class as long as they wanted, and Marta became one of the stalwarts, often reassuring others who were feeling overwhelmed by the material and the language barrier. "I was afraid to come to this class the first time," she told a Senegalese woman who was ready to give up. "I have been in this country for more than 20 years, but the first time I came to this class, it was like I was in the country for the first day."

A close evaluation of Hispanic acculturation data suggests there was scant reason to worry that their growing presence in the country would dilute America's national identity or lead to cultural separatism. The 2000 Fairfax County survey of Salvadoran immigrants like Call found that while 83 percent had arrived in the United States with no English at all, most of their children by the time of the survey spoke English well enough to translate for them. In a 2007 article, four political scientists examined available data for Hispanic immigrants and found that they "acquire English and lose Spanish rapidly beginning with the second generation" and that their educational attainment and political attitudes suggest "a traditional pattern of political assimilation." A scholar at the RAND Corporation, after comparing the trajectories of various ethnic groups in America, found that "education advances made by Latinos are actually greater than those achieved by either Europeans or Asian migrants," meaning that as a group their educational attainment rose steadily from generation to generation. Hispanics were joining the American mainstream, just as previous immigrants had.

A broader and more difficult question was whether immigrants who became American citizens would genuinely embrace the American ideology. The woman from U.S. Citizenship and Immigration Services (USCIS) who presided at the naturalization ceremony at Oakton High School told the assembled immigrants to cheer as their origin countries were announced, and then she encouraged them to applaud again and wave their flags when they officially became Americans, as if they had been reborn. She said they should speak English whenever they could, take part in elections, and otherwise fulfill their civic responsibilities, but she also told them they should feel free to continue speaking their native language, celebrate their own cultural backgrounds, and stay true to their own religions.

The question of what it should actually mean to become American had been debated for decades. The term "assimilation" was resisted by some immigrant advocates because it suggested that people arriving from other lands were obliged to give up their distinctive histories and embrace the dominant culture in their new homeland. When almost all newcomers to America shared a European background, the question was less pressing, but that changed with the arrival of a much more diverse immigrant population after 1965. In 2006, the George W. Bush administration organized the Task Force on New Americans with representatives from 12 cabinet departments. In its report, "Building an Americanization Movement for the Twenty-first Century," the group attempted to balance the celebration of ethnic diversity and the promotion of national unity by distinguishing between the cultural and political aspects of a new citizen's identity. "The cultural sphere—traditions, religion—is up to the individual," it concluded. "The Task Force focuses on the shared common identity that binds us as Americans in the political sphere." Government policies, it said, should concern "not cultural but political assimilation," which the group defined as "embracing the principles of American democracy, identifying with U.S. history, and communicating in English."

Distinguishing between the political and cultural spheres of the American identity, however, did not address the question of whether the United States should have a common *political culture*, meaning the values, attitudes, and beliefs that shape the nation's approach to politics. Issues such as minority rights, civil liberties, the role of the state, and the place of religion in public life were largely unresolved. What, for example, was the significance of the national motto, *E pluribus unum*, which is usually translated as "Out of many, one"? One of the most provocative offerings about American identity came from the liberal historian Arthur Schlesinger, Jr., who claimed that a "cult of ethnicity has arisen among non-Anglo whites and among nonwhite minorities" and that it was endangering a distinctive American identity. "It belittles *unum* and glorifies *pluribus*," he wrote in his book *The Disuniting of America*. He detected a slackening commitment to America's unique goal, which he said "was not to preserve old cultures, but to forge a new American culture."

Schlesinger's critics countered that his "*unum*" was simply a white Anglo-Saxon construct reflective of an earlier, less diverse America, and that it could not possibly bind all Americans in the post-1965 period, whether laudable or not. "A nation of more than 130 cultural groups cannot hope to have all of them Anglo-Saxonized," wrote Molefi Kete Asante in his book *The Painful Demise of Eurocentrism*. Asante, a professor of African American Studies at Temple University, argued that Schlesinger and others who wrote critically of multiculturalism were not only out of touch with the contemporary U.S. reality but were actually advocating a vision that would divide Americans, not bring them together. "Since the American idea is not a static but a dynamic one," Asante said, "we must constantly reinvent ourselves in the light of our diverse experiences. One reason this nation works the way it does is our diversity. Try to make Africans and Asians copies of Europeans…and you will force the disunity Schlesinger fears."

Even the multiculturalists like Asante, however, recognized that "Americanization" brought certain obligations. Many immigrants were not accustomed to living in diverse communities, and accepting American values meant learning to respect people of different racial and cultural backgrounds. Americans of white Anglo-Saxon parentage had to appreciate the Asian or African experience, but Asians and Africans were also obliged to appreciate each other. The U.S. Commission on Immigration Reform chaired by Barbara Jordan of Texas devoted an entire chapter of its final report to "Americanization," focusing on the importance of "a covenant between immigrant and nation." The United States, the commission concluded, "assumes an obligation to those it admits, as immigrants assume an obligation to the country they chose." The commission emphasized that immigration is a voluntary act, and that those foreigners who choose to become U.S. citizens must necessarily accept certain principles, including the elevation of individual rights over collective rights. "Unlike other countries, including those from which many immigrants come," the commission said, "rights in the United States are not defined by ethnicity, religion, or membership in any group nor can immigrants be denied rights because they are members of a particular ethnic, religious, or political group." Whether such a formulation is inherently European or universal might be debated, but it would seem to put limits on the celebration of diversity per se. To adopt a position of pure cultural relativism would be to accept some customs or traditions that are antithetical to broadly accepted American values and norms. Forced marriage or genital mutilation are not to be tolerated,

G

while freedom of expression and women's rights are not to be abridged, regardless of how other cultures or countries view such issues.

The elaboration of an American political culture that guarantees freedoms but also respects diversity is inevitably a challenge in an era when so many people of such different backgrounds are coming together. "The mutual antipathy of tribes is one of the oldest things in the world," Schlesinger observed. "Mass migrations produce mass antagonisms. The fear of the Other is among the most instinctive human reactions." While his detractors rejected Schlesinger's diagnosis of what ailed the American nation, they could not dispute the potential for conflict he identified in a more diverse America. The bigger questions were what diversity meant and how to deal with it. The critics of immigration regularly cited the prospect of increased ethnic conflict as a reason for limiting the foreign influx. Otis Graham, one of the founders of the modern restriction movement, highlighted the possibility of "weakening social cohesion, mounting class and ethnoracial division, and even regional separatism." Schlesinger argued that the multiculturalists were making things worse by not promoting commonality; the multiculturalists countered that the solution was to respect different cultural traditions.

Robert Putnam, a Harvard political scientist famous for his analysis of how and when Americans bond with each other, addressed the issue in a 2006 lecture he titled "E Pluribus Unum: Diversity and Community in the Twenty-first Century." Noting the increased ethnic diversity in the United States and other advanced countries due to rising immigration, Putnam said the consequence in the short run was reduced social solidarity. "New evidence from the U.S.," he wrote, "suggests that in ethnically diverse neighborhoods, residents of all races tend to 'hunker down.' Trust (even of one's own race) is lower, altruism and community cooperation rarer, friends fewer." But this was only a short-term phenomenon. "In the long run," he said, "successful immigrant societies have overcome such fragmentation by creating new, cross-cutting forms of solidarity and more encompassing identities." Social behavior in this vein featured what he called "bridging" interactions between individuals of different cultural backgrounds, and he saw this as an area that could be supported by public policy and institutions. "My hunch," he said, "is that at the end we shall see that the challenge is best met not by making 'them' like 'us,' but rather by creating a new, more capacious sense of 'we.'" ∎

AUTHOR PROFILE

Tom Gjelten (b. 1948) is an acclaimed journalist who has worked at National Public Radio (NPR) since 1982. During that time, he has covered varied issues both as a foreign and domestic correspondent. Gjelten was reporting from the Pentagon on September 11, 2001 when it was hit and served as NPR's lead Pentagon reporter at the beginning of the war in Afghanistan. Much of his work has focused on notions of nation-building and immigration both in the United States and around the world. He is the author of several books, including *A Nation of Nations: A Great American Immigration Story*, published in 2015. "Should Immigration Require Assimilation?" was first published in *The Atlantic* on Oct. 3, 2015.

Coming to Class Consciousness

By bell hooks

As a child I often wanted things money could buy that my parents could not afford and would not get. Rather than tell us we did not get some material thing because money was lacking, mama would frequently manipulate us in an effort to make the desire go away. Sometimes she would belittle and shame us about the object of our desire. That's what I remember most. That lovely yellow dress I wanted would become in her storytelling mouth a really ugly mammy-made thing that no girl who cared about her looks would desire. My desires were often made to seem worthless and stupid. I learned to mistrust and silence them. I learned that the more clearly I named my desires, the more unlikely those desires would ever be fulfilled.

I learned that my inner life was more peaceful if I did not think about money, or allow myself to indulge in any fantasy of desire. I learned the art of sublimation and repression. I learned it was better to make do with acceptable material desires than to articulate the unacceptable. Before I knew money mattered, I had often chosen objects to desire that were costly, things a girl of my class would not ordinarily desire. But then I was still a girl who was unaware of class, who did not think my desires were stupid and wrong. And when I found they were I let them go. I concentrated on survival, on making do.

When I was choosing a college to attend, the issue of money surfaced and had to be talked about. While I would seek loans and scholarships, even if everything related to school was paid for, there would still be transportation to pay for, books, and a host of other hidden costs. Letting me know that there was no extra money to be had, mama urged me to attend any college nearby that would offer financial aid. My first year of college I went to a school close to home. A plain-looking white woman recruiter had sat in our living room and explained to my parents that everything would be taken care of, that I would be awarded a full academic scholarship, that they would have to pay nothing. They knew better. They knew there was still transportation, clothes, all the hidden costs. Still they found this school acceptable. They could drive me there and pick me up. I would not need to come home for holidays. I could make do.

After my parents dropped me at the predominately white women's college, I saw the terror in my roommate's face that she was going to be housed with someone black, and I requested a change. She had no doubt also voiced her concern. I was given a tiny single room by the stairs—a room usually denied a first-year student—but I was a first-year black student, a scholarship girl who could never in a million years have afforded to pay her way or absorb the cost of a single room. My fellow students kept their distance from me. I ate in the cafeteria and did not have to worry about who would pay for pizza and drinks in the world outside. I kept my desires to myself, my lacks and my loneliness; I made do.

149

I rarely shopped. Boxes came from home, with brand-new clothes mama had purchased. Even though it was never spoken she did not want me to feel ashamed among privileged white girls. I was the only black girl in my dorm. There was no room in me for shame. I felt contempt and disinterest. With their giggles and their obsession to marry, the white girls at the women's college were aliens. We did not reside on the same planet. I lived in the world of books. The one white woman who became my close friend found me there reading. I was hiding under the shadows of a tree with huge branches, the kinds of trees that just seemed to grow effortlessly on well-to-do college campuses. I sat on the "perfect" grass reading poetry, wondering how the grass around me could be so lovely and yet when daddy had tried to grow grass in the front yard of Mr. Porter's house it always turned yellow or brown and then died. Endlessly, the yard defeated him, until finally he gave up. The outside of the house looked good but the yard always hinted at the possibility of endless neglect. The yard looked poor.

Foliage and trees on the college grounds flourished. Greens were lush and deep. From my place in the shadows I saw a fellow student sitting alone weeping. Her sadness had to do with all the trivia that haunted our day's classwork, the fear of not being smart enough, of losing financial aid (like me she had loans and scholarships, though her family paid some), and boys. Coming from an Illinois family of Czechoslovakian immigrants she understood class.

When she talked about the other girls who flaunted their wealth and family background there was a hard edge of contempt, anger, and envy in her voice. Envy was always something I pushed away from my psyche. Kept too close for comfort envy could lead to infatuation and on to desire. I desired nothing that they had. She desired everything, speaking her desires openly without shame. Growing up in the kind of community where there was constant competition to see who could buy the bigger better whatever, in a world of organized labor, of unions and strikes, she understood a world of bosses and workers, of haves and have-nots.

White friends I had known in high school wore their class privilege modestly. Raised, like myself, in church traditions that taught us to identify only with the poor, we knew that there was evil in excess. We knew rich people were rarely allowed into heaven. God had given them a paradise of bounty on earth and they had not shared. The rare ones, the rich people who shared, were the only ones able to meet the divine in paradise, and even then it was harder for them to find their way. According to the high school friends we knew, flaunting wealth was frowned upon in our world, frowned upon by God and community.

The few women I befriended my first year in college were not wealthy. They were the ones who shared with me stories of the other girls flaunting the fact that they could buy anything expensive—clothes, food, vacations. There were not many of us from working class backgrounds; we knew who we were. Most girls from poor backgrounds tried to blend in, or fought back by triumphing over wealth with beauty or style or some combination of the above. Being black made me an automatic outsider. Holding their world in contempt pushed me further to the edge. One of the fun things the "in" girls did was choose someone and trash their room. Like so much else deemed cute by insiders, I dreaded the thought of strangers entering my space and going through my things. Being outside the in crowd made me an unlikely target. Being contemptuous made me first on the list. I did not understand. And when my room was trashed it unleashed my rage and deep grief over not being able to protect my space from violation and invasion. I hated that girls who had so much, took so much for granted, never considered that those of us who did not have mad money would not be able to replace broken things, perfume poured out, or talcum powder spread everywhere—that we did not know everything could be taken care of at the dry cleaner's because we never took our clothes there. My rage fueled by contempt was deep, strong, and long lasting. Daily it stood as a challenge to their fun, to their habits of being.

Nothing they did to win me over worked. It came as a great surprise. They had always believed black girls wanted to be white girls, wanted to possess their world. My stoney gaze, silence, and absolute refusal to cross the threshold of their world was total mystery; it was for them a violation they needed to avenge. After trashing my room, they tried to win me over with apologies and urges to talk and understand. There was nothing about me I wanted them to understand. Everything about their world was overexposed, on the surface.

One of my English professors had attended Stanford University. She felt that was the place for me to go—a place where intellect was valued over foolish fun and games and dress up, and finding a husband did not overshadow academic work. She had gone to Stanford. I had never thought about the state of California. Getting my parents to agree to my leaving Kentucky to attend a college in a nearby state had been hard enough. They had accepted a college they could reach by car, but a college thousands of miles away was beyond their imagination. Even I had difficulty grasping going that far away from home. The lure for me was the promise of journeying and arriving at a destination where I would be accepted and understood.

All the barely articulated understandings of class privilege that I had learned my first year of college had not hipped me to the reality of class shame. It still had not dawned on me that my parents, especially mama, resolutely refused to acknowledge any difficulties with money because her sense of shame around class was deep and intense. And when this shame was coupled with her need to feel that she had risen above the low-class backwoods culture of her family, it was impossible for her to talk in a straightforward manner about the strains it would put on the family for me to attend Stanford.

All I knew then was that, as with all my desires, I was told that this desire was impossible to fulfill. At first it was not talked about in relation to money, it was talked about in relation to sin. California was an evil place, a modern-day Babylon where souls were easily seduced away from the path of righteousness. It was not a place for an innocent young girl to go on her own. Mama brought the message back that my father had absolutely refused to give permission.

I expressed my disappointment through ongoing unrelenting grief. I explained to mama that other parents wanted their children to go to good schools. It still had not dawned on me that my parents knew nothing about "good" schools. Even though I knew mama had not graduated from high school I still held her in awe. Mama and daddy were awesome authority figures—family fascists of a very high order. As children we knew that it was better not to doubt their word or their knowledge. We blindly trusted them.

A crucial aspect of our family fascism was that we were not allowed much contact with other families. We were rarely allowed to go to someone's house. We knew better than to speak about our family in other people's homes. While we caught glimpses of different habits of being, different ways of doing things in other families, we knew that to speak of those ways at our home, to try to use them to influence or change our parents, was to risk further confinement.

Our dad had traveled to foreign countries as a soldier but he did not speak of these experiences. Safety, we had been religiously taught in our household, was always to be found close to home. We were not a family who went on vacations, who went exploring. When relatives from large cities would encourage mama to let us children go back with them, their overtures were almost always politely refused. Once mama agreed that I could go to Chicago to visit an elderly cousin, Schuyler—a name strange and beautiful on our lips.

Retired Cousin Schuyler lived a solitary life in a basement flat of the brownstone he shared with Lovie, his wife of many years. Vocationally a painter, he did still lifes and nudes. When they came to visit us, Mama had shown them the painting I had done that won a school prize. It was a portrait of a poor lonely boy with sad eyes. Despite our class background all of us took art classes in school. By high school the disinterested had forgotten about art and only those of us who were committed to doing art, to staying close to an artistic environment, remained. For some that closeness was just a kindly voyeurism. They had talent but were simply not sufficiently interested to use it. Then there were folks like me, full of passion and talent, but without the material resources to do art. Making art was for people with money.

I understood this when my parents adamantly refused to have my painting framed. Only framed work could be in the show. My art teacher, an Italian immigrant who always wore black, showed me how to make a frame from pieces of wood found in the trash. Like my granddaddy he was a lover of found objects. Both of them were men without resources who managed to love beauty and survive. In high school art classes we talked about beauty—about aesthetics. But it was after class that I told the teacher how I had learned these things already from my grandmother.

Each year students would choose an artist and study their work and then do work in that same tradition. I chose abstract expressionism and the work of Willem de Kooning. Choosing to paint a house in autumn, the kind of house I imagined living in, with swirls of color—red, yellow, brown—I worked for hours after class, trying to give this house the loneliness I felt inside. This painting was my favorite. I showed it to Cousin Schuyler along with the image of the lonely boy.

It remains a mystery how Schuyler and Lovie convinced mama that it would be fine to let me spend some time with them in Chicago—my first big city. Traveling to Chicago was my first sojourn out of the apartheid south. It was my first time in a world where I saw black people working at all types of jobs. They worked at the post office delivering mail, in factories, driving buses, collecting garbage—black people with good jobs. This new world was awesome. It was a world where black people had power. I worked in a little store owned by a black male friend of my aunt. The wife of this friend had her own beauty parlor but no children. They had money.

Lovie talked to me about class. There were low-class folks one should not bother with. She insisted one should aim high. These were big city ideas. In our small town community we had been taught to see everyone as worthy. Mama especially preached that you should never see yourself as better than anyone, that no matter anyone's lot in life they deserved respect. Mama preached this even though she aimed high. These messages confused me. The big city was too awesome and left me afraid.

Yet it also changed my perspective, for it had shown me a world where black people could be artists. And what I saw was that artists barely survived. No one in my family wanted me to pursue art; they wanted me to get a good job, to be a teacher. Painting was something to do when real work was done. Once, maybe twice even, I expressed my desire to be an artist. That became an occasion for dire warning and laughter, since like so many desires it was foolish, hence the laughter. Since foolish girls are likely to do foolish things dire warnings had to come after the laughter. Black folks could not make a living as artists. They pointed to the one example—the only grown-up black artist they knew, Cousin Schuyler, living in a dark basement like some kind of mole or rat.

Like everything else the choice to be an artist was talked about in terms of race, not class. The substance of the warnings was always to do with the untalked-about reality of class in America. I did not think about being an artist anymore. I struggled with the more immediate question of where to continue college, of how to find a place where I would not feel like such an alien.

When my parents refused to permit me to attend Stanford, I accepted the verdict for awhile. Overwhelmed by grief, I could barely speak for weeks. Mama intervened and tried to change my father's mind as folks she respected in the outside world told her what a privilege it was for me to have this opportunity, that Stanford University was a good school for a smart girl. Without their permission I decided I would go. And even though she did not give her approval mama was willing to help.

My decision made conversations about money necessary. Mama explained that California was too far away, that it would always "cost" to get there, that if something went wrong they would not be able to come and rescue me, that I would not be able to come home for holidays. I heard all this but its meaning did not sink in. I was just relieved I would not be returning to the women's college, to the place where I had truly been an outsider.

There were other black students at Stanford. There was even a dormitory where many black students lived. I did not know I could choose to live there. I went where I was assigned. Going to Stanford was the first time I flew somewhere. Only mama stood and waved farewell as I left to take the bus to the airport. I left with a heavy heart, feeling both excitement and dread. I knew nothing about the world I was journeying to. Not knowing made me afraid but my fear of staying in place was greater.

H

Since we do not talk about class in this society and since information is never shared or talked about freely in a fascist family, I had no idea what was ahead of me. In small ways I was ignorant. I had never been on an escalator, a city bus, an airplane, or a subway. I arrived in San Francisco with no understanding that Palo Alto was a long drive away—that it would take money to find transportation there. I decided to take the city bus. With all my cheap overpacked bags I must have seemed like just another innocent immigrant when I struggled to board the bus.

This was a city bus with no racks for luggage. It was filled with immigrants. English was not spoken. I felt lost and afraid. Without words the strangers surrounding me understood the universal language of need and distress. They reached for my bags, holding and helping. In return I told them my story—that I had left my village in the South to come to Stanford University, that like them my family were workers, they worked the land—they worked in the world. They were workers. They understood workers. I would go to college and learn how to make a world where they would not have to work so hard.

When I arrived at my destination, the grown-ups in charge cautioned me about trusting strangers, telling me what I already knew, that I was no longer in my town, that nothing was the same. On arriving I called home. Before I could speak, I began to weep as I heard the far-away sound of mama's voice. I tried to find the words, to slow down, to tell her how it felt to be a stranger, to speak my uncertainty and longing. She told me this is the lot I had chosen. I must live with it. After her words there was only silence. She had hung up on me—let me go into this world where I am a stranger still.

Stanford University was a place where one could learn about class from the ground up. Built by a man who believed in hard work, it was to have been a place where students of all classes would come, women and men, to work together and learn. It was to be a place of equality and communalism. His vision was seen by many as almost communist. The fact that he was rich made it all less threatening. Perhaps no one really believed the vision could be realized. The university was named after his son who had died young, a son who had carried his name but who had no future money could buy. No amount of money can keep death away. But it could keep memory alive. And so we work and learn in buildings that remind us of a young son carried away by death too soon, of a father's unrelenting grief remembered.

Everything in the landscape of my new world fascinated me, the plants brought from a rich man's travels all over the world back to this place of water and clay. At Stanford University adobe buildings blend with Japanese plum trees and leaves of kumquat. On my way to study medieval literature, I ate my first kumquat. Surrounded by flowering cactus and a South American shrub bougainvillea of such trailing beauty it took my breath away, I was in a landscape of dreams, full of hope and possibility. If nothing else would hold me, I would not remain a stranger to the earth. The ground I stood on would know me.

Class was talked about behind the scenes. The sons and daughters from rich, famous, or notorious families were identified. The grown-ups in charge of us were always looking out for a family who might give their millions to the college. At

Stanford my classmates wanted to know me, thought it hip, cute, and downright exciting to have a black friend. They invited me on the expensive vacations and ski trips I could not afford. They offered to pay. I never went. Along with other students who were not from privileged families, I searched for places to go during the holiday times when the dormitory was closed. We got together and talked about the assumption that everyone had money to travel and would necessarily be leaving. The staff would be on holiday as well, so all students had to leave. Now and then the staff did not leave and we were allowed to stick around. Once, I went home with one of the women who cleaned for the college.

Now and then when she wanted to make extra money mama would work as a maid. Her decision to work outside the home was seen as an act of treason by our father. At Stanford I was stunned to find that there were maids who came by regularly to vacuum and tidy our rooms. No one had ever cleaned up behind me and I did not want them to. At first I roomed with another girl from a working-class background—a beautiful white girl from Orange County who looked like pictures I had seen on the cover of *Seventeen* magazine. Her mother had died of cancer during her high school years and she had since been raised by her father. She had been asked by the college officials if she would find it problematic to have a black roommate. A scholarship student like myself, she knew her preferences did not matter and as she kept telling me, she did not really care.

Like my friend during freshman year she shared the understanding of what it was like to be a have-not in a world of haves. But unlike me she was determined to become one of them. If it meant she had to steal nice clothes to look the same as they did, she had no problem taking these risks. If it meant having a privileged boyfriend who left bruises on her body now and then, it was worth the risk. Cheating was worth it. She believed the world the privileged had created was all unfair—all one big cheat; to get ahead one had to play the game. To her I was truly an innocent, a lamb being led to the slaughter. It did not surprise her one bit when I began to crack under the pressure of contradictory values and longings.

Like all students who did not have seniority, I had to see the school psychiatrists to be given permission to live off campus. Unaccustomed to being around strangers, especially strangers who did not share or understand my values, I found the experience of living in the dorms difficult. Indeed, almost everyone around me believed working-class folks had no values. At the university where the founder, Leland Stanford, had imagined different classes meeting on common ground, I learned how deeply individuals with class privilege feared and hated the working classes. Hearing classmates express contempt and hatred toward people who did not come from the right backgrounds shocked me. Naively, I believed them to be so young to hold those views, so devoid of life experiences that would serve to uphold or make sense of these thoughts. I had always worked. Working-class people had always encouraged and supported me.

To survive in this new world of divided classes, this world where I was also encountering for the first time a black bourgeois elite that was as contemptuous of working people as their white counterparts were, I had to take a stand, to get clear my own class affiliations. This was the most difficult truth to face. Having been taught all my life to believe that black people were inextricably bound in solidarity

155

by our struggles to end racism, I did not know how to respond to elitist black people who were full of contempt for anyone who did not share their class, their way of life.

At Stanford I encountered for the first time a black diaspora. Of the few black professors present, the vast majority were from African or Caribbean backgrounds. Elites themselves, they were only interested in teaching other elites. Poor folks like myself, with no background to speak of, were invisible. We were not seen by them or anyone else. Initially, I went to all meetings welcoming black students, but when I found no one to connect with I retreated. In the shadows I had time and books to teach me about the nature of class—about the ways black people were divided from themselves.

Despite this rude awakening, my disappointment at finding myself estranged from the group of students I thought would understand, I still looked for connections. I met an older black male graduate student who also came from a working-class background. Even though he had gone to the right high school, a California school for gifted students, and then to Princeton as an undergraduate, he understood intimately the intersections of race and class. Good in sports and in the classroom, he had been slotted early on to go far, to go where other black males had not gone. He understood the system. Academically, he fit. Had he wanted to, he could have been among the elite but he chose to be on the margins, to hang with an intellectual artistic avant garde. He wanted to live in a world of the mind where there was no race or class. He wanted to worship at the throne of art and knowledge. He became my mentor, comrade, and companion.

When we were not devoting ourselves to books and to poetry we confronted a real world where we were in need of jobs. Even though I taught an occasional class, I worked in the world of the mundane. I worked at a bookstore, cooked at a club, worked for the telephone company. My way out of being a maid, of doing the dirty work of cleaning someone else's house, was to become a schoolteacher. The thought terrified me. From grade school on I feared and hated the classroom. In my imagination it was still the ultimate place of inclusion and exclusion, discipline and punishment—worse than the fascist family because there was no connection of blood to keep in check impulses to search and destroy.

Now and then a committed college professor opened my mind to the reality that the classroom could be a place of passion and possibility, but, in general, at the various colleges I attended it was the place where the social order was kept in place. Throughout my graduate student years, I was told again and again that I lacked the proper decorum of a graduate student, that I did not understand my place. Slowly I began to understand fully that there was no place in academe for folks from working-class backgrounds who did not wish to leave the past behind. That was the price of the ticket. Poor students would be welcome at the best institutions of higher learning only if they were willing to surrender memory, to forget the past and claim the assimilated present as the only worthwhile and meaningful reality.

Students from nonprivileged backgrounds who did not want to forget often had nervous breakdowns. They could not bear the weight of all the contradictions they had to confront. They were crushed. More often than not they dropped out with no trace of their inner anguish recorded, no institutional record of the myriad ways their take on the world was assaulted by an elite vision of class and privilege. The records merely indicated that even after receiving financial aid and other support, these students simply could not make it, simply were not good enough.

At no time in my years as a student did I march in a graduation ceremony. I was not proud to hold degrees from institutions where I had been constantly scorned and shamed. I wanted to forget these experiences, to erase them from my consciousness. Like a prisoner set free I did not want to remember my years on the inside. When I finished my doctorate I felt too much uncertainty about who I had become. Uncertain about whether I had managed to make it through without giving up the best of myself, the best of the values I had been raised to believe in—hard work, honesty, and respect for everyone no matter their class—I finished my education with my allegiance to the working class intact. Even so, I had planted my feet on the path leading in the direction of class privilege. There would always be contradictions to face. There would always be confrontations around the issue of class. I would always have to reexamine where I stand. ∎

AUTHOR PROFILE

bell hooks (b. 1952) is a teacher, author, and renowned critical theorist and activist. hooks received her B.A. from Stanford University, her M.A. from the University of Wisconsin, and her Ph.D. from the University of California, Santa Cruz. The focus of hooks' writing has been the intersectionality of race, capitalism, and gender, and what she describes as their ability to produce and perpetuate systems of oppression and class domination. She has published over 30 books and numerous scholarly articles, appeared in documentary films, and participated in public lectures. Notable books include *Ain't I a Woman: Black Women and Feminism* (1981), *Feminist Theory from Margin to Center* (1984), *Teaching to Transgress: Education as the Practice of Freedom* (1994), *Killing Rage: Ending Racism* (1995), *Reel to Real: Race, Sex, and Class at the Movies* (1996), and *The Will to Change: Men, Masculinity, and Love* (2004). She has held positions as Professor of African-American Studies and English at Yale University, Associate Professor of Women's Studies and American Literature at Oberlin College in Oberlin, Ohio, as Distinguished Lecturer of English Literature at the City College of New York, and Scholar in Residence at The New School in Manhattan. In 2014, she founded the bell hooks Institute at Berea College in Berea, Kentucky. "Coming to Class Consciousness" is chapter two of her book, *Where We Stand: Class Matters* (2000).

H

A Small Italian Town Can Teach the World How to Defuse Controversial Monuments

By Carlo Invernizzi-Accetti

Coming to terms with national history isn't always easy. Whether because of civil war, political oppression, or simply a change of values, monuments and other vestiges of the past often remind us that what we held dear in other ages doesn't necessarily chime with what we cherish today. The bitter controversy—and deadly protests—sparked earlier this year by the proposed removal of a statue of Gen Robert E Lee in Charlottesville, Virginia, are a ringing reminder of this.

The small northern Italian town of Bolzano may provide the model for a better way of dealing with such thorny issues. For several decades, what are now the town's financial offices have been housed in a fascist-era building displaying a massive bas-relief of Benito Mussolini on horseback, bearing the slogan "Credere, Obbedire, Combattere" ("Believe, Obey, Combat") on the side. Although Italy's fascist past is officially condemned, the monument stood untouched until a 2011 directive from the national government formally required the municipal administration to do something about it.

In the face of calls to both "destroy" and "preserve" the monument, the town opted for what appears in retrospect a far smarter strategy.

A public bid was launched, soliciting ideas over how to "defuse and contextualize" the politically charged frieze. Open to artists, architects, historians, and "anyone involved in the cultural sphere", the bid explicitly stated that the intention was to "transform the bas-relief into a place of memory…so that it will no longer be visible directly, but accessible thoughtfully, within an appropriately explanatory context".

Almost 500 proposals were submitted and evaluated by a jury composed of local civil society figures, including a history professor, a museum curator, an architect, an artist and a journalist. This jury recommended five proposals, voted upon by the municipal council. All the proposals and proceedings were documented online and open to public scrutiny.

The winning proposal is as powerful as it is simple. Superimposed upon the bas-relief is now an LED-illuminated inscription of a quote by the German Jewish philosopher Hannah Arendt that reads "Nobody has the right to obey" in the three local languages: Italian, German and Ladin.

As the two artists who originally made the proposal, Arnold Holzknecht and Michele Bernardi, elucidate in their explanatory text, the "minimalism" of the intervention is explicitly meant to contrast the "grandiloquence" of the fascist-era style, whereas the content of the quotation is meant as a "direct answer" to the "invitation to blind obedience" contained in the fascist slogan.

What is most important, however, is that the original monument remains visible through the inscription. This is meant to emphasize that memory—and therefore history—is not a "blank slate" on which we can arbitrarily write whatever happens to be congenial to us in the present. Rather, it is a process of sedimentation, by which the past is never completely effaced, but constantly reinterpreted through the lens of the present.

The transformed monument therefore invites people to reflect on the town's complex history in a way that is neither simply celebratory nor in denial, but rather contextualized—and for that reason all the more challenging and profound.

A sign of its success is that it almost completely failed to generate controversy, either nationally or locally. Inaugurated with a purposely sober ceremony on 5 November, the installation only managed to stir the predictable recriminations of representatives from the local neo-fascist party, one of whom decried it as a "Taliban act" intended to "efface a portion of the country's history". The very fact that these objections so patently failed to grasp the point of the installation has given them little following.

This local experiment with the politics of memory nonetheless deserves greater attention. Virtually all existing countries have to face difficult questions over how to relate to past instances of violence, injustice and oppression—often publicly sanctioned.

Pretending the past never happened is clearly not a promising way of learning from it. But neither is passively accepting the past's own way of representing itself to the future. Which is why contextualizing monuments from a troubled era, through a creative procedure that is at once inclusive, transparent and educational, may actually be the best solution.

This is, after all, another way of reading the message contained in the quote from Hannah Arendt inscribed over the fascist monument in Bolzano. To say that "nobody has the right to obey" is a reminder that our actions are always the result of a choice—and therefore judgment—in the present.

The quote by Hannah Arendt implies that we cannot in good faith disclaim responsibility for things we have the power to act upon—such as the monuments we inherit from our history. Even letting them stand untouched is a way of affirming something in the present. The question is what we want that message to be.

Apparently, during the deliberations that preceded the decision to remove the statue of Robert E Lee in Charlottesville, Virginia, a proposal was made to add more "historical context" to the monument. That might have been an opportunity for the city to come to terms more openly and inclusively with its troubled past, but the proposal was ultimately rejected.

In contrast, the town of Bolzano has resolutely taken a stand in favor of freedom and civic courage. It is only to be hoped that other administrations facing similar problems around the world can live up to this model. ■

──────────────────────────────────── **AUTHOR PROFILE**

Carlo Invernizzi-Accetti is Assistant Professor of Political Science at The City College of New York and Associate Researcher at the Center for European Studies at the Institut d'Etudes Politiques de Paris. He holds a Ph.D. in Political Science from Columbia University and conducts research on democracy, populism, human rights, secularism, and constitutionalism. His book *Relativism and Religion: Why Democratic Societies Do Not Need Moral Absolutes* was published by Columbia University Press in 2015. Dr. Invernizzi-Accetti is also a commentator for several international media outlets and his opinion piece on "A Small Italian Town Can Teach the World How to Defuse Controversial Monuments" appeared in *The Guardian* on December 6, 2017.

Maps in the Head

By Kate Jeffery

In Lewis Carroll's *The Hunting of the Snark* (1876), the hapless snark-hunting crew found themselves presented with a navigational challenge by their captain, the Bellman:

> He had bought a large map representing the sea,
> Without the least vestige of land:
> And the crew were much pleased when they found it to be
> A map they could all understand.

Refreshingly uncluttered, the Bellman's map had nothing on it:

> 'Other maps are such shapes, with their islands and capes!
> But we've got our brave Captain to thank'
> (So the crew would protest) 'that he's bought us the best—
> A perfect and absolute blank!'

Even a perfectly blank map, however, could be useful if it had a grid reference, something to indicate compass direction, a scale, and a marker for current position. Sadly, the Bellman's map had none of these things:

> 'What's the good of Mercator's North Poles and Equators,
> Tropics, Zones, and Meridian Lines?'
> So the Bellman would cry: and the crew would reply
> 'They are merely conventional signs!...'

So, the map was truly blank and not much use for navigating.

We humans have been mapping space for many centuries, and our maps have greatly improved over this time so that now they are *very* useful for navigating. In antiquity, maps such as the beautiful *Mappa Mundi* did have features of the landscape—islands and capes—that were arranged in roughly the right relationship to each other; but the scale was wrong, the shapes of the coastlines were wrong, and there was no convention to place North at the top of the page as we do nowadays. They were exquisite as illustrations, but little use for navigating because they lacked metric (measurement) information such as distance and direction. They also had nothing to measure distances and directions *from*, which in modern maps are called reference points, lines and planes. As maps evolved over the centuries, however, map-makers added metric information in the form of direction (North and South) and distances (latitude and longitude lines), as well as reference points (North and South poles), reference lines (the Greenwich Meridian and the Equator) and, eventually, when we started to move above and below ground, a reference plane (sea level). A map with all this information is useful even without islands and capes.

Maps are for humans, but how do animals, which began navigating millions of years before parchment was invented, manage to find *their* way around? Do animal (and human) brains contain a map, and if so does it have islands and capes, North Poles and Equators, reference lines and so on? And if they do, where is it, and how does it work? How could a jelly-like blob of protoplasm contain anything as structured as a map?

These questions have intrigued biologists for many decades, particularly because animals can perform astonishing feats such as navigating their way from the North Pole to the South and back again, like the Arctic tern; or returning home after being transported hundreds of miles away, like the homing pigeon. How animals (both human and non-human) work out their location is just beginning to be understood by brain scientists. There *are* maps in the brain, as it happens. The properties of these maps, which neuroscientists call 'cognitive maps', have turned out to be highly intriguing, and are helping us to understand not just how animals navigate, but also more general principles about how the brain forms, stores and retrieves knowledge.

The neuroscientist John O'Keefe discovered cognitive maps in the 1970s. His research ultimately won him a share of the 2014 Nobel Prize in Physiology or Medicine. O'Keefe was not looking for maps in the brain. Newly arrived at University College London (UCL) from McGill University in Canada, he was actually interested in memory. Specifically, he was trying to understand a discovery that had been made a few years earlier by the neurosurgeon William Beecher Scoville and his colleague, the neuropsychologist Brenda Milner, which seemed to provide clues about how memories are formed and stored. Scoville and Milner were fascinated by one of Scoville's neurosurgical patients, a young man known to the world by his initials 'HM'. He had undergone surgery to cure his epilepsy and, tragically, developed amnesia as a result. Scoville and Milner thought his amnesia might be due to damage to his hippocampus. The idea that the hippocampus might be linked with memory was very exciting to brain scientists, as they had started to think that memory might not have *a* special location in the brain.

Previous attempts to pin down where memories are stored had failed dismally. In the early 20th century, the Russian physiologist Ivan Pavlov, who had been studying learning in dogs, had suggested that memory consists of a complex web of associations formed between 'representations' in an animal's brain. The genius and dominance of Pavlov's idea meant that for many decades the prevailing view of learning was one in which even complex behaviours might be explained simply by the formation of associations between so-called stimuli and either other stimuli or responses. Famously, he conditioned dogs to form an association between the sound of a bell and the appearance of food. Translated into the language of neuroscience, this same process of association consisted of the formation of connections between neurons activated by the bell, which we might say 'represent' the bell, and the neurons activated by food. This idea received a boost when the Canadian psychologist Donald Hebb suggested that memories could be formed by changing the connections between simultaneously active neurons across the brain, to make their communication easier in future—a simple and yet profoundly influential idea. By following Hebb's rule, the simultaneous activity of the bell neuron and the food neuron should cause the connection between them to become stronger, so that next time the animal heard the bell, its food neuron would more easily be stimulated—memory retrieval in action.

Neuroscientists speculated about what this would look like in physical terms, in the brain itself. When a representation is activated, in recalling a memory for instance, what do neurons actually do? The brain is just a lump of flesh and blood, and yet our memories feel like replayed movies, very graphic and dynamic. We clearly don't have tiny movies playing in our brains when we think or remember, so how could this actually work, and whereabouts in the brain does it happen?

The answer to all this has been something of a Holy Grail for psychologists and neuroscientists. The American psychologist Karl Lashley was an early researcher in this area. He followed Pavlov's approach of studying very simple learning under tightly controlled conditions, hypothesising that if an animal learned a new association, then it should be possible to find the site of this association in the brain by making small lesions in it at specific points, to see precisely when the animal suddenly forgot what it had just learned. His attempts failed completely, and in 1950 he concluded, with joking despair: 'I sometimes feel, on reviewing the evidence of the localisation of the memory trace, that the necessary conclusion is that learning just is not possible.' Scientists began to doubt that memory was located in *a* place in the brain. Perhaps, instead, it was distributed in various regions. This distributed view of memory had, however, to be re-thought in 1957 when Scoville and Milner published their study of HM. At last someone seemed to have found a specific place in the brain—the hippocampus—in which damage caused profound memory problems.

Might the hippocampus be a memory organ buried deep in the brain? This was the question that led O'Keefe, in his new lab at UCL, to try to record the firing of single neurons from the hippocampus, to see if he could see memories being formed. His task was not an easy one. Neurons work by 'talking' among themselves, via nerve impulses or 'action potentials'—each neuron receives impulses sent to it from other neurons, and if it receives enough of these, it in turn generates an impulse of its own. These signals are minute—a few millivolts in size—and can be detected only by placing a tiny detector right next to a few neurons, and monitoring the electrical blips produced as the cells chatter to each other. By listening to this chatter with recording equipment, it is possible to work out what types of things each neuron is interested in. Using this technique, O'Keefe and his student Jonathan Dostrovsky set about recording hippocampal neurons to find out what they do on a normal day in a normal rat that was just foraging around for food. They made a remarkable discovery. Some neurons in the hippocampus would become active only when the rat walked into a particular place in its environment. After many control experiments to see if the cells were being activated by particular sights, sounds or smells, O'Keefe concluded that these cells were being stimulated simply by the rat's being in a particular place, and so he named these neurons 'place cells'.

Instead of memory, O'Keefe seemed to have stumbled on a map in the brain, and he said as much in *The Hippocampus as a Cognitive Map* (1978), co-written with the neuropsychologist Lynn Nadel. Their basic idea was that neurons in the hippocampus form a memory of the animal's environment, so that when the animal goes to a particular place, neurons representing that place become active, as if reminded about that place. However, this idea of a map in the hippocampus was not well-received, and generated a great deal of controversy. In fact, the idea that the brain *could* make a map pre-dated O'Keefe by some decades, and it had not been well-received back then either. The American psychologist Edward Tolman had already suggested this in 1948, on the basis of his studies of how rats find their way around mazes.

Tolman was working in the Behaviourist era that Pavlov had initiated. Pavlov's idea that all learning takes place by the formation of connections between representations is simple and yet very powerful, and it still holds sway today. However, for most of the previous century, the competing notion of cognitive 'representation' was an extremely limited one, and just meant activation of neurons by simple sensory stimuli (bells and food, etc). Psychologists were resistant to attributing behaviour to such invisible and magical-seeming internal processes as 'thought' and 'imagination' if there might be a simpler explanation in plain sight. Behaviourists explained learning as animals linking very simple sets of associations—'if I turn left here, a good thing will happen', and so on.

Tolman, however, discovered that rats were able to do things in mazes that they shouldn't be able to do according to Behaviourism. They could figure out shortcuts and detours, for example, even if they hadn't learned about these. How could they possibly do this? Tolman was convinced animals must have something like a map in their brains, which he called a 'cognitive map', otherwise their ability to discover shortcuts would make no sense. Behaviourists were skeptical. Some years later, when O'Keefe and Nadel laid out in detail why they thought the hippocampus might be Tolman's cognitive map, scientists were still skeptical.

One of the difficulties was that nobody could imagine what a map in the brain would be like. Representing associations between simple things, such as bells and food, is one thing; but how to represent *places*? This seemed to require the mystical unseen internal 'black box' processes (thought and imagination) that Behaviourists had worked so hard to eradicate from their theories. Opponents of the cognitive map theory suggested that what place cells reveal about the brain is not a map, so much as a remarkable capacity to associate together complex sensations such as images, smells and textures, which all happen to come together *at* a place but aren't in themselves spatial.

Is the hippocampus a map, or an all-purpose association device used for all types of sensory stimuli? How could we even decide between these two views? To understand this, we need to turn to the critical aspect of a map that makes it useful for navigation, which is that it needs to have metric information concerning distance and direction—the keystones that the Bellman's map in *The Hunting of the Snark* lacked. No amount of chaining together stimulus-response associations could inject these spatial components into a representation: the brain needs to have a way of *calculating* distances and directions based on its incoming sensory data. This type of inference is exactly the type of 'magical' internal process that Behaviourists dislike, and it wasn't until two further crucial discoveries came along that they had to admit defeat and concede that the brain might in fact be capable of metric inference.

The first discovery was made by the American physiologist Jim Ranck, who in 1984 was recording neurons from a part of the brain near the hippocampus and found that some of them fired when the animal faced in a particular direction. When several of these neurons were recorded together, Ranck and Jeffrey Taube, his colleague at the SUNY Health Sciences Center in Brooklyn, New York, realised that different brain cells fired when the rat faced different directions, as though each had the job of telling the rat's brain which way it was facing. It was as if the rat had an internal compass, except one with a different 'North' set for different rooms. Importantly, these 'head direction cells' worked the same way whether in the light or in the dark, with eyes open or closed, and anywhere in the room, so it didn't matter exactly what the rat could see, smell or touch, it mattered only which way it faced. Also, importantly, every cell always had the same firing direction relationship to every other cell: if cell A's preferred firing direction was to the left of cell B's in one room, this was so in every room. Thus, direction seems to be an intrinsic property of the system—it seems to be only the orientation of the whole representation relative to the outside world that depends on sensations and perceptions.

So, there *is* metric information about direction in the brain. What about distance? This brings us to the second major challenge to Behaviourism: the discovery of grid cells by Torkel Hafting and Marianne Fyhn, then part of a team at the Norwegian University of Science and Technology headed by Edvard and May-Britt Moser. The Mosers had been fascinated by the hippocampus since the very early days of their doctoral studies. Not long after qualifying, they visited O'Keefe's lab in London to learn how to record these mysterious place cells that were so exercising neuroscientists. They then returned to Norway to establish a new lab of their own, where they imported O'Keefe's technique and started studying inputs to the hippocampus. Their reasoning was that, to understand how place cells 'know' where the rat is, it is necessary to see what the upstream neurons are saying to them.

What the team found was rather unexpected. In the entorhinal cortex, which is the part of the brain that sends more information to the hippocampus than almost anywhere else, they found a new type of spatial cells. These cells, like place cells, fired only when the rat went into specific places in the environment, which in itself was not so surprising. What *was* surprising, though, was that they didn't just fire in *one* place, they fired in *many* places. More surprisingly still, these places together formed a remarkable, regular pattern in which each firing location was the same distance from all the neighbouring ones. This meant that the entire array of fields formed a regular hexagonal pattern, like oranges when packed in a box, as illustrated below. The distance between the fields could be small (30 cm or so) or large, depending on the cell, and was so regular that its discoverers named the cells 'grid cells'.

The importance of grid cells lies in the apparently minor detail that the patches of firing (called 'firing fields') produced by the cells are evenly spaced. That this makes a pretty pattern is nice, but not so important in itself—what *is* startling is that the cell somehow 'knows' how far (say) 30 cm is—it must do, or it wouldn't be able to fire in correctly spaced places. This even spacing of firing fields is something that couldn't possibly have arisen from building up a web of stimulus associations over the life of the animal, because 30 cm (or whatever) isn't an intrinsic property of most environments, and therefore can't come through the senses—it must come from *inside the rat*, through some distance-measuring capability such as counting footsteps, or measuring the speed with which the world flows past the senses. In other words, metric information is inherent in the brain, wired into the grid cells as it were, regardless of its prior experience. This was a surprising and dramatic discovery. Studies of other animals, including humans, have revealed place, head direction and grid cells in these species too, so this seems to be a general (and thus important) phenomenon and not just a strange quirk of the lab rat.

Grid cells were discovered in 2005, and more than a decade later we still don't know exactly what they are for, but they are believed to be the brain's equivalent of the grid reference on a map. Whatever their function, their existence does prove, however, that these structures in the brain—hippocampus, entorhinal cortex and a host of their neighbours—collaborate in forming a metric representation of space. This is a real map. It might not *look* like a conventional map because it's not written on parchment and isn't labelled with printed text and a compass rose. However, the neurons in these regions respond in a way that shows that they are somehow stimulated, not by bells and food, as the Behaviourists believed, but by abstract properties of the animal's experience, such as how far it has walked and what place it has reached. The discovery of grid cells confirmed O'Keefe's cognitive map proposal, and the Mosers and O'Keefe together shared the 2014 Nobel Prize in Physiology or Medicine 'for their discoveries of cells that constitute a positioning system in the brain'.

But where does this leave memory? This is where research in the hippocampus began: do place cells have anything to do with memory?

Yes, we think they do, and research now aims to uncover precisely what. One of the most important implications for humans, arising from study of the hippocampus, is its involvement in Alzheimer's disease, which begins in the entorhinal cortex (where the grid cells are) and spreads throughout the hippocampus and thence to the rest of the brain. The first symptom of Alzheimer's disease is often disorientation (e.g., getting lost on the way back from the shops), but this progresses rapidly to a more general amnesia. Scientists now know that the hippocampus is *both* a map *and* a memory system. For some reason, nature long ago decided that a map was a handy way to organise life's experiences. This makes a lot of sense, since knowing where things happened is a critical part of knowing how to act in the world. The quest now is to understand how memories get attached to this map. Armed with this knowledge about memory, we might one day be able to study memories directly, and even, perhaps, manipulate them—to soften traumatic memories, for example, or repair damaged ones such as those affected in Alzheimer's disease. ■

J

──────────────────────────── AUTHOR PROFILE

Kate Jeffery, originally from New Zealand, is a behavioral neuroscientist who founded and directs a laboratory at the Institute of Behavioural Neuroscience at University College London. Her laboratory explores "the cognitive map," exploring the ways that the brain handles navigation and cognition, as well as how the brain organizes memories, or the "architecture of cognition." She has published scholarly articles in journals such as *Nature Neuroscience*, the *Journal of Neuroscience*, and *Behavioural Brain Research*. "Maps in the Head" originally appeared in the digital magazine *Aeon* on January 25, 2017.

Place, Ethics, and Everyday Eating: A Tale of Two Neighbourhoods

By Josée Johnston, Alexandra Rodney, and Michelle Szabo

Introduction: Ethical Eating, Class, and Place

Sociologists, food scholars, and market researchers have devoted considerable attention to the social determinants of 'ethical eating'. The term 'ethical eating' is used in various ways, but, here, refers to food choices thought to ameliorate social and/or ecological injustices (e.g. fair trade, organics). Ethical eating[1] is best thought of as a socially constructed, contested discourse containing myriad contradictions, rather than an objectively superior set of eating practices. Within ethical eating discourse, some issues are emphasized more than others (e.g. environment in North America) (Johnston, 2008; Johnston and Szabo, 2011) and privileged groups are generally better positioned to engage with this discourse (Johnston et al., forthcoming). Ethical eating discourse has an undeniable moral tone, as well as a connection to class privilege (Govindasamy et al., 1998; Lockie, 2009). Food preferences have long been associated with displays of cultural capital (Bourdieu, 1984), and ethical eating practices are no exception (Johnston and Baumann, 2010).

Ethical eating practices create and reproduce classed consumption habits, yet ethical consumption is not only about what people can afford to buy. Some high-income consumers don't engage with ethical eating, while certain low-income shoppers go to great lengths to do so (Johnston, 2008; Johnston and Szabo, 2011). To shed light on this complex situation, it is important to recognize that ethical eating is not simply an abstract or moral idea, but is concretized in physical and material relationships. As Bourdieu argues in his later work, cultural capital is located not only in social but in *physical* space (1999, 2005; see also Lury, 1997; Savage, 2010; Skeggs, 2004). Ethical stores are often located in affluent neighbourhoods and may not feel accessible to those with fewer economic and cultural resources (Barnett et al., 2010; Johnston and Szabo, 2011). Further, ethical consumption may be a part of the food cultures of specific regions (Beagan et al., 2010).

While place and class clearly work together to shape ethical consumption, more research is needed to understand how this interaction plays out in everyday eating practices (Starr, 2009). To address this gap, we investigate how ethical eating varies across neighbourhoods with different retail environments and income levels. We focus on ethical eating, but also discuss its relationship to *healthy* eating—a necessary consideration given the tendency of some interviewees to conflate food ethics with health. Our analysis draws from 40 qualitative interviews with parents and their teenage children (ages 13–19) in two Toronto neighbourhoods: the upper-income neighbourhood of Riverdale, and the gentrifying neighbourhood of Parkdale.

We argue that understandings of ethical eating are significantly shaped by place-specific neighbourhood cultures that reflect and reproduce classed ways of eating. To conceptualize these cultures, we draw from the sociological study of culture and cognition, and develop the idea of a neighbourhood 'prototype'. The neighbourhood prototype reflects residents' perceptions of the typical eater in their neighbourhood, thereby incorporating people's perceptions of the material environment, as well as neighbourhood standards or ideals. By charting how people understand the prototypical neighbourhood eater, we shed light on the complex intersections between place, class and eating practices. People compare themselves—both positively and negatively—to a neighbourhood prototype that sets a standard for 'normal' eating practices.

Understanding the link between neighbourhood food culture and ethical eating directly relates to the reproduction of a stratified food system where marginalized populations lack the economic capital, cultural capital, and geographic mobility required to access high-status foods. If ethical eating constitutes a moral 'gold standard' for food consumption, then it is important to understand how access to this standard is facilitated by class and neighbourhood culture. Furthermore, because an individualistic, voluntary notion of ethical eating tends to dominate public discourse[2] (e.g. Pollan, 2006), understanding the links between place, class and ethical eating can help challenge insinuations that lower-class eaters are morally irresponsible.

Below, we review literature examining the intersection of place, health and ethical consumption. Next, we describe our interview sample and methods. Finally, we look at each site to better understand how the neighbourhood food environment and prototype relate to class and the eating practices described by participants.

Place, Neighbourhood, and Ethical Eating

Recent scholarship points to the importance of place in relation to ethical consumption. First, the presence of retailers selling ethical products in an area, and residents' awareness of these retailers, is related to ethical food purchases (Beagan et al., 2010; Brown et al., 2009; Popkin et al., 2005; Squires et al., 2001; Weatherell et al., 2003). The interrelation of store location and income also influences ethical eating. Ethical stores tend to be located in more affluent neighbourhoods, making access more difficult for non-residents or public transportation users (Baker et al., 2009; Ellaway and Macintyre, 2000; Govindasamy et al., 1998; Moore and Roux, 2006; Morland et al., 2002; Smith and Morton, 2009). For low-income individuals especially, barriers to engaging with ethical food opportunities include access, distance and cost (Baker et al., 2009; Beagan et al., 2010; Govindasamy et al., 1998; Smith and Morton, 2009). More broadly, scholars are recognizing that ethical consumption is intimately tied to 'systems of provision'; in other words, commodity chains, marketing and retail environments set broad parameters for what individual choices are possible (Seyfang and Paavola, 2008).

A second way ethical consumption relates to place is through geographically-based food and consumption cultures (DeSoucey, 2010; Oluwabamide and Akpan, 2010; Schultz, 2002; Storey et al., 2002). For example, consumers in census tracts where ethical consumption is already relatively common are more likely

to engage in ethical practices (Starr, 2009). Starr (2009) in the USA and Beagan et al. (2010) in Canada found that some regions were more engaged in ethical consumption than others. In Beagan et al. (2010), participants on Canada's west coast felt that their ethical purchasing decisions contributed to the prevalence of ethical stores and markets in their area, suggesting that discourses and resources for ethical eating can be mutually reinforcing.

These place-specific consumer cultures have a significant class dimension (Bourdieu, 1999, 2005; see also Savage, 2010). If we understand class not as a static condition, but as something that is continually made through symbolic and material struggles (Skeggs, 2004; Wacquant, 1991), then both place and consumption appear implicated in this class-making process. Place-based identifications often emerge as a 'shorthand way of speaking class' that makes overt references to class unnecessary (Skeggs, 2004: 15; see also Gidley and Rooke, 2010). While consumer spaces are theoretically open for all to enjoy, particular sites and regions (e.g. gentrified neighbourhoods, global cities) are distinguished by their classed consumption habits (Zukin, 2010). Butler and Robson (2003) use the term 'metropolitan habitus' to describe the distinct disposition and consumption habits of London's middle classes (see also Webber, 2007), and argue that neighbourhoods develop 'mini-habituses' influenced by specific ideas of the neighbourhood (2003: 190–2). A 'geographical imaginary' can also work to 'fix' less privileged groups in marginalized locations; working-class neighbourhoods are marked by a kind of 'pathological lack' that often carries associations of moral promiscuity (Gidley and Rooke, 2010: 97; Skeggs, 2004). Meanwhile, the middle classes enjoy the comfort that comes with participating in socially valorized consumption practices—like eating organic food (Guthman, 2008).

In sum, prior studies suggest that cities and neighbourhoods develop particular classed ways of consuming that both reflect and reproduce class identities. While culture and food scholars demonstrate how neighbourhoods and regions have place-specific, classed ways of consuming, what is less understood is exactly how these classed consumption habits are maintained and reproduced. How do neighbourhood residents influence each other, how are their consumption practices shaped by their retail environment, and how do they understand their neighbourhood as imposing certain consumption standards? In this article, we build on the aforementioned literature to address these questions. More specifically, we investigate how the intersection of place, class and material resources shapes perceptions of a typical neighbourhood diet and ethical eating.

To conceptualize the perceptions and habitual consumption decisions around food, we turn to cultural sociology, and Bourdieu's concept of the habitus—a concept that describes how a system of class-based dispositions are internalized, and subtly influence perceptions and actions (1984: 170). Bourdieu's work *Distinction* (1984) showed how privileged classes in 1970s France distinguished themselves through their 'good' taste in foods, and more recent work suggests a continued ability to display cultural capital through food choices, including ethical foods (Bennett et al., 2009; Johnston and Baumann, 2010; Mellor et al., 2010). The concept of habitus, and Bourdieu's work more generally, suggests that people unconsciously enact their objective social structure, and that access to cultural assets or resources are based on people's social position.

One critique of the habitus concept is its black box quality (e.g. Boudon, 1998). In other words, how do we know the processes by which the habitus is constructed? Recent research in social psychology gives empirical force to the idea of habitus, affirming that many decisions are rooted in intuitive, habitual ways of thinking and acting (Chaiken and Trope, 1999). Sociologists have drawn from social psychology, psychology and neuroscientific research to illuminate how subconscious rules of thought create possibilities for thinking and acting (Douglas, 1966; Fleck, 1979; Vaisey, 2008, 2009). This cultural and cognition research builds on past sociological insights—like Giddens' (1984) distinction between 'practical' or automatic consciousness (intuitive decisions made during daily routines), and 'discursive' or deliberate consciousness (formal articulations and rationalizations for action).[3] Not only is automatic consciousness influential in what we think, feel and do, but *most* cognition appears to occur at this level (Vaisey, 2009: 1681). These insights help explain why people's food ideals do not always match with actual food habits (Caplan, 1997: 5–6), and suggest that sociologists need to better appreciate how culture shapes food preferences in ways that are habitual and automatic.

Building on the idea that the habitus is shaped by place (e.g. Butler with Robson, 2003), we argue that residents articulate a place-based habitus through their descriptions of a prototypical neighbourhood eater that includes both positive and negative attributes. Employing the concept of 'prototypes' (developed by psychologist Eleanor Rosch, 1978, but taken up by sociologists, e.g. Cerulo, 2010), we map out habitual ideas shaping everyday food practices. Prototypes are the best example of a particular category (e.g. a 'chair' is a prototypical piece of furniture), and function as a kind of mental shorthand that allows for processing complex information with minimal cognitive effort (Rosch and Lloyd, 1978: 37, 28). A prototype is akin to Weber's (1949) conception of an ideal-type, but relies on social-psychological understandings of how people think and make classifications. While a Weberian ideal-type is an analytical construct developed by researchers and rooted in attempts to evaluate social phenomena (see Weber, 1949; Bruun, 2001; Eliaeson, 2000), the prototype is a way of getting at what Bourdieu (1977) called the 'logic of practice': the habitual, semi-conscious thought processes people employ to recognize and make sense of the neighbourhood eating style. People's awareness of, and self-positioning with, reference to the neighbourhood's prototypical eating style can be understood as one way habitus operates at the level of automatic consciousness. More specific to the topic of food, place and ethical eating, the prototype concept helps us understand how people implicitly make connections between a neighbourhood, its typical diet, the resources available to residents, and their own food practices.

In response to interview questions and photo elicitation, our interviewees painted a picture of a prototypical neighbourhood eating style that was both ideational and material: it included normative statements about dietary ideals, but also referenced material constraints, physical infrastructure, and supports for different eating styles.[4] The prototypical neighbourhood diet was not a distant or abstract idea, but served as a reference point used in combination with other reference points (e.g. the 'good' mother, parent, or family [James and Curtis, 2010; Lawler, 2000; Taylor, 2010]) to evaluate family food practices. In the section on

analysis, we map out neighbourhood prototypes, and the mechanisms by which place of residence, community norms and resources interact to shape participants' involvement in ethical consumption.

Data and Methods

Our study draws on interviews with residents of two neighbourhoods in Toronto, a city with a population of 2.48 million. In each neighbourhood we interviewed at least one adult and one teen (ages 13–19) from 10 families, totaling 20 families and 47 participants. Parents and teens were interviewed separately in the family home. Each participant was interviewed twice resulting in 40 interviews. In addition to interviews, we asked participants to take approximately 20 photos of 'food in their life'.[5]

The two neighbourhoods, South Parkdale and North Riverdale (hereafter 'Parkdale' and 'Riverdale'), are relatively close to each other geographically, but differ significantly. Riverdale is located just east of the downtown core. The population is somewhat diverse, but tends towards a middle, or upper middle class base that self-identifies as 'white' or 'Caucasian'. The most recent census data (Statistics Canada, 2010) indicate that Riverdale is relatively affluent and well educated. A substantial percentage of the population has a university education (46%), as compared to the Toronto average of 27 per cent. The average household income, in 2006 dollars, was $96,006 (City of Toronto, 2006). In terms of the retail strip, Riverdale has a number of trendy clothing and lifestyle stores, upscale cafes, specialty food shops and a green-living store. It is home to a large worker-owned food coop, The Big Carrot, that sells a range of organic, local and 'natural' groceries, and is housed in a plaza full of other similar retailers.

Parkdale is a gentrifying neighbourhood that maintains a reputation for drugs and prostitution. Low-rent apartments coexist with large Victorian houses, many of which have been bought and renovated by upper middle class Torontonians (Slater, 2005). There is a good deal of income disparity, though the average Parkdale income is about 13 per cent below the city average (Slater, 2005). The population is ethnically and racially diverse. Approximately 56 per cent of residents are 'visible minorities', with Tibetan, Filipino, Black, Chinese and South Asian being the five most populous ethno-racial groups (Statistics Canada, 2006). The main Parkdale retail strip has greengrocers, a discount chain grocery store, fast food outlets, convenience stores and a handful of relatively new trendy restaurants. In comparison to Riverdale's main street, the Parkdale strip is somewhat stark, and displays greater class and ethno-racial diversity.

The participant families reflect the diversity of the two neighbourhoods. While there was not a perfect homology between status and neighbourhood, most Riverdale participants were 'white', and most had higher incomes, class designations, and education levels than Parkdale participants (see Table 1).[6] In both neighbourhoods, mothers volunteered to be interviewed more readily than fathers, while the composition of male and female teenagers was roughly equal. This predominance of women produced gendered descriptions of family food practices, and while gender is not our primary focus in this article, we recognize the importance of gender and class intersectionality in these food practices.[7] We began the data analysis process by coding interview transcripts using the qualitative data

Place, Ethics, and Everyday Eating: A Tale of Two Neighbourhoods
Josée Johnston, Alexandra Rodney, and Michelle Szabo

J

management software AtlasTi. Interviews were first coded for themes related to how local food cultures, socioeconomic status, and the family context interact to shape family food habits, including ethical eating. Additional codes were added as new themes emerged. We recorded participants' and families' *overall* approach to ethical eating (i.e. experiences of and thoughts about ethical eating) and how this related to other participants and families. We noted salient differences between the approaches and experiences of Riverdale and Parkdale families to ethical eating, and their conceptualizations of a 'prototypical' neighbourhood eating style.

Table 1. Demographic summary

Family Characteristics	Parkdale	Riverdale	Total Families
Income			
High	2	5	7
Middle	1	1	2
Low	7	4	11
Education[a]			
University degree or more	3	8	11
Some post-secondary	5	1	6
High school or less	2	1	3
Race/Ethnicity			
White (Anglo-Saxon, European)	5	9	14
Non-white, mixed heritage	5	1	6
Class[b]			
Upper-middle	2	5	7
Lower-middle	5	3	8
Working class/working poor/underclass	3	2	5
Gender			
Parents (F/M)	9/2	10/1	n/a[c]
Teenagers (F/M)	5/7	9/4	n/a

Notes:
[a] Based on the family member with the highest education level.
[b] Families were assigned to class categories based on occupation, since this characteristic usefully combines education, income, and occupational prestige (Gilbert, 2008; Goldthorpe, 1987; Lamont, 1992). When couples differed, the class of the partner with the higher class was used. When immigrant families were underemployed, we placed them in the class category corresponding to their occupation of training. Upper middle class participants generally held professional or managerial jobs. Lower middle class participants included lower-level managers and administrators, lower-status white collar and some highly skilled blue collar workers. Working class/working poor/underclass participants had low-skill manual or clerical jobs, unstable work situations, or were supported by public assistance.
[c] More than one parent or teen were interviewed in some families.

Analysis: Neighbourhood Food Environments and Prototypical Eating Styles

This section maps out a prototypical eating style in each neighbourhood, and examines what part ethical eating plays in this prototype. First, we examine how the physical environment shaped possibilities for ethical consumption in each neighbourhood. While the analysis is influenced by our neighbourhood observations, it is primarily informed by participant depictions through interviews and photographs. Second, we analyse how participants constructed and related to the prototypical eater in their neighbourhood.

Perceptions of Neighbourhood Food Environments

The Riverdale Food Environment: 'Healthy-ethical' Choices Abound. Riverdale is a predominantly upper middle class neighbourhood, and familiarity with ethical eating discourse was very common in our interviews, even amongst participants with lower incomes.[8] References to healthy and ethical eating went hand in hand, which is not surprising given that 'health food' stores are often places to find ethical products, and some products (e.g. organics) are understood to have health and eco-social benefits. The term 'organic' was often conflated with ethical, and the ubiquity of organic produce in the retail environment promoted a sense that the neighbourhood offered a variety of health-promoting, ethical food choices.

A key element of the Riverdale food environment emphasized by participants was the tremendous diversity of food choices, including ethical products. When asked what kind of store or restaurant Riverdale lacked, most participants could think of no obvious omissions, and they emphasized the neighbourhood's variety. Neighbourhood affluence, and the presence of young professionals interested in 'ethical/healthy' food, was thought to contribute to this panoply of upper middle class 'healthy-ethical' food options. Bojana (48, lower middle class, Serbian-Canadian) noted: 'The whole area of Riverdale is a very good community for farmers' markets, for example. There are enough people with money to buy these things.' Bojana's comments speak to the affluent customer base and increased market development in neighbourhoods such as Riverdale, leading to intensified consumption of ethical products (Squires et al., 2001).

Participants' photographs also demonstrated a perception of Riverdale as having an abundance of healthful, ethical food options enabling residents to engage in these practices. Photographs depicted ethical food establishments like The Big Carrot, as well as close-up shots of organic mushrooms, local apples and a juice bar. While there are some fast food outlets in Riverdale, these were almost completely absent from participant photos. Fast food was seen by most participants as a neighbourhood blight. Several participants explained how their children refused to eat fast food, and detailed how a fast food chicken franchise (Swiss Chalet) had been forced out of business. Patricia (47, lower middle class, Japanese-Canadian) noted that residents celebrated its closure and that 'there was almost a stigma in the neighbourhood that you didn't want to buy there'.

In keeping with earlier research on fast food and class (e.g. Bugge, 2011), Riverdale's abundance of healthful, ethical food options appeared to confer social status on the area and its residents. For example, Claude (52, upper middle class,

Place, Ethics, and Everyday Eating: A Tale of Two Neighbourhoods
Josée Johnston, Alexandra Rodney, and Michelle Szabo

J

French), described the Riverdale eating style as 'sophisticated because of these [multiple food] options'. His response suggests a conflation between the neighbourhood retail options and its residents' appreciation of 'diversity', a term with moral and social weight in cosmopolitan cities (Butler with Robson, 2003: 165). In sum, abundant retail options in Riverdale were seen as both enabling healthy-ethical shopping and enabled *by* the 'sophisticated' and 'diverse' tastes of its residents. Moreover, social pressures (e.g. the stigma against fast food) reproduced the upper middle class neighbourhood culture and retail landscape.

The Parkdale Food Environment: Less Choice, More Fast Food. In contrast to the glowing descriptions of retail variety in Riverdale, our interviews revealed little sense of a healthy, ethical foodscape in Parkdale. Residents mentioned some neighbourhood stores selling ethical products, including a butcher selling sustainably raised meats and a fair trade coffee shop. However, these stores were all located on the gentrified *edges* of the neighbourhood, while most interviewees lived in the core. Unsurprisingly, these stores were frequented mainly by the two upper middle class families in our sample who lived on the gentrified eastern edge of Parkdale, and had vehicle access to stores within and outside the neighbourhood. The other eight Parkdale families, who did not own cars and were conscious of public transit expenses, made do with stores and restaurants within the neighbourhood core.

Despite the ethno-cultural variety in stores that Parkdale residents found pleasant and convenient, neighbourhood retailers were often described as lacking. For participants with an interest in ethical food issues, central Parkdale, where lower-income participants lived, offered little in the way of ethical products, especially affordable ones. One example comes from Marianne (49, lower middle class, European/Middle Eastern), a single mother living on a limited income. She was interested in products like sustainably raised fish, but didn't know where to purchase them locally, other than at a health food store she found 'outrageously expensive'. She also noted the costliness of going outside the neighbourhood for ethical products: 'That's five dollars [return transit fare] added on to the price of a piece of salmon.' Wendy (60, working-poor/underclass, white), a single grandmother on social assistance, similarly noted that she wanted to buy local produce 'for environmental reasons', but had trouble finding it at her neighbourhood grocery store.

Although some interviewees expressed concerns about ethical eating, this was not the primary concern for most Parkdale participants. A few participants displayed signs of food insecurity, and even for those who were food secure, food quality and healthfulness were key concerns. Instead of conflating healthy food with ethical food, as Riverdale participants did, Parkdale residents frequently contrasted healthy food with fast food. Shamar (15, lower middle class family, Tibetan) said: 'The restaurants and food stores here aren't that healthy for you… All there is is fast food everywhere.' Other teens echoed this description of the ubiquity of fast food, and this was also reflected in participant photos. While there were images of grocery stores and 'ethnic' restaurants (e.g. Caribbean, Thai), photos of Burger King, McDonald's and takeaway pizza shops were much more common. A few residents saw fast food options as convenient, but many, such as

Sarama (15, working-poor/underclass family, Eritrean-Canadian), saw drawbacks. She was critical of Parkdale's food environment, particularly since she had medical problems attributed to her diet, and identified fast food outlets around her school as a 'temptation'. She noted: 'We should have less fast foods in the area so it's less [easy] for us to go there.' Some participants also identified a dearth of stores with fresh, high quality items. For instance, Kim (49, lower middle class, white), noted that some stores near her home had 'old' and 'dusty' products, and wished there were more options for high quality, affordable foods.

While Riverdale participants associated the healthy-ethical retail environment with their own sophisticated food tastes and saw themselves as having power over their foodscape (as when residents drove out Swiss Chalet), there was little evidence that Parkdale residents saw their food environment as changeable. This is in keeping with previous research on the sense of 'given-ness' in lower class participants' narratives about their circumstances (Lareau, 2002: 769; Savage, 2010: 131). It also reflects the fact that Parkdale residents generally had fewer financial resources and thus diminished market influence. Parkdale narratives did, however, suggest how the *limitations* of participants' food environment might influence their self-definition and social status. For example, in reference to farmers' markets (which she did not patronize), Wendy said:

> Sometimes I think they're charging much more because their stuff is unique, because it's freshly grown nearby, it's organic…for the caché of all that…[I wonder] if they couldn't charge a little more reasonable price for your everyday person.

The 'caché' of ethical food is evident to Wendy, but as 'your everyday person' she sees it as out of her reach.

Participants portrayed Parkdale as a neighbourhood that at best did not facilitate, and at worst provided barriers to, ethical and healthy eating. The neighbourhood core was characterized as dominated by fast food, and lacking high quality, or 'ethical' food options. While the neighbourhood's gentrified outer edges offered more options, they were primarily accessed by affluent, mobile residents, who also described travelling throughout the city to get specific food products. Further, there was little evidence that Parkdale participants—especially those with lower incomes—saw themselves as empowered to change their food environment. The food environments in both Riverdale and Parkdale reflect how place, social class and food culture are mutually reinforcing, and how participants embody these food environments and reflect them in daily food practices.

Prototypical Eating Styles in Riverdale and Parkdale

Drawing from descriptions of neighbourhood eating styles as well as participants' food habits, we examine how interviewees depicted a prototypical neighbourhood diet, and address the classed nature of food ideals.

The Riverdale Prototype: An Idealized Ethics-Health Hybrid. When asked to describe the typical eating style in Riverdale, most participants depicted an idealized health-conscious, ethical consumer favouring organic foods. Participants with

Place, Ethics, and Everyday Eating: A Tale of Two Neighbourhoods
Josée Johnston, Alexandra Rodney, and Michelle Szabo

J

high *and* low incomes frequently named The Big Carrot as a store where a typical Riverdale resident shopped, and as a place to take visitors. Marina (47, upper middle class, white), a mother of three, characterized it as 'a real Riverdale place, a big beautiful store to get healthy, organic food', while Ted (52, lower middle class, white), suggested that The Big Carrot 'influences a lot of people in the neighbourhood'. Patricia (47, lower middle class, Japanese-Canadian), described residents' attention to food ethics:

> If I had to sum up [Riverdale residents] it would probably be quite knowledgeable, savvy about food…two benchmarks are the Carrot Common and Sun Valley [another health-ethics grocery store]…that ethical basis for food plus local. And another tenet of Riverdale as well is that we would look into alternative or complementary lifestyle and food choices, medicines. So we would have a general support system with that type of lifestyle.

Patricia's comments echo other residents' perceptions of the prototypical Riverdale eater as interested in health and food ethics. Her use of the term 'savvy', like Claude's use of 'sophisticated' earlier, also emphasizes the status given these food habits.

While the Riverdale prototype serves as an idealized standard, it was also construed as difficult to emulate due to money and time constraints. Even though The Big Carrot was depicted as the prototypical Riverdale store, none of the Riverdale participants regularly shopped there because of perceived cost barriers (despite the relatively high incomes of some participants—see Table 1). Bojana (48, lower middle class, Serbian-Canadian) declared: 'I would like to be able to buy things non-stop from Big Carrot where I know it's good quality, it's organic, locally supplied. But my financial situation is not so good so I have to compromise these things.'

When the prototypical Riverdale diet could not be attained, some participants described feelings of guilt and anxiety. For example, in reference to the 'local' dimension of the ethical eating discourse, several expressed remorse for not using their backyard space to grow food, as in Patricia's case: 'I feel badly [about not growing food]…I feel that I am almost being indulgent or wasteful about the space that I have.' Negative emotions were also articulated when the prototypical eating style was perceived as status-driven, especially when it came to children's consumption. As Krista (43, upper middle class, white) put it:

> I think there's a bit of one-upmanship that goes on. Especially when you have kids in school…the one-upmanship also going on in the schoolyard, that you don't send your kids with prepackaged lunches…And the kids do it too, 'Oh I hate McDonald's'.

While some residents did occasionally eat fast food, fast food chains were frequently referenced as a foil to the prototypical Riverdale diet. Residents evoked the image of McDonald's as representative of 'low-quality', 'unhealthy', and

'socially irresponsible' food, thus defining what does *not* fit within the neighbour-hood prototype. For example, Krista said that McDonald's serves 'lowest common denominator foods', and proudly spoke about how her kids wouldn't eat there even if she offered to take them.

This reprobation of fast foods, often associated with the lower classes (Bugge, 2011; Warde, 1999), is in keeping with a long history in western culture of stig-matizing lower-class bodies and the perceived excesses of their consumption habits (Gidley and Rooke, 2010: 99, 103). There is an equally long history of women being held responsible for the 'good' or 'bad' food habits of their families (James and Curtis, 2010). It is no wonder, then, that many Riverdale participants who did not follow the prototypical diet, especially mothers, felt guilty and ashamed. Marina, for instance, was self-conscious about not buying organic: 'We're not into [organics]. Most of my friends do eat organic food…A lot of people in Riverdale eat organic.' Neither Marina or her husband trusted organic certification and she noted that she 'could give a crap about the environment', yet she still felt pres-sure to justify her choice. She mentioned several times that they 'couldn't afford' organics, even though the family has a high income. While Marina's sense of not living up to neighbourhood standards did not cause her to change her buying practices, the neighbourhood prototype directly influenced the habits of many other participants, both men and women. When participants could not meet neighbourhood standards, they described strategies for *approximating* them—by buying local, in-season foods rather than certified organics, or purchasing non-certified products from trusted sources.

Our interviews reveal that the prototypical Riverdale eating style revolves around health and food ethics, two concerns that carry significant social status and moral weight (Bugge, 2011; James and Curtis, 2010; Mellor et al., 2010) and are most easily acted on by residents with high incomes. They also reveal the socio-emotional mechanisms (e.g. guilt, shame) through which this prototype is reproduced.

The Parkdale Prototype: Fast Food, Food Insecurity, and Multicultural Diets.
The prototypical diet described by Parkdale residents was less idealized than the Riverdale prototype, was centrally concerned with fast food, and made little reference to a neighbourhood *ethical* eating standard. In fact, the lack of such as standard was critiqued by one lower-middle-class family committed to ethical eating. The son, Marcus (18, lower middle class, Barbadian-Middle Eastern), criti-cized Parkdale residents for what he perceived as their inattention to food politics. The mother, Marianne (49, lower middle class, European/Middle Eastern), spoke about wanting to teach others about ethical eating, such as her local greengrocer, whom she was encouraging 'to label things and get more local, get more direct from farmers'. That Marianne felt a need to educate her (most likely lower class) neighbours and local shopkeepers about food ethics again speaks to the power of food and bodies as markers of class and sophistication (Gidley and Rooke, 2010). But what we would like to emphasize here is what Marianne's experience tells us about the Parkdale prototype. Marianne saw a void of knowledge about, and com-mitment to, ethical eating in her physical and social environment. This is a clear contrast with Riverdale participants, who perceived an abundance of ethical eating information around them.

Attitudes towards fast food differed significantly across the two neighbour-hoods. In Parkdale, fast food was associated with health problems, but was also seen, particularly by teenagers, as the source of peer pressure and social status. Sarama (15, working-poor/underclass family, Eritrean-Canadian) was worried about her health and weight but ate fast food nonetheless because 'it's a teenager thing'. She explained: 'Everyone's eating out and you don't want to bring [food] from home 'cause everybody's watching you'. For Sarama and other teens, fast food signaled freedom from parents (the supposed source of homemade food) and from 'adult' health concerns. (In contrast, Riverdale participants described both adults and youth being *negatively* judged for liking fast food or 'junky' food.) For Parkdale adults, social pressure to eat fast food was less evident, but there were signs that the prototypical Parkdale diet centred to some degree around fast food. When we asked Marika (46, lower middle class, Ukrainian) her impressions of eating in Parkdale, she mentioned the ubiquity and popularity of fast food places: 'You can find probably eight or ten takeaway shops in this particular intersection, and people are shopping there all the time.' Unlike many Riverdale participants who told us about their own (rare) fast food purchases with embarrassment or qualification, Marika added matter-of-factly that her family frequented these places, even for family outings (a key moment for 'family displays' and other-judgment around food [James and Curtis, 2010]). Though fast food eating was not equally sanctioned by all Parkdale participants, it was seen as somewhat 'nor-mal' in the neighbourhood.

The prototypical understanding of Parkdale diets is undoubtedly related to the area's reputation, even among its own residents, as a haven for drug addicts, the unemployed, the poor and the mentally ill. When asked about typical eating habits in Parkdale, Marika (46, lower middle class, Ukrainian) described the neighbourhood as a place where people 'are living on welfare and don't have much money to shop'. April (13, underclass, white), a teen living on social assistance with her grandmother, referenced 'junkies [drug addicts]' in Parkdale, who 'don't eat too much'. As Gidley and Rooke (2010: 97) point out, cultural associations between poor neighbourhoods and their residents are often so strong that resi-dents may be stigmatized 'by virtue of merely residing there'. We suggest that a similar process of association is going on in terms of the Parkdale prototypical eater, with residents imagining somebody who not only eats fast food, but has trouble accessing enough food, period. With this prototypical eater as a reference point, ethical eating concerns appeared outside the purview of most of Parkdale participants, especially those with lower incomes.

In terms of how the prototypical eating style impacted Parkdale participants, we again see a contrast with Riverdale. While Riverdale participants felt shameful about falling short of emulating the health-ethical prototype, Parkdale partici-pants seemed to feel either on par with, or, in the case of middle class residents, superior to, the neighbourhood prototype. For example, Kim (49, lower middle class, white) admitted to being 'so judgmental' when she saw fellow grocery shop-pers checking out with 'cases of pop and five bags of chips'. We attribute this to the 'low bar' of the Parkdale prototype and the neighbourhood's overall reputa-tion. Participants noted that fellow residents were 'going to the food bank' or 'liv-ing on welfare' and thus set a low standard of comparison in terms of a culturally

acceptable (i.e. middle class) diet. But whether they felt on par with, or superior to, the Parkdale prototype, the result was similar in terms of *ethical* eating: the neighbourhood prototype provided little social pressure to engage with ethical eating practices.

While the prototypical eating style in Parkdale was dominated by negative qualities, there were some positive dimensions that are important to mention briefly. In particular, some participants spoke passionately about the vibrant, multicultural aspects of Parkdale eating styles. Azzezza (44, working-poor/under-class, Eritrean) described potlucks at the local community centre where her family was able to discover new foods and make friends of other ethno-cultural back-grounds. Marianne appreciated being able to find food from all over the world: 'This neighbourhood really prides itself on its multicultural [character].' Thus, the prototypical Parkdale eater was less idealized than the Riverdale prototype, but it was multidimensional: participants invoked images of a fast food diet that is mini-mally engaged with ethical eating discourses, but also referenced a cosmopolitan eating style with food choices from multiple culinary backgrounds.

Discussion and Conclusion

While engagement with ethical eating discourse clearly depends on individual taste proclivities, sociologists have charted the influence of social factors on tastes, including cultural and economic capital, the influence of particular food cultures, and most significant for this article, place, or neighbourhood. Our interpretive analysis emphasizes the richness of investigating the mutual influence of these factors through discussions of food ideals and practices. Place, in the form of a neighbourhood retail environment and culture, shapes expectations of food choices, including engagement with ethical eating discourse. At the same time, the material resources available to neighbourhood residents impact the expecta-tions and standards of local food cultures, as well as the ability of residents to meet these standards.

Our research into neighbourhood food culture centres around the concept of 'prototype', a conceptual tool capturing the automatic associations gleaned from residents' verbal and photographic impressions of a typical neighbourhood diet. To be clear, the prototype does not reflect a uniform neighbourhood diet. Instead, it is best understood as a cluster of characteristics representing the 'best fit' for how diet in a particular place is understood and related to. In the wealthier neighbourhood of Riverdale, the prototypical neighbourhood diet reflected upper middle class economic and cultural resources, clustered around concepts of good health, ethical eating and prioritized local and organic foods. Although none of the residents interviewed felt they could fully achieve these standards, most aspired to them nonetheless, in part, we suggest, because of social pressures caus-ing them to feel judged, guilty, or uncomfortable when failing to comply. While some residents spoke of the high cost of healthy, ethical eating in Riverdale, most perceived the neighbourhood favourably as offering multiple options for healthy, ethical food choices.

In the gentrifying neighbourhood of Parkdale, the dietary prototype was less aspirational, and reflected the material constraints of its low-income residents. Ethical food concerns were not central characteristics of the neighbourhood prototype, which was instead focused on fast food—as a temptation, as a readily accessible and affordable meal choice, and as a source of status for teenagers. Our analysis suggests that there is no single way of relating to a prototypical neighbourhood diet, and that this relationship depends on available economic and cultural resources. Upper middle class gentrifiers in Parkdale had similar ideas about Parkdale's 'low' culinary standards and ubiquitous fast food options, but used their resources to exceed neighbourhood standards and access ethical food options at the outer edge of the neighbourhood or in different parts of the city. For low-income Parkdale residents, minimal resources restricted their food practices spatially to the neighbourhood core, which was perceived as offering minimal choice. Even in a gentrifying neighbourhood like Parkdale, we observed a local food culture shaped by a legacy of poverty and urban problems—a legacy which made it difficult (logistically, culturally, materially) for low-income residents to take advantage of newer food trends like farmers' markets.

This work demonstrates how sociological research can productively use interpretive approaches to study how place-specific food cultures intersect with social class, and to map the cognitive processes guiding food choices. Together, these two neighbourhood prototypes work to reproduce a larger social understanding of affluent eaters as 'ethical', and lower-income residents as relatively 'unethical', fast food eaters. While ethical foods have become a way of displaying cultural sophistication and moral concern, we show that place and privilege are just as important as personal taste and ethics in shaping daily food choices. ∎

Acknowledgements

The Canadian Institute for Health Research (CIHR) generously funded this research. The principal investigators on this grant are Brenda Beagan (Dalhousie), and Gwen Chapman (UBC). Other investigators include Elaine Powers, Helen Valiantos, and post-doctoral fellows Deborah McPhail and Sonya Sharma. We are grateful for all ideas and inspiration provided by these researchers, but accept all limitations as our own.

References

Baker D, Hamshaw K and Kolodinsky J (2009) Who shops at the market? Using consumer surveys to grow farmers' markets: Findings from a regional market in Northwestern Vermont. *Journal of Extension* 47(6): 1–9.

Barnett C, Cloke P, Clarke N and Malpass A (2010) *Globalizing Responsibility: The Political Rationalities of Ethical Consumption*. RGS-IBG Book Series. London: Wiley-Blackwell.

Beagan BL, Ristovski-Slijepcevic S and Chapman GE (2010) People are just becoming more conscious of how everything's connected: 'Ethical' food consumption in two regions of Canada. *Sociology* 44(4): 751–69.

Bennett T, Savage M, Silva E, Warde A, Gayo-Cal M and Wright D (2009) *Culture, Class, Distinction*. New York: Routledge.

Boudon R (1998) Social mechanisms without black boxes. In: Hedstrom P and Swedberg R (eds) *Social Mechanisms: An Analytical Approach to Social Theory*. Cambridge: Cambridge University Press.

Bourdieu P (1977) *Outline of a Theory of Practice*. New York: Cambridge University Press.

Bourdieu P (1984) *Distinction: A Social Critique of the Judgment of Taste*. Nice R (transl.). Cambridge, MA: Harvard University Press.

Bourdieu P (1999) *The Weight of the World*. Cambridge: Polity Press.

Bourdieu P (2005) *The Social Structures of the Economy*. Cambridge: Polity Press.

Brown E, Dury S and Holdsworth M (2009) Motivations of consumers that use local, organic fruit and vegetable box schemes in Central England and Southern France. *Appetite* 53(2): 183–88.

Bruun HH (2001) Weber on Rickert: From value relation to ideal type. *Max Weber Studies* 1(2): 138–60.

Bugge AB (2011) Lovin' it? A study of youth and the culture of fast food. *Food, Culture & Society* 14(1): 71–89.

Butler T with Robson G (2003) *London Calling: The Middle Classes and the Remaking of Inner London*. Oxford: Berg.

Cairns K, Johnston J and Baumann S (2010) Caring about food: Doing gender in the foodie kitchen. *Gender and Society* 24(5): 591–615.

Caplan P (1997) Approaches to the study of food, health and identity. In: Caplan P (ed.) *Food, Health and Identity*. New York: Routledge, 1–31.

Cerulo K (2010) Mining the intersections of cognitive sociology and neuroscience. *Poetics* 38: 115–32.

Chaiken S and Trope Y (1999) *Dual-Process Theories in Social Psychology*. New York: Guilford Press.

City of Toronto (2006) South Parkdale neighbourhood profile: North Riverdale neighbourhood profile. Available at: http://www.toronto.ca/demographics/ profiles _ map _and _index.htm (accessed 16 May 2011).

DeSoucey M (2010) Gastronationalism: Food traditions and authenticity politics in the European Union. *American Sociological Review* 75(3): 432–55.

Doucet A (2006) *Do Men Mother? Fathering, Care and Domestic Responsibility*. Toronto: University of Toronto Press.

Douglas M (1966) *Purity and Danger: An Analysis of Concepts of Pollution and Purity*. London: Routledge and Kegan Paul.

Eliaeson S (2000) Max Weber's methodology: An ideal type. *Journal of the History of the Behavioural Sciences* 36(3): 241–63.

Ellaway A and Macintyre S (2000) Shopping for food in socially contrasting localities. *British Food Journal* 102(1): 52–9.

Fleck L (1979) *Genesis and Development of a Scientific Fact*. Chicago University of Chicago Press.

Fox B (2009) *When Couples Become Parents: The Creation of Gender in the Transition to Parenthood*. Toronto: University of Toronto Press.

Giddens A (1984) *The Constitution of Society. Outline of a Theory of Structuration*. Berkeley, CA: University of California Press.

Gidley B and Rooke A (2010) Asdatown: The intersections of classed places and identities. In: Taylor Y (ed.) *Classed Intersections: Spaces, Selves, Knowledges*. Farnham: Ashgate.

Gilbert D (2008) *The American Class Structure in an Age of Growing Inequality*. London: Sage.

Goldthorpe JH (with Llewellyn C and Pane C) (1987) *Social Mobility and Class Structure in Modern England*. New York: Oxford University Press.

Govindasamy R, Zurbriggen M, Italia J, Adelaja A, Nitzsche P and VanVranken R (1998) *Farmers Markets: Consumer Trends, Preferences, and Characteristics*. New Jersey Agricultural Experiment Station. P-02137-77-98. Newark: Department of Agricultural, Food, and Resource Economics, Rutgers, The State University of New Jersey.

Guthman J (2008) Neoliberalism and the making of food politics in California. *Geoforum* 39: 1171–83.

Hochschild A (1989) *The Second Shift: Working Parents and the Revolution at Home*. New York: Viking Penguin.

James A and Curtis P (2010) Family displays and personal lives. *Sociology* 44(6): 1163–80.

Johnston J (2008) The citizen-consumer hybrid: Ideological tensions and the case of Whole Foods Market. *Theory and Society* 37: 229–70.

Johnston J and Baumann S (2010) *Foodies: Democracy and Distinction in the Gourmet Foodscape*. New York: Routledge.

Johnston J and Szabo M (2011) Reflexivity and the Whole Food Market shopper: Shopping for change, or cruising for pleasure? *Agriculture and Human Values* 28(3): 303–19.

Johnston J, Szabo M and Rodney A (2011) Good food, good people: Understanding the cultural repertoire of ethical eating. *Journal of Consumer Culture* 11(3): 293–318.

Lamont M (1992) *Money, Morals, and Manners: The Culture of the French and the American Upper-Middle Class*. Chicago: University of Chicago Press.

Lareau A (2002) Invisible inequality: Social class and childrearing in black families and white families. *American Sociological Review* 67: 747–76.

Lawler S (2000) *Mothering the Self: Mothers, Daughters, Subjects*. London: Routledge.

Lizardo O (2004) The cognitive origins of Bourdieu's *Habitus*. *Journal for the Theory of Social Behavior* 34(4): 375–401.

Lockie S (2009) Responsibility and agency within alternative food networks: Assembling the 'citizen consumer'. *Agriculture and Human Values* 26(3): 193–201.

Lury C (1997) *Consumer Culture*. Cambridge: Polity Press.

Mellor J, Blake M and Crane L (2010) When I'm doing a dinner party I don't go for the Tesco cheeses, it's that sort of level, you know?' Class distinctions, friendship and home entertaining. *Food, Culture & Society* 13: 115–34.

Moore LV and Roux AVD (2006) Associations of neighbourhood characteristics with the location and type of food stores. *American Journal of Public Health* 96(2): 325–31.

Morland K, Wing S, Roux AD and Poole C (2002) Neighbourhood characteristics associated with the location of food stores and food service places. *American Journal of Preventive Medicine* 22(1): 23–9.

Oluwabamide AJ and Akpan NS (2010) Environmental and cultural patterns in nutrition: A comparison of food patterns in two Nigerian societies. *Anthropologist* 12(2): 95–8.

Pollan M (2006) *The Omnivore's Dilemma: A Natural History of Four Meals.* New York: Penguin.

Popkin BM, Duffey K and Gordon-Larsen P (2005) Environmental influences on food choice, physical activity and energy balance. *Physiology and Behaviour* 86(5): 603–13.

Rosch E and Lloyd B (1978) *Cognition and Categorization.* Philadelphia, PA: Lawrence Erlbaum.

Rose N (1992) Governing the enterprising self. In: Heelas P and Morris P (eds) *The Values of Enterprise Culture: The Moral Debate.* New York: Routledge.

Savage M (2010) The politics of elective belonging. *Housing, Theory and Society* 27(2): 115–35.

Schultz PW (2002) Knowledge, education and household recycling: Examining the knowledge-deficit model of behaviour change. In: Dietz T and Stern P (eds) *Education, Information and Voluntary Measures in Environmental Protection.* Washington, DC: National Academy of Sciences, 67–82.

Seyfang G and Paavola J (2008) Inequality and sustainable consumption: Bridging the gaps. *Local Environment* 13(8): 669–84.

Skeggs B (2004) *Class, Self, Culture.* New York: Routledge.

Slater T (2005) *Toronto's South Parkdale Neighbourhood.* Toronto: Centre for Urban and Community Studies, University of Toronto.

Smith C and Morton L W (2009) Rural food deserts: Low-income perspectives on food access in Minnesota and Iowa. *Journal of Nutrition Education and Behaviour* 41 (3): 176–87.

Squires L, Juric B and Cornwell TB (2001) Level of market development and intensity of organic food consumption: Cross-cultural study of Danish and New Zealand consumers. *Journal of Consumer Marketing* 18(5): 392–409.

Starr MA (2009) The social economics of ethical consumption: Theoretical considerations and empirical evidence. *Journal of Socio-Economics* 38(6): 916–25.

Statistics Canada (2006) *Census tract profiles for 0004.00, 0005.00, 0007.01, 0007.02, Toronto (CMA), Ontario.*

Statistics Canada (2010) *Census tract profile for 0071.00, Toronto (CMA) and Ontario.*

Storey M, Neumark-Sztainer D and French S (2002) Environmental influences on adolescent eating behaviours. *Journal of the Dietetic Association* 102: S40–S51.

Szabo M (2011) The challenges of 're-engaging with food': Connecting employment, household patterns and gender relations to convenience food consumption in North America. *Food, Culture & Society* 14(4): 547–66.

Taylor Y (2010) Privileged locations? Sexuality, class and geography. In: Taylor Y (ed.) *Classed Intersections: Spaces, Selves, Knowledges.* Farnham: Ashgate.

Vaisey S (2008) Socrates, Skinner, and Aristotle: Three ways of thinking about culture in action. *Sociological Forum* 23(3): 603–13.

Place, Ethics, and Everyday Eating: A Tale of Two Neighbourhoods
Josée Johnston, Alexandra Rodney, and Michelle Szabo

J

Vaisey S (2009) Motivation and justification: A dual-process model of culture in action. *American Journal of Sociology* 114(6): 1675–715.

Walzer S (1989) *Thinking about the Baby: Gender and Transitions into Parenthood.* Philadelphia, PA: Temple University Press.

Wacquant L (1991) Making class: The middle-class(es) in social theory and social structure. In: McNall SG, Levin RF and Fantasia R (eds) *Bringing Class Back in Contemporary Historical Perspectives.* Boulder, CO: Westview Press.

Warde A (1999) Convenience food: Space and timing. *British Food Journal* 101(7): 518–27.

Weatherell C, Tregear A and Allinson J (2003) In search of the concerned consumer: UK public perceptions of food, farming and buying local. *Journal of Rural Studies* 19(2): 233–44.

Webber R (2007) The metropolitan habitus: Its manifestations, locations, and consumption profiles. *Environment and Planning* 39: 182–207.

Weber M (1949) Objectivity in social science. In: Shils EA and Finch HA (eds) *The Methodology of the Social Sciences.* York: Simon & Schuster, The Free Press.

Zukin S (2010) *Naked City: The Death and Life of Authentic Urban Places.* Oxford: Oxford University Press.

Notes

1. While we emphasize the contested nature of the term 'ethical eating', we refrain from using quotation marks from this point on in the article for reasons of legibility.

2. The focus on individual choice as a way of constructing subjects and managing collective responsibilities is not unique to the realm of food. See Rose (1992).

3. Also, Lizardo's (2004) work suggests that Bourdieu's development of the 'habitus' concept can be seen as a form of cognitive sociology, as it demonstrates the 'cognitive structures that agents bring to bear in their practical knowledge of the social worlds thus structured' (2004: 375).

4. Visual and verbal images of the 'typical' neighbourhood diet were often invoked automatically and impressionistically by respondents, suggesting that automatic consciousness (Giddens, 1984) plays a role in the conceptualization of prototypical neighbourhood diets.

5. Following the first interview, participants were asked to take food photos (e.g. favourite/disliked foods, local restaurants) to be discussed in the second interview.

6. Given the small sample size and the qualitative nature of our data, it was not possible to control for income or social class in our neighbourhood comparison. Instead, our intention was to use interpretive analysis to explore how class, income and neighbourhood work together to create prototypical eating styles. For an elaboration of how ethical eating varied by social class in this sample (Johnston et al., 2011).

7. We are aware of the unequal maternal burden for domestic care work in western societies, including food provision and forging a family food identity (Doucet, 2006; Fox, 2009; Hochschild, 1989; James and Curtis,

2010; Mellor et al., 2010; Walzer, 1989). These unequal burdens clearly influenced the gender balance in our sample, and shape responsibility for providing ethical food products within the home. Regarding ethical eating and place, male and female participants expressed similar conceptions of their neighbourhood retail environment and the prototypical eater. While we touch on some of the ways in which food habits and ideals were gendered and racialized, our primary focus in this article is social class (but see Cairns et al., 2010; Szabo, 2011).

8. In Riverdale, three families were weakly engaged with ethical eating discourse; seven had moderate or high engagement. In Parkdale, five families were weakly engaged; five had moderate or high engagement (see Johnston et al., forthcoming).

AUTHOR PROFILE

Josée Johnston is a professor of Sociology at the University of Toronto. She has a Ph.D. and an M.A. in Sociology from the University of Alberta, and a B.A. in Political Science from McGill University. Her major substantive interest is the sociological study of food. Her work examines discourses of ethical consumption, and investigates how consumers seek social transformation within the constraints of contemporary market forces. Johnston has published five books. The most recent, entitled *Introducing Sociology Using the Stuff of Everyday Life*, was published in 2016. She has contributed a wealth of scholarship to her field, and "Place, Ethics, and Everyday Eating" appeared in *Sociology* in 2012.

Alexandra Rodney received her Ph.D. in Sociology from University of Toronto. She is currently a postdoctoral fellow at the University of Guelph, working on the Gender Equity and Excellence Through Leadership Initiative. Her research areas include cultural studies, gender studies, feminist theory, and qualitative-ethnography.

Michelle Szabo is Professor of Environmental Studies and Sociology at Sheridan Institute of Technology and Advanced Learning in Oakville, Canada. She was a 2014–2016 SSHBC Postdoctoral Research Fellow in Sociology at the University of Toronto. Her research focus includes the sociologies of gender, consumption, and food.

The Dirt on Ocean Garbage Patches

By Jocelyn Kaiser

Chances are you've heard of the great Pacific Garbage Patch. It is, according to countless press and TV reports, a "trash vortex," "the world's largest rubbish dump," and a "vast mass of floating debris" midway between Hawaii and California. According to Charles Moore, a sailor-turned-scientist who discovered the patch in 1997 and has been interviewed on *The Oprah Show*, the *Late Show with David Letterman*, and *Good Morning America*, it is a plastic soup twice the size of Texas.

Although many media stories conjure up a chunky soup of bottles and tires, it is mostly an unstrained consommé of small bits of floating plastic. And the patch Moore found isn't the only one. A similar accumulation of plastic particles—which include weathered fishing line, Styrofoam, wrappers, and raw resin pellets—has shown up in the North Atlantic Ocean. But the potential harm to marine life is far from clear. "We just don't know the importance," says biological oceanographer James Leichter of the Scripps Institution of Oceanography in San Diego, California, who points out that "there's a lot more water than plastic."

Accumulating tiny plastic debris was first discovered in 1972, when researchers at the Woods Hole Oceanographic Institution in Massachusetts found plastic particles up to 0.5 centimeters in diameter in their surface plankton nets in the North Atlantic's Sargasso Sea (*Science*, 17 March 1972, p. 1240). Since then, there have been a dozen or so similar reports mainly from the North Atlantic and the North Pacific.

It was Moore who brought the problem to public attention. In 1997, he sailed from Hawaii to Long Beach, California, across a notoriously calm area, where for a solid week he spotted at least one bottle or piece of plastic every hour, he says. Moore went back with some scientists and a plankton tow net. In a 2001 paper in *Marine Pollution Bulletin*, they reported the highest average plastic count on record in the Pacific—334,271 pieces per square kilometer—and a startling 6:1 ratio of plastic to zooplankton by weight. They worried that the plastic was exposing animals to toxins, pointing to a Japanese study showing that polypropylene pellets can suck up pollutants from seawater.

Independent Seattle oceanographer Curtis Ebbesmeyer, known for using spilled shipments of shoes and rubber ducks to study ocean currents, suggested that Moore had found a "garbage patch" within the North Pacific subtropical gyre—one of several major ocean gyres, or large, wind-driven, circular current systems with a quiet center.

While scientists commend Moore's efforts to raise public awareness of marine pollution, some question the 6:1 ratio he came up with. Doubts have also been raised about the patch's size.

Nevertheless, there's clearly a lot of plastic out there. When graduate students from Scripps spent 19 days in the same area last summer sampling sea life, they

snagged plastic on every one of 126 plankton tows. Often, the half-liter jar of residue strained from a single 0.5-kilometer tow contained so many plastic chips that the jar "looked like a snow globe," says graduate student Miriam Goldstein, who led the trip. "That is not normal."

Similar findings have come from off the U.S. East Coast. Last winter, the Sea Education Association (SEA), a nonprofit in Falmouth, Massachusetts, that takes students on sailing research trips, reported high—but consistent year-to-year—microplastic counts over a 1450-kilometer transect in the western North Atlantic Ocean that SEA has been sampling for 22 years. Oceanographic modeler Nikolei Maximenko of the University of Hawaii, Manoa, had predicted this patch's location; he has pinpointed other likely patches in the Indian Ocean, South Pacific, and South Atlantic.

Whether the plastic is damaging marine ecosystems is, however, an open question. In the past, researchers have mostly focused on larger threats: abandoned fishing nets that trap turtles and seals; plastic bags that block the digestive tracts of turtles; and the toothbrushes; and bottle caps that seabirds mistake for food, sometimes starving as a result or dying from a blockage. But toxin-laden microplastics may add another risk to marine life. Benthic worms, mussels, krill, sea cucumbers, and birds will ingest tiny plastic particles, according to various studies, some by marine ecologist Richard Thompson of the University of Plymouth in the United Kingdom. "There's quite a lot of signals out there that we need to be concerned," says Thompson. But nobody has yet confirmed that significant amounts of chemicals wind up in animals' tissues.

Nor does anyone know where all this plastic ultimately goes. Does it simply get too small to trap with a net? Does it sink to the sediments? Wash onto shore? (Large numbers of microplastics have been found on a Hawaii beach.) One worrisome find from the Scripps trip: a hatchetfish, a midwater dweller, with a plastic chip in its stomach. "It's going somewhere," says SEA oceanographer Kara Lavender Law. She and others would like to find out where. ■

AUTHOR PROFILE

Jocelyn Kaiser is a staff writer for *Science* magazine. She received two degrees, first in Chemical Engineering from Princeton and then in Journalism from Indiana University. Before joining *Science* she spent two years in New York as a researcher for General Electric and was an intern for *Science News*. Beginning as an intern for *Science*, Kaiser has been a staff writer since 1995. She initially covered world ecological problems with a wide scope of topics. Her current work focuses on corporate research and policy including issues such as financial stakeholder conflicts and the changing nature of biodefense labs and biomedicine. "The Dirt on Ocean Garbage Patches" appeared in *Science* on June 18, 2010.

Who Am I? Who Are My People?

By Gwyn Kirk and Margo Okazawa-Rey

K

Identity formation is the result of a complex interplay among individual decisions and choices, particular life events, community recognition and expectations, and societal categorization, classification, and socialization. It is an ongoing process that involves several key questions:

Who am I? Who do I want to be?
Who do others think I am and want me to be?
Who and what do societal and community institutions, such as schools,
    religious institutions, the media, and the law, say I am?
Where/what/who are my "home" and "community"?
Which social group(s) do I want to affiliate with?
Who decides the answers to these questions, and on what basis?

Answers to these questions form the core of our existence....

The *American Heritage Dictionary* (1993) defines *identity* as

the collective aspect of the set of characteristics by which a thing is defi-
    nitely known or recognizable;
a set of behavioral or personal characteristics by which an individual is
    recognizable as a member of a group;

The same dictionary defines *to identify* as "to associate or affiliate (oneself) closely with a person or group; to establish an identification with another or others."

These definitions point to the connections between us as individuals and how we are perceived by other people and classified by societal institutions. They also involve a sense of individual agency and choice regarding affiliations with others. Gender, race, ethnicity, class, nationality, sexual orientation, age, religion, disability, and language are all significant social categories by which people are recognized by others. Indeed, on the basis of these categories alone, others often think they know who we are and how we should behave. Personal decisions about our affiliations and loyalties to specific groups are also shaped by these categories. For example, in many communities of color women struggle over the question of race versus gender. Is race a more important factor than gender in shaping their lives? If a Latina speaks out publicly about sexism within the Latino community, is she betraying her people? This separation of categories, mirrored by our segregated social lives, tends to set up false dichotomies in which people often feel that they have to choose one aspect of their identity over another. It also presents

189

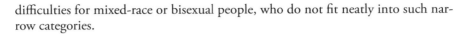

difficulties for mixed-race or bisexual people, who do not fit neatly into such narrow categories.

Being Myself: The Micro Level

At the micro level, individuals usually feel the most comfortable as themselves. Here one can say, for example, "I am a woman, heterosexual, middle class, with a movement disability; but I am also much more than those categories." At this level we define ourselves and structure our daily activities according to our own preferences. At the micro level we can best feel and experience the process of identity formation, which includes naming specific forces and events that shape our identities. At this level we also seem to have more control of the process, although there are always interconnections between events and experiences at this level and the other levels.

Critical life events, such as entering kindergarten, losing a parent through death, separation, or divorce, or the onset of puberty, may all serve as catalysts for a shift in how we think about ourselves. A five-year-old Vietnamese American child from a traditional home and community may experience the first challenge to her sense of identity when her kindergarten teacher admonishes her to speak only in English. A White, middle-class professional woman who thinks of herself as "a person" and a "competent attorney" may begin to see the significance of gender and "the glass ceiling" for women when she witnesses younger, less experienced male colleagues in her law office passing her by for promotions. A woman who has been raped who attends her first meeting of a campus group organizing against date rape feels the power of connection with other rape survivors and their allies. An eighty-year-old woman, whose partner of fifty years has just died, must face the reality of having lost her lifetime companion, friend, and lover. Such experiences shape each person's ongoing formulation of self, whether or not the process is conscious, deliberate, reflective, or even voluntary.

Identity formation is a lifelong endeavor that includes discovery of the new; recovery of the old, forgotten, or appropriated; and synthesis of the new and old, as illustrated by several writers in this chapter who reflect on how their sense of identity has developed over the course of their lives. At especially important junctures during the process, individuals mark an identity change in tangible ways. An African American woman may change her name from the anglicized Susan to Aisha, with roots in African culture. A Chinese Vietnamese immigrant woman, on the other hand, may adopt an anglicized name, exchanging Nu Lu for Yvonne Lu as part of becoming a U.S. citizen. Another way of marking and effecting a shift in identity is by altering your physical appearance: changing your wardrobe or makeup; cutting your hair very short, wearing it natural rather than permed or pressed, dyeing it purple, or letting the gray show after years of using hair coloring....

Community Recognition, Expectations, and Interactions: The Meso Level

It is at the meso level—at school, in the workplace, or on the street—that people most frequently ask "Who are you?" or "Where are you from?" in an attempt to categorize us and determine their relationship to us. Moreover, it is here that people experience the complexities, conflicts, and contradictions of multiple identities, which we consider later.

The single most visible signifier of identity is physical appearance…. Questions such as "Where do you come from?" and questioning behaviors, such as feeling the texture of your hair or asking if you speak a particular language, are commonly used to interrogate people whose physical appearances especially, but also behaviors, do not match the characteristics designated as belonging to established categories. At root, we are being asked, "Are you one of us or not?" These questioners usually expect singular and simplistic answers, assuming that everyone will fit existing social categories, which are conceived of as undifferentiated and unambiguous. Among people with disabilities, for example, people wanting to identify each other may expect to hear details of another's disability rather than the fact that the person being questioned also identifies equally strongly as, say, a woman who is White, working class, and bisexual.

Community, like home, may be geographic and emotional, or both, and provides a way for people to express group affiliations. "Where are you from?" is a commonplace question in the United States among strangers, a way to break the ice and start a conversation, expecting answers like "I'm from Tallahassee, Florida," or "I'm from the Bronx." Community might also be an organized group like Alcoholics Anonymous, a religious group, or a political organization like the African American civil rights organization, the National Association for the Advancement of Colored People (NAACP). Community may be something much more abstract, as in "the women's community" or "the queer community," where there is presumed to be an identifiable group. In all of these examples there is an assumption of some kind of shared values, goals, interests, culture, or language.

At the community level, individual identities and needs meet group standards, expectations, obligations, responsibilities, and demands. You compare yourself with others and are subtly compared. Others size up your clothing, accent, personal style, and knowledge of the group's history and culture. You may be challenged directly, "You say you're Latina. How come you don't speak Spanish?" "You say you're working class. What are you doing in a professional job?" These experiences may both affirm our identities and create or highlight inconsistencies, incongruities, and contradictions in who we believe we are, how we are viewed by others, our role and status in the community, and our sense of belonging.

Social Categories, Classifications, and Structural Inequality: Macro and Global Levels

Classifying and labeling human beings, often according to real or assumed physical, biological, or genetic differences, is a way to distinguish who is included and who is excluded from a group, to ascribe particular characteristics, to prescribe social roles, and to assign status, power, and privilege. People are to know their places. Thus social categories such as gender, race, and class are used to establish and maintain a particular kind of social order. The classifications and their specific features, meanings, and significance are socially constructed through history, politics, and culture. The specific meanings and significance were often imputed to justify the conquest, colonization, domination, and exploitation of entire groups of people, and although the specifics may have changed over time,

191

this system of categorizing and classifying remains intact. For example, Native American people were described as brutal, uncivilized, and ungovernable savages in the writings of early colonizers on this continent. This justified the genocide of Native Americans by White settlers and the U.S. military and public officials, as well as the breaking of treaties between the U.S. government and Native American tribes. Today, Native Americans are no longer called savages but are often thought of as a vanishing species, or a non-existent people, already wiped out, thereby rationalizing their neglect by the dominant culture and erasing their long-standing and continuing resistance....

These social categories are at the foundation of the structural inequalities present in our society. In each category there is one group of people deemed superior, legitimate, dominant, and privileged while others are relegated—whether explicitly or implicitly—to the position of inferior, illegitimate, subordinate, and disadvantaged.

Category	Dominant	Subordinate
Gender	Men	Women, transgender people
Race	White	Peoples of color
Class	Middle and upper class	Poor, working class
Nation	U.S./First World	Second, Third Worlds
Ethnicity	European	All other ethnicities
Sexual orientation	Heterosexual	Lesbian, gay, bisexual, transgender
Religion	Christian	All other religions
Physical ability	Able-bodied	Persons with disabilities
Age	Youth	Elderly persons
Language	English	All other languages

This hierarchy of advantage and disadvantage has meant that the preponderance of analytical writing about identity has been done by those in subordinate positions: women of color, lesbians, bisexual women, and working-class women.... For White people descended from European immigrants to this country, the advantages of being White are not always fully recognized or acknowledged.... As a result, White people in the United States tend to think of all identities as equal: "I'm Italian American, you're Polish American. I'm Irish American, you're African American." This assumed equivalence ignores the very big differences between an individualist symbolic identity and a socially enforced and imposed racial identity....

Maintaining Systems of Structural Inequality

Maintaining this system of inequality requires the objectification and dehumanization of subordinated peoples. Appropriating their identities is a particularly effective method of doing this, for it defines who the subordinated group/person is or ought to be. This happens in several ways:

Using the values, characteristics, features of the dominant group as the supposedly neutral standard against which all others should be evaluated. For example, men are generally physically larger and stronger than women. Many of the clinical trials for new pharmaceutical drugs are conducted using men's bodies and activities as the standard. The results, however, are applied equally to both men and women. Women are often prescribed the same dosage of a medication as men are even though their physical makeup is not the same. Thus women, as a distinct group, do not exist in this research.

Using terms that distinguish the subordinate from the dominant group. Terms such as "non-White" and "minority" connote a relationship to another group, White in the former case and majority in the latter. A non-White person is the negative of the White person; a minority person is less than a majority person. Neither has an identity on her or his own terms.

Stereotyping. Stereotyping involves making a simple generalization about a group and claiming that all members of the group conform to this generalization. Stereotypes are behavioral and psychological attributes; they are commonly held beliefs about groups rather than individual beliefs about individuals; and they persist in spite of contradictory evidence. Lesbians hate men. Latinas are dominated by macho Latinos. Women with physical disabilities are asexual. Fat women are good-humored but not healthy. As Andre asserts, "A 'stereotype' is pejorative; there is always something objectionable in the beliefs and images to which the word refers."

Exoticizing and romanticizing. These two forms of appropriation are particularly insidious because on the surface there is an appearance of appreciation. For example, Asian American women are described as personifying the "mysterious orient," Native American women as "earth mothers" and the epitome of spirituality, and Black women as perpetual towers of strength. In all three cases, seemingly positive traits and cultural practices are identified and exalted. This "positive" stereotyping prevents people from seeing the truth and complexity of who these women are.

Given the significance of identity appropriation as an aspect of oppression, it is not surprising that many liberation struggles have included projects and efforts aimed at changing identities and taking control of the process of positive identity formation and representation. Before liberation struggles, oppressed people often use the same terminology to name themselves as the dominant group uses to label them. One crucial aspect of liberation struggles is to get rid of pejorative labels and use names that express, in their own terms, who people are in all their humanity. Thus the name a group uses for itself gradually takes on more of an insider perspective that fits the evolving consciousness growing out of the political movement.

As with individual identity, naming ourselves collectively is an important act of empowerment. One example of this is the evolution of the names African Americans have used to identify themselves, moving from Colored, to Negro, to Black to Afro-American, and African American. Similarly, Chinese Americans gradually rejected the derogatory label "Chink," preferring to be called Orientals and now Chinese Americans or Asians. These terms are used unevenly, sometimes according to the age and political orientation of the person or the geographic region, where one usage may be more popular than another. Among the very

diverse group of people connected historically, culturally, and linguistically to Spain, Portugal, and their former colonies (parts of the United States, Mexico, the Caribbean, and Central and South America), some use more inclusive terms such as Latino or Hispanic; others prefer more specific names such as Chicano, Puerto Rican, Nicaraguan, Cuban, and so on....

Colonization, Immigration, and the U.S. Landscape of Race and Class

Other macro-level factors affecting people's identities include colonization and immigration.... This ideology that the United States is "a land of immigrants" obscures several important issues excluded from much mainstream debate about immigration: Not all Americans came to this country voluntarily. Native American peoples and Mexicans were already here on this continent, but the former experienced near-genocide and the latter were made foreigners in their own land. African peoples were captured, enslaved, and forcibly imported to this country to be laborers. All were brutally exploited and violated—physically, psychologically, culturally, and spiritually—to serve the interests of those in power. The relationships between these groups and this nation and their experiences in the United States are fundamentally different from the experiences of those who chose to immigrate here, though this is not to negate the hardships the latter may have faced. These differences profoundly shaped the social, cultural, political, and economic realities faced by these groups throughout history and continue to do so today.

...Early in the history of this country, for example, the Naturalization Law of 1790 (which was repealed as recently as 1952) prohibited peoples of color from becoming U.S. citizens, and the Slave Codes restricted every aspect of life for enslaved African peoples. These laws made race into an indelible line that separated "insiders" from "outsiders." White people were designated insiders and granted many privileges while all others were confined to systematic disadvantage. As Mary C. Waters points out, the stories that White Americans learn of how their grandparents and great-grandparents triumphed in the United States "are usually told in terms of their individual efforts." The role of labor unions, community organizations, and political parties, as well as the crucial importance of racism, is usually left out of these accounts, which emphasize individual effort and hard work.

On coming to the United States, immigrants are drawn into the racial landscape of this country. In media debates and official statistics, this is still dominated by a Black/White polarization in which everyone is assumed to fit into one of these two groups. Demographically, the situation is much more complex and diverse, but people of color, who comprise the more inclusive group, are still set off against White people, the dominant group. Immigrants identify themselves according to nationality—for example, as Cambodian or Guatemalan. Once in the United States they learn the significance of racial divisions in this country and may adopt the term *people of color* as an aspect of their identity here....

This emphasis on race tends to mask differences based on class, another important distinction among immigrant groups. For example, the Chinese and Japanese people who came in the nineteenth century and early twentieth century to work on plantations in Hawai'i, as loggers in Oregon, or building roads

Who Am I? Who Are My People?
Gwyn Kirk and Margo Okazawa-Rey

K

and railroads in several western states were poor and from rural areas of China and Japan. The 1965 immigration law made way for "the second wave" of Asian immigration. It set preferences for professionals, highly skilled workers, and members of the middle and upper-middle classes, making this group "the most highly skilled of any immigrant group our country has ever had." The first wave of Vietnamese refugees who immigrated between the mid-1970s and 1980 were from the middle and upper classes, and many were professionals; by contrast, the second wave of immigrants from Vietnam was composed of poor and rural people. The class backgrounds of immigrants affect not only their sense of themselves and their expectations but also how they can succeed as strangers in a foreign land. For example, a poor woman who arrives with no literacy skills in her own language will have a more difficult time learning to become literate in English than one who has several years of formal schooling in her country of origin that may have included basic English.

Multiple Identities, Social Location, and Contradictions

The social features of one's identity incorporate individual, community, societal, and global factors, as discussed in the accounts that follow. The point where all the features embodied in a person overlap is called social location. Imagine a diagram made up of overlapping circles, with a circle representing one specific feature of identity such as gender, class, ability, age, and so on. A person's social location is the point at which a part of each circle touches all others—where all elements are present simultaneously. Social location is a way of expressing the core of a person's existence in the social and political world. It places us in particular relationships to others, to the dominant culture of the United States, and to the rest of the world. It determines the kinds of power and privilege we have access to and can exercise, as well as situations in which we have less power and privilege.

Because social location is where all the aspects of one's identity meet, our experience of our own complex identities is sometimes contradictory, conflictual, and paradoxical. We live with multiple identities that can be both enriching and contradictory and that push us to confront questions of loyalty to individuals and groups.... ■

─────────────────────────────── AUTHOR PROFILE

Gwyn Kirk and Margo Okazawa-Rey are both scholar-activists writing on wide-ranging topics including militarism and violence against women; ecology and environmental justice; and gender politics. In 2013, Kirk and Okazawa-Rey co-edited the 6th edition of *Women's Lives: Multicultural Perspectives.* Their essay "Identities and Social Locations," which appeared in *Reading for Diversity and Social Justice* in 2010, interrogates the intricate social entanglements and intersections that we orchestrate to compose a sense of identity.

Facing It

By Yusef Komunyakaa

My black face fades,
hiding inside the black granite.
I said I wouldn't
dammit: No tears.
I'm stone. I'm flesh.
My clouded reflection eyes me
like a bird of prey, the profile of night
slanted against morning. I turn
this way—the stone lets me go.
I turn that way—I'm inside
the Vietnam Veterans Memorial
again, depending on the light
to make a difference.
I go down the 58,022 names,
half-expecting to find
my own in letters like smoke.
I touch the name Andrew Johnson;
I see the booby trap's white flash.
Names shimmer on a woman's blouse
but when she walks away
the names stay on the wall.
Brushstrokes flash, a red bird's
wings cutting across my stare.
The sky. A plane in the sky.
A white vet's image floats
closer to me, then his pale eyes
look through mine. I'm a window.
He's lost his right arm
inside the stone. In the black mirror
a woman's trying to erase names:
No, she's brushing a boy's hair. ■

———— AUTHOR PROFILE

Yusef Komunyakaa (b. 1941) was born in Bogalusa, Louisiana. He has published several volumes of poetry over the past forty years. Komunyakaa's poetic trademarks include jazz rhythms, colloquial language, striking imagery, and complex themes. In 1994, he won the Tufts Poetry Award, as well as the Pulitzer Prize in Poetry for *Neon Vernacular: New and Selected Poems*. His other publications include *The Emperor of Water Clocks* (2015) and *Dien Cai Dau* (1988), which won the Dark Room Poetry Prize, and where his poem "Facing It" can be found. Komunyakaa currently teaches Creative Writing at New York University.

The Ones Who Walk Away from Omelas

(Variations on a theme by William James)

By Ursula K. Le Guin

The central idea of this psychomyth, the scapegoat, turns up in Dostoyevsky's Brothers Karamazov, *and several people have asked me, rather suspiciously, why I gave the credit to William James. The fact is, I haven't been able to re-read Dostoyevsky, much as I loved him, since I was twenty-five, and I'd simply forgotten he used the idea. But when I met it in James's "The Moral Philosopher and the Moral Life," it was with a shock of recognition. Here is how James puts it:*

Or if the hypothesis were offered us of a world in which Messrs. Fourier's and Bellamy's and Morris's utopias should all be outdone, and millions kept permanently happy on the one simple condition that a certain lost soul on the far-off edge of things should lead a life of lonely torment, what except a specific and independent sort of emotion can it be which would make us immediately feel, even though an impulse arose within us to clutch at the happiness so offered, how hideous a thing would be its enjoyment when deliberately accepted as the fruit of such a bargain?

The dilemma of the American conscience can hardly be better stated. Dostoyevsky was a great artist, and a radical one, but his early social radicalism reversed itself, leaving him a violent reactionary. Whereas the American James, who seems so mild, so naïvely gentlemanly—look how he says "us," assuming all his readers are as decent as himself!—was, and remained, and remains, a genuinely radical thinker. Directly after the "lost soul" passage he goes on,

All the higher, more penetrating ideals are revolutionary. They present themselves far less in the guise of effects of past experience than in that of probable causes of future experience, factors to which the environment and the lessons it has so far taught us must learn to bend.

The application of those two sentences to this story, and to science fiction, and to all thinking about the future, is quite direct. Ideals as "the probable causes of future experience"—that is a subtle and an exhilarating remark!

Of course I didn't read James and sit down and say, Now I'll write a story about that "lost soul." It seldom works that simply. I sat down and started a story, just because I felt like it, with nothing but the word "Omelas" in mind. It came from a road sign: Salem (Oregon) backwards. Don't you read road signs backwards? POTS. WOLS nerdlihc. Ocsicnarf Nas…Salem equals schelomo equals salaam equals Peace. Melas.

O melas. Omelas. Homme hélas. "Where do you get your ideals from, Ms Le Guin?"
From forgetting Dostoyevsky and reading road signs backwards, naturally. Where else?

. . . .

With a clamor of bells that set the swallows soaring, the Festival of Summer came to the city Omelas, bright-towered by the sea. The rigging of the boats in harbor sparkled with flags. In the streets between houses with red roofs and painted walls, between old moss-grown gardens and under avenues of trees, past great parks and public buildings, processions moved. Some were decorous: old people in long stiff robes of mauve and grey, grave master workmen, quiet, merry women carrying their babies and chatting as they walked. In other streets the music beat faster, a shimmering of gong and tambourine, and the people went dancing, the procession was a dance. Children dodged in and out, their high calls rising like the swallows' crossing flights over the music and the singing. All the processions wound towards the north side of the city, where on the great water-meadow called the Green Fields boys and girls, naked in the bright air, with mud-stained feet and ankles and long, lithe arms, exercised their restive horses before the race. The horses wore no gear at all but a halter without bit. Their manes were braided with streamers of silver, gold, and green. They flared their nostrils and pranced and boasted to one another; they were vastly excited, the horse being the only animal who has adopted our ceremonies as his own. Far off to the north and west the mountains stood up half encircling Omelas on her bay. The air of morning was so clear that the snow still crowning the Eighteen Peaks burned with white-gold fire across the miles of sunlit air, under the dark blue of the sky. There was just enough wind to make the banners that marked the racecourse snap and flutter now and then. In the silence of the broad green meadows one could hear the music winding through the city streets, farther and nearer and ever approaching, a cheerful faint sweetness of the air that from time to time trembled and gathered together and broke out into the great joyous clanging of the bells.

Joyous! How is one to tell about joy? How describe the citizens of Omelas?

They were not simple folk, you see, though they were happy. But we do not say the words of cheer much any more. All smiles have become archaic. Given a description such as this one tends to make certain assumptions. Given a description such as this one tends to look next for the King, mounted on a splendid stallion and surrounded by his noble knights, or perhaps in a golden litter borne by great-muscled slaves. But there was no king. They did not use swords, or keep slaves. They were not barbarians. I do not know the rules and laws of their society, but I suspect that they were singularly few. As they did without monarchy and slavery, so they also got on without the stock exchange, the advertisement, the secret police, and the bomb. Yet I repeat that these were not simple folk, not dulcet shepherds, noble savages, bland utopians. They were not less complex than us. The trouble is that we have a bad habit, encouraged by pedants and sophisticates, of considering happiness as something rather stupid. Only pain is intellectual, only evil interesting. This is the treason of the artist: a refusal to admit the banality of evil and the terrible boredom of pain. If you can't lick 'em, join 'em. If it hurts, repeat it. But to praise despair is to condemn delight, to embrace violence is to lose hold of everything else. We have almost lost hold; we can no longer describe a happy man, nor make any celebration of joy. How can I tell you about the people of Omelas? They were not naïve and happy children—though their children were, in fact, happy. They were mature, intelligent, passionate adults whose lives were not wretched. O miracle! but I wish I could describe it better. I wish I could convince you. Omelas sounds in my words like a city in a fairy tale, long ago and far away, once upon a time. Perhaps it would be best if you imagined it as your own fancy bids, assuming it will rise to the occasion, for certainly I cannot suit you all. For instance, how about technology? I think that there would be no cars or helicopters in and above the streets; this follows from the fact that the people of Omelas are happy people. Happiness is based on a just discrimination of what is necessary, what is neither necessary nor destructive, and what is destructive. In the middle category, however—that of the unnecessary but undestructive, that of comfort, luxury, exuberance, etc.—they could perfectly well have central heating, subway trains, washing machines, and all kinds of marvelous devices not yet invented here, floating light-sources, fuelless power, a cure for the common cold. Or they could have none of that: it doesn't matter. As you like it. I incline to think that people from towns up and down the coast have been coming in to Omelas during the last days before the Festival on very fast little trains and double-decked trams, and that the train station of Omelas is actually the handsomest building in town, though plainer than the magnificent Farmers' Market. But even granted trains, I fear that Omelas so far strikes some of you as goody-goody. Smiles, bells, parades, horses, bleh. If so, please add an orgy. If an orgy would help, don't hesitate. Let us not, however, have temples from which issue beautiful nude priests and priestesses already half in ecstasy and ready to copulate with any man or woman, lover or stranger, who desires union with the deep godhead of the blood, although that was my first idea. But really it would be better not to have any temples in Omelas—at least, not manned temples. Religion yes, clergy no. Surely the beautiful nudes can just wander about, offering themselves like divine soufflés to the hunger of the needy and the rapture of the flesh. Let them join the processions. Let tambourines be struck above the copulations, and the glory of desire be proclaimed upon the gongs, and (a not unimportant point) let the offspring of these delightful rituals be beloved and looked after by all. One thing I know there is none of in Omelas is guilt. But what else should there be? I thought at first there were no drugs, but that is puritanical. For those who like it, the faint insistent sweetness of *drooz* may perfume the ways of the city, *drooz* which first brings a great lightness and brilliance to the mind and limbs, and then after some hours a dreamy languor, and wonderful visions at last of the very arcana and inmost secrets of the Universe, as well as exciting the pleasure of sex beyond all belief; and it is not habit-forming. For more modest tastes I think there ought to be beer. What else, what else belongs in the joyous city? The sense of victory, surely, the celebration of courage. But as we did without clergy, let us do without soldiers. The joy built upon successful slaughter is not the right kind of joy; it will not do; it is fearful and it is trivial. A boundless and generous contentment, a magnanimous triumph felt not against some outer enemy but in communion with the finest and

fairest in the souls of all men everywhere and the splendor of the world's summer: this is what swells the hearts of the people of Omelas, and the victory they celebrate is that of life. I really don't think many of them need to take *drooz*.

Most of the processions have reached the Green Fields by now. A marvelous smell of cooking goes forth from the red and blue tents of the provisioners. The faces of small children are amiably sticky; in the benign grey beard of a man a couple of crumbs of rich pastry are entangled. The youths and girls have mounted their horses and are beginning to group around the starting line of the course. An old woman, small, fat, and laughing, is passing out flowers from a basket, and tall young men wear her flowers in their shining hair. A child of nine or ten sits at the edge of the crowd, alone, playing on a wooden flute. People pause to listen, and they smile, but they do not speak to him, for he never ceases playing and never sees them, his dark eyes wholly rapt in the sweet, thin magic of the tune.

He finishes, and slowly lowers his hands holding the wooden flute.

As if that little private silence were the signal, all at once a trumpet sounds from the pavilion near the starting line: imperious, melancholy, piercing. The horses rear on their slender legs, and some of them neigh in answer. Sober-faced, the young riders stroke the horses' necks and soothe them, whispering, "Quiet, quiet, there my beauty, my hope…" They begin to form in rank along the starting line. The crowds along the racecourse are like a field of grass and flowers in the wind. The Festival of Summer has begun.

Do you believe? Do you accept the festival, the city, the joy? No?

Then let me describe one more thing.

In a basement under one of the beautiful public buildings of Omelas, or perhaps in the cellar of one of its spacious private homes, there is a room. It has one locked door, and no window. A little light seeps in dustily between cracks in the boards, secondhand from a cobwebbed window somewhere across the cellar. In one corner of the little room a couple of mops, with stiff, clotted, foul-smelling heads, stand near a rusty bucket. The floor is dirt, a little damp to the touch, as cellar dirt usually is. The room is about three paces long and two wide: a mere broom closet or disused tool room. In the room a child is sitting. It could be a boy or a girl. It looks about six, but actually is nearly ten. It is feeble-minded. Perhaps it was born defective, or perhaps it has become imbecile through fear, malnutrition, and neglect. It picks its nose and occasionally fumbles vaguely with its toes or genitals, as it sits hunched in the corner farthest from the bucket and the two mops. It is afraid of the mops. It finds them horrible. It shuts its eyes, but it knows the mops are still standing there; and the door is locked; and nobody will come. The door is always locked; and nobody ever comes, except that sometimes—the child has no understanding of time or interval—sometimes the door rattles terribly and opens, and a person, or several people, are there. One of them may come in and kick the child to make it stand up. The others never come close, but peer in at it with frightened, disgusted eyes. The food bowl and the water jug are hastily filled, the door is locked, the eyes disappear. The people at the door never say anything, but the child, who has not always lived in the tool room, and can remember sunlight and its mother's voice, sometimes speaks. "I will be good," it says. "Please let me out. I will be good!" They never answer. The child used to scream for help at night, and cry a good deal, but now it only makes a kind of whining, "eh-haa, eh-haa," and it speaks less and less often. It is so thin there are no calves to its legs; its belly protrudes; it lives on a half-bowl of corn meal and grease a day. It is naked. Its buttocks and thighs are a mass of festered sores, as it sits in its own excrement continually.

They all know it is there, all the people of Omelas. Some of them have come to see it, others are content merely to know it is there. They all know that it has to be there. Some of them understand why, and some do not, but they all understand that their happiness, the beauty of their city, the tenderness of their friendships, the health of their children, the wisdom of their scholars, the skill of their makers, even the abundance of their harvest and the kindly weathers of their skies, depend wholly on this child's abominable misery.

This is usually explained to children when they are between eight and twelve, whenever they seem capable of understanding; and most of those who come to see the child are young people, though often enough an adult comes, or comes back, to see the child. No matter how well the matter has been explained to them, these young spectators are always shocked and sickened at the sight. They feel disgust, which they had thought themselves superior to. They feel anger, outrage, impotence, despite all the explanations. They would like to do something for the child. But there is nothing they can do. If the child were brought up into the sunlight out of that vile place, if it were cleaned and fed and comforted, that would be a good thing, indeed; but if it were done, in that day and hour all the prosperity and beauty and delight of Omelas would wither and be destroyed. Those are the terms. To exchange all the goodness and grace of every life in Omelas for that single, small improvement: to throw away the happiness of thousands for the chance of the happiness of one: that would be to let guilt within the walls indeed.

The terms are strict and absolute; there may not even be a kind word spoken to the child.

Often the young people go home in tears, or in a tearless rage, when they have seen the child and faced this terrible paradox. They may brood over it for weeks or years. But as time goes on they begin to realize that even if the child could be released, it would not get much good of its freedom: a little vague pleasure of warmth and food, no doubt, but little more. It is too degraded and imbecile to know any real joy. It has been afraid too long ever to be free of fear. Its habits are too uncouth for it to respond to humane treatment. Indeed, after so long it would probably be wretched without walls about it to protect it, and darkness for its eyes, and its own excrement to sit in. Their tears at the bitter injustice dry when they begin to perceive the terrible justice of reality, and to accept it. Yet it is their tears and anger, the trying of their generosity and the acceptance of their helplessness, which are perhaps the true source of the splendor of their lives. Theirs is no vapid, irresponsible happiness. They know that they, like the child, are not free. They know compassion. It is the existence of the child, and their knowledge of its existence, that makes possible the nobility of their architecture, the poignancy of their music, the profundity of their science. It is because of the child that they are so gentle with children. They know that if the wretched one were not there snivelling in the dark, the other one, the flute-player, could make no joyful

music as the young riders line up in their beauty for the race in the sunlight of the first morning of summer.

Now do you believe in them? Are they not more credible? But there is one more thing to tell, and this is quite incredible.

At times one of the adolescent girls or boys who go to see the child does not go home to weep or rage, does not, in fact, go home at all. Sometimes also a man or woman much older falls silent for a day or two, and then leaves home. These people go out into the street, and walk down the street alone. They keep walking, and walk straight out of the city of Omelas, through the beautiful gates. They keep walking across the farmlands of Omelas. Each one goes alone, youth or girl, man or woman. Night falls; the traveler must pass down village streets, between the houses with yellow-lit windows, and on out into the darkness of the fields. Each alone, they go west or north, towards the mountains. They go on. They leave Omelas, they walk ahead into the darkness, and they do not come back. The place they go towards is a place even less imaginable to most of us than the city of happiness. I cannot describe it at all. It is possible that it does not exist. But they seem to know where they are going, the ones who walk away from Omelas. ■

AUTHOR PROFILE

Ursula K. Le Guin (1929–2018) was an American author and literary theorist from Berkeley, California. Though primarily known for her science fiction and fantasy titles, Le Guin was also a prominent author of children's books, poetry, and essays. A graduate of both Radcliffe College and Columbia University, Le Guin initially gained acclaim for her four-part science fiction book series known as the "Hanish Cycle." This series culminates with *The Left Hand of Darkness* (1969), which is generally considered Le Guin's most praised work and the winner of the Nebula and Hugo awards. Her publications would continue to win many awards across writing genres and her books have been finalists for the American Book Award and the Pulitzer Prize. In 2016, the Library of America published from Le Guin *The Complete Orsinia: Malafrena, Stories and Songs*, including works not previously available to the general public. "The Ones Who Walk Away from Omelas" has been reprinted widely, and was first published in 1973.

New Monuments Honor People Forced from Their Homes to Make Way for Shenandoah National Park

By Bill Lohmann

Sherman Shifflett's father was a true mountain man: rugged, resourceful and resilient.

Born in a log cabin on top of a mountain in Rockingham County, Harvey Shifflett wasn't what you'd call book smart—he didn't attend school past the second grade and he could barely sign his name—but he was plenty sharp. He could do math without pencil and paper, and he kept his family fed, even in the leanest times. He was brainy in the ways of living, and when he put his mind to it he could figure out how to do just about anything.

However, he could never quite come to grips with living off the mountain.

His was among the hundreds of families forced from their homes in the 1930s to make way for Shenandoah National Park as state authorities used eminent domain to acquire private property that would be turned over to the federal government for the park. After leaving Rockingham in 1933, the Shiffletts settled in the foothills of Albemarle County, but Harvey Shifflett's heart never relocated.

Decades later, still bitter at the way his family had been treated and still longing for his mountain home, he would have his children drive him to the park on weekend mornings where he would sit for hours on one of the stone walls along Skyline Drive—not far from his old home place. The old man spent the time whittling, watching the tourists drive by and soaking in the beauty that once was his.

"My dad wasn't upset about the money. He was upset about the way they were treated; he said they were treated real 'shabbily,'" said Sherman Shifflett, 74, who was born after the family moved to Albemarle, though his four oldest siblings were born on the mountain. Shifflett's father was told later their home had been burned to the ground, a common practice to discourage former residents from returning or squatters from settling in.

"Several generations had been up there on top of the mountain," said Shifflett, now retired after a career in teaching and administration at Louisa High School, old family photographs scattered about his kitchen table during an interview at his Louisa home. "They were fiercely independent. They worked hard. They eked out a living."

"My dad never stopped talking about it. He was really hurt. He never got the mountains out of his system."

• • • • • • • • • • • • •

The story of the people who lost their homes in the creation of Shenandoah National Park was largely untold or poorly told for years and is now fading from view altogether as the youngest of those forced from the mountains are well into their 80s. The Blue Ridge Heritage Project is breathing new life into the story of displacement—although Sherman Shifflett says his father never used the term "displaced" to describe his experience, believing "evicted" better captured the feeling—by promoting the development of a monument site in each of the eight counties where land was acquired. The monuments will recognize those who were displaced and educate visitors about the lives and culture of the people who dwelled in the mountains.

The first monuments went up in Albemarle and Madison counties. The Rappahannock monument will be dedicated in April, while ones in Page and Greene are in the works with Augusta, Rockingham and Warren to come. The monuments are being developed by committees within each county that will oversee site selection, design and fundraising. The monuments will differ slightly in terms of materials and construction, but the focal points of each will be a stone chimney. The symbolism is quite intentional, said Bill Henry, who founded the nonprofit Blue Ridge Heritage Project.

"If you go up in the park today, you'll find quite a few chimneys still standing," Henry said. "The first chimney I came across in the backcountry was a very powerful experience. I didn't know the whole story back then. It was like, 'Wow, somebody lived here.'

"Once I learned about the people being evicted and the houses being burned...the chimneys left standing really had a lot of meaning to me. The chimneys show the determination and spirit of the mountain people."

Henry, a retired school teacher, has no personal connection to the displaced people. He became interested in their story when he began attending meetings of The Children of Shenandoah, a group of descendants of the displaced that was formed in 1994. Their mission was to preserve the heritage of their ancestors, in part, by encouraging the park to more fully tell their story to visitors in a way that wasn't demeaning, which they felt was the tone of earlier narratives.

Henry, who grew up in Fairfax County and regularly visited the park with his family, went to the meetings because he was interested in learning about the park's history.

"I started going to hear the speakers, and then I got to wondering why all these people were so damn angry," he recalled.

· · · · · · · · · · · · ·

Lisa Custalow, who co-founded the descendants group with her husband, Curtis King Custalow, acknowledged there was considerable anger. Her mother was born on High Top Mountain and she was not even school age when her family had to leave their home. Custalow's grandparents rented their home, so they weren't compensated for their trouble.

"I remember as a young child I would ask my mom, 'Why did you have to leave the mountain?'" recalled Custalow, who grew up in Charlottesville and still lives there. "She would become quiet. She would have tears in her eyes, and she would say, 'When the government tells you you have to go, you have to go.'

"That was my signal to be quiet because you don't want to make Mama sad."

As she grew older, Custalow would stop at the Harry F. Byrd Visitor Center, where the exhibits put the most positive spin on the story of how the park was created, but in doing so cast a negative light on the mountain people.

"What we were angry about was the truth wasn't being told," Custalow said. "You can't take the park back. We could never move back. But at least we wanted the truth to be told about our families and how they lived."

The Children of Shenandoah got the attention of park officials, and the two entities worked to revamp the exhibits and videos, focusing considerable attention on the experiences of the people who were displaced. Depending on your perspective, those who developed the park might not come off looking so swell. Claire Comer, an interpretive specialist for the park assigned to the visual media department, said The Children of Shenandoah was "a fantastic partner for us to get that perspective." The collaboration, she said, was part of an ongoing effort by the park to tell the story "very comprehensively and objectively."

"We wanted to just present the facts…and let people draw their own conclusions," Comer said. "It's made for wonderful discussion for school groups and visitors alike: What is the greater good? What about eminent domain? Is it a good or bad thing? Is the end result of the park worth the heartache of those people who were displaced?

"This is really a story of colliding passions," she said, noting that on one side were those who wanted to preserve the beauty of the area while establishing a viable economy that was not an "extracting" industry, namely tourism, while on the other were the people who called the mountains home.

Comer brings an empathy to the story as her family also was touched—though in not such a dramatic way: Her great-grandfather had to sell his mountain land that he used for grazing cattle in the summer. He had to give up a cabin, though not his family farm, which was nearby but not on land that became part of the park. Still, she understands the sense of place and loss that infuses the feelings of descendants of the displaced. That's why she considers her work incorporating a more complete account "a really fulfilling part of my career. Having come from the local area, it was really a great thing for me to have the opportunity to tell that story," she said.

Custalow is "extremely pleased" with how the park responded, but said her group's biggest accomplishment might have been inspiring Henry—someone without a personal stake in the issue—to take an interest in their efforts and carry it forward.

. . . .

Having sensed the pain that was still palpable among descendants, Henry thought more could be done to honor the displaced. He began working on the idea for the Blue Ridge Heritage Project in 2012—asking Custalow to serve on the board—and eventually proposed a single site with eight monuments. Later, a monument in each county was suggested, making the logistics more complicated but the final result more compelling, he said.

"One of the things I've learned is it's not just one story, but it's thousands of stories," Henry said during an interview on a cold, blustery day at the Madison monument next to the now-closed Criglersville Elementary School on Old Blue Ridge Turnpike, which in the days before the park was a main thoroughfare over the mountains to the Shenandoah Valley. "They had different experiences, and they had different ways of dealing with it. Everybody's family saw their part of it, and quite often they don't know how big this was, which is one thing that's really great about having eight counties with eight sites."

Jim Lillard led the effort for the Madison monument, having picked out the fieldstones that went into the building of the chimney. His family goes back centuries in the area, several of his ancestors having fought in the American Revolution, and his grandfather had to abandon his 154-acre farm. It made Lillard feel better when he searched the records and discovered his grandfather had been offered $1,700 by the state, held out for $2,117 and wound up buying a 216-acre farm with a two-story house elsewhere in Madison for $2,000.

Asked if he was gratified to have the first monument in Madison, he replied, "I surely am."

. . . .

As one of the first national parks in the East when it was established in 1926, Shenandoah presented challenges the park system had not encountered in the open spaces of the West on land already owned by the government—namely residents. It wasn't entirely the park system's fault. It had been led somewhat astray by local promoters of the notion of a national park in the Blue Ridge, including a local businessman who operated the Skyland Resort (in what is now the park). Park advocates submitted a questionnaire to the search committee scouting out possible locations that described the mountain land as "pristine and uninhabited."

Though not crowded, the area was far from uninhabited. A census taken in 1934 showed approximately 435 families needed to be relocated before the park was dedicated in 1936, but the NPS's Comer said no one is sure of the total number of people who were displaced in the decade between when it was authorized and when it was dedicated.

County records show landowners who were paid for their property, but those who were tenant farmers or migrant workers or simply didn't have a legal deed—as those who had lived for generations in a remote area might certainly not have—were not compensated at all. Some sold willingly, while others resisted to the end. A few older residents were given life rights to live out their days in their homes. Everyone else was ushered out, sometimes with eviction notices and a visit from local law enforcement.

The people scattered. Some traveled a few miles into the foothills to settle, while others relocated in far-away places such as Baltimore, where jobs were more plentiful. The government established resettlement communities in several counties for those with no place in particular to go, charging a monthly rent in a sort of rent-to-own arrangement.

Larry Lamb, who helped get the Albemarle monument constructed and also serves on the Greene monument committee, has family ties to residents displaced in four counties. The Blue Ridge Heritage Project is important, he said, because most people who visit the park today have no understanding of how it was created or the lives it adversely affected.

"It lets people know that part of the story," he said.

Lamb, 65, who retired as a service engineer in the University of Virginia radiology department and lives in Albemarle, said he harbors "no hard feelings" toward the park, which he's been visiting since he was a child. "I've always loved it," he said.

He has hiked into the backcountry, visiting family gravesites and the remains of a log building at the farm where his great-great-grandparents lived.

"When you get up there, it's unbelievably beautiful," he said. "Those mountain people knew how to pick sites to build their homes. They were very smart."

∎

L

AUTHOR PROFILE

Bill Lohmann is a columnist for the *Richmond Times-Dispatch*. He graduated from the University of Richmond in 1979 with a BA in journalism before becoming a sports writer for the *Charlottesville Daily Progress*. Lohmann wrote for the United Press International in bureaus in Richmond, Orlando, and finally in Atlanta where he served as a regional feature writer. Lohmann came to *The Richmond News Leader* in 1988 as a reporter on the city desk, and then joined the *Richmond Times-Dispatch* when both papers merged in 1992. He has been a feature writer and columnist since and is also the author of four books, including most recently, *Backroads & Byways of Virginia* (2010). "New Monuments Honor People…" appeared in the *Richmond Times-Dispatch* on March 11, 2017.

When an App Is Called Racist

By Andrew Marantz

On August 7th of last year, Crain's ran an article about SketchFactor, an app that was set to launch the next day. It would allow users to report having seen or experienced something "sketchy" in a particular location; these reports would then be geotagged and overlaid on a Google map, creating a sketchiness heat map of a neighborhood or city. The idea was to help urban walkers be more street-smart, but the implications seemed insensitive at best, racist at worst. Allison McGuire, the app's co-creator, had recently moved from Washington, D.C., to the West Village. Both she and her co-founder, Daniel Herrington, were white and in their twenties. At one point, the Crain's reporter asked McGuire whether her company "could be vulnerable to criticisms regarding the degree to which race is used to profile a neighborhood."

"We understand that people will see this issue," she said. Still, she argued, "sketchy" can mean many things. "As far as we're concerned, racial profiling is 'sketchy.'" She was confident that the app would reflect her good intentions.

A few hours later, Gothamist published a more pointed piece, under the headline "Tone-Deaf App Helps Naive Travelers Avoid 'Sketchy' Neighborhoods." McGuire didn't mind. "We were just excited to be mentioned somewhere else," she told me recently. "Then I started getting texts and e-mails saying, 'Have you seen the front page of Gawker?'" The headline there was more blunt: "Smiling Young White People Make App for Avoiding Black Neighborhoods." There was a photograph of McGuire and Herrington, back to back, grinning. It probably didn't help that the app's icon was a black bubble with googly eyes.

The writer Jamelle Bouie tweeted, "Are you afraid of black people? Latinos? The poors? Then this app is just for you!" Maxwell Strachan, writing for the Huffington Post, pointed out some of the problems with establishing a "rating system based on the personal views of Americans, a people historically known to mask the occasional racist view behind words like 'dangerous'"—or, for that matter, "sketchy." Many people pointed out that the app, which was ostensibly designed to "empower everyone," would, in practice, empower only people who owned smartphones. SketchFactor's Twitter feed was inundated with such hashtags as #racist, #classist, and #gentrification. The next day, the same journalist at Crain's wrote an article about the Internet's "full-throated condemnation" of the company. "I was in shock," McGuire said. "And the app wasn't even live yet."

SketchFactor never fully recovered. Businesses are path-dependent—what happens early has a disproportionately strong effect on what comes later—and this is especially true of businesses that rely on user-generated content. Unlike, say, a Web publication, whose tone can be set by its writers and commenters, the tenor of a social platform is largely determined by who is doing the socializing. SketchFactor was unexpectedly popular—it was, for a time, the third-most down-loaded navigation app, behind Google Maps and Waze—but many of its first users were drawn in by the controversy. Some early "sketch reports" were actually pleas for the app to be taken down. Others were jokes (116th and Broadway:

"pretentious undergrads") or incomprehensible clutter (Atlanta: "This's guy just kicked his dog ahhhhhhhhhhh"); still others were puerile outbursts or racist screeds. McGuire and her team encouraged users to downvote or report offensive posts, but they couldn't remove them fast enough. Whether the idea was inherently racist or not, the app began to seem irredeemably toxic. The company released an update the following week and another one in October, but by winter they had stopped working on the app. In February of this year, they acknowledged that SketchFactor was not going to succeed. They decided to pivot.

Like "disrupt" and "10x" and "culture fit," "pivot" is an overused bit of tech-world jargon; but it's also a useful word with a simple definition. Let's say you try to start a company and the idea doesn't take hold, as most ideas don't. You can disband the company. Or you can keep your staff and some key part of your idea, jettison everything else, and rebuild. This is a pivot (though a better term might be "flatworm," after the invertebrates that can be cut in half and then regenerate themselves). In 2005, Noah Glass and Evan Williams launched Odeo, a podcasting platform. The next year, they pivoted—Glass and Williams stayed on, but they worked on new platforms that had nothing to do with podcasting. Eventually, they changed their name to Twitter.

Most companies pivot when they receive too little attention; SketchFactor's pivot came after receiving too much negative attention. In February, McGuire changed her company's name. (Had SketchFactor been named more innocuously in the first place, it might have attracted a different kind of audience; then again, it might have attracted no audience at all.) She and Herrington hired new staff and rebuilt around what she claims was always her core proposition: making city streets more walkable.

As of today, SketchFactor is gone. The new app will be called Walc. It recently closed a half-million-dollar round of seed funding, and it will launch in the fall. In the new app, users will not be asked to submit reports, and sketchiness will not be mentioned.

Tech entrepreneurs like to talk about failure, but they usually do so in the gauzy, uplifting tone of teleological hubris. Successful entrepreneurs fail up. They fail better. They move fast and break things. Starting a company is difficult, but the travails that befall a founder—the "trough of sorrow," for example—are mere way stations on the path to glory.

McGuire bristled at the suggestion that her company's pivot was a concession to public criticism. "We realized that we had built a social platform, and what we wanted to build was more of a utility," she told me. "So we corrected. It's that simple." She did not express any self-doubt, and she gave little credence to the notion that SketchFactor was racist. "I've only ever been about helping people," she said. "The fact that we were misconstrued was really painful for me." I asked whether she had ever considered moving out of the West Village—say, to Brooklyn, where "sketch reports" were more plentiful—to field-test the app, or to see how locals responded to it. She said that she hadn't.

When we spoke, in June, she referred to SketchFactor in the past tense; but it was still live in the Apple, Google, and Amazon app stores. Hundreds of people had downloaded it since February, and sketch reports continued to trickle in, like graffiti in a ghost town. I asked her why she hadn't removed the app. After all,

it was not generating income—it cost nothing to download and contained no ads—and she did not plan to transfer SketchFactor's user data to Walc. Ed Smith, an entrepreneur who has launched a handful of major apps including the ride-sharing service Sidecar, told me that, if he were in a similar situation, he would take down any dormant app that had the potential to "hurt my brand." This is a "very simple" process, he said. "It can take just a few moments."

McGuire's explanation, essentially, was carelessness. "As soon as we decided we were pivoting, we just didn't touch SketchFactor at all. It takes time and energy and resources to do anything—editing it, pulling it, whatever. Our focus was on Walc." In general, entrepreneurs who are moving fast and breaking things are not always equally concerned about cleaning up after themselves.

As I talked to McGuire, I tried to gauge how chastened she felt. Was her pivot only an economic decision, or was it also an ethical one? Did she think of herself solely as a victim of cyberbullying, or could she understand why her critics saw her as a perpetrator of it? Those questions seemed to rest on another: was SketchFactor just a failed business, or had it caused enduring harm?

One Friday a few weeks before my interview with McGuire, I walked through Bedford-Stuyvesant, a traditionally African-American neighborhood in Brooklyn that is undergoing rapid and contentious gentrification. I had SketchFactor open on my phone. On the map, my route was riddled with red bubbles, indicating a five on the app's one-to-five "sketchiness" scale. When I found myself at a location corresponding to one of the bubbles, I approached the people near me, showed them the map on my screen, and asked for their thoughts.

Location: Nostrand Avenue at Myrtle Avenue, near the Marcy Houses

Sketch Report: "Same guy asks me about once a week to buy milk for him, follows me for a bit. Feels threatening."

Early afternoon. No beggars in evidence, lacteally inclined or otherwise. Instead there were, from east to west: a Duane Reade; a deli; Lucky Liquor & Wine; Brooklyn Cooperative, a credit union; and Brooklyn Stoops, a new-looking burgers-and-beer place. Four middle-aged women waited for a bus. I showed them the app. "This corner ain't so sketchy," one of them said. "You want sketchy? Go down to Marcy and Greene. Don't tell them I sent you."

A young woman named Lupe Chino walked by, popped out her earbuds, and wrinkled her brow. Her companion Terrence Harper, a young man wearing a Billionaire Boys Club T-shirt, said, of the app, "Theoretically, it sounds good. If my friend tells me someplace is sketchy, I might listen. But a stranger?"

A man in his fifties, wearing a chocolate-colored chef's apron, walked outside and introduced himself as Chef Jay, the proprietor of Brooklyn Stoops. "I know these people," he said, gesturing toward Chino and Harper. "They come in all the time. I know they're good people. But if you just look at an app and it says 'sketchy,' you'd just avoid a place without going to see it for yourself."

Chino and Harper headed inside the restaurant. Chef Jay continued: "I'm from Harlem. I have four restaurants. I targeted this location a few years ago because I know this neighborhood is coming up. To me, an app talking about sketchy places? That's basically judging people before you know them, which is pretty much the worst thing you can do, in my opinion. People can go on Yelp and find out whether I make the best chicken in this neighborhood. Which I do, by the way."

Location: Nostrand Avenue at DeKalb Avenue

Sketch Report: "Lots of people making up stories on sketch factor and trying to annoy other races."

An awning on the northeast corner: Sugarhill Supper Club, Restaurant & Disco. Up a flight of stairs is an old-fashioned ballroom: mirrored walls, a grand piano on a raised stage, a framed photo of Hillary Clinton with her arm around the owner. Dawn Albert, the manager on duty, said, of the app, "That is not a good idea." She raised an eyebrow. "We're not on there, are we?"

A few blocks south is The Civil Service Café, a smartly appointed coffeehouse with rough-hewn wood tables and a Strada MP espresso machine. Behind the bar, the owner, Ayo Balogun, held a piece of pound cake in his hand. "Does this place look sketchy?" he said. "I'm eating cake." He looked at SketchFactor and scoffed. "Look, I'm conflicted," he said. "I'm a black guy. I understand why this kind of thing is offensive. But I also own a business that caters to hipsters." The app could, in theory, be good for business, signalling that the area is safer than it used to be. "Obviously, you hate to see the old-school, politically driven, redlining kind of gentrification. I'd like to think that what's happening here is a less aggressive, more organic process." He shrugged. "I moved here from Chelsea, so who am I to talk?"

Location: Herbert Von King Park, Marcy and Tompkins Avenues between Lafayette and Greene Avenues

Sketch Reports: "I've been solicited several times to buy drugs in this park, and in the mornings the recent ex-cons collect here to do pull ups on the playground equipment."

"A little Hispanic girl threw a socket wrench at me while I was jogging. She didn't want any white people playing in her park."

Every Friday afternoon, on the corner of Marcy and Lafayette, at one of the entrances to the park, an anarchist collective called In Our Hearts gives away clothes, books, and kitchen supplies. Lisa Weir, one of the volunteers, sat in a portable lawn chair. She wore a jean jacket, bright green socks, a nose ring in her septum, and a loose Afro shaved on the sides. "Look around," she said. "I'm in this park multiple times a week. I see people walking their dogs at the dog park. I see people teaching yoga classes. Is that sketchy? Look, I understand that now everyone wants to move here, and they're right—Brooklyn is dope. But for them to come from wherever and immediately start judging what goes on here? I would ask them this: what's sketchy, thirty black people on a corner, or six squad cars on a corner? I might have a different answer to that than Al from Seattle would."

An S.U.V. parked nearby. A woman got out, crossed the street, and kissed Weir on the cheek. "Namaste," Weir said. The woman handed her a wad of cash, ran back to the car, and drove off. "See, she owns a restaurant, and I'm a bike messenger, and I just did some work for her," Weir said. "What if you didn't know that? Would that seem sketchy to you?"

I strolled through the park. Tiff Baldomero, a young woman with a tight ponytail, waved her hand dismissively. "Frankly, if people want to be worried about this neighborhood, that would be great for keeping my rent low."

Lisa Weir jogged past me. "African-American female running through the park!" she shouted. "Sketchy!"

In our interview, I asked McGuire where SketchFactor had gone wrong. "Was there anything you could have done differently?" I said.

"Was there anything that *I* could have done differently?" she said. "To make Gawker not write what they wrote about me? No. I have no control over Gawker."

I pointed out that the headline had referred to "Smiling Young White People"; if her co-founder had not been white, people might have seen her company differently. She changed the subject. Later, she said that, before she met Herrington, she had planned to found SketchFactor with two female friends. "One of them is gay and one of them is black," she said. "We all had our own experiences, our own ideas about what we wanted to help people avoid in the streets." I was surprised. I had read everything I could find about SketchFactor; if the company's origin story included two other co-founders, this was the first I was hearing about it. I asked McGuire several times to share their names, or to make them available for comment, but she refused.

Some of the people I met in Bed-Stuy, and others on Twitter, had suggested that SketchFactor was a cynical attempt to profit from bigotry. It seemed to me that McGuire's motives were innocent, or that she thought they were. Still, inadvertently or not, the app had played on racist stereotypes; and it might have reduced local businesses' profits or poured fuel on the fire of gentrification. The concept of sketchiness is inseparable from prejudice: if American cities were not riven by inequality and fear, there would have been no market for SketchFactor. In light of all this, it seemed that the best way for McGuire to fail up would be to acknowledge some culpability, and to promise that Walc would do better.

"Is there anything you regret?" I asked.

"I regret that we were misinterpreted by the media," she said. "I lost twenty pounds in two weeks."

McGuire, who received unwelcome attention from Internet trolls, has reasons to feel aggrieved. Still, I was surprised at how she was choosing to frame her story. In the recent book "So You've Been Publicly Shamed," the journalist Jon Ronson meets several people who have been brought low by online hordes. Some of them are indignant; others are self-lacerating. All of them, with one exception, offer some sort of apology. (The exception, a man who was accused of hosting a Nazi-themed sex orgy, is so unflappable, so anomalous in his inability to feel shame, that it becomes one of the book's central mysteries.) Not all of the apologies are good ones. The one offered by the monologist Mike Daisey, whose work conflated truth and fiction, is particularly evasive. But even Daisey, at one point, manages to spit out the words "I'm sorry."

This was the first interview McGuire had granted in months. Setting it up had required weeks of negotiation. She had clearly spent time and money crafting a media plan; yet that plan did not seem to include a one-sentence apology, even a qualified one of the "I'm sorry you got upset" variety. Perhaps she had been advised to project unalloyed confidence. This seemed, at the very least, like a bad tactical decision.

Many tech founders appear to inhabit a world without accountability—if not above the law, then above the social convention of occasionally eating crow. For all their talk of failed elevator pitches and failed redesigns and failed companies, they are loath to talk about interpersonal or moral failures, which are both more embarrassing and more important. As one entrepreneur, explicitly channelling the spirit of Steve Jobs, wrote on Medium, "Dive in. Do. Stop over-thinking it." In this world, there are no bad ideas, only bad market fits.

In life, if not in business, not all ideas are good. Some cause real harm. Talking about race can be uncomfortable, and white people, who have the luxury to opt out of such conversations, often do so. It's unpleasant to admit that you've made a mistake, and it takes work to do better in the future. It would be dangerous if the tech élite got into the habit of dismissing such work as weakness, or as a waste of time.

For the rest of our interview, we talked about Walc. McGuire said, "Google Maps makes you figure out where you are by looking at a blue dot and turning around and around—we call this the smartphone pirouette—until you figure out which way the arrow is facing. Our innovation is to give you landmark-based directions: walk away from the Chase Bank, toward the McDonald's. We plan to do integration with those businesses, consumer deals that pop up seamlessly as you pass storefronts. We want to be a friend in your pocket. There are some shortcuts that every New Yorker knows: You don't have to walk around the block—you can just cut through the playground. That's the kind of thing that can help you walk smart."

"So let's say it's midnight," I said. "You want to walk from the Upper East Side to the Upper West Side. Clearly, the quickest route is through Central Park. But many New Yorkers would say that's unsafe. Would your app take that sort of thing into account?"

"Right now, we're not focussed on that," she said. ■

AUTHOR PROFILE

Andrew Marantz is a freelance nonfiction writer living in Brooklyn, NY. His writing has appeared in such publications as *New York* magazine, *Slate*, *Heeb*, and the *New York Times*. He attended Brown University and was awarded a Royce Fellowship in 2006 to participate in Brown's Swearer Center which connects students to programs and activities that promote community engagement, social innovation, and engaged scholarship. Marantz traveled extensively through this experience and still writes about a broad spectrum of topics. Upon graduation from Brown, he attended the NYU School of Journalism. Since 2011, he has been a contributing editor for *The New Yorker*, in which "When an App Is Called Racist" appeared on July 29, 2015.

Life-Centered Ethics, and the Human Future in Space

By Michael N. Mautner

I. Introduction

Biotechnology can transform life extensively, especially in the new environments of space. These developments will raise profound questions in bioethics and space ethics. Life-centered (biocentric) principles can provide guidance. These ethics can be generalized as biotic ethics, which value organic gene/protein life itself, and as panbiotic ethics, which seek to expand our family of organic life in the universe.

Expansion in space may be in fact imperative for our future. In contrast to fragile and limited Life on Earth, multiple worlds in space can secure our survival, and provide rich resources.[1]

These visions are developing into concrete programs.[2] For example, large-scale space colonies,[3] and the terraforming of Mars,[4] are studied. Seeding new solar systems deeper in space with life was proposed,[5] motivated by life-expanding panbiotic ethics.[6] Adapting life to these new environments can affect the future of evolution.[7]

---

[1] N.A. Rynin. *K.E. Tsiolkovskii: Life, Writings, and Rockets*. Leningrad, 1971. (Vol. 3, No. 7 of Interplanetary Flight and Communication. Leningrad Academy of Sciences of the USSR. Translated by the Israel Program for Scientific Translations, Jerusalem). 'The Earth is the cradle of the human mind, but one cannot live in the cradle forever'. A. Starchild. 2000. *Science Fiction of Konstantin Tsiolkovsky*. New York, NY: International Specialized Books Services; F. Dyson. 1979. Time Without End: Physics and Biology in an Open Universe. *Rev. Modern Phys.* 1979; 51: 447–468; F. Dyson. 1988. *Infinite in All Directions*. New York, NY: Harper and Row.

[2] S. O'Keefe, NASA Administrator. *Pioneering the Future*. 'To improve life here, to extend life to there, to find life beyond'. April 12, 2002. Syracuse University. Similar programs were announced by the European Space Agency, India, China, and Japan.

[3] G.K. O'Neill. The Colonization of Space. *Physics Today* 1974; 27: 32–38; G.K. O'Neill. 1977. *The High Frontier*. New York, NY: William Morrow.

[4] M.J. Fogg. Terraforming: A Review for Environmentalists. *The Environmentalist* 1993; 13: 7–12.

[5] M.N. Mautner. 2000. *Seeding the Universe with Life: Securing Our Cosmological Future*. Washington, DC.: Legacy Books. (www.panspermia-society.com)

[6] M.N. Mautner & G.L. Matloff. Directed Panspermia: A Technical Evaluation of Seeding Nearby Solar Systems. *Bull. Astr. Soc.* 1977; 9: 501 and *J. British Interplanetary Soc.* 1979; 32: 419–424; M.N. Mautner. Directed Panspermia. 2. Technological Advances Toward Seeding Other Solar Systems, and the Foundations of Panbiotic Ethics. *J. British Interplanetary Soc.* 1995; 48: 435–440; Directed Panspermia. 3. Strategies and Motivations for Seeding Star-Forming Clouds. *J. British Interplanetary Soc.* 1997; 50: 93–98. (www.panspermia-society.com)

[7] A. Rosenfeld. 1975. *The Second Genesis: The Coming Control of Life*. New York, NY: Vintage Books: 281; A.C. Clark. 1984. *Profiles of the Future*. New York, NY: Warner Books; 210; M.H. Hart. 1985. Interstellar Migration, the Biological Revolution, and the Future of the Galaxy. In *Interstellar Migration and Human Experience*, B.R. Finney & E.M. Jones, eds. Berkeley, CA: University of California Press: 278– 291. Ethical aspects of evolution in space are also discussed in M.A.G. Michaud. 2007. *Contact with Alien Civilisations*. New York, NY: Copernicus Books.

The potentials for life in space are supported by experimental astro-ecology.[8] Plant cultures on meteorite/asteroid materials suggest that the Solar System can support populations of trillions.[9] These resources can make territorial conflicts obsolete, assure human survival, and increase biological and cultural diversity.

Life in space opens ethical and philosophical questions that have been discussed starting with Tsiolkovski,[10] and addressed more recently in several books.[11] In parallel, biocentric ethics are also advancing. Life-centered principles have been established since antiquity, as in the edict 'choose life',[12] and in Buddhist principles,[13] and they are receiving new attention by environmental ethics.[14]

Space ethics and biocentric ethics are both at early stages. They are usually considered separately, although a connection was suggested for seeding other solar systems with life, motivated by life-centered principles.[15] This paper will propose further basic connections between life-centred ethics and space ethics.

Space adaptation through designed evolution may affect the future profoundly, especially when our designs become self-fulfilling. Our survival can then be secured only if it is pursued deliberately. In that future our guiding ethics can have far-reaching consequences.

This paper intends to contribute to a discourse on life-centered astroethics and on its effects on the future. In particular, it will postulate that expansion in space, combined with life-centered ethics, can best secure our long-term survival.

II. Science-Based Arguments for Biocentric Ethics

Before biocentric ethics are applied to space, these life-centred principles need to be justified rationally. Of course all ethics are subjective, but scientific insights can provide rational foundations.

---

[8] M.N. Mautner. Biological Potential of Extraterrestrial Materials. 1. Nutrients in Carbonaceous Meteorites, and Effects on Biological Growth. *Planetary and Space Science.* 1997; 45: 653–664; Planetary Resources and Astroecology. Planetary Microcosm Models of Asteroid and Meteorite Interiors. Implications for Space Populations and Panspermia. *Astrobiology* 2002; 2: 59–76; M.N. Mautner. Directed Panspermia, Astroethics, and our Cosmological Future. *Int. J. Astrobiology* 2004; Supplement 1: 116 (www.Astro-Ecology.com)

[9] M.N. Mautner. Life in the Cosmological Future: Resources, Biomass and Populations. *J. British Interplanetary Soc.* 2005; 58: 167–180.

[10] Tsiolkovski, *op. cit.* note 1.

[11] E.C. Hargrove, ed. 1986. *Beyond Spaceship Earth – Environment Ethics and the Solar System.* Sierra Club Books; P.C.W. Davies. 1995. *Are We Alone? Philosophical Implications of the Discovery of Extraterrestrial Life.* London: Basic Books; B.R. Finney. 1985. Voyagers Into Ocean Space. In *Interstellar Migration and Human Experience.* B.R. Finney & E.M. Jones, eds. Berkeley: CA: University of California Press: 164–180.

[12] Bible. Old Testament *Deuteronomy*: ch. 30 vv. 15, 19.

[13] A. Hunt-Badiner, ed. 1990. *Dharma Gaia: A Harvest of Essays in Buddhism and Ecology.* Berkeley, CA: Parallax; B. Gruzalski. Gandhi's Contribution to Environmental Thought and Action. *Environmental Ethics* 2002; 24: 227–242.

[14] A. Schweitzer. 1990. *Out of My Life and Thought.* New York, NY: Holt: 131. '(being good:) to preserve life, to promote life, to raise to its highest value life which is capable of development'; P.W. Taylor. 1986. *Respect for Nature: A Theory of Environmental Ethics.* Princeton, NJ: Princeton University Press: 45; J.R. Des Jardins. 1997. *Environmental Ethics: An Introduction to Environmental Philosophy.* Belmont: Wadsworth. G.E. Moore. 1988. *Principia Ethica.* NY: Prometheus Books. 'With regard to some rules.... where the instincts to preserve and propagate life were strong....'

[15] Mautner, *op. cit.* note 5; Mautner & Matloff, *op. cit.* note 6.

Molecular biology shows that all organic cellular life share a common feature, self-reproduction through gene/protein cycles. Biotic ethics value these core patterns of biology themselves, and strive to perpetuate them. Expansion in space can broaden these principles into panbiotic ethics that value all organic cellular gene/protein life, present and future, and seek to maximize life in all accessible habitats.

Although these ethics value all cellular gene/protein life, from a human point of view life may best enjoy conscious existence, further motivating self-propagation.

Molecular Self-Replication and the Definition of Life

When seeking to define Life, we ask: What objects in Nature are we willing to accept as fellow living beings? In this sense, 'what is Life?' is a question of judgement, rather than of science. However, science can reveal common features that help define fellow life.

Most definitions of life recognize reproduction and evolution as essential features. Of all known phenomena, only organic biological life reproduces actively, and evolves. A plausible definition may then state: 'Life is a process whose outcome is the self-reproduction of complex molecular patterns'. Importantly, Life is then a *process* that requires a constant flow of information, matter and energy.

More specifically, biological matter is composed of genetic information contained in DNA sequences that code proteins, which in turn help reproducing the DNA sequences. All organic cellular life uses these self-reproducing gene/protein cycles.

The Unique Position of Life in Nature

Complexity assigns a unique position to life. Proteins, DNA and membranes are all made of complex molecules that are structured precisely for their functions. Complex enzymes catalyze specific reactions, and complex t-RNA molecules convert DNA codes to amino acids in proteins. Even the most simple cell possesses thousands of finely tuned complex molecules that act in coordination. This complexity is unique to life.

Biology also depends on the precise coincidence of seemingly independent physical laws.[16] The universe contains just enough matter and energy to avoid fast collapse or expansion, allowing liveable conditions for eons. Stars such as the Sun last for billions of years and host habitable planets, due to a coincidence of the laws of gravity, nuclear physics, gas convection, and magnetic fields. Biology is based on carbon, formed in stars due to coincidental nuclear resonances. Electromagnetism bonds molecules with just the right strength, allowing chemistry and biology to exist.

Life therefore depends on the laws of gravity, nuclear forces, chemistry, thermodynamics and cosmology. These laws are seemingly independent of each other, but they coincide precisely to allow life to exist. In this sense, the physical universe itself comes to a unique point in life.

---

[16] L.J. Henderson. 1970. *The Fitness of the Environment.* Glouster: Peter Smith: 312. J. Gribbin & M. Rees. 1989. *Cosmic Coincidences.* New York, NY: Bantam Books: 269; F. Hoyle. 1983. *The Intelligent Universe.* London: Michael Joseph: 218; P.C.W. Davies. 2007. *Cosmic Jackpot: Why Our Universe Is Just Right for Life.* New York, NY: Houghton Mifflin.

The Unity of Life

We have a special feeling for other living beings, an empathy called 'biophilia'.[17] This special relation exists even among very different life-forms. For example, we readily recognize a cactus being closer to us than a rock. We also recognize microorganisms as fellow life, and astrobiology searches for microorganisms in space to ease our cosmic loneliness. We sense that all living beings are one family who share mutual affinity and dependence.

This sense of unity is supported by science. From microorganisms to humans, we all share common designs. Every living cell is surrounded by selective membranes; processes energy through biochemical cycles using enzymes and ATP; has a complex genome coded in DNA sequences; and uses a common code and mechanism for translating three-letter DNA codes to amino acids in proteins. Ultimately, the proteins help to reproduce the DNA code, completing the gene/protein cycle.[18]

Further, phylogenetic trees indicate that all terrestrial life can be traced to a common ancestor.[19] Organisms as different from us as yeasts share half; mice, over 90%, chimpanzees, over 95%, and different human individuals share over 99% of our genome.[20]

These scientific insights give a deeper meaning to the unity of all Life. Our complex molecular patterns are common to all organic gene/protein life and distinguish us from any other phenomena of nature.

Observational Equivalence, and Life and Purpose

Expanding life in space will require action with purpose. 'The purpose of life' has been pondered since antiquity, but today it can be examined with scientific insights. One useful principle is 'observational equivalence': If two phenomena are identical in all observables, then they are identical in fact. Examples are the relativistic equivalence of gravity and acceleration, and Turing's test of intelligence.[21]

Applied to behaviour, self-perpetuation is usually included in the definition of life. All organisms act for survival and propagation, *as if* they pursued these outcomes deliberately. This of course does not imply conscious planning. However, if the *observed* behavior of organisms appears to pursue survival and propagation, then the *equivalent effective observable purpose* of life is survival and propagation. Therefore life may be seen to have an intrinsic purpose, and since the universe contains life, it contains purpose. In brief, the purpose of life is to live.

We, as living beings, share this effective purpose. The shared drive for self-propagation can then define a human purpose: to safeguard and perpetuate life. To this effect, we can expand life and seek to advance it into a controlling force in nature. These objectives can give human existence a cosmic purpose.

---

[17] E.O. Wilson & S. McVay, eds. 1993. *The Biophilia Hypothesis*. Washington, DC: Island Press.

[18] W.K. Purves et al. 2001. *Life: The Science of Biology*. Sunderland, MA: Worth Publishers, Inc.

[19] S.L. Baldauf, J.D. Palmer & W.F. Doolittle. The Root of the Universal Tree and the Origin of Eukaryotes Based on Elongation Factor Phylogeny. *Proc. Nat. Academy Sci. USA* 1996; 93: 7749–7754.

[20] A. Gibbons. Which of Our Genes Make Us Humans. *Science* 1998; 81: 1432–1434.

[21] S. Goldberg. 1984. *Understanding Relativity: Origin and Impact of a Scientific Revolution*. Cambridge, MA: Birkhauser; A. Turing. Computing Machinery and Intelligence. *Mind* 1950; 256: 433–460.

M

From a subjective point of view as conscious humans, we may wish to maximize conscious life. In fact, the conscious enjoyment of life can further motivate self-continuation.

In summary, life is united by its unique complexity, by the physical laws that precisely allow life, and by self-reproduction through gene/protein cycles. Life also has a special value for us as living beings. Therefore both objective science and our subjective judgement can support life-centered ethics and its purpose to propagate life.

III. Space Bioethics: Prospects and Questions

Astro-Ethics and Survival in a Controlled Future

In space, life can access limitless resources through astronomical times, helped by designed evolution in new environments. With such mastery of nature, our objectives become self-fulfilling.

With biotechnology that adapts us to space we can also control our biological future. However, these powers also entail dangers. In particular, tests by survival will always apply, both in natural and in designed evolution. Fit life-forms will survive, while failed designs will perish. This logic of life has guided, and will continue to guide, evolution. These tests of survival must be taken into account when designing future life.

In a designed future, what we pursue, we shall accomplish. Therefore, to prevail, survival must be pursued deliberately. This pursuit can be secured by ethics that aim to propagate life. Therefore, life-centered ethics themselves must be always propagated to secure our continued survival.

Ultimately it may depend on our ethics whether life will realize its cosmic potentials.

Astro-Ecology and Space Populations. Should We Create Populations of Trillions?

Life-centered ethics suggest that we should use space to advance life, and panbiotic ethics suggest that we should use space to maximize life. Of course, the quality of future life also matters, and in particular, we may wish to maximize conscious life.

Quantitatively, we may wish to maximize life over specific, maybe astronomically long, times. We can define a possible measure of the amounts of life in terms of biomass summed over of the time that it exists (Biomass Integrated Over Times Available (BIOTA) measured in kg-years).[22]

The potential amount of life in the Solar System can be estimated based on the available resources, such as the carbonaceous asteroids and comets that contain water, organic carbon and mineral nutrients. These resources can support, at high standards, human populations of thousands of trillions, more than one

---

[22] In mathematical terms, the objective is to maximize the term BIOTA (Biomass Integrated Over Time Available), defined as the integral of B(t)dt, where B(t) is total biomass as a function of time and the integration is over the habitable lifetime of the universe. The ultimate maximum would be achieved by converting all matter to biomass and maximizing its longevity. (Mautner, *op. cit.* note 9)

hundred thousand times the Earth's present population.[23] Cometary resources can yield biomass a hundred times larger; and a population equal to that of one million Earths. Extended to the galaxy, if one in ten stars has habitable environments, the above immense amounts can be multiplied further by ten billion.

Should we aim to create such immense amounts of life in billions of solar systems? Panbiotic ethics that seek to maximize life support these objectives. Further, this expansion will allow new lines of evolution, rich biodiversity, and ever advancing civilizations.

The potential time-scales of future life are also astronomical. For example, the expected lifetime of the Solar System is five billion years, while star-bound civilizations may exist for hundreds of trillions of years.[24] With these data, we can calculate the immense amounts of time-integrated BIOTA that resources in the Solar System permit.[25]

These immense populations may be created relatively rapidly, but biological wastage could exhaust life in the Solar System in half a million years. On the other hand, smaller but still very large populations could last through five billion future years of the Sun.

Should we construct immense shorter-lived populations or smaller but longer-lived populations? It would seem preferable that life should exist as long as possible.

The Ultimate Prospects. Should we Propagate Life if the Future Is Finite?

Considering the amounts of matter in the universe and its duration in time, we can estimate the ultimate amounts of possible life in the universe.

If all matter was converted to biomass, some of it would have to be then converted to energy to sustain biology. On this basis, we can calculate the ultimate extent of possible life in the galaxy and in the universe, in the form of populations of trillions that last trillions of eons.[26] This potential scope of life is indeed immense, but by current cosmology, still finite.

Is there a point to maximizing life if it is finite? Panbiotic ethics that seek to maximize life would answer in the affirmative. The vast scope of future life will allow great biological diversity, and rich experiences for intelligent beings. These potentials can further encourage us to secure and expand life.

---

[23] The 1e22 kg carbonaceous asteroids contain 2% carbon, 10% water, and phosphorus and nitrogen, the limiting element. This could yield a human biomass of 3e20 kg (exponential notation, 3e20 = 3×10^{20}) in a population of 6e18, a hundred million present Earth populations. Alternatively these resources can yield 6e20 kg general biomass, and if 100,000 kg biomass supports one human, the population in the Solar System would be 6e15 (six thousand trillion) humans, equal to about 100,000 present Earth populations.

[24] F. Adams & G. Laughlin. 1999. *The Five Ages of the Universe*. New York, NY: Touchstone.

[25] With 6e20 kg asteroid-based biomass, in the five billion future years of the Sun the time-integrated biomass (BIOTA) in the Solar System will be 3e30 kg-years. Cometary resources can yield a biomass still a hundred times larger. (Mautner, *op. cit.* note 9)

[26] The estimated 1e41 kg baryonic matter in the galaxy can be converted gradually to biomass and then to energy, sustaining a steady-state biomass of 3e11 kg, possibly as ten billion humans, comparable to the current world population. In this manner life would last for an incomprehensible 1e37 years until protons decay, yielding BIOTA of 3e48 kg-years. For life in the universe these numbers may be multiplied by one hundred billion galaxies, allowing a time-integrated biomass of 3e59 kg-years of biological life in the universe. (Mautner, *op. cit.* note 9)

Is the duration of life in the universe really finite? Cosmology will be controlled by dark matter and dark energy, both of whose natures are unknown. We have evidence about the past fourteen billion years since the Big Bang, but this is fleetingly short compared with trillions of future eons. Our descendants may have to observe cosmology for many eons until they can predict, and maybe control, the ultimate future.

For now, we need to secure Life for future generations. They may then understand Nature more deeply, and seek to extend life indefinitely.

Seeding Other Solar Systems with Life

We can soon start expanding life by seeding other solar systems. Human travel to other stars has major obstacles,[27] but we can soon start directed panspermia, sending microorganisms to other solar systems to plant the essential patterns of gene/protein life. We can also include eukaryotic organisms, hardy plant spores and the cysts of microscopic animals to start higher evolution.[28]

Solar sails or seeded comets can launch microbial capsules to nearby stars, or to clusters of new stars in interstellar clouds where they can seed many new solar systems.[29] Some of this new life may evolve into civilizations that can promote Life further in the galaxy.

These directed panspermia missions will be launched easily from space colonies, even by individuals or small groups. Should we proceed?

At present there is no scientific evidence for extraterrestrial life. The complexity of even a single cell suggests that the origins of life may be highly improbable and that it may not have occurred elsewhere even on billions of planets. Life on Earth may be unique, and the fate of life is then in our hands.

Seeding other planetary systems could prevent the study of pristine space but seeding a few hundred new solar systems will secure and propagate life while leaving hundreds of billions of pristine stars for exploration.

Conclusive proofs of extraterrestrial life could be provided by interstellar probes, but at achievable velocities, this would require millions of years. In the absence of such proof, we need to seed other solar systems to assure that life will indeed exist elsewhere in the universe.

However, the technology to seed space and, eventually, life itself in this Solar System, have finite durations. Should we accept the certain end of our family of gene/protein life, in order to avoid a small chance of interfering with putative alien life elsewhere?

The chances of interfering with other life-forms can be minimized by targeting young solar systems where life, especially advanced life, would not have yet started. Even if our microbial missions encounter other life, they may merge with local life and generate new biology. In either case, life will benefit.

Biotic ethics concerns first our own family of gene/protein life. If this family of life is unique to Earth, its fate is in our hands. Panbiotic ethics can then motivate us to seed other solar systems to secure life, with cosmic consequences.

---

[27] E.F. Mallove & G.L. Matloff. 1989. *The Starflight Handbook: A Pioneer's Guide to Interstellar Travel.* New York, NY: Wiley; J.H. Mauldin. 1992. *Prospects for Interstellar Travel (Science and Technology, Vol 80)* San Diego, CA: Univelt.

[28] Mautner, *op. cit.* note 5; Mautner & Matloff, *op. cit.* note 6.

[29] Mautner & Matloff, *op. cit.* note 6.

Fundamental Changes in Biology. How Far Can We Transform, but Still Preserve, Life?

Biology will have to adapt to space. Authors from Tsiolkovsky to Freeman Dyson, and much science fiction, realized that we may need to design new human traits in space.[30]

Resistance to radiation may be achieved by adapting human cells with genes from *Deinococcus radiodurans* and other microorganisms. Humans in space may need photosynthetic organs to use solar energy directly. They will need to adapt to reduced gravity, possibly reduce body size, develop new limbs for solar sailing and use engineered mechanical organs. Controlling these organs may require modified brains interfaced with computers. Long-distance space travel may require longevity of millennia, and artificial reproduction.

These technologies are developing, but their products still remain gene/protein life. Current research, however, also addresses basic biology itself. Novel proteins incorporate new amino acids for mechanical strength and for extreme conditions.[31] Correspondingly, DNA may be expanded with new nucleic bases to code for new proteins.

These developments can transform the very core of gene/protein life. Is this permitted by ethics that aim to preserve life? They may be allowed if the modified biology retains gene/protein reproduction. For example, the new biochemical components may be related to the natural amino acids and to DNA bases, or propagate otherwise through gene/protein cycles. These fundamental changes still preserve essentially gene/protein life.

However, biological life would be eliminated if humans were replaced by robots.[32] Although robots can be useful, to preserve biology, control should remain with biological beings. Specifically, control should remain with biological brains that have vested interest to perpetuate organic gene/protein life.

Biocentric ethics aims to propagate life. What does this mean when we can transform life? What is the essence of life that we should propagate? How far can we change, and still preserve, life? Biotechnology can soon turn these questions into actionable, practical choices.

Human Survival

Similar questions apply to human survival. If humans are altered, does humankind still survive? Do we aim to preserve the present human species, or help its evolutionary progress?

Even if humans are altered, we would not become extinct if our genes are preserved and extended in advanced post-humans. This is in fact the natural course of evolution.

Biotic ethics value gene/protein life itself, and panbiotic ethics would favor evolution that helps to secure life. Similarly, if advanced post-human species can better secure life, then biotic ethics would approve continued human evolution.

---

[30] J.W. Valentine. 1985. The Origins of Evolutionary Novelty and Galactic Colonization. In *Interstellar Migration and Human Experience*. B.R. Finney & E.M. Jones, eds. Berkeley, CA: University of California Press: 266–276; Hart, *op. cit.* note 7.

[31] J.L. Cleland & C.S. Craik, eds. 1996. *Protein Engineering: Principles and Practice*. Chichester: Wiley.

[32] I. Aleksander & P. Barnett. 1983. *Reinventing Man: The Robot Becomes Reality*. New York, NY: Penguin Books.

Biocentric Ethics, Moral and Religious Values, Purpose and Determinism

By biocentric ethics, actions that secure life are morally good, and actions that threaten life are evil. These principles are ancient: 'I put before you good and evil, life and death....choose life.'[33] This text identifies life as the essential moral good, and death as evil. So do more recent sources such as Schweitzer[34], and discussions of panbiotic ethics.[35]

By life-centered ethics, self-extinction is the ultimate evil. By these principles, dangers that threaten all life constitute infinite risk. No finite cause can justify an infinite risk/benefit ratio. Therefore, biotic ethics cannot accept even a small danger to all Life.

Conversely, endeavors that secure Life, such as expansion in space, are morally imperative. This endeavor will involve large-scale human collaborations, which require justice, peace, compassion, and truth. Human curiosity, ambition, and intelligence are also needed. These values are, therefore, consistent with biotic ethics.

Life-centered ethics are consistent with both religious and secular principles. In religious terms, a Creator who formed life will also desire its propagation. For secular ethics, life-centered principles suggest a rationally based human purpose and related moral and social values.

Having defined a purpose, can we in fact realize it? Is the future open or pre-determined, and can we control it? We cannot test experimentally if Nature is deterministic, because we can only observe one path of events that unfolds in time and cannot see if alternative paths are possible. However, lacking scientific proof that we can affect the future, we still make plans and often realize them.

Although the future cannot be predicted in detail, we can formulate principles that can guide it. Ultimately, biology will define the possible forms and scope of life, and survival will shape its evolution. These laws made us into a force of life in the universe, and will continue to advance us in the future.

Relations between Biocentric, Biotic and Panbiotic Ethics

Biocentric ethics value living organisms, species, and ecosystems.[36] More generally, a biotic ethics can be defined that values the core pattern of Life itself, that is, self-propagation through gene/protein cycles. This can be broadened further to panbiotic ethics, which seek to maximize life in space and time, and to incorporate in Life all the accessible resources.[37]

All life-centered ethics aim to secure our family of gene/protein life. Traditional biocentric ethics favor the conservation of existing species. Biotic ethics favor the evolution of new life-forms that help to secure gene/protein life in

---

[33] Bible, *op. cit.* note 12.

[34] Schweitzer, *op. cit.* note 14.

[35] Mautner, *op. cit.* note 5; Mautner & Matloff, *op. cit.* note 6.

[36] Schweitzer, *op. cit.* note 14.

[37] Technically, panbiotic ethics aim to realize the full biotic potential of gene/protein life using the carrying capacity of the universe. (See these terms in J.M. Anderson. 1981. *Ecology for the Environmental Sciences: Biosphere, Ecosystems and Man.* London: Edward Arnold; M. Begon, M. Mortimer & D.J. Thompson. 1996. *Population Ecology: a Unified Study of Animals and Plants.* Oxford: Blackwell Science.

space. Panbiotic ethics favor the perpetual expansion of life with the continuing divergence of new species.

Summary

Adapting Life to space will require major biological changes, helped by designed evolution. Our designs will then become self-fulfilling, and we shall need to propagate life deliberately in order to secure our survival. Life-centered ethics can motivate this quest, secure the future, and shape it with far-reaching, even cosmic, consequences. Therefore life-centered ethics themselves need always to be propagated.

Indeed, judging by observed behavior, the effective purpose of life is self-propagation. Briefly, the self-contained purpose of life is to live. Being part of life then defines a human purpose, to safeguard and propagate life. This also defines moral values: Acts that support life are good and acts that destroy life are evil.

Life-centered ethics can be supported by scientific insights: the biological unity of all gene/protein life, and the special place of complex life in nature, which precisely permits biology to exist.

Life-centered ethics can be generalized as biotic ethics that value the basic patterns of organic gene/protein life, and as panbiotic ethics that seek to expand life in the universe. The panbiotic objectives can be quantified, to maximize the time-integrated biomass in living matter. To maximize life, we can soon start to settle our Solar System, and to seed with life new solar systems beyond.

The expansion of life will increase biological complexity, diversity and intelligence, leading to new species who can further propagate life in the universe. From the human viewpoint, future life may best enjoy conscious existence, further motivating self-propagation. Indeed, control must always remain with organic gene/protein life that has a vested interest to continue organic life.

Whether future evolution will be designed or natural, selection by survival will always apply: Species that seek to propagate life will survive and species that do not, will perish. Therefore, in a designed future we shall always need to seek survival deliberately, and these life-centered principles will always need to be propagated.

Ultimately, biology will define the possible forms and scope of life, and survival will shape its evolution. These laws made us into a force of life in the universe, and will continue to advance life in the future.

Given the projections of cosmology, life can expect an immense future. With the powers of intelligence, this future is in our hands. For now, we need to establish ethics that will secure life for future generations. Our descendants may then understand nature more deeply and seek to extend life indefinitely. In that future, our human existence will find a cosmic purpose. ■

M

─────────────────────────────── AUTHOR PROFILE

Michael N. Mautner (b. 1942) was born in Hungary, where he was saved by a courageous woman, Irene Gigor-Horvath. He obtained a B.Sc. from the Hebrew University, an M.Sc. from Georgetown University, and a Ph.D. from Rockefeller University, New York. Current research interests are ion kinetics and thermochemistry, gas-phase acidities and basicities, and ionic processes in astrochemistry and bioenergetics, with over 200 publications in these areas. He served on the faculty of Rockefeller University and as Research Chemist at NIST, and was also affiliated with The University of Canterbury and Lincoln University in New Zealand. He is currently Affiliate Research Professor at Virginia Commonwealth University. Over the course of his career, Mautner became increasingly aware of the great challenges and opportunities opened up by science and technology. He believes that new ethics are required to ensure that science will serve, rather than threaten, life on Earth and in space. A life-centered ethics can be based on our core identity as part of the organic, gene/protein family of life. This basic identity then leads to a human purpose to secure and expand life, which is best achieved in space. With this philosophy, we can secure a future for life in the galaxy for trillions of years. Establishing this future for life can give our human existence a cosmic purpose. His other research interests include space colonization, and the science and ethics of seeding other solar systems with life; more information is available at www.panspermia-society.com. "Life-Centered Ethics, and the Human Future in Space" was published in *Bioethics* in 2009.

Making American Places: Civic Engagement Rightly Understood

By Ted V. McAllister

The loss of place is, in part, a casualty of our culture's drive for liberation from necessity—not only from the limitations of physical space, but the limitations of any and all aspects of our given identity, including our pasts. This sense of liberation has long been a healthy element of American life. But the health of both the individual and society depends on the existence of certain democratic dispositions that need exercise and expression in acts of civic engagement. This requires local institutions in which citizens can deliberate on questions of public good. Without such institutions, our democratic dispositions will wither and die, and democratic self-rule with them. The "liberation" from place, argues Ted V. McAllister, is no liberation at all, while the commitment to place is the path to self-reliant freedom.

M

Place, the story usually goes, is about limits, and defending the importance of place is really a species of repression. There is much truth in this line of reasoning. For so many people in history, place was either such a basic fact of their lives that they never came to see it conceptually or, if they did, saw it as a sort of prison. In villages or neighborhoods all over the world and throughout history—as diverse as fifteenth-century France and early twentieth-century Tennessee (or, for that matter, contemporary Afghanistan)—the experience of place has often been oppressive. It is an experience of prying eyes, leaving no privacy, no relief from the tedium of small expectations, no meaningful escape to a larger world of possibility—not even a reasonable hope of a liberated imagination to dream of other possibilities. For so many of our ancestors, place was just another word for hopelessness.

Do we really need a place in the world today? Isn't the world itself our "place"—our global community? Perhaps for previous generations, the world was too large to be a place and so they were forced to find or carve out a little space to call their own, a provincial home for protection against unruly nature and lawless strangers. We moderns are liberated from the unchosen restraints of our ancestors, for we have largely mastered space with transportation and communication technologies. Who needs the walls of their fortress cities against the barbarians? Certainly for many, portable wealth and countless "connected" locations around the globe liberate them from any meaningful dependence on one place, one society, one polis. We have escaped the limits of geography.

This presumed liberation from physical space (or at least from connection to specific physical spaces) also suggests deeper forms of liberation, including giving ourselves to the creative urge to re-form and reinvent our identities. In this sense, the very idea of place is restrictive. Whereas we might once have said that someone should know his place (which, beyond the racist overtones this language has

taken, suggests that we ought to play roles that are given to us, that we did not choose), we now assert that a person should find space in the world for his particular experiment in living. Because we are no longer bound by inherited roles or even strong familial or social pressures to fulfill the expectations that often come from a strong sense of place, we prefer to think of the world as a space big enough for us to find our true selves or create new selves. By mastering physical space we turn the world into metaphorical space for individual expression. Liberation from specific places also means release from bonds of social institutions like family or church. The expansiveness of this world allows us to create or join whatever social networks we choose, designing a social, political, artistic, and sexual life that reaches from Little Rock to Timbuktu, from our laptop to the ether.

Perhaps the most overlooked form of liberation promised by the gurus of modern emancipation comes in the form of historylessness. Human beings have usually had a "place" in history, the felt presence of ancestors, of inherited culture, a sense that as individuals and groups they played an appointed role in a story not of their making. But as the pace of technological, social, and cultural change accelerates, we increasingly experience our environment in a way that exposes no clear dependence on the distant or middle past. The ways of our grandparents are so hopelessly ill-suited to the contemporary environment that one might well consider knowledge of history a useless form of antiquarianism. The conquest of space is also the conquest of history, if not of time. No longer bound to our places of birth, we can more easily ignore the history attending any temporary places we might later inhabit. We have not only turned place into space but we have abandoned history for the ever-present now. As I will argue, to the degree that we live free from the constraints of the cultural and political spaces that we call communities and from the grounding role of history, we sever ourselves from the creative energies of richly encumbered lives. This form of liberation leads to a form of powerlessness.

American Space and Place

Like most of the contributors to this volume, I believe that the modern liberation of the individual from the constraints of place constitutes as much a limitation as an emancipation. To put the claim bluntly, place constrains but it also empowers, and a radical emancipation from place does not lead to creative freedom but to boredom, emotional and spiritual fragmentation, and tyranny. Thus, it is important to create, preserve, and improve real places for real people (not abstract individuals of indeterminate identity) to find attachments, to empower them to engage meaningfully and well with neighbors toward collective purposes, and to help them understand their particular role in the larger story of humanity. The task must be a constructive one, active rather than passive. It is not a matter of simply not getting in the way of communities but rather of thinking more positively about policies that can cultivate or protect healthy places as lively habitats for citizens, families, businesses, and civil society. To affirm that America needs healthy places requires a theoretical defense of the importance of place to human flourishing but also demands a serious reflection on policies to fit that philosophical and anthropological vision.

But, is it possible that Americans love space more than place? Our cultural mythology is particularly rich with the liberating power of wide-open spaces, the awesome beauty of trackless wilderness, the adventure of the frontiersman untethered to place, the romance and fresh possibilities of the open road, the power of placeless space to inspire self-discovery and creativity. We are often in need of "space" to clear our heads—space to breathe when obligations make us claustrophobic. Many of us need to put space between ourselves and our loved ones, lest we lose our identity in the tight bonds of familial or communal affection. We talk about real and metaphorical space in terms of freedom, creativity, opportunity, and a profound individualism—emotionally connecting "space" with our very identities, our sense of self. It seems that without "space" we cannot find ourselves or create ourselves.

Space can also be forbidding, mysterious, dark—the source for experiences of ennui, loss, and fear. Driving through the vast open spaces of the Great Plains or the western deserts produces, in many a sensitive soul, a sense of spiritual nausea. The horizon is vast, the terrain appears unchanging, time slows down as miles go by without detectable landmarks. One can easily feel insignificant, small, meaningless in such a space—a space that bears little trace of human contact and evokes no sense whatsoever of history. With little effort the sojourner through such spaces meditates on the formless, the timeless, on the infinite—that is, on the terror of boundlessness.

However much we need space for adventure and growth, we need, perhaps even more, boundaries that give structure to our lives, that turn space into something knowable and that help form the architecture that preserves memory. What is needed is an art of place-making. for we can say with G. K. Chesterton that "Art consists of limitation.... The most beautiful part of every picture is the frame."[1] The art of turning space into place is the art of limiting in order to create. Indeed, American history is as much the tale of place-making as of seeking space. We Americans are peerless in the practice of this art and we have made America itself into a "place," a huge but not boundless place that incorporates both a built environment and open spaces into a meaningful whole. America is bound by shared history, language, cultural affinities. and collective purposes that emerge from democratic participation—from civic engagement rightly understood. And yet it is reasonable to argue that America is a place only because of the rich and robust nature of its many different and distinct places. Loyalty and attachment to "America" requires, in most cases, complex and almost invisible cords of affection to particular people, local institutions, and places.

In American lore, devotion to these particular places, or to the insistence of building such places, is almost as great as our myth of intrepid individuals bound for virgin land. We celebrate foundings, which, among other things, are acts of turning space into place. The Separatists (so called Pilgrims) established order in the wilds of America with the Mayflower Compact. At nearly the same time, the Puritans created a robust social and political order on their "errand into the wilderness." What was the Northwest Ordinance of 1787 but the imposition of order on space—the mechanism by which space can be turned into social and political places favorable to human needs? The United States Constitution was the product of a deliberate and deliberative effort to create a new political structure to help

227

solidify a single, multifarious, coherent place. Every story of the lone frontiersman unfolds against the backdrop of one of the greatest place-making adventures in human history—the constant settling and organizing of towns that brought order and stability to previously lawless spaces. Devotion to place was an important part of the story of the Civil War and how it was fought. And in the twentieth century, fascination with what kinds of places we could build and what those places could do to and for us pushed urban development to new heights, governed the development of the post-1945 "crabgrass frontier" of suburbia, and led to the creation of a national transportation infrastructure. Say what you will about the American love for space and freedom, but few peoples have shown the same genius for creating places and order.

Civic Engagement Rightly Understood

...American devotion to freedom emerged from social and political life, not from solitary individuals seeking protection of what is theirs by nature. Because democracy serves as a solvent to relationships that bind individuals together through mutual forms of obligation, it tends to reduce society to a loose association of individuals whose connections are products of affection, desire, and mutually agreed-upon contract. The origins of American freedom are essential to explaining how democratic instincts were altered by circumstance.

The township, Tocqueville argued (following Aristotle), is a natural form of association, found throughout history. But, however natural the township, history knows very few cases where township freedom (the freedom to govern themselves without interference) lasted long enough for citizens to establish deep habits of self-rule and emotional attachments to their own town. Because American townships (or at least New England townships), during a long period of salutary neglect, produced countless and distinct varieties of these self-governing communities, they also produced a patriotism attached to each town wrought by these ongoing habits of self-rule. By investing as many citizens as possible in the regular acts of government, these townships foster a distinct sense of ownership or meaningful participation—for their citizens it was truly "our town."

The constellation of choices, laws, traditions, and habits that emerge from this robust form of self-rule produces something akin to the "native country." "In this manner," wrote Tocqueville of the multiplication of civic duties, "life in a township makes itself felt in a way at each instant; it manifests itself each day by the accomplishment of a duty or by the exercise of a right."[2] The constant and regular action of political life gives a very specific character, look, even feel to each town. "The Americans are attached to the city by a reason analogous to the one that makes inhabitants of the mountains love their country. Among them, the native country has *marked and characteristic features*; it has more of a *physiognomy* than elsewhere."[3] The shape of a town, its features, its laws, its history, its way of doing things, gives rise to attachments, to the love of the particular, the eccentric, the known in ways that no generic expression of a town can produce. Most important of all, Tocqueville claims that the very particularistic character of each town, and therefore the means of producing loyalty, a sense of duty, and love of what is one's own, is the product of what we might call civic engagement rightly understood.

228

Civic engagement does not mean organized appeals to a distant government, nor does it include any conception in which the citizens construe their relationship to the government, local or distant, in a manner similar to a client or a customer. Civic engagement rightly understood, in whatever particular form it takes, requires that citizens engage as citizens in a deliberative process in which they understand themselves to be partners in governance. Governance, in this use of the word, is not limited to, nor must it be primarily, an expression of an organized government that supplies services. Indeed, the more centralized the administrative functions of the town, the fewer the opportunities for self-government. A large administrative apparatus leaves individuals free to live largely unconnected from social and political arrangements, free to live and let live, free to cultivate a lifestyle. Individualists, thus produced, see no need to rely on their fellow citizens or their closest neighbors or their fellow congregants or their lodge members. The well-functioning administration (local, state, and federal) liberates them from mutual dependence and thereby robs them of township freedom.

Civic engagement, therefore, must incorporate a sense of self-reliance rather than individualism. Habituated to solving problems with their neighbors as those problems emerge, citizens do not reflexively turn to the administrative state when a bridge washes out, when the little league needs a place to play, when a family loses its income. Civic engagement surely includes citizens working through the political process to make changes (often to get that bridge or baseball diamond built) but it must also open up social space for other groups, clusters of volunteers, and nongovernmental institutions to solve problems. The common denominator of all such civic engagement is the investing of citizens in the task of governing with some or all their neighbors and the fostering of a sense of ownership that can only come from each town developing its distinctive physiognomy.

By contrast, Tocqueville's admiration for the way American democracy produced countless native countries and for the salutary effect of this prodigious expression of self-rule also meant that he saw the risks of tyranny as great to the extent that America lost this habit of local self-rule. Freedom depends on local self-rule. At the end of his second volume, as Tocqueville anticipated what would happen if democracy were to be abandoned to its savage instinct and thereby stripped of its virtues, he placed the loss of native country as the very expression of despotism:

> I want to imagine with what new features despotism could be produced in the world: I see an innumerable crowd of like and equal men who revolve on themselves without repose, procuring the small and vulgar pleasures with which they fill their souls. Each of them, withdrawn and apart, is like a stranger to the destiny of all the others: his children and his particular friends form the whole human species for him; as for dwelling with his fellow citizens, he is beside them, but he does not see them; he touches them and does not feel them; he exists only in himself and for himself alone, and if a family still remains for him, one can at least say that he no longer has a native country.[4]

Understood this way, strong places that are distinct, that have a purchase on the attention and affection of their citizens, that engage at least a large minority in robust self-rule (civic engagement rightly understood), are the necessary condition for the protection of American freedom. The problem we face today, as I noted earlier, is that people must want this kind of freedom, this political and civic involvement that requires them to give up individualism for communal self-reliance. Healthy freedom, at least in the American story, requires places that move citizens to love where they live, to find themselves part of a local story (history), and to invest their time and energy in the evolution of a place strange, distinct, and perhaps even a little weird. To paraphrase Edmund Burke, to make us love our native country, our native country ought to be lovely.[5] ■

Notes

1. G. K. Chesterton, "The Toy Theatre," in *Tremendous Trifles* (New York: Dodd, Mead & Co., 1909), 182–183, archive.org/stream/cu31924013463140#page/n195/mode/2up.
2. Alexis de Tocqueville, *Democracy in America*, trans. and ed. Harvey C. Mansfield and Delba Winthrop (Chicago: University of Chicago Press, 2000), 64–65.
3. *Ibid.*, 65 (emphasis added).
4. *Ibid.*, 663.
5. Edmund Burke, "Reflections on the Revolution in France," in *The Writings and Speeches of Edmund Burke—Volume VIII: The French Revolution 1790–1794*, ed. L. G. Mitchell (New York: Oxford University Press, 1998), 129.

———————————————————— AUTHOR PROFILE

Ted V. McAllister received his Ph.D. in American Intellectual and Cultural History from Vanderbilt University in 1994. Currently he is Edward L. Gaylord Chair and Associate Professor of Public Policy at Pepperdine University's School of Public Policy. He is the author of *Revolt Against Modernity: Leo Strauss, Eric Voegelin, and the Search for a Postliberal Order* (1996), and is co-authoring a survey of American history entitled *The Promise and Paradox of Freedom*. He has also written or edited numerous articles, most of which focus on his research interests of public policy and the role of intellectuals in American democratic culture. "Making American Places: Civic Engagement Rightly Understood" was published in *Why Place Matters: Geography, Identity, and Civic Life in Modern America* in 2014, for which he was a co-editor.

Why Place Matters

Introduction

By Wilfred M. McClay

The most famous words about the city of Oakland, California came from the pen of Gertrude Stein. There was, she declared, no "there" there.[1] This line has been widely understood as a casually dismissive judgment upon that city, and it has been used and reused countless times, as a barb directed at a variety of objects. Unfortunately, her quip is also the chief thing that many people, particularly non-Californians, are likely to know about Oakland. Its better-off neighbor Berkeley, home of the most eminent of the University of California campuses, and always eager to demonstrate its cultural *élan*, has even created a gently witty piece of public art called "HERETHERE" that plays on Stein's words.[2] The installation stands at the border of the two cities, with the word "HERE" on the Berkeley side, and the word "THERE" on the Oakland side. As you might expect, Oaklanders don't much like it. There has even been a T-party rebellion, so to speak, in which an intrepid army of knitters covered up the "T" on the Oakland side with a huge and elaborate tea-cozy.[3] This is how they conduct cultural warfare in the Bay Area, where some people clearly have too much time on their hands.

Yet the irony of it all is that when Stein penned those words in her autobiography, they were not meant as a snappy put-down. She was thinking of something entirely different. Oakland had been extremely important to her when she lived there as a child, as a rare stable place in an unsettled and peripatetic upbringing. But when she discovered later in life that her childhood home there had been torn down, leaving her with nothing familiar to return to, Oakland lost its meaning for her. The blooming, buzzing confusion of the city no longer had a nucleus around which she could orient it. Saying that there was no "there" there was a poignant way to express this personal disorientation—a disorientation felt by many of us in the modern world, particularly when the pace of change causes us to lose our grip on the places that matter most to us.

There is no evading the fact that we human beings have a profound need for "thereness," for visible and tangible things that persist and endure, and thereby serve to anchor our memories in something more substantial than our thoughts and emotions. Nor can we ever predict in advance the points at which our foundational sense of place will be most vulnerable, though surely a childhood home is a very likely candidate. In any event, when one of those anchors disappears or changes, as it did for Stein, we are left alone, bereft and deserted, our minds and hearts burdened by the weight of uprooted and disconnected memories which can no longer be linked to any visible or tangible place of reference in the world outside our heads. So the memories wither in time like cut flowers, and the more general sense of place, of "thereness," is lost with them, like abandoned farmland slowly reclaimed by the primeval forest.

The Places of Our Lives

Although "place" is the most general of words, the things to which it points are very specific. "Place" as a concept is highly abstract, but places in particular are concrete, palpable, intimately meaningful. Each place is different. Each of us comes from just such a particular and unreproducible somewhere, and considers some place (or places) "home."

Each of us knows, too, that "a sense of place" is as much an achievement as a given condition. Although one could argue that a "place" is ultimately merely a point on some coordinate system, such a flat-footed assertion misses the inherently phenomenological character of place. Which explains why not all places are equal, and some places seem to us to be more fully "places" than others. In a frenetically mobile and ever more porous and inexorably globalizing world, we stand powerfully in need of such stable and coherent places in our lives—to ground us and orient us, and mark off a finite arena, rich with memory, for our activity as parents and children, as friends and neighbors, and as free and productive citizens.

And we know that the sense of place, even when it is very strong, is also very fragile and easily lost. Stein's famous line about Oakland is testimony to that. By the same token, the ghostly imprint of a sense of place may persist even when the physical conditions for it have vanished, like the sensations that linger after a limb has been amputated. Such is the utterly quotidian incident described in a haunting little column that Verlyn Klinkenborg wrote several years ago for the *New York Times*, a demonstration that the sense of place can apply especially powerfully to the most commonplace and unremarkable things. The column was a response to the closing of a Korean market in his neighborhood—not an event of obvious importance, and yet Klinkenborg found himself maintaining "a mental map" of the place:

> I know just where the seltzer is in a store that no longer exists. I can walk straight to the dried pineapple, but only in the past. Some part of me had quietly made an inventory of the necessities—the analgesics and toothbrushes and small shampoos—that had migrated to the front counter, which was a drugstore in itself. There are other places to buy all these things, and not far away. But there is still a perfectly good Korean market in my head.
>
> We carry with us these footprints of vanished places: apartments we moved out of years ago, dry cleaners that went out of business, restaurants that stopped serving, neighborhoods where only the street names remain the same. This is the long-gone geography of New York. I look up at the buildings and try to imagine all the lives that have passed through them.[4]

We are sometimes left, he concludes, in the strange position of "knowing our way around a world that can no longer be found."[5]

What Stein's and Klinkenborg's accounts share is their depiction of an ordinary but disquieting phenomenon: the translation of *place* into *space*—the transformation of a setting that had once been charged with human meaning into one from which the meaning has departed, something empty and inert, a mere space. We all have experienced this, some of us many times. Think of the strange emotion we feel when we are moving out of the place where we have been living, and we finish clearing all our belongings out of the apartment or the house or the dorm room—and we look back at it one last time, to see a space that used to be the center of our world, reduced to nothing but bare walls and bare floors. Even when there are a few remaining signs of our time there—fading walls pockmarked with nail holes, scuffs in the floor, spots on the carpet—they serve only to render the moment more poignant, since we know that these small injuries to the property will soon be painted over and tidied up, so that in the fullness of time there will be no trace left of us in that spot.

Blurring Distinctiveness

One should not be too melodramatic about this. Such changes and transitions, however painful they may sometimes be, are part of a healthy and dynamic human existence. What is different now is not that they happen but that they have become so pervasive, reflecting a social and psychological fluidity that seems to mark our times. As we have become ever more mobile and more connected and absorbed in a panoply of things that are not immediately present to us, our actual and tangible places seem less and less important to us, more and more transient or provisional or interchangeable or even disposable. The pain of parting becomes less, precisely because there is so little reason to invest oneself in "place" to begin with. Sometimes it almost seems as if we are living like plants without roots, drawing our sustenance not from the earth beneath our feet but from the satellites that encircle us and the computer clouds that feed and absorb our energies.

It has not always been thus, of course; and we forget how recently things were, as they had been from the beginning of time, almost entirely different. It was not much more than a century ago that the lives of most Americans were confined within a narrow local radius, in what historian Robert Wiebe revealingly called "island communities."[6] The ability of these island communities, and the individuals who comprised them, to communicate across large distances was limited by the vast seas of space and time—by the distances that separated them, and the immense time it took to traverse those distances. The term "real time," to the extent it would have had any meaning at all, referred to strictly local time, measured by reference to the sun's reaching its zenith at that particular location. Far from being a puzzle or an enigma, one's "place in the world" was a given for a great many, if not most, men and women. With rare exceptions, the person that one became and the life that one lived were inextricably linked to the geographical location where one was born and raised. Such factors remained even if one moved, as Americans always have, since one's origins lingered on as a structural mold of one's worldly existence, nearly as hard and fast as one's biological makeup. One could only move so far, and so fast.

But a cascading array of technological and social innovations has, with astonishing speed, rendered those considerations obsolete. Inexpensive travel and instantaneous telecommunications have almost eliminated the isolation of provincial life everywhere in the world, and resulted in the unprecedented mobility of both individuals and entire populations, the blurring of national identities

M

and porousness of boundaries, and the relentless global flow of labor, capital, and goods. All these forces erase distances and erode barriers that had formerly been considered an inescapable part of the human condition. And the term "real time" now refers, not to local time, but to its opposite—the possibility of near-universal simultaneity, so that, for example, I can have a lively conversation in "real time" with anyone on any part of the planet.

This revolution shouldn't be a surprise to us, since it has been coming at us steadily ever since the invention of the locomotive and the telegraph. And make no mistake, there is much to celebrate in these developments. They give crucial support to one of the most powerful and fundamental, and universally appealing, of all American ideas: the idea of freedom. We embrace freedom because we believe fervently in the fullest breadth of individual human possibility, and share a deep conviction that no one's horizons in life should be dictated by the conditions of his or her birth. Nothing is more quintessentially American than that conviction. But interestingly, the word "place" rarely plays any role in this freedom narrative, and in fact, what role it plays tends to be negative. One's place of origin is seen as an impediment, something to be overcome. "Place" may even point toward notions of social hierarchy that Americans generally find anathema. Many of us can still remember when the idea of "knowing your place" was used to promote racial segregation and the social and legal subordination of women.

But very little of that is relevant anymore, and it would be a grave error to think that the problems of the past are the same as those today. We now have a new set of problems, which have been engendered precisely by our dazzling achievements. One of those problems is the widespread sense that something is now seriously out of balance in the way we live. All the technological wizardry and individual empowerment have unsettled all facets of life, and given rise to profound feelings of disquiet and insecurity in many Americans. No one can yet reckon the human costs of such radical changes, but they may turn out to be far higher than we have imagined.

Accompanying this disquiet is a gnawing sense that something important in our fundamental human nature is being lost, abandoned or sacrificed in this headlong rush, and that this "something" remains just as vital to our full flourishing as human beings as it was in the times when we had far fewer choices on offer. Could it be the case that the global-scale interconnectedness of things may be coming at too high a price? Could it be the case that the variety and spontaneous diversity of the world as we have known it for all the prior centuries of human history is being gradually leveled and effaced, and insensibly transformed into something standardized, artificial, rootless, pastless, and bland—a world of interchangeable airport terminals and franchise hotels and restaurants, a world of smooth surfaces designed to facilitate perpetual movement rather than rooted flourishing? A world of space rather than place, in which there are no "theres" there?

Could it be the case that one of the chief things neglected by this pattern of ceaseless movement is precisely the opportunity to live dignified and purposeful lives of self-government and civic engagement, the kind of lives that thinkers since the time of Aristotle have regarded as the highest expression of human flourishing? Is the living of such lives even conceivable in a world without "theres"?

These concerns should not be confused with feelings of nostalgia, such as one finds in sentimental discourse about lost "community," often emanating from individuals who would not for a second tolerate the kind of constraints on individual liberty that "thick" communities of the past always required. For better or worse, while a wholesale rollback of modernity may be conceivable as a thought experiment, it is simply not a serious practical option. But that does not mean accepting an unacceptable status quo, in which human flourishing itself is rendered impossible. Instead, we should seek to discover how, given the American people as they are, and American economic and social life as it now exists—and not as those things can be *imagined* to be—we can find means of resisting the steady homogenization of the world. This means cultivating a strong sense of place wherever we find it—and thereby cultivating the human goods that depend upon an enduring sense of place and are impossible without it.

Living "Places"

In both its literal and its figurative meanings, "place" refers not only to a geographical spot but to a defined niche in the social order: one's place in the world. Thus, when we say that we have "found our place," we are speaking not only of a physical location, but of the achievement of a stable and mature personal identity within a coherent social order, so that we can provide an answer to the questions: "Who are you? Where did you come from? Where is your home? Where do you fit in the order of things?" Hence, it is not surprising that a disruption or weakening in our experience of geographical place will be reflected in similar disruptions in our sense of personal identity. The two things go together.

But any effort to affirm the importance of place brings us into tension with the same disorienting forces that are shrinking and transforming our world. A national government and a global economy always tend in the direction of consolidation and uniformity, toward the imposition of a universal standard. A stress upon the importance of "place" represents a counterforce to these huge structural tendencies. For place is always grounded in the particular, even the provincial. Such affirmation is not mere attachment to the abstraction of "place" but to *this* place, scaled to our innate human sensibility: toward *specific* hometowns and neighborhoods and countrysides and landscapes, each having its own enveloping aura of thoughts and desires and memories—that is to say, its own history, its own customs and traditions, its own stories, its foodways and folkways, its relics, and its own burial grounds.

Furthermore, what makes a "place" is not merely a loyalty to its past, but the vitality of its present, and the lure of its future. Far from being static, a "place" must be a node of continuous human activity: political, economic, and cultural. These are the forces that make a living "place" different from a museum. A living "place" has to offer scope for the creative energies of its people.

We should not imagine that the erosion of "place" is an "optional" issue, or an "aesthetic" one, the sort of concern best taken up when times are flush and there are less pressing items on our plate. Nor should we dismiss a renewed emphasis on "place" as fanciful, or backward-looking, or fetishistic, a foolish and futile attempt to resurrect something whose time has passed. Instead, it can be argued that, like it or not, we must recover a more durable and vibrant sense of

M

place if we are to preserve the healthy dynamism of our society as it now exists, and promote the highest measure of human happiness and flourishing. Or, to put it in the words of historian William Leach, "People require a firm sense of place so they can dare to take risks. A society whose common store of memories has been beaten down or shattered is open to further disruption; for such a society cannot defend or protect itself from the stronger incursions of those who know what they want and how to get it."[7]

A firmer sense of "place," in short, may be an essential basis of our freedom, and the necessary grounding for a great many other human goods. Simone Weil wrote eloquently of the human need for roots[8]; but roots cannot be summoned down from the clouds, transported over a fiber-optic network, or carried around in a suitcase. They have to find some "there" that can become an enduring "here" for them.

The abandonment of such roots in the quest to inhabit some technologically simulated stratosphere of pure fluidity, to be at once all things in all places, and thereby escape once and for all every imprisoning feature of the particularities that have been given to us, including ultimately the limitations of our bodies themselves, will carry a fearsome hidden cost. "We exist by distinction," said George Santayana, "by integration round a specific nucleus according to a particular pattern."[9] Let that nucleus be lost—as it became lost for Gertrude Stein—and so too are we. ■

Notes

1. Gertrude Stein, *Everybody's Autobiography* (New York: Cooper Square Publishers, 1971), 289.
2. The sculpture was installed in 2005 by artists Steve Gillman and Katherine Keefer, as part of the "Gateway Series" of public art commissioned by the Berkeley Civic Arts Commission. "The South Berkeley Gateway Project," Official Web Site of the City of Berkeley, California, www.ci.berkeley.ca.us/ContentPrint.aspx?id=19660.
3. Carolyn Jones, "Berkeley: No tea cozy for 'There' sculpture," *San Francisco Chronicle*, June 2, 2010, available at www.sfgate.com/bayarea/article/Berkeley-No-tea-cozy-for-There-sculpture-3263028.php.
4. Verlyn Klinkenborg, "Remembered Spaces," *New York Times*, July 17, 2007, A20, available at www.nytimes.com/2007/07/17/opinion/17tue4.html.
5. *Ibid.*
6. Robert Wiebe, *The Search for Order: 1877–1920* (New York: Hill & Wang, 1967), xiii.
7. William Leach, *Country of Exiles* (New York: Pantheon Books, 1999), 30.
8. Simone Weil, *The Need for Roots: Prelude to a Declaration of Duties Towards Mankind*, trans. Arthur Wills (New York: Routledge, 2001), originally published as *L'Enracinement: prélude à une déclaration des devoirs envers l'être humain* (Paris: Éditions Gallimard, 1949).
9. George Santayana, *The Genteel Tradition* (Lincoln, Neb.: University of Nebraska Press, 1998), 157.

—————————————————————— AUTHOR PROFILE

Wilfred M. McClay earned his Ph.D. in history from The Johns Hopkins University in 1987. His research interests focus on the intellectual and cultural history of the United States, with particular attention to the social and political thought of the 19th- and 20th-centuries. He was the recipient of fellowships from the Woodrow Wilson International Center for Scholars, the National Endowment for the Humanities, and the National Academy of Education. He is currently a Senior Scholar at the Woodrow Wilson International Center for Scholars and a Senior Fellow at the Ethics and Public Policy Center. He has authored many works, including *The Student's Guide to U.S. History*, *Religion Returns to the Public Square: Faith and Policy in America*, and *Figures in the Carpet: Finding the Human Person in the American Past*. He was an editor and contributor for *Why Place Matters: Geography, Identity, and Civic Life in Modern America*, published in 2014.

M

Here

By Richard McGuire

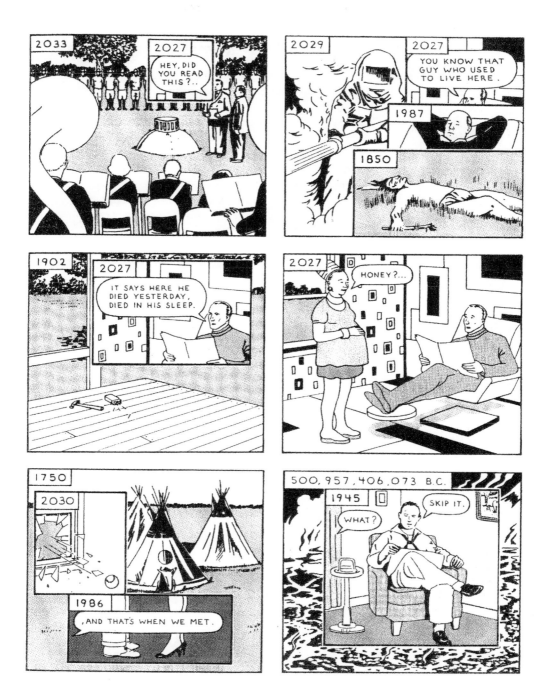

M

—————————————————————— **AUTHOR PROFILE**

Richard McGuire (b. 1957) is an illustrator, graphic designer, comic book artist, animator, children's book author, musician, and toy designer. His illustrations have been published in the *New York Times*, *The New Yorker*, *Le Monde*,
and other publications. His work frequently appears on the cover of *The New
Yorker*. He is a founding member and bassist for the band Liquid Liquid.
McGuire has also written and illustrated four children's books and has created
award winning animation design for television for PBS Kids. The original comic
strip "Here," a six-page version published in *Raw* magazine, has personal
roots based on his childhood home in Perth Amboy, New Jersey. An updated
book-length version of *Here* was published by Pantheon in December 2014.

The Limits of Utopia

By China Miéville

Dystopias infect official reports.

The Intergovernmental Panel on Climate Change (IPCC) demands a shift in our emissions by a third to avoid utter disaster. KPMG, in the leaden chattiness of corporate powerpoint-ese, sees the same horizon. NASA part-funds a report warning that systemic civilizational collapse 'is difficult to avoid.'

We may quibble with the models, but not that the end of everything is right out there, for everyone to discuss.

The stench and blare of poisoned cities, lugubrious underground bunkers, ash landscapes…Worseness is the bad conscience of betterness, dystopias rebukes integral to the utopian tradition. We hanker and warn, our best dreams and our worst standing together against our waking.

Fuck this up, and it's a desiccated, flooded, cold, hot, dead Earth. Get it right? There are lifetimes-worth of pre-dreams of New Edens, from le Guin and Piercy and innumerable others, going right back, visions of what, nearly two millennia ago, the Church Father Lactantius, in *The Divine Institutes*, called the 'Renewed World'.

> [T]he earth will open its fruitfulness, and bring forth the most abundant fruits of its own accord; the rocky mountains shall drop with honey; streams of wine shall run down, and rivers flow with milk; in short, the world itself shall rejoice, and all nature exult, being rescued and set free from the dominion of evil and impiety, and guilt and error.

And it's never only the world that's in question: for Lactantius, as for all the best utopias, it's humanity too. The world will rejoice because we at last will be capable of inhabiting it, free from the evil and impiety and guilt and error with which we've excoriated it. The relationship between humanity and what we'd now call the environment will be healed.

But so rich a lineage has hardly stopped countless environmentalisms from failing, not merely to change the world, but to change the agenda about changing the world.

We who want another, better Earth are understandably proud to keep alternatives alive in this, an epoch that punishes thoughts of change. We need utopias. That's almost a given in activism. If an alternative to this world were inconceivable, how could we change it?

But utopia has its limits: utopia can be toxic.

What price hopelessness, indeed? But what price hope?

In 1985 the city government announced that it would locate a trash incinerator in South Central Los Angeles, a year after California Waste Management paid half a million tax-payers' dollars to the consultancy firm Cerrell Associates for advice on locating such controversial toxic facilities. The Cerrell Report is a how-to,

M

a checklist outlining the qualities of the '"least resistant" personality profile'. Target the less educated, it advises. The elderly. 'Middle and higher-socioeconomic strata neighborhoods', it says, 'should not fall at least within the one-mile and five-mile radii of the proposed site.'

Target the poor.

That this is the strategy is unsurprising: that they admit it raises eyebrows. 'You know,' one wants to whisper, 'that we can hear you?'

In fact the local community did resist, and successfully. But what are sometimes called the Big Ten green groups—The Sierra Club, Friends of the Earth, the National Resources Defense Council, the Wilderness Society, and others—refused the request to join the campaign. Because, they said, it was not an environmental, but a 'community health' issue.

The fallacies of Big Green. Start with heuristics like *rural* versus *urban*, *nature* versus *the social*, and in the face of oppressive power you easily become complicit, or worse, in environmental injustice, in racism. Such simplistic urbophobic utopianism can unite the most nostalgic conservative, seeking solace in a national park with the most extropian post-hippy touting an eco-start-up.

For Lactantius, it was God who would heal a broken nature. This is a more secular age—sort of. But not everyone leaves such messianism aside: some incorporate it into a new, and newly vacuous, totality.

In 1968, Stewart Brand opened the first *Whole Earth Catalogue* with an image of the Blue Planet, Spaceship Earth, a survival pod in which we mutually cuddle. Beside it the text read, 'We are as gods and might as well get good at it.'

Here, says the image, is a beautiful Gaian totality. Here, say the words, is the ecological subject: 'We'. Which obviously leaves unanswered, in the famous punchline to the blistering, uneasy joke, Tonto's question to the Lone Ranger: 'Who is "we"?'

Faced with the scale of what's coming, there's a common and baleful propriety, a self-shackling green politeness. 'Anything', the argument goes, 'is better than nothing.' Hence solutions to tempt business, and the pleading for ecologically-inflected economic rationality. Capitalism, we are told by Jonathan Porritt, an eminent British environmentalist, is the only game in town.

And businesses do adapt, according to their priorities. Whatever the barking of their pet deniers, the oil companies all have Climate Change Divisions—less to fight that change than to plan for profit during it. Companies extend into newly monetised territories. Thus the brief biofuels boom, and that supposed solution to the planet's problems drives rapid deforestation and food riots, before the industry and market tanks. The invisible hand is supposed to clean up its own mess, with Emissions Trading Schemes and offsetting. Opportunities and incentives for shady deals and inflated baseline estimates increase, as, relentlessly, do the emissions. EU carbon bonds remain junk. New financial instruments proliferate: weather derivatives that make climate chaos itself profitable. What are called 'catastrophe bonds' change hands in vast quantities, because one of the minor casualties of capitalism is shame.

Citizens fret about their own refuse, which we should, absolutely, minimise. But in the UK only ten percent of waste is down to households. Recall that the very concept of litter was an invention of the American packaging industry, in

1953, in response to a local ban on disposable bottles. The caul of atomised and privatised guilt under which we're encouraged to labour is a quite deliberate act of misdirection.

At a grander scale, the most conciliatory green organizations obfuscate the nexus of ecological degradation, capitalism and imperialism in which they're caught up. In 2013 the US Environmental Protection Agency presented its National Climate Leadership Award, for 'tackling the challenge of climate change with practical, common-sense, and cost-saving solutions', to Raytheon.

It isn't clear whether Raytheon's drones will be embossed with the award's symbol, so their commitment to sustainability can flash like a proud goldfish fin as they rain death on Afghan villages.

In the service of profit, even husbanding trees supposedly to counteract emissions can be violence. Far worse than merely a failure, UN-backed emission-reduction forest offsetting schemes—known as REDD—legitimate monocultures and seize land, in the name of the planet, all so corporations can continue to pollute. In Uganda, 22,000 farmers are evicted for the UN-Accredited New Forests Company plans. In Kenya, Ogiek people are threatened with violent expulsion from the Mau Forest, in a project blessed by the UN. And in case we need an unsubtle metaphor, the Guaraquecaba Climate Action Project in Brazil, bankrolled by Chevron, General Motors and American Electric Power, locks the Guarani people away from their own forest, and to do so it employs armed guards called 'Forca Verde'—*Green Force*.

This is environmentalism as dispossession, what the Indigenous Environmental Network calls Carbon Colonialism.

And stocks of heavy industry go up. The recent IPCC report left financial markets unmoved: the value such markets continue to grant oil, coal and gas reserves ignores the international targets according to which the bulk of such reserves not only are still in the earth, but must remain so. This carbon bubble declaims that the choice is climate catastrophe or another financial one.

Or, of course, both.

Forget any spurious *human* totality: there is a very real, dangerous, other modern totality in commanding place, one with which too much environmentalism has failed to wrestle. As Jason Moore puts it, 'Wall Street is a way of organizing Nature.'

The very term 'Anthropocene', which gives with one hand, insisting on human drivers of ecological shift, misleads with its implied 'We'. After all, whether in the deforestation of what's now Britain, the extinction of the megafauna in North America, or any of countless other examples, *Homo sapiens*, a*nthropos*, has always fed back into its *–cene*, the ecology of which it is constituent, changing the world. Nor was what altered to make these previously relatively local effects planetary and epochal, warranting a new geochronological term, the birth (as if, in too many accounts, by some miracle) of heavy industry, but a shift in the political economy by which it and we are organised, an accelerating cycle of profit and accumulation.

Which is why Moore, among others, insists that this epoch of potential catastrophe is not the 'Anthropocene', but the 'Capitalocene'.

M

Utopias are necessary. But not only are they insufficient: they can, in some iterations, be part of the ideology of the system, the bad totality that organises us, warms the skies, and condemns millions to peonage on garbage scree.

The utopia of togetherness is a lie. Environmental justice means acknowledging that there is no whole earth, no 'we', without a 'them'. That we are not all in this together.

Which means fighting the fact that fines for toxic spills in predominantly white areas are five times what they are in minority ones. It means not only providing livings for people who survive by sifting through rejectamenta in toxic dumps but squaring up against the imperialism of garbage that put them there, against trash neoliberalism by which poor countries compete to become repositories of filth.

And it means standing directly against military power and violence. Three times as many land-rights and environmental activists were murdered in 2012 than a decade before. Environmental justice means facing down Shell not only for turning Nigeria's Ogoniland into a hallucinatory sump, a landscape of petrochemical Ragnarok, but for arming the Nigerian state for years, during and after the rule of Sani Abacha.

Arms trading, dictatorships and murder are environmental politics.

Those punching down rely not on the quiescence, but on the *weakness* of those against whom they fight. The Cerrell Report is clear: 'All socioeconomic groupings tend to resent the nearby siting of major facilities, but the middle and upper-socioeconomic strata possess better resources to effectuate their opposition.'

The poor should be targeted, in other words, not because they will not fight, but because, being poor, they will not win. The struggle for environmental justice is the struggle to prove that wrong.

• • • • • • • • • • • • •

So we start with the non-totality of the 'we'. From there not only can we see the task but we can return to our utopias, to better honor the best of them.

Those rivers of milk and wine can stop being surplus. There's nothing foolish about such yearnings: they are glimmerings in eyes set on human freedom, a leap from necessity. Far from being merely outlandish, these are abruptly aspects of a grounded utopia incorporating political economy, a yearning on behalf of those who strive without power. In the medieval peasant utopia Cockaigne it rains cheese. Charles Fourier imagined the seas turned to lemonade. The Big Rock Candy Mountain. These are dreams of sustenance out of reach of the dreamers, of the reduction of labour, of a world that will let exhausted humanity rest.

We can dispense with the most banal critiques of utopia. That it is unconvincing as a blueprint, as if that is what it should ever be. That it is drab, boring, faceless and colourless and always the same. The smear that the visionary aspiration for better things always makes things worse. These canards serve stasis.

There are sharper criticisms to be made, for the sake of our utopias themselves and of the day-to-day interventions without which they risk being—and this, itself, is one of those criticisms—valves to release pressure.

Utopia, for one thing, has never been the preserve of those who cleave to liberation. Settlers and expropriators have for centuries asserted their good environmental sense against the laziness of feckless natives, in realizing the potential of land spuriously designated empty, of making so-called deserts so-called bloom. Ecotopia has justified settlement and empire since long before the UN's REDD schemes. It has justified murder.

There is a vision of the world as a garden, under threat. Choked with toxic growth. Gardening as war. And the task being one of 'ruthlessly eliminating the weeds that would deprive the better plants of nutrition, the air, light, sun.'

Here the better plants are Aryans. The weeds are Jews.

SS-Obergruppenfuhrer and *Reichsminister* of Agriculture in the Third Reich, Walther Darré coagulated soil science, nostalgia, pagan kitsch, imperialism, agrarian mystique and race hate in a vision of green renewal and earth stewardship predicated on genocide. He was the most powerful theorist of *Blut und Boden*, 'Blood and Soil', a Nazi ecotopia of organic farmlands and restocked Nordic forests, protected by the pure-blooded peasant-soldier.

The tree may not have grown as Darré hoped, but its roots didn't die. A whole variety of fascist groups across the world still proclaim their fidelity to ecological renewal, green world, and agitate ostentatiously against climate change, pollution and despoliation, declaring against those poisons in the service of another, the logic of race.

Of course reactionary apologists for Big Pollute routinely slander ecological activists as fascists. That doesn't mean those committed to such activism should not be ruthless in ferreting out any real overlaps: very much the opposite.

Aspects of eliminationist bad utopia can be found much more widely than in the self-conscious Far Right. Swathes of ecological thinking are caught up with a nebulous, sentimentalised spiritualist utopia, what the ecofeminist Chaia Heller calls 'Eco-la-la'. Crossbred with crude Malthusianism, in the combative variant called Deep Ecology, the tweeness of that vision can morph into brutality, according to which the problem is overpopulation, humanity itself. At its most cheerfully eccentric lies the Voluntary Human Extinction Movement, advocating an end to breeding: at the most vicious are the pronouncements of David Foreman of Earth First!, faced with the Ethiopian famine of 1984: '[T]he worst thing we could do in Ethiopia is to give aid—the best thing would be to just let nature seek its own balance, to let the people there just starve'.

This is an ecological utopia of mass death. That we could also call an apocalypse.

Apocalypse and utopia: the end of everything, and the horizon of hope. Far from antipodes, these two have always been inextricable. Sometimes, as in Lactantius, the imagined relationship is chronological, even of cause and effect. The one, the apocalypse, the end-times rending of the veil, paves the way for the other, the time beyond, the new beginning.

Something has happened: now they are more intimately imbricated than ever. 'Today,' the bleak and sinister philosopher Emile Cioran announces, 'reconciled with the terrible, we are seeing a contamination of utopia by apocalypse…The two genres…which once seemed so dissimilar to us, interpenetrate, rub off on

each other, to form a third'. Such reconciliation with the terrible, such interpenetration, is vivid in these Deep Ecological hankerings for a world slashed and burned of humans. The scourging has become the dream.

This is not quite a dystopia: it's a third form—apocatopia, utopalypse—and it's all around us. We're surrounded by a culture of ruination, dreams of falling cities, a peopleless world where animals explore. We know the clichés. Vines reclaim Wall Street as if it belongs to them, rather than the other way round; trash vastness, dunes of garbage; the remains of some great just-recognizable bridge now broken to jut, a portentous diving board, into the void. Etcetera.

It's as if we still hanker to see something better and beyond the rubble, but lack the strength. Or as if there's a concerted effort to assert the 'We' again, though negatively—'We' are the problem, and thus this We-lessness a sublime solution. The melancholy is disingenuous. There's enthusiasm, a disavowed investment in these supposed warnings, these catastrophes. The apocalypse-mongers fool no one. Since long before Shelley imagined the day when 'Westminster Abbey shall stand, shapeless and nameless ruins, in the midst of an unpeopled marsh', these have been scenes of beauty.

We've all scrolled slack-mouthed through images of the Chernobyl zone, of Japan's deserted Gunkanjima island, of the ruins of Detroit, through clickbait lists of Top Ten Most Awesomely Creepy Abandoned Places. This shouldn't occasion guilt. Our horror at the tragedies and crimes behind some such images is real: it coexists with, rather than effaces, our gasp of awe. We don't choose what catches our breath. Nor do the images that enthrall us read off reductively to particular politics. But certainly the amoral beauty of our apocatopias can dovetail with something brutal and malefic, an eliminationist disgust.

We can't not read such camply symptomatic cultural matter diagnostically. What else can we do with the deluge of films of deluge, the piling up, like debris under Benjamin's angel of history, of texts about the piling up of debris?

Symptoms morph with the world. One swallow, of however high a budget, does not a summer make, but one doesn't have to be a Žižek to diagnose a cultural shift when, in Guillermo Del Toro's recent *Pacific Rim*, Idris Elba bellows, 'Today we are cancelling the apocalypse.' Perhaps we've had our fill of the end, and with this line we usher in a different kind of aftermath—the apocalypse that fails. We're back, with muscular new hope.

A similar shift is visible in the rise of geoengineering, ideas once pulp fiction and the ruminations of eccentrics. Now, planet-scale plans to spray acid into the stratosphere to become mirrored molecules to reflect radiation, to scrub CO_2 from the atmosphere, to bring up benthic waters to cool the oceans, are written up by Nobel laureates, discussed in the *New Yorker* and the *MIT Technology Review*. A new hope, a new can-do, the return of human agency, sleeves rolled up, fixing the problem. With *Science*.

This planet-hacking, however, is utterly speculative, controversial, and—according to recent work at Germany's Helmholtz Centre—by the most generous possible projections thoroughly inadequate to halt climate chaos. It is, by any reasonable standards, absurd that such plans seem more rational than enacting the social measures to slash emissions that are entirely possible *right now*, but which would necessitate a transformation of our political system.

It's a left cliché to pronounce that these days it's easier to imagine the end of the world than the end of capitalism: Andreas Malm points out that with the trope of geoengineering, it's easier to imagine the deliberate transformation of the entire planet than of our political economy. What looks at first like a new Prometheanism is rather capitulation, surrender to the status quo. Utopia is here exoneration of entrenched power, the red lines of which are not to be crossed.

What price hope indeed?

• • • • • • • • • • • • • •

Seventy percent of the staff at the mothballed Union Carbide factory in Bhopal, India, had been docked pay for refusing to break safety routines. Staffing levels were inadequate, readings taken half as often as intended. None of the six safety systems worked as it should, if at all. The trade union had protested, and been ignored.

On 3 December 1984, twenty-seven tonnes of methyl isocyanate spewed from the plant. Between 8,000 and 10,000 people died that night. 25,000 have died since. Half a million were injured, around 70,000 permanently and hideously. The rate of birth defects in the area is vastly high. The groundwater still shows toxins massively above safe levels.

Initially, the Indian government demanded $3.3 billion in compensation, which Union Carbide spent $50 million fighting. At last, in 1989, the company settled out of court for $470 million, 15 percent of that initial sum. The survivors received, as lifetime compensation, between $300 and $500 each. In the words of Kathy Hunt, Dow-Carbide's public affairs officer, in 2002, '$500 is plenty good for an Indian.'

Why rehearse these terrible, familiar facts? Not only because, as is well known, Warren Anderson, Carbide's ex-CEO, has never been extradited to face Indian justice, despite an arrest warrant being issued. Nor because Carbide, and Dow Chemicals, which bought it in 2001, deny all responsibility, and refuse to clean the area or to respond to Indian court summonses. There is another reason.

In 1989, the Wall Street Journal reported that US executives were extremely anxious about this first major test of a US corporation's liability for an accident in the developing world. At last, in October 1991, came the key moment for this discussion: the Indian Supreme Court upheld Carbide's offer and dismissed all outstanding petitions against it, thereby offering the company legal protection. And its share price immediately spiked high. Because Wall Street knew its priorities had prevailed. That it was safe.

A real-world interpenetration of apocalypse and utopia. Apocalypse for those thousands who drowned on their own lungs. And for the corporations, now reassured that the poor, unlike profit, were indeed dispensable? An everyday utopia.

This is another of the limitations of utopia: we *live* in utopia; it just isn't ours.

So we live in apocalypse too.

• • • • • • • • • • • • • •

Earth: to be determined. Utopia? Apocalypse? Is it worse to hope or to despair? To that question there can only be one answer: yes. It is worse to hope or to despair.

Bad hope and bad despair are mutually constitutive. Capitalism gets you coming or going. 'We' can fix the problem 'we' made. And when 'we', geoengineers, fail, 'we' can live through it, whisper 'our' survivalist bad consciences, the preppers hoarding cans of beans.

Is there a better optimism? And a right way to lose hope? It depends who's hoping, for what, for whom—and against whom. We must learn to hope with teeth.

We won't be browbeaten by demands for our own bureaucratised proposals. In fact there is no dearth of models to consider, but the radical critique of the everyday stands even in the absence of an alternative. We can go further: if we take utopia seriously, as a total reshaping, its scale means we can't think it from this side. It's the process of making it that will allow us to do so. It is utopian fidelity that might underpin our refusal to expound it, or any roadmap.

We should utopia as hard as we can. Along with a fulfilled humanity we should imagine flying islands, self-constituting coraline neighborhoods, photosynthesizing cars bred from biospliced bone-marrow. Big Rock Candy Mountains. Because we'll never mistake those dreams for blueprints, nor for mere absurdities.

What utopias are are new Rorschachs. We pour our concerns and ideas out, and then in dreaming we fold the paper to open it again and reveal startling patterns. We may pour with a degree of intent, but what we make is beyond precise planning. Our utopias are to be enjoyed and admired: they are made of our concerns and they tell us about our now, about our pre-utopian selves. They are to be interpreted. And so are those of our enemies.

To understand what we're up against means to respect it. The Earth is not being blistered because the despoilers are stupid or irrational or making a mistake or have insufficient data. We should fight our case as urgently as we can, and win arguments, but we shouldn't fool ourselves: whatever the self-delusion, guilt, or occasional tears of a CEO, in a profit-maximizing world it's *rational* for the institutions of our status quo to do what they do. Individuals and even sometimes some organizations may resist that in specific cases, but only by refusing that system's logic. Which the system itself of course cannot do.

The fight for ecological justice means a fight against that system, because there is massive profit in injustice. This battle won't always be over catastrophic climate change or land expropriation: in neoliberalism, even local struggles for fleeting moments of green municipal life are ultimately struggles against power. The protests that shook the Turkish state in 2013 started with a government plan to build over Gezi Park, one of the last green spaces in the city.

Rather than touting togetherness, we fight best by embracing our not-togetherness. The fact that there are sides. Famously, we approach a tipping point. Rather than hoping for cohesion, our best hope lies in conflict. Our aim, an aspect of our utopianism, should be this strategy of tension.

There is bad pessimism as well as bad optimism. Against the curmudgeonly surrender of, say, James Lovegrove, there are sound scientific reasons to suggest that we're not yet—quite—at some point of no return. We need to tilt at a different tipping point, into irrevocable *social* change, and that requires a different pessimism, an unflinching look at how bad things are.

Pessimism has a bad rap among activists, terrified of surrender. But activism without the pessimism that rigor should provoke is just sentimentality.

There is hope. But for it to be real, and barbed, and tempered into a weapon, we cannot just default to it. We have to test it, subject it to the strain of appropriate near-despair. We need utopia, but to try to think utopia, in this world, without rage, without fury, is an indulgence we can't afford. In the face of what is done, we cannot think utopia without hate.

Even our ends-of-the-world are too Whiggish. Let us put an end to one-nation apocalypse. Here instead is to antinomian utopia. A hope that abjures the hope of those in power.

It is the supposedly sensible critics who are the most profoundly unrealistic. As Joel Kovel says, 'we can have the accumulation of capital, and we can have ecological integrity, but we can't have both of them together'. To believe otherwise would be quaint were it not so dangerous.

In 2003, William Stavropoulos, CEO of Dow—who has, recall, no responsibility to the chemically maimed of Bhopal—said in a press release, 'Being environmentally responsible makes good business sense.'

And that, in the pejorative sense, is the most absurd utopia of all. ■

M

AUTHOR PROFILE

China Miéville is an English speculative fiction author. He is best known for his Bas-Lag trilogy that begins with the novel *Perdido Street Station* (2000), which is exemplary of the sub-genre of the New Weird, with which he is most closely defined: blending traditional science fiction and fantasy tropes with dark or dystopic themes, often in urban settings, in such a way as to challenge readers' ideas and comfort zones. However, Miéville has said that he wants to write a novel in every genre, which resulted in the noir crime thriller *The City & The City* (2009), the current Focused Inquiry theme-reading selection. In addition to his novels, Miéville has also written issues of the comic books *Hellblazer* and *Justice League*. Miéville holds a Ph.D. in international relations from the London School of Economics and has been a member of the International Socialist Organization and the Socialist Workers Party. He is currently the editor of the leftist political literary magazine *Salvage*.

The Outer Space Treaty of 1967

By NASA

Treaty on principles governing the activities of states in the exploration and use of outer space, including the moon and other celestial bodies.

Opened for signature at Moscow, London, and Washington on 27 January, 1967

THE STATES PARTIES. TO THIS TREATY,

INSPIRED by the great prospects opening up before mankind as a result of man's entry into outer space,

RECOGNIZING the common interest of all mankind in the progress of the exploration and use of outer space for peaceful purposes,

BELIEVING that the exploration and use of outer space should be carried on for the benefit of all peoples irrespective of the degree of their economic or scientific development,

DESIRING to contribute to broad international co-operation in the scientific as well as the legal aspects of the exploration and use of outer space for peaceful purposes,

BELIEVING that such co-operation will contribute to the development of mutual understanding and to the strengthening of friendly relations between States and peoples,

RECALLING resolution 1962 (XVIII), entitled "Declaration of Legal Principles Governing the Activities of States in the Exploration and Use of Outer Space", which was adopted unanimously by the United Nations General Assembly on 13 December 1963,

RECALLING resolution 1884 (XVIII), calling upon States to refrain from placing in orbit around the earth any objects carrying nuclear weapons or any other kinds of weapons of mass destruction or from installing such weapons on celestial bodies, which was adopted unanimously by the United Nations General Assembly on 17 October 1963,

TAKING account of United Nations General Assembly resolution 110 (II) of 3 November 1947, which condemned propaganda designed or likely to provoke or encourage any threat to the peace, breach of the peace or act of aggression, and considering that the aforementioned resolution is applicable to outer space,

CONVINCED that a Treaty on Principles Governing the Activities of States in the Exploration and Use of Outer Space, including the Moon and Other Celestial Bodies, will further the Purposes and Principles of the Charter of the United Nations,

HAVE AGREED ON THE FOLLOWING:

Article I

The exploration and use of outer space, including the moon and other celestial bodies, shall be carried out for the benefit and in the interests of all countries, irrespective of their degree of economic or scientific development, and shall be the province of all mankind.

Outer space, including the moon and other celestial bodies, shall be free for exploration and use by all States without discrimination of any kind, on a basis of equality and in accordance with international law, and there shall be free access to all areas of celestial bodies.

There shall be freedom of scientific investigation in outer space, including the moon and other celestial bodies, and States shall facilitate and encourage international co-operation in such investigation.

Article II

Outer space, including the moon and other celestial bodies, is not subject to national appropriation by claim of sovereignty, by means of use or occupation, or by any other means.

Article III

States Parties to the Treaty shall carry on activities in the exploration and use of outer space, including the moon and other celestial bodies, in accordance with international law, including the Charter of the United Nations, in the interest of maintaining international peace and security and promoting international co-operation and understanding.

Article IV

States Parties to the Treaty undertake not to place in orbit around the earth any objects carrying nuclear weapons or any other kinds of weapons of mass destruction, install such weapons on celestial bodies, or station such weapons in outer space in any other manner.

The moon and other celestial bodies shall be used by all States Parties to the Treaty exclusively for peaceful purposes. The establishment of military bases, installations and fortifications, the testing of any type of weapons and the conduct of military manoeuvres on celestial bodies shall be forbidden. The use of military personnel for scientific research or for any other peaceful purposes shall not be prohibited. The use of any equipment or facility necessary for peaceful exploration of the moon and other celestial bodies shall also not be prohibited.

Article V

States Parties to the Treaty shall regard astronauts as envoys of mankind in outer space and shall render to them all possible assistance in the event of accident, distress, or emergency landing on the territory of another State Party or on the high seas. When astronauts make such a landing, they shall be safely and promptly returned to the State of registry of their space vehicle.

In carrying on activities in outer space and on celestial bodies, the astronauts of one State Party shall render all possible assistance to the astronauts of other States Parties.

States Parties to the Treaty shall immediately inform the other States Parties to the Treaty or the Secretary-General of the United Nations of any phenomena they discover in outer space, including the Moon and other celestial bodies, which could constitute a danger to the life or health of astronauts.

Article VI

States Parties to the Treaty shall bear international responsibility for national activities in outer space, including the moon and other celestial bodies, whether such activities are carried on by governmental agencies or by non-governmental entities, and for assuring that national activities are carried out in conformity with the provisions set forth in the present Treaty. The activities of non-governmental entities in outer space, including the moon and other celestial bodies, shall require authorization and continuing supervision by the appropriate State Party to the Treaty. When activities are carried on in outer space, including the moon and other celestial bodies, by an international organization, responsibility for compliance with this Treaty shall be borne both by the international organization and by the States Parties to the Treaty participating in such organization.

Article VII

Each State Party to the Treaty that launches or procures the launching of an object into outer space, including the moon and other celestial bodies, and each State Party from whose territory or facility an object is launched, is internationally liable for damage to another State Party to the Treaty or to its natural or juridical persons by such object or its component parts on the Earth, in air space or in outer space, including the moon and other celestial bodies.

Article VIII

A State Party to the Treaty on whose registry an object launched into outer space is carried shall retain jurisdiction and control over such object, and over any personnel thereof, while in outer space or on a celestial body. Ownership of objects launched into outer space, including objects landed or constructed on a celestial body, and of their component parts, is not affected by their presence in outer space or on a celestial body or by their return to the Earth. Such objects or component parts found beyond the limits of the State Party of the Treaty on whose registry they are carried shall be returned to that State Party, which shall, upon request, furnish identifying data prior to their return.

Article IX

In the exploration and use of outer space, including the moon and other celestial bodies, States Parties to the Treaty shall be guided by the principle of co-operation and mutual assistance and shall conduct all their activities in outer space, including the moon and other celestial bodies, with due regard to the corresponding interests of all other States Parties to the Treaty. States Parties to the Treaty shall pursue studies of outer space, including the moon and other celestial bodies, and conduct exploration of them so as to avoid their harmful contamination and also adverse changes in the environment of the Earth resulting from the introduction of extraterrestrial matter and, where necessary, shall adopt appropriate measures for this purpose. If a State Party to the Treaty has reason to believe that an activity or experiment planned by it or its nationals in outer space, including the moon and other celestial bodies, would cause potentially harmful interference with activities of other States Parties in the peaceful exploration and use of outer space, including the moon and other celestial bodies, it shall undertake appropriate international consultations before proceeding with any such activity or experiment. A State Party to the Treaty which has reason to believe that an activity or experiment planned by another State Party in outer space, including the moon and other celestial bodies, would cause potentially harmful interference with activities in the peaceful exploration and use of outer space, including the moon and other celestial bodies, may request consultation concerning the activity or experiment.

Article X

In order to promote international co-operation in the exploration and use of outer space, including the moon and other celestial bodies, in conformity with the purposes of this Treaty, the States Parties to the Treaty shall consider on a basis of equality any requests by other States Parties to the Treaty to be afforded an opportunity to observe the flight of space objects launched by those States.

The nature of such an opportunity for observation and the conditions under which it could be afforded shall be determined by agreement between the States concerned.

Article XI

In order to promote international co-operation in the peaceful exploration and use of outer space, States Parties to the Treaty conducting activities in outer space, including the moon and other celestial bodies, agree to inform the Secretary-General of the United Nations as well as the public and the international scientific community, to the greatest extent feasible and practicable, of the nature, conduct, locations and results of such activities. On receiving the said information, the Secretary-General of the United Nations should be prepared to disseminate it immediately and effectively.

Article XII

All stations, installations, equipment and space vehicles on the moon and other celestial bodies shall be open to representatives of other States Parties to the Treaty on a basis of reciprocity. Such representatives shall give reasonable advance notice of a projected visit, in order that appropriate consultations may be held and that maximum precautions may be taken to assure safety and to avoid interference with normal operations in the facility to be visited.

Article XIII

The provisions of this Treaty shall apply to the activities of States Parties to the Treaty in the exploration and use of outer space, including the moon and other celestial bodies, whether such activities are carried on by a single State Party to the Treaty or jointly with other States, including cases where they are carried on within the framework of international inter-governmental organizations.

Any practical questions arising in connexion with activities carried on by international inter-governmental organizations in the exploration and use of outer space, including the moon and other celestial bodies, shall be resolved by the States Parties to the Treaty either with the appropriate international organization or with one or more States members of that international organization, which are Parties to this Treaty.

N

Article XIV

1. This Treaty shall be open to all States for signature. Any State which does not sign this Treaty before its entry into force in accordance with paragraph 3 of this Article may accede to it at any time.

2. This Treaty shall be subject to ratification by signatory States. Instruments of ratification and instruments of accession shall be deposited with the Governments of the United Kingdom of Great Britain and Northern Ireland, the Union of Soviet Socialist Republics and the United States of America, which are hereby designated the Depositary Governments.

3. This Treaty shall enter into force upon the deposit of instruments of ratification by five Governments including the Governments designated as Depositary Governments under this Treaty.

4. For States whose instruments of ratification or accession are deposited subsequent to the entry into force of this Treaty, it shall enter into force on the date of the deposit of their instruments of ratification or accession.

5. The Depositary Governments shall promptly inform all signatory and acceding States of the date of each signature, the date of deposit of each instrument of ratification of and accession to this Treaty, the date of its entry into force and other notices.

6. This Treaty shall be registered by the Depositary Governments pursuant to Article 102 of the Charter of the United Nations.

Article XV

Any State Party to the Treaty may propose amendments to this Treaty. Amendments shall enter into force for each State Party to the Treaty accepting the amendments upon their acceptance by a majority of the States Parties to the Treaty and thereafter for each remaining State Party to the Treaty on the date of acceptance by it.

Article XVI

Any State Party to the Treaty may give notice of its withdrawal from the Treaty one year after its entry into force by written notification to the Depositary Governments. Such withdrawal shall take effect one year from the date of receipt of this notification.

Article XVII

This Treaty, of which the Chinese, English, French, Russian and Spanish texts are equally authentic, shall be deposited in the archives of the Depositary Governments. Duly certified copies of this Treaty shall be transmitted by the Depositary Governments to the Governments of the signatory and acceding States.

IN WITNESS WHEREOF the undersigned, duly authorised, have signed this Treaty.

DONE in triplicate, at the cities of London, Moscow and Washington, the twenty-seventh day of January, one thousand nine hundred and sixty-seven. ■

——————————————————————— AUTHOR PROFILE

The National Aeronautics and Space Administration (NASA) is a United States governmental organization that was created in 1958 in response to early Soviet space achievements. Developed through a combination of the National Advisory Committee for Aeronautics (NACA) and other governmental organizations, it was intended as a centralized entity for U.S. civil aerospace research and development. Since its inception, it has been a global leader in scientific and technical development both in air and space. In the early years, Project Apollo became one of the main priorities of NASA in response to a statement from John F. Kennedy that "the nation should commit itself to achieving the goal, before this decade is out, of landing a man on the Moon and returning him safely to Earth." Today, NASA remains a leader in advocating aerospace exploration, and their discoveries and projects have largely been responsible for providing new ways of viewing the Earth and the universe. "The Outer Space Treaty of 1967" was presented to the Office of Outer Space Affairs in the United Nations, and opened for signature by three leading nations: The Russian Federation, the United Kingdom, and the United States of America. It includes the basic framework for international space law.

N

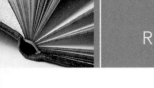
Res. No. 1723: Resolution Declaring a Symbolic Ban on the Negative Use of the Word 'Ghetto'

By The New York City Council

Resolution declaring a symbolic ban on the negative use of the word "ghetto" in New York City.

By Council Members Baez and Seabrook

Whereas, The word "ghetto" is derived from the Venetian term, "ghèto," a conjugation of an Italian word that means "to pour" or "to cast"; and

Whereas, The term "Ghèto" was first applied to Jews living in Venice, who were forced to live behind walls on an island near an iron foundry; and

Whereas, Though the ghettoization of Jews has taken place throughout history, it is most closely associated with the ghettos created during World War II by the Nazis where Jews throughout occupied Europe were sequestered into small areas with little food, water and sanitation; and

Whereas, In the modern-day United States, the term ghetto is most often applied to low-income urban neighborhoods populated by ethnic and racial minorities; and

Whereas, The existence of these neighborhoods is a legacy of our country's history of discrimination, which by law or by custom forced certain groups to live in specific neighborhoods; and

Whereas, Residents of these enclaves often miss the economic opportunities that are frequently found in more affluent areas, thereby perpetuating the downtrodden nature of the neighborhood; and

Whereas, Over time, the word "ghetto" has evolved in popular culture to pejoratively describe something perceived to be of low quality or taste; and

Whereas, "Ghetto" has also acquired a more comical definition, referring to the perceived quirky and unique style and behaviors that accompany a lifestyle with limited financial resources; and

Whereas, Invariably, the colloquial use of the term "ghetto" is linked to the African American and Latino communities; and

Whereas, "Ghetto", whether it is referring to a geographic location or a particular style and attitude, is almost always used in the pejorative; and

Whereas, Linking a racial or ethnic group to terminology used to describe a state of poverty only serves to further dehumanize and disenfranchise that particular group; and

Whereas, While a government must never limit one's free speech, however incendiary or offensive its expression may be, it is imperative that individuals understand the power of their words and their potential to inflict great harm on the community; now, therefore, be it

Resolved, That the Council of the City of New York declares a symbolic ban on the negative use of the word "ghetto" in New York City. ∎

AUTHOR PROFILE

As the main legislative body in New York City, the **New York City Council** has 51 members from 51 council districts throughout the city. They are charged with introducing and voting on legislation having to do with all aspects of city life, including negotiating the city budget, monitoring public agencies, and assessing land use in the city. Given the unique history, size and demographic makeup of New York City, the policies and recommendations of the City Council often reach national attention. In 2008, in part a response to an earlier debate over the use of the "n-word" in public discourse, New York City Council members Maria Baez and Larry Seabrook proposed this "symbolic ban" in an attempt to reevaluate the use of terms such as "ghetto" to marginalize certain portions and populations of the city.

N

The Racial Segregation of American Cities Was Anything But Accidental

By Katie Nodjimbadem

It's not surprising to anyone who has lived in or visited a major American metropolitan region that the nation's cities tend to be organized in their own particular racial pattern. In Chicago, it's a north/south divide. In Austin, it's west/east. In some cities, it's a division based around infrastructure, as with Detroit's 8 Mile Road. In other cities, nature—such as Washington, D.C.'s Anacostia River— is the barrier. Sometimes these divisions are man-made, sometimes natural, but none are coincidental.

A narrative of racially discriminatory landlords and bankers—all independent actors—has long served as an explanation for the isolation of African-Americans in certain neighborhoods in large cities. But this pervasive assumption rationalizing residential segregation in the United States ignores the long history of federal, state and local policies that generated the residential segregation found across the country today.

In *The Color of Law: A Forgotten History of How Our Government Segregated America*, Richard Rothstein, a research associate at the Economic Policy Institute, aims to flip the assumption that the state of racial organization in American cities is simply a result of individual prejudices. He untangles a century's worth of policies that built the segregated American city of today. From the first segregated public housing projects of President Franklin Roosevelt's New Deal, to the 1949 Housing Act that encouraged white movement to the suburbs, to unconstitutional racial zoning ordinances enacted by city governments, Rothstein substantiates the argument that the current state of the American city is the direct result of unconstitutional, state-sanctioned racial discrimination.

Smithsonian.com spoke with Rothstein about his findings and his suggestions for change.

Your book aims to turn over misconceptions on how American cities came to be racially segregated. What are some of the biggest misconceptions people have, and how did they influence your research and writing of this book?

There's one overall misconception. And that is that the reason that neighborhoods in every metropolitan area in the country are segregated by race is because of a series of accidents driving prejudice and personal choices.

Income differences, private discrimination of real estate agents, banks and all of these come under the category of what the Supreme Court called, and what is now generally known as, *de facto* segregation, something that just happened by accident or by individual choices. And that myth, which is widespread across the political spectrum, hobbles our ability to remedy segregation and eliminate the enormous harm that it does to this country.

The truth is that segregation in every metropolitan area was imposed by racially explicit federal, state and local policy, without which private actions of prejudice or discrimination would not have been very effective. And if we understand that our segregation is a governmentally sponsored system, which of course we'd call *de jure* segregation, only then can we begin to remedy it. Because if it happened by individual choice, it's hard to imagine how to remedy it. If it happened by government action, then we should be able to develop equally effective government actions to reverse it.

Why do you think there is this national amnesia about the history of these policies?

When we desegregated the buses, people could sit anywhere on the bus they wanted. When we desegregated restaurants, people could sit anywhere in the restaurant that they wanted. Even when we desegregated schools, if the ruling was enforced, the next day, children could go to the school in their neighborhood. But residential segregation is a much more difficult thing to do. If we prohibit the effects of residential segregation, it's not as though the next day people can up and move to suburbs that once excluded them by federal policy.

So given how difficult it is and how disruptive it would be to the existing residential patterns in the country, people avoid thinking about it, rather than having to confront something that's very difficult. And once people start to avoid thinking about it, then fewer and fewer people, as time goes on, remember the history at all.

How did the Great Depression contribute to the problem?

In the Great Depression, many lower-middle class and working-class families lost their home. They couldn't keep up with their payments. So the Public Works Administration constructed the first civilian public housing ever in this country. Initially, it was primarily for white families in segregated white projects, but at some point, a few projects were built for African-Americans in segregated African-American projects. This practice often segregated neighborhoods that hadn't previously been that way.

In Langston Hughes' autobiography, he describes how he lived in an integrated neighborhood in Cleveland. His best friend in high school was Polish. He dated a Jewish girl. That neighborhood in Cleveland was razed by the WPA, which built two segregated [ones], one for African-Americans, one for whites. The Depression gave the stimulus for the first civilian public housing to be built. Were it not for that policy, many of these cities might have developed with a different residential pattern.

How did the Roosevelt administration justify these New Deal policies, like the WPA, if segregation wasn't constitutional?

The main justification they used was that segregation was necessary because if African-Americans lived in those neighborhoods, the property values of those neighborhoods would decline. But, in fact, the FHA had no evidence of this claim. Indeed, the opposite was the case. The FHA had research that demonstrated that property values rose when African-Americans moved into white neighborhoods, but it ignored its own research.

263

African-Americans had fewer options for housing. African-Americans were willing to pay more to purchase homes than whites were for identical homes, so when African-Americans moved into a white neighborhood, property values generally rose. Only after an organized effort by the real estate industry to create all-black suburbs and overcrowd them and turn them into slums did property values decline. But that was the rationale and it persisted for at least three decades, perhaps more.

How did the Housing Act of 1949 contribute to the issue of segregation?

President Harry Truman proposed the act because of an enormous civilian housing shortage. At the end of World War II, veterans returned home, they formed families; they needed places to live. The federal government had restricted the use of building materials for defense purposes only, so there was no private housing industry operating at that time.

Conservatives in Congress in 1949 were opposed to any public housing, not for racial reasons, because most housing was for whites. But they opposed any government involvement in the private housing market, even though the sector wasn't taking care of the housing needs of the population.

So they decided to try to defeat the public housing bill by proposing a "poison pill amendment" to make the entire bill unpalatable. It said from now on that public housing could not discriminate, understanding that if northern liberals joined conservatives in passing that amendment, southern Democrats would abandon the public housing program and along with conservative Republicans, defeat the bill entirely.

So liberals in Congress fought against the integration amendment led by civil rights opponents [resulting in a] 1949 housing program that permitted segregation. When the civilian housing industry picked up in the 1950s, the federal government subsidized mass production builders to create suburbs on conditions that those homes in the suburbs be sold only to whites. No African-Americans were permitted to buy them and the FHA often added an additional condition requiring that every deed in a home in those subdivisions prohibit resale to African-Americans.

Eventually, we had a situation everywhere in the country where there were large numbers of vacancies in the white projects and long waiting lists for the black projects. The situation became so conspicuous that the government and local housing agencies had to open up all projects to African-Americans. So these two policies, the segregation of public housing in urban areas and the subsidization of white families to leave urban areas and go to the suburbs, created the kind of racial patterns that we're familiar with today.

How did the Supreme Court decision in *Buchanan v. Warley* set the U.S. on a path of racial housing segregation?

In the early 20th century, a number of cities, particularly border cities like Baltimore, St. Louis, and Louisville, Kentucky, passed zoning ordinances that prohibited African-Americans from moving onto a block that was majority white. In 1917, the Supreme Court found in *Buchanan v. Warley* that such ordinances were unconstitutional, but not for racial reasons. The Court found it unconstitutional because such ordinances interfered with the rights of property owners.

As a result, planners around the country who were attempting to segregate their metropolitan areas had to come up with another device to do so. In the 1920s, Secretary of Commerce Herbert Hoover organized an advisory committee on zoning, whose job was to persuade every jurisdiction to adopt the ordinance that would keep low-income families out of middle-class neighborhoods. The Supreme Court couldn't explicitly mention race, but the evidence is clear that the [Commerce Department's] motivation was racial. Jurisdictions began to adopt zoning ordinances that were exclusive on economics, but the true purpose was, in part, to exclude African-Americans. So they developed ordinances that for example, prohibited apartment buildings from being built in suburbs that had single-family homes. Or they required single-family homes to have large setbacks and be set on multiple acres, all as an attempt to make the suburb racially exclusive.

Even though the Buchanan decision was handed down in 1917, many cities continued to have racial ordinances in flagrant violation of the decision. Richmond, Virginia, passed an ordinance that said people couldn't move on to a block where they were prohibited from marrying the majority of people on that block. And since Virginia had an anti-miscegenation law that prohibited blacks and whites from marrying, the state claimed that this provision didn't violate the Buchanan decision. Many of these devices were used to evade the Court's decision. Some cities adopted ordinances that prohibited African-Americans from *living* on a block that was majority white. So the Buchanan decision wasn't totally effective, but it did stimulate the drive for economic zoning to keep African-Americans out of white neighborhoods.

People say that housing segregation happens because African-Americans simply can't afford to live in middle class neighborhoods, but you argue that this is overly simplistic.

For one thing, when these practices of public segregation were most virulent, many African-Americans *could* afford to live in white suburbs. Large subdivisions developed with FHA support like Levittown, New York, were built on conditions that they be all white. The homes in those places sold, in today's dollars, about $100,000 apiece. They cost twice the national median income and were easily affordable to African-Americans as well as whites, but only working-class whites were permitted to buy into those homes.

In the next several generations, those homes sell for seven-to-eight times the median national income—unaffordable to working-class families. So the segregation that took place when the homes were first built created a permanent system that locked African-Americans out of it as appreciation grew. White families gained in home equity, in wealth, from the appreciation of their homes. African-Americans who were forced to live in apartments and not be homeowners gained none of that appreciation.

The result is that today African-American average incomes are about 60 percent of white incomes, but African-Americans' average wealth is about 5 percent of white wealth. That enormous difference is almost entirely attributable to unconstitutional federal housing policy in the mid-20th century.

How did reverse-redlining impact the African-American community in the financial crisis of 2008?

Reverse-redlining is a term used to describe the targeting by banks and mortgage lenders of minority communities for exploitative loans, called subprime loans. They were typically loans designed to induce African-American and Latino homeowners to refinance their homes at a low-interest rate that then exploded into a very high rate once they're locked into the mortgage. In many cases, these subprime loans were issued to African-American families who qualified for conventional loans, but they were denied those mortgages. The result was that foreclosure [rates] in minority communities far-exceeded that in white communities. Federal regulators were certainly aware of the fact that banks they supervised were targeting African-American communities with these loans. This was their job. So the federal government was complicit in this reverse-redlining in the period leading up to 2008. The result was devastation of middle-class and lower-middle-class African-American communities.

If the federal government was complicit in this, what is the obligation of the federal government now as the nation continues to recover from that crisis and the legacy of residential discrimination?

The obligation is under our constitution. If it's a constitutional violation, it's the obligation of our government to fashion a remedy. It's not as though simply saying "we're no longer segregating" creates a situation where segregated families can pick up and move to integrated neighborhoods. But there is an obligation to remedy segregation.

That's the reason why learning this history is important. If people believe that this all happened without government direction, then there is no constitutional obligation to desegregate. It might be a good policy, but there's no obligation.

There are many remedies. For example, Congress could prohibit the use of exclusionary zoning ordinances in suburbs that were segregated and prohibit those ordinances from being enforced until such time the suburb became diverse. That would permit developers to create townhouses and modest apartment buildings or single-family homes in all-white suburbs that currently prohibit all of those things. There are many policies we could follow, but we're not likely to have the political support to develop them without understanding the role of government in creating the segregation in the first place. ■

AUTHOR PROFILE

Katie Nodjimbadem is a graduate of Northwestern University. At the time of this article, she was a staff reporter for *Smithsonian* magazine covering history, art, and science. She is currently a Fulbright fellow in Abidjan, Cote d'Ivoire.

Alcatraz

By Sharon Olds

When I was a girl, I knew I was a man
because they might send me to Alcatraz
and only men went to Alcatraz.
Every time we drove to the city,
I'd see it there, white as a white
shark in the shark-rich Bay, the bars like
milk-white ribs. I knew I had pushed my
parents too far, my inner badness had
spread like ink and taken me over, I could
not control my terrible thoughts,
terrible looks, and they had often said
they would send me there—maybe the very next
time I spilled my milk, *Ala*
Cazam, the aluminum doors would slam, I'd be
there where I belonged, a girl-faced man in the
prison no one had escaped from. I did not
fear the other prisoners,
I knew who they were, men like me who had
spilled their milk one time too many,
not been able to curb their thoughts—
what I feared was the horror of the circles: circle of
sky around the earth, circle of
land around the Bay, circle of
water around the island, circle of
sharks around the shore, circle of
outer walls, inner walls,
steel girders, chrome bars,
circle of my cell around me, and there at the
center, the glass of milk and the guard's
eyes upon me as I reached out for it. ■

AUTHOR PROFILE

Sharon Olds (b. 1942) was born in San Francisco, California, but raised in Berkeley. The themes of her poems include family, sex, the body, and abuse, which all can be found in her first volume of poetry "Satan Says" (1980). Olds is the recipient of several major literary awards, including the National Book Critics Circle Award for *The Dead and the Living* (1984) and *Strike Sparks: Selected Poems 1980–2002* (2002). She also won the Pulitzer Prize in Poetry for her collection *Stag's Leap* (2013) about the divorce from her husband after 32 years. Her most current collection is titled *Odes* (2016). Currently, Olds teaches Creative Writing at New York University. Her poem "Alcatraz" can be found in *The Gold Cell* (1987).

267

For the Forgotten African-American Dead

By Brian Palmer

To get to East End Cemetery in Henrico County, Va., an abandoned African-American graveyard, my wife, Erin, and I drive through a predominantly black Richmond neighborhood—our neighborhood. Decades of neglect have turned this once beautiful burial ground into woodland. We're part of a volunteer effort that has reclaimed about two and a half of East End's 16 acres since it began in 2013.

Thick, tangled vegetation has swallowed headstones and grave markers. The chest-high spring and summer growth is gone or going, so we're left with the year-round die-hards that have grown every which way over the decades—English ivy, brambles, privet. Chinese sumac sprouts everywhere and has grown tree-high and tree-thick, competing with and winning against cedar and oak. Beneath it, we find pockets of illegally dumped trash. We also find headstones, fragments and corners of which Erin spots beneath the carpet of ivy. I tend to find them with my feet, by tripping over them.

Even sections we call "clear" will look scruffy and forlorn to people accustomed to manicured cemeteries. There is no lawn, just a patchwork—weeds, dead brown leaves, bare earth. Headstones are cracked, askew, even shattered, by nature or by vandals. Encroaching tree roots have buckled and broken concrete curbs that once enclosed family plots.

Before we take the first of two turns to enter East End and Evergreen—an adjacent African-American cemetery that is just as overgrown and almost three times as large—we pass a neatly landscaped graveyard, the Confederate Section of Oakwood Cemetery. Oakwood is owned by the City of Richmond; this particular section, however, gets an extra helping of taxpayer money from the State Legislature every year. In fact, dozens of Confederate cemeteries across the state have been receiving such allotments, for roughly 100 years.

The cash goes to private entities like the Sons of Confederate Veterans and the Stonewall Confederate Memorial Association through the Virginia Division of the United Daughters of the Confederacy. From 2007 to mid-2016, Virginia's General Assembly handed the Daughters more than $700,000.

The United Daughters of the Confederacy was founded in the 1890s on the twin myths of the tragic yet noble Lost Cause of the Confederacy and the happy black folks who just loved them some slavery. That my tax dollars flow into their coffers doesn't sit well with this descendant of enslaved people who escaped the Confederacy and fought for the United States in the Civil War—in the waning days of the conflict, my great-grandfather Mat liberated himself from a farm in Goochland County, Va., and joined the 115th Infantry Regiment of the United States Colored Troops. He signed up here in Richmond. My great-grandmother Julia's family escaped Gloucester County, Va., for Union-held territory in York County.

Both East End and Evergreen Cemetery, which lies in the City of Richmond, were established because "white" cemeteries wouldn't accept black burials. Neither benefits from the Virginia Legislature's largess. In fact, state, county and city agencies have spent years studiously ignoring these deteriorating African-American historic sites.

There are small signs that this is changing. In June 2016, the Virginia Outdoors Foundation, a quasi-state agency set up to preserve open spaces, awarded East End and Evergreen a $400,000 grant. Most of the funds will go toward purchasing the properties and legal costs, so other money must be found to sustain the restoration.

Bills introduced in the General Assembly to provide any funds to save historic African-American cemeteries in Virginia have died—or been killed—in committee. Later this month, when the Legislature opens its 45-day session, Virginia's lawmakers will have another chance to get on the right side of history. On Dec. 29, Delores McQuinn, a Democratic state delegate from Richmond, introduced House Bill 1547, drafted in collaboration with the administration of Gov. Terry McAuliffe. Beginning in 2018, it would allot roughly $35,000 a year to preserve historical graves and cemeteries "of African-Americans who lived at any time between January 1, 1800, and January 1, 1900." The appropriation would become part of the Code of Virginia, just like the Confederate graves provision.

"These cemeteries hold some of the iconic leaders of the past who in many ways have never been given their due honor," Ms. McQuinn told me. Funds have been earmarked for Revolutionary War and Confederate graves, which "deserve that honor and attention," she said. "This is just extending it to sites that have been left out of the equation." The amount of the appropriation is quite small. The symbolism, however, is huge.

East End and Evergreen are the only cemeteries identified so far as potential recipients of this aid, which would go to vetted nonprofits. "Nobody has ever really looked at how many African-American cemeteries there are" in Virginia or across the South, Dr. Michael Trinkley, an archaeologist who works with the Chicora Foundation, told me. But "you can't have the history of the South without having the history of African-Americans."

There are abandoned and neglected historic African-American cemeteries across the South and the country as a whole. In a 2015 story in The Nation, my colleague Seth Freed Wessler traced the decline of Greenwood Cemetery in St. Louis County, Mo., where a volunteer cleanup effort collapsed for lack of government or institutional support. We have seen at least one success story, a collaboration between members of the St. John A Baptist Church, local colleges and other community groups that restored and now care for South Asheville Cemetery in North Carolina. It's a beautiful but tiny cemetery, a fraction of the combined acreage of East End and Evergreen.

Great women and men are buried at East End and Evergreen, as great as any of the Confederate souls at rest in Oakwood—or those honored with imposing statues along Richmond's Monument Avenue. Many Richmonders know of Maggie L. Walker, the first African-American female bank president. She is buried at Evergreen with members of her family. A few know of John Mitchell Jr., buried

P

at Evergreen with his mother, Rebecca. At the turn of the 20th century, Mitchell built The Richmond Planet into one of the nation's most progressive black newspapers, and later served on the City Council. Next to no one knows about Rosa D. Bowser, an educator and suffragist, or Richard F. Tancil, a doctor and bank president. Both are buried at East End. Mitchell, Tancil, Bowser—and so many others at rest in these burial grounds—were born enslaved.

People often ask me how these cemeteries got so bad. Why can't they be like the Confederate Section of Oakwood or Hollywood Cemetery, the immaculate burial ground of thousands of Confederate soldiers? The subtext is: Why can't black people take care of their own stuff?

One short and incomplete answer is that many people moved away. Others lost their connection to the cemetery and their forebears—or simply couldn't find their loved ones beneath the foliage. The current and former owners of both cemeteries, which had no perpetual-care funds, have given up on the properties.

But a precious few folks do still maintain their plots—descendants of the Knights, the Taylors, the Jonathans, the Bowsers and the Walkers.

There's a longer, more accurate answer that begins with a core fact: The roots of today's neglect are in Jim Crow. Black Richmonders suffered from a withering assault on their political rights, economic opportunities and dignity that was initiated—resumed, really—by the white elite after Reconstruction. Central to this attack was the theft of suffrage through a series of laws that created nearly insurmountable barriers to blacks—and many poor whites—hoping to exercise their 15th Amendment rights. By the early 1900s, 90 percent of black men had been cut from voting rolls.

Jim Crow drove many black people from their neighborhoods, some away from the city, and many into poverty. And while white supremacy was not as brutal in Virginia as it was in the Deep South, lynching did happen here. Joseph McCoy was murdered by a mob in Alexandria in 1897, the year East End opened. A little terror goes a long way.

Contrast this with Confederate cemeteries around the state. Privately owned Hollywood Cemetery appears to receive little—if any—taxpayer support now. But go back a century and you'll see its owners got a leg up from their brothers in the General Assembly. In 1914, after years of annual payments to Confederate groups, the Legislature appropriated $8,000 to provide perpetual care for Hollywood's Confederate graves. That's $190,000 in 2016 dollars.

Other states have practiced their own forms of preferential treatment. When creating its Department of Conservation and Natural Resources, Alabama approved up to $25,000 a year, for "any committee of citizens" wanting to erect a Confederate monument or to supplement funds raised by organizations like the United Daughters of the Confederacy.

Mississippi's state code allows county boards of supervisors to donate money to locate and care for graves and graveyards of "Confederate soldiers or sailors who died in the Confederate service" and to purchase "land on which any of the said graveyards may be situated." I have found no law that authorizes similar annual funding for the graves and graveyards of people enslaved in the former Confederate States of America. Virginia's would be the first—if the General Assembly does the right thing and passes House Bill 1547. ∎

─────────────────────────── AUTHOR PROFILE

Brian Palmer, a New York native, is a visual journalist based in Richmond, VA. Before going freelance in 2002, he was a CNN correspondent. Prior to that, he was Beijing Bureau Chief for *U.S. News & World Report*. In 2015, he served as a scholar-in-residence in VCU's Division of Learning Innovation and Student Success. Currently, he is a visiting professor at the Columbia Graduate School of Journalism as well as an adjunct professor at VCU. His documentary *Full Disclosure* appeared in 2011 on *The Documentary Channel*. That film, along with several magazine articles and photo exhibitions, grew out of three media embeds in Iraq with the U.S. Marines. His current documentary work, *Make the Ground Talk*, led to the photography project of Virginia's neglected African American cemeteries depicted in "For the Forgotten African-American Dead," which appeared in *The New York Times* on January 7, 2017.

P

Yes, Wonderful Things

Excerpt from *Rubbish: The Archaeology of Garbage*

By William Rathje and Cullen Murphy

On a crisp October morning not long ago the sun ascended above the Atlantic Ocean and turned its gaze on a team of young researchers as they swarmed over what may be the largest archaeological site in the world. The mound they occupied covers three thousand acres and in places rises more than 155 feet above a low-lying island. Its mass, estimated at 100 million tons, and its volume, estimated at 2.9 billion cubic feet, make it one of the largest man-made structures in North America. And it is known to be a treasure trove—a Pompeii, a Tikal, a Valley of the Kings—of artifacts from the most advanced civilization the planet has ever seen. Overhead sea gulls cackled and cawed, alighting now and then to peck at an artifact or skeptically observe an archaeologist at work. The surrounding landscape still supported quail and duck, but far more noticeable were the dusty, rumbling wagons and tractors of the New York City Department of Sanitation.

The site was the Fresh Kills landfill, on Staten Island, in New York City, a repository of garbage that, when shut down, in the year 2005, will have reached a height of 505 feet above sea level, making it the highest geographic feature along a fifteen-hundred-mile stretch of the Atlantic seaboard running north from Florida all the way to Maine. One sometimes hears that Fresh Kills will have to be closed when it reaches 505 feet so as not to interfere with the approach of aircraft to Newark Airport, in New Jersey, which lies just across the waterway called Arthur Kill. In reality, though, the 505-foot elevation is the result of a series of calculations designed to maximize the landfill's size while avoiding the creation of grades so steep that roads built upon the landfill can't safely be used.

Fresh Kills was originally a vast marshland, a tidal swamp. Robert Moses's plan for the area, in 1948, was to dump enough garbage there to fill the marshland up—a process that would take, according to one estimate, until 1968—and then to develop the site, building houses, attracting light industry, and setting aside open space for recreational use. ("The Fresh Kills landfill project," a 1951 report to Mayor Vincent R. Impelliteri observed, "cannot fail to affect constructively a wide area around it. It is at once practical and idealistic.") Something along these lines may yet happen when Fresh Kills is closed. Until then, however, it is the largest active landfill in the world. It is twenty-five times the size of the Great Pyramid of Khufu at Giza, forty times the size of the Temple of the Sun at Teotihuacan. The volume of Fresh Kills is approaching that of the Great Wall of China, and by one estimate will surpass it at some point in the next few years. It is the sheer physical stature of Fresh Kills in the hulking world of landfills that explains why archaeologists were drawn to the place.

To the archaeologists of the University of Arizona's Garbage Project, which is now entering its twentieth year, landfills represent valuable lodes of information that may, when mined and interpreted, produce valuable insights—insights not into the nature of some past society, of course, but into the nature of our own. Garbage is among humanity's most prodigious physical legacies to those who have yet to be born; if we can come to understand our discards, Garbage Project archaeologists argue, then we will better understand the world in which we live. It is this conviction that prompts Garbage Project researchers to look upon the steaming detritus of daily existence with the same quiet excitement displayed by Howard Carter and Lord George Edward Carnarvon at the unpillaged, unopened tomb of Tutankhamun.

"Can you see anything?" Carnarvon asked as Carter thrust a lighted candle through a hole into the gloom of the first antechamber.

"Yes," Carter replied. "Wonderful things."

Garbage archaeology can be conducted in several ways. At Fresh Kills the method of excavation involved a mobile derrick and a thirteen-hundred-pound bucket auger, the latter of which would be sunk into various parts of the landfill to retrieve samples of garbage from selected strata. At 6:15 a.m. Buddy Kellett of the company Kellett's Well Boring, Inc., which had assisted with several previous Garbage Project landfill digs, drove one of the company's trucks, with derrick and auger collapsed for travel, straight up the steep slope of one of the landfill mounds. Two-thirds of the way up, the Garbage Project crew directed Kellett to a small patch of level ground. Four hydraulic posts were deployed from the stationary vehicle, extending outward to keep it safely moored. Now the derrick was raised. It supported a long metal rod that in turn housed two other metal rods; the apparatus, when pulled to its full length, like a telescope, was capable of penetrating the landfill to a depth of ninety-seven feet—enough at this particular spot to go clear through its bottom and into the original marsh that Fresh Kills had been (or into what was left of it). At the end of the rods was the auger, a large bucket made of high-tension steel: four feet high, three feet in diameter, and open at the bottom like a cookie cutter, with six graphite-and-steel teeth around the bottom's circumference. The bucket would spin at about thirty revolutions per minute and with such force that virtually nothing could impede its descent. At a Garbage Project excavation in Sunnyvale, California, in 1988, one of the first things the bucker hit in the cover dirt a few feet below the surface of the Sunnyvale Landfill was the skeleton of a car. The bucket's teeth snapped the axle, and drilled on.

The digging at Fresh Kills began. Down the whirring bucket plunged. Moments later it returned with a gasp, laden with garbage that, when released, spewed a thin vapor into the chill autumnal air. The smell was pungent, somewhere between sweet and disagreeable. Kellett's rig operator, David Spillers, did his job with the relaxation that comes of familiarity, seemingly oblivious to the harsh grindings and sharp clanks. The rest of the archaeological crew, wearing cloth aprons and heavy rubber gloves, went about their duties with practiced efficiency and considerable speed. They were veteran members of the Garbage Project's A-Team—its landfill-excavating arm—and had been through it all before.

Again a bucketful of garbage rose out of the ground. As soon as it was dumped Masakazu Tani, at the time a Japanese graduate student in anthropology at the University of Arizona (his Ph.D. thesis, recently completed, involves

identifying activity areas in ancient sites on the basis of distributions of litter), plunged a thermometer into the warm mass. "Forty-three degrees centigrade," Tani called out. The temperature (equivalent to 109.4 degrees Fahrenheit) was duly logged. The garbage was then given a brusque preliminary examination to determine its generic source and, if possible, its date of origin. In this case the presence of telltale domestic items, and of legible newspapers, made both tasks easy. Gavin Archer, another anthropologist and a research associate of the Garbage Project, made a notation in the running log that he would keep all day long: "Household, circa 1977." Before the next sample was pulled up Douglas Wilson, an anthropologist who specializes in household hazardous waste, stepped up to the auger hole and played out a weighted tape measure, eventually calling out, "Thirty-five feet." As a safety precaution, Wilson, like any other crew member working close to the sunken shaft on depth-measure duty, wore a leather harness tethered to a nearby vehicle. The esophagus created by the bucket auger was just large enough to accept a human being, and anyone slipping untethered a story or two into this narrow, oxygen-starved cavity would die of asphyxiation before any rescue could be attempted.

Most of the bucketfuls of garbage received no more attention than did the load labeled "Household, circa 1977." Some basic data were recorded for tracking purposes, and the garbage was left on a quickly accumulating backdirt pile. But as each of what would finally be fourteen wells grew deeper and deeper, at regular intervals (either every five or every ten feet) samples were taken and preserved for full-dress analysis. On those occasions Wilson Hughes, the methodical and serenely ursine co-director and field supervisor of the Garbage Project, and the man responsible for day-to-day logistics at the Fresh Kills dig, would call out to the bucket operator over the noise of the engine: "We'll take the next bucket." Then Hughes and Wilson would race toward the rig in a running crouch, like medics toward a helicopter, a plywood sampling board between them. Running in behind came a team of microbiologists and civil engineers assembled from the University of Oklahoma, the University of Wisconsin, and Procter & Gamble's environmental laboratory. They brought with them a variety of containers and sealing devices to preserve samples in an oxygen-free environment—an environment that would allow colonies of the anaerobic bacteria that cause most of the biodegradation in landfills (to the extent that biodegradation occurs) to survive for later analysis. Behind the biologists and engineers came other Garbage Project personnel with an assortment of wire mesh screens and saw horses.

Within seconds of the bucket's removal from the ground, the operator maneuvered it directly over the sampling board, and released the contents. The pile was attacked first by Phillip Zack, a civil engineering student from the University of Wisconsin, who, as the temperature was being recorded, directed portions of the material into a variety of airtight conveyances. Then other members of the team moved in—the people who would shovel the steaming refuse atop the wire mesh; the people who would sort and bag whatever didn't go through the mesh; the people who would pour into bags or cannisters or jars whatever did go through the mesh; the people who would label everything for the trip either back to Tucson and the Garbage Project's holding bins or to the laboratories of the various microbiologists. (The shortest trip was to the trailer-laboratory that Procter & Gamble scientists had driven from Cincinnati and parked at the edge of the landfill.) The whole sample-collection process, from dumping to sorting to storing, took no more than twelve minutes. During the Fresh Kills dig it was repeated forty-four times at various places and various depths.

As morning edged toward afternoon the bucket auger began to near the limits of its reach in one of the wells. Down through the first thirty-five feet, a depth that in this well would date back to around 1984, the landfill had been relatively dry. Food waste and yard waste—hot dogs, bread, and grass clippings, for example—were fairly well preserved. Newspapers remained intact and easy to read, their lurid headlines ("Woman Butchered—Ex-Hubby Held") calling to mind a handful of yesterday's tragedies. Beyond thirty-five feet, however, the landfill became increasingly wet, the garbage increasingly unidentifiable. At sixty feet, a stratum in this well containing garbage from the 1940s and 1950s, the bucket grabbed a sample and pulled it toward the surface. The Garbage Project team ran forward with their equipment, positioning themselves underneath. The bucket rose majestically as the operator sat at the controls, shouting something over the noise. As near as anyone can reconstruct it now, he was saying, "You boys might want to back off some, 'cause if this wind hits that bucket...." The operator broke off because the wind did hit that bucket, and the material inside—a gray slime, redolent of putrefaction—thoroughly showered the crew. It would be an exaggeration to suggest that the victims were elated by this development, but their curiosity was certainly piqued, because on only one previous excavation had slime like this turned up in a landfill. What was the stuff made of? How had it come to be? What did its existence mean? The crew members doggedly collected all the usual samples, plus a few extras bottles of slime for special study. Then they cleaned themselves off.

It would be a blessing if it were possible to study garbage in the abstract, to study garbage without having to handle it physically.[1] But that is not possible. Garbage is not mathematics. To understand garbage you have to touch it, to feel it, to sort it, to smell it. You have to pick through hundreds of tons of it, counting and weighing all the daily newspapers, the telephone books, the soiled diapers, the foam clamshells that once briefly held hamburgers, the lipstick cylinders coated with grease, the medicine vials still encasing brightly colored pills, the empty bottles of scotch, the half-full cans of paint and muddy turpentine, the forsaken toys, the cigarette butts. You have to sort and weigh and measure the volume of

---

[1] A note on terminology. Several words for the things we throw away—"garbage," "trash," "refuse," "rubbish"—are used synonymously in casual speech but in fact have different meanings. *Trash* refers specifically to discards that are at least theoretically "dry"—newspapers, boxes, cans, and so on. *Garbage* refers technically to "wet" discards—food remains, yard waste, and offal. *Refuse* is an inclusive term for both the wet discards and the dry. *Rubbish* is even more inclusive: It refers to all refuse plus construction and demolition debris. The distinction between wet and dry garbage was important in the days when cities slopped garbage to pigs, and needed to have the wet material separated from the dry; it eventually became irrelevant, but may see a revival if the idea of composting food and yard waste catches on. We will frequently use "garbage" in this book to refer to the totality of human discards because it is the word used most naturally in ordinary speech. The word is etymologically obscure, though it probably derives from Anglo-French, and its earliest associations have to do with working in the kitchen.

R

all the organic matter, the discards from thousands of plates: the noodles and the Cheerios and the tortillas; the pieces of pet food that have made their own gravy; the hardened jelly doughnuts, bleeding from their side wounds; the half-eaten bananas, mostly still within their peels, black and incomparably sweet in the embrace of final decay. You have to confront sticky green mountains of yard waste, and slippery brown hills of potato peels, and brittle ossuaries of chicken bones and T-bones. And then, finally, there are the "fines," the vast connecting mixture of tiny bits of paper, metal, glass, plastic, dirt, grit, and former nutrients that suffuses every landfill like a kind of grainy lymph. To understand garbage you need thick gloves and a mask and some booster shots. But the yield in knowledge—about people and their behavior as well as about garbage itself—offsets the grim working conditions.

To an archaeologist, ancient garbage pits or garbage mounds, which can usually be located within a short distance from any ruin, are always among the happiest of finds, for they contain in concentrated form the artifacts and comestibles and remnants of behavior of the people who used them. While every archaeologist dreams of discovering spectacular objects, the bread-and-butter work of archaeology involves the most common and routine kinds of discards. It is not entirely fanciful to define archaeology as the discipline that tries to understand old garbage, and to learn from that garbage something about ancient societies and ancient behaviors. The eminent archaeologist Emil Haury once wrote of the aboriginal garbage heaps of the American Southwest: "Whichever way one views the mounds—as garbage piles to avoid, or as symbols of a way of life—they nevertheless are features more productive of information than any others." When the British archaeologist Sir Leonard Woolley, in 1916, first climbed to the top of the ancient city of Carchemish, on the Euphrates River near the modern-day Turkish-Syrian border, he moistened his index finger and held it in the air. Satisfied, he scanned the region due south of the city—that is, downwind—pausing to draw on his map the location of any mounds he saw. A trench dug through the largest of these mounds revealed it to be the garbage dump Woolley was certain it was, and the exposed strata helped establish the chronological sequence for the Carchemish site as a whole. Archaeologists have been picking through ancient garbage ever since archaeology became a profession, more than a century ago, and they will no doubt go on doing so as long as garbage is produced.

Several basic points about garbage need to be emphasized at the outset. First, the creation of garbage is an unequivocal sign of a human presence. From Styrofoam cups along a roadway and urine bags on the moon there is an uninterrupted chain of garbage that reaches back more than two million years to the first "waste flake" knocked off in the knapping of the first stone tool. That the distant past often seems misty and dim is precisely because our earliest ancestors left so little garbage behind. An appreciation of the accomplishments of the first hominids became possible only after they began making stone tools, the debris from the production of which, along with the discarded tools themselves, are now probed for their secrets with electron microscopes and displayed in museums not as garbage but as "artifacts." These artifacts serve as markers—increasingly frequent and informative markers—of how our forebears coped with the evolving physical and social world. Human beings are mere place-holders in time, like zeros in a long number; their garbage seems to have more staying power, and a power to inform across the millennia that complements (and often substitutes for) that of the written word. The profligate habits of our own country and our own time—the sheer volume of the garbage that we create and must dispose of—will make our society an open book. The question is: Would we ourselves recognize our story when it is told, or will our garbage tell tales about us that we as yet do not suspect?

That brings up a second matter: If our garbage, in the eyes of the future, is destined to hold a key to the past, then surely it already holds a key to the present. This may be an obvious point, but it is one whose implications were not pursued by scholars until relatively recently. Each of us throws away dozens of items every day. All of these items are relics of specific human activities—relics no different in their inherent nature from many of those that traditional archaeologists work with (though they are, to be sure, a bit fresher). Taken as a whole the garbage of the United States, from its 93 million households and 1.5 million retail outlets and from all of its schools, hospitals, government offices, and other public facilities, is a mirror of American society. Of course, the problem with the mirror garbage offers is that, when encountered in a garbage can, dump, or landfill, it is a broken one: our civilization is reflected in billions of fragments that may reveal little in and of themselves. Fitting some of the pieces back together requires painstaking effort—effort that a small number of archaeologists and natural scientists have only just begun to apply.

A third point about garbage is that it is not an assertion but a physical fact—and thus may sometimes serve as a useful corrective. Human beings have over the centuries left many accounts describing their lives and civilizations. Many of these are little more than self-aggrandizing advertisements. The remains of the tombs, temples, and palaces of the elite are filled with personal histories as recorded by admiring relatives and fawning retainers. More such information is carved into obelisks and stelae, gouged into clay tablets, painted or printed on papyrus and paper. Historians are understandably drawn to written evidence of this kind, but garbage has often served as a kind of tattle-tale, setting the record straight.

It had long been known, for example, that French as well as Spanish forts had been erected along the coast of South Carolina during the sixteenth century, and various mounds and depressions have survived into our own time to testify to their whereabouts. Ever since the mid-nineteenth century a site on the tip of Parris Island, South Carolina, has been familiarly known as the site of a French outpost, built in 1562, that is spelled variously in old documents as Charlesfort, Charlesforte, and Charles Forte. In 1925, the Huguenot Society of South Carolina successfully lobbied Congress to erect a monument commemorating the building of Charlesfort. Subsequently, people in nearby Beaufort took up the Charlesfort theme, giving French names to streets, restaurants, and housing developments. Gift shops sold kitschy touristiana with a distinctly Gallic flavor. Those restaurants and gift shops found themselves in an awkward position when, in 1957, as a result of an analysis of discarded matter discovered at Charlesfort, a National Park Service historian, Albert Manucy, suggested that the site was of

Spanish origin. Excavations begun in 1979 by the archaeologist Stanley South, which turned up such items as discarded Spanish olive jars and broken majolica pottery from Seville, confirmed Manucy's view: "Charlesfort," South established, was actually Fort San Marcos, a Spanish installation built in 1577 to protect a Spanish town named Santa Elena. (Both the fort and the town had been abandoned after only a few years.)

Garbage, then, represents physical fact, not mythology. It underscores a point that can not be too greatly emphasized: Our private worlds consist essentially of two realities—mental reality, which encompasses beliefs, attitudes, and ideas, and material reality, which is the picture embodied in the physical record. The study of garbage reminds us that it is a rare person in whom mental and material realities completely coincide. Indeed, for the most part, the pair exist in a state of tension, if not open conflict. ■

AUTHOR PROFILE

William Rathje (1945–2012) was an archaeologist and professor emeritus of Anthropology at the University of Arizona. In addition to Mesoamerica and early civilizations, Dr. Rathje focused much of his work on modern material culture, specifically the study of garbage. He was a founder and director of the Tucson Garbage Project, which uses field research in residential waste and landfills to study American consumer habits, often challenging long-held assumptions. *Rubbish: The Archaeology of Garbage*, which contains the current excerpt, was published in 1992.

Cullen Murphy is currently editor-at-large for *Vanity Fair* magazine, but for over 20 years he was managing editor of *The Atlantic*. In addition to his editing work and co-authoring *Rubbish* with William Rathje, he has authored numerous books on a range of subjects, including *The World According to Eve: Women and the Bible in Ancient Times and Our Own* (1998), *Are We Rome?: The Fall of an Empire and the Fate of America* (2007), and a collection of essays titled *Just Curious* (1995). For twenty-five years he wrote the *Prince Valiant* comic strip, along with his father, the illustrator John Cullen Murphy. His latest book, *Cartoon County: My Father and His Friends in the Golden Age of Make-Believe*, published in 2017, draws on that experience.

Story of Cities #44: Will Dadaab, the World's Largest Refugee Camp, Really Close?

By Ben Rawlence

Kenya's third biggest city, after Nairobi and Mombasa, is not a city at all but a refugee camp—the world's largest. This year the Dadaab refugee complex is 25 years old: young for a city, but old for a camp that was only ever supposed to be a temporary sanctuary.

Dadaab was built in 1992 for 90,000 refugees fleeing the war in Somalia. Today it is home to an estimated half a million people, 350,000 of them registered refugees—an urban area the size of Bristol, Zurich or New Orleans. Last week Kenya announced plans to close it by May of next year, to the unhappiness of many who live there.

Noor Tawane, now a middle-aged father of seven and businessman in the camp, was one of Dadaab's first residents. Over the past four years, while researching a book about the camps, I have learned his story. He arrived in Dadaab on a donkey cart in 1992, at the age of seven, with his mother and father: a thin, wizened man with hennaed hair and light eyes called Idris.

The family had fled the violence that engulfed southern Somalia following the collapse of the government of Siad Barre. Idris was a prosperous farmer with a lot of land on the banks of the Juba river that he was reluctant to abandon. "The most beautiful land ever is that place," Tawane says proudly—but he cannot remember directly. This is his father's memory talking.

One day, Tawane's elder brothers had gone to work on the farm outside their home town of Jama'ame. When they didn't return, Idris went looking for them— and discovered his two boys lying dead amid the maize stalks, a bullet in each of them. So the rest of the family ran.

Refugees were massing at the border with Kenya and a town of tents and huts sprang up—a bit like the "Jungle" camp in Calais today. These waves of new arrivals prompted the Kenyan government to make a more permanent (but still temporary) arrangement: it invited the UN's refugee agency to build three planned camps around the small dusty border town of Dadaab, 90km inside Kenya. And it was into one of these, a camp called Hagadera, that Tawane, his parents and his remaining brothers and sisters were shown one morning in late 1992.

Hagadera, in Somali, means "the place of the tall trees". It was also a place of sandy gullies formed by sporadic streams in the rainy season, where nomads brought their camels. Twelve kilometres to the north was the town of Dadaab— hitherto a tiny settlement of 5,000 semi-nomadic people—where the UN and the other aid agencies made their own camp of tents next to the police post. To the north of Dadaab were two more camps, Ifo and Dagahaley; like Hagadera, each was designed to hold 30,000 people.

R

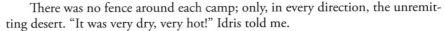

There was no fence around each camp; only, in every direction, the unremitting desert. "It was very dry, very hot!" Idris told me.

North-east Kenya is lonely country and the government wanted the refugees penned in as far away as possible from everyone else. It stopped the refugees from moving further into Kenya with a roadblock on the road south and another at the Tana river in Garissa town, 100km to the south.

The UN planners designed the three camps on a grid pattern, arranged in lettered sections and numbered blocks bisected by roads wide enough for police patrol cars. The principles that have always guided the camp architecture are visibility and control, a bit like a prison—the camp follows the structure of punishment, but there has been no crime.

Tawane's family was shown to a rectangle of sand in block E5 of Hagadera. The size of a plot corresponds to the number of people in each family: a UN unit of measurement (also used to calculate rations) known as "family-size".

Tawane's family was given a tent, and they set about planting thorn cuttings along the perimeter of their plot for a fence. Every two weeks, a truck would arrive with food for the distribution of rations: maize flour, wheat, beans. "The children couldn't adapt to the relief food," Idris recalled. "For six months they were always getting sick; I was always taking them to the hospital."

Water arrived by truck, too, every few days, before the drilling machines came and boreholes were dug. In those early days, water was only 20 metres below the surface of the desert—but by 2016, a new borehole struck water only after going down 400 metres. Half a million people use a lot of water.

Soon after they were settled in Hagadera, a group of volunteers built a school out of wood and corrugated-iron sheets. Tawane's earliest memories are of running down the sandy alleyways between the blocks, then across the open expanse in front of them, to the little school. "I learned my ABC there, in Arabic," he said, "writing lessons on a narrow wooden board."

In each camp, in the centre of the grid, the UN planners marked out an area for a market, with plots for stalls. The new arrivals had arranged themselves in their sections and blocks, appointing community leaders to liaise with the UN, the Kenyan government, and agencies that had suddenly appeared to run the camps' clinics.

In many cases, those who had been in positions of authority back home, such as Tawane's father, slipped easily into leadership roles in the camps. As a businessman with some assets, he was among those invited to set up a shop in the market. The UN rations are dry and many people would wish to sell them in order to buy other things including vegetables, meat, tea or sugar. But Tawane's father refused the offer: "We'll be going home soon," Idris told them.

"I never had the expectation of staying in this place," he said to me. "I know I have the name of 'refugee', but I never accepted settling here as a permanent solution." Idris died earlier this year, after 25 years in the camp, still waiting to return to his farm.

He had, though—after some years of resistance—invested in a butchery business, and bequeathed his sons a network of shops around the camp, plus three donkey carts with insulated steel boxes on their back, each sporting the word "MEAT" in red paint.

In time, of course, the economy of the camp grew. People would go hungry for years in order to save the capital to start a business—but these days, in the market, you can buy everything from an iPhone to an ice-cream.

In time, too, the UN formalised the ad-hoc appointment of block and section leaders into municipal elections. Each camp has an elected chairman and woman, plus an overall chair who represents the three camps in discussions about everything from the siting of boreholes and problems with refuse collection, to communal relations between the different groups in the camp. After finishing high school, Tawane ran for office as youth chairman of Hagadera: "I am different because I have been to trainings on democracy and I know what it is about," he said.

Tawane won—and used his two terms to preach a message of inclusivity and gender mainstreaming, buzzwords he had learned from UN workshops. "Women have more choice in Dadaab," he said. "NGOs teach them about female genital mutilation and forced marriage and so on. Dadaab is a more free place for women than Somalia."

These days, Dadaab is a veritable melting pot, with Sudanese, Ethiopians, Congolese, Ugandans and even a lone Rwandan refugee from the 1994 genocide adding to the mix. The camp is not a democracy, more a kind of consultative autocracy, with the Kenyan government and the UN the ultimate overseers—in some areas content to operate a kind of laissez-faire governance, but in other respects fierce about enforcing restrictions.

The perversity of these restrictions has grown more acute as the camps have aged. Tawane's home for a quarter of a century is made of mud and sticks because the refugees are not allowed to pour concrete or make permanent structures. He has been through the Kenyan school system and acquired diplomas by distance learning, yet he is not allowed to work for the UN or the agencies that run the camp because he is not a Kenyan. "Sometimes I wonder, why has God left me like this?" Tawane complains.

But he has not accepted his fate lying down. While the government has always forbidden proper sanitation and electricity in the camp, to avoid this giant slum becoming "permanent", Tawane and his friends have invested in a generator and provide power, illegally, to nearly 400 households for a monthly fee.

Tawane's ingenuity exemplifies both the triumph and the tragedy of the camp system in dealing with large-scale refugee flows. Underlying their foundation is a fiction of temporariness—a fiction the Kenyan government is willing to enforce with bulldozers if necessary.

The government recently required the UN to dismantle some newly built homes because they "looked too much like real houses", and it has torn down illegal power lines too. If the refugees were allowed to work, to make their businesses prosper, to pay tax even—it seems clear that everyone would be better off. As Tawane himself complained: "What could I have achieved if I hadn't been born a refugee?"

Despite the restrictions, however, Dadaab is working after a fashion. And even though Mogadishu appears to be stabilising, for people such as Tawane, who have made a life—and a living—in the camp, the uncertainty of life back in Somalia is not an attractive alternative.

"The UN and Kenya government are saying: 'Go back home'," said Tawane, "But for me, go back where? The house we had has been taken by other clans—and Al-Shabaab is still in control."

Moreover, the economic reach of the Dadaab camps has become a part of the national landscape: powerful interests have taken root. Many Kenyans are coming to work here—for the agencies in running water, education and health services; as security guards, hoteliers and drivers; and also working for refugee businesses in the camp market that long ago outgrew its allotted space: metalworkers, tailors, computer technicians, traders of everything from sugar to sportswear. This is the largest market between Nairobi and Mogadishu, turning over $20m–$30m a year.

The roads through the camp are also a hub for a multimillion-dollar smuggling ring that enriches certain officials in the Kenyan government. Some members of the police, nominally in charge of security in the camps, are paid bribes to look the other way.

By day, a government spokesman might blame Dadaab refugees for terrorist attacks in Kenya and call for the camp to be closed; by night, however, this illicit trade is pouring cash into the campaign coffers of some politicians, although the government has denied this. "The Kenyans are very good at smuggling," said Tawane. "They prefer money rather than maintaining a good security in the camp."

For these reasons, and because of the remoteness of a durable peace across much of southern Somalia, Dadaab seems very likely to remain, despite last week's announcement of its impending closure.

This sprawling urban slum in the middle of an inhospitable desert—the most inappropriate place for a city—is sustained by a curious mix of political intrigue, bureaucratic inertia, and the simple fact that for two generations now, it has become "home". While this refugee complex does not appear on any official atlas of Kenya, the Dadaab camp is, so the saying goes, very much "on the map". ■

AUTHOR PROFILE

Ben Rawlence is a British journalist, human rights advocate, and author. He studied Swahili and History at the School of Oriental and African Studies at the University of London and he received a Master's degree from the University of Chicago in International Relations. Rawlence worked as a researcher for the Human Rights Watch in Africa. He is also the author of *City of Thorns: Nine Lives in the World's Largest Refugee Camp* (2016), a work that explores the experiences of refugees living in Dadaab, and *Radio Congo: Signals of Hope from Africa's Deadliest War* (2012), a book about his travels in Congo in the aftermath of a deadly war there. "Story of Cities #44" was originally published in *The Guardian* newspaper's 50-part series on the history of urbanization across the world.

The New Meaning of Mobility

By Christine Rosen

What is "mobility" and what is it for? The word has commonly been used to describe upward movement on the socioeconomic scale, the sort of classic American success story of which fiction and real life have given us countless examples. This figurative meaning is related to the more literal sense of mobility as freedom for movement across physical space—which itself has an iconic role in the American tale, from the explorers through the pioneers and the Beats. Americans understood the two meanings of *mobility* as of a piece: moving out and moving up, both a means of striking out for new prospects. It was liberation, pursued in the spirit of self-reliance, exploration, and reinvention.

Today, when we speak of being "mobile," we refer to the myriad technologies that allow us to remain in constant contact with each other regardless of where we are. This kind of mobility isn't like that of immigrants struggling to break out of poverty, or of the pioneers heading west. That kind was engaged with places: escaping the confines of the old place, searching for opportunities in the new. For today's mobile citizens, place matters very little; it is an obstacle that technology painlessly overcomes, with our ever-present smartphones telling us always where we are, what's around us, and, thanks to GPS, how to get where we are going.

The cutting edge of mobility is "location awareness": smartphone content that automatically responds and reacts to your physical location. For instance, websites like Yelp allow you to see nearby restaurants and businesses. And Twitter, Facebook, and other social networking sites allow you to "geotag" your updates, so that friends and followers will know precisely where you are. Panasonic makes a camera with a built-in GPS that can automatically geotag every photograph you take, allowing picture-sharing sites to show where the photo was taken.

Although we rarely pause to consider whether this kind of mobility is good, we are beginning to see what it means for those who hope to profit from our use of it. AT&T recently unveiled ShopAlerts, a "geo-fencing" service: as the *New York Times* Media Decoder blog reported, "marketers can create a geo-fence around an event, like a concert, a retail location or a geographic area," and when a person with a smartphone steps into the geofenced area, he is bombarded with offers of products to buy. This is but one example of how mobility has begun to deepen the commercialization of public space, moving it from mere ads and billboards to a point where every individual sojourn into public space becomes an opportunity for targeted commercial exploitation. In this sense, the digitization of public space seems to be following the path that the Internet took two decades ago, moving rapidly away from its initial status as a freewheeling, unencumbered realm and turning it into something that more closely resembles a shopping mall.

Consider an interview Eric Schmidt gave to the *Wall Street Journal* in August 2010 when he was still CEO of Google, in which he stated rather matter-of-factly, "We know roughly who you are, roughly what you care about, roughly who your friends are." This is true for millions of users of GPS-enabled smartphones—and,

R

as users of Apple's iPhone and Google's Android discovered this spring, data on their locations and movements are stored and transmitted back to the parent companies, meaning that they know too *where* you are, and where you were.

Why do Google and Apple want to know where you are and where you've been? So that one day in the near future, when you are walking home from work, Google can remind you to get milk and urge you to stop into a nearby store to buy it. Schmidt foresees, in the *Journal* author's paraphrasing, that "a generation of powerful handheld devices is just around the corner that will be adept at surprising you with information that you didn't know you wanted to know." Schmidt calls this "serendipity," and promises that it "can be calculated now. We can actually produce it electronically."

How desirable, really, is this "electronic serendipity"? It is no small historical irony that the technology that is meant to liberate us from place also allows such ubiquitous location tracking: You can go anywhere, but you can also be found anywhere. The possibility encapsulated in the old form of mobility—the freedom to escape one's past, the chance to start anew—is undermined by the technologies of the new mobility, which make it increasingly difficult for us, even from moment to moment in far-off places, to be free from society, from each other, and from ourselves.

Curiously, although we are ever more inextricably linked together in this way, human ties are not necessarily strengthening as a result. As many sociologists have documented, we frequently find ourselves "alone together," whether we are immersed in our individual cell-phone conversations in public or updating our Facebook pages at home while our family members engage in their own electronic entertainments. We are now available for communication with practically anyone at any time, yet large numbers of Americans report feelings of loneliness, fewer families sit down together to share meals, and the number of Americans living alone is the highest it has ever been. We have more hours of leisure time than any previous generation, and yet we spend most of them watching television. And while we are "connected" to large numbers of people via social networking, studies show we have fewer close friends than did previous generations.

As Sherry Turkle puts it in her new book, which takes *Alone Together* as its title, "we expect more from technology and less from each other." Perhaps we are justified in sensing something paradoxical at work in the progress of our technologies of mobility: their promise—to connect us to people and places—is belied by the reality that our connections to people and places seem only to be weakening.

Mobile But Tethered

To be rooted is perhaps the most important and least recognized need of the human soul," Simone Weil argued in the mid-twentieth century. Even our virtual playgrounds pay homage to the deeply felt need for place: MySpace was, until recently, called "a place for friends"; Second Life mimics real-life places with its homes, offices, and restaurants. What is different about mobile playgrounds is that mobile devices force real life and virtual life (and real places and virtual places) to try to coexist in a way they never have before.

We want to see this as a good, enabling thing—I can fire off that e-mail to the office and then get back to relaxing on my vacation!—but it is instructive to go to a playground today: even on a weekend, you will see parents engrossed in their iPhones and BlackBerrys while their children make increasingly loud bids for their attention. The November 2, 2009 cover of *The New Yorker* sadly and beautifully satirized this trend: it shows an illustration of children out trick-or-treating, basked in the glow of houselights, while their parents bask in the glow of the smartphones in which *they* are rapt. Even our leisure time, it seems, has been colonized by our need to stay connected—and it is a constant struggle to set limits on our engagement with the virtual world so that we can attend to the real one in front of us.

And when we decide to leave home entirely, we find it difficult to leave the demands of work behind. Consider the cruise ship industry: every year, more than three million people board a Carnival Cruise ship to take a vacation. They spend a great deal of time eating—and gambling—and then eating some more. The perpetual buffets that have long been a staple of the cruise ship lifestyle cater to one kind of hunger; Carnival now caters to another—one that seems counterintuitive in vacationers eager to get away from it all: staying connected. With their twenty-four-hour Internet cafés, onboard WiFi, and an advertising campaign that features bikini-clad patrons lounging on deck chairs with laptop computers, Carnival Cruise Lines has enthusiastically responded to the demands of patrons who seek an ideal of maritime escape but still want to check their e-mail several times a day.

This, too, is the strange new world of leisure: never disconnected, and never really free from the demands of daily life. Notwithstanding all the talk of mobility, we find ourselves tethered in novel ways—not to a hometown, or to a particular social background, but to our devices themselves and the feeling of connection they provide, which we seemingly cannot sit still without.

This kind of ubiquitous connection transforms our sense of place. First, it brings the Outside in: it eliminates the boundary between work life and home life, and in the process disrupts many of the rituals of private life. Family members constantly checking in and out of virtual worlds exist in a state that has been dubbed "continuous partial attention," which is hardly conducive to healthy family life. Neither is this erosion between work and home life at all like the days when the two were merged, with children tending to the family farm and family members producing goods out of home-based workshops, for this new shift does not bring with it the binding up of family members together in some shared activity or practice. Quite the opposite: what family members do around each other at home has less and less to do with each other.

Our new mobility also brings the Inside out by transforming public space. Every public space is now potentially a scene for the private if we can reach out to those we know via technology. The oft-told tales of being forced to listen to someone else's cell-phone conversation are but one example. More broadly, our new mobility brings the Inside out in the sense that we bring our personal connections with us wherever we go. We can talk to our neighbor when we're on the other side of the world, and update our Facebook page while climbing Mt. Kilimanjaro. This connectivity comes with a cost: the joy of being away from familiar places and discovering new ones unencumbered, the freedom of *dis*connection.

R

285

A related consequence of our increasing mobility is the homogenization of experience. We take our devices with us wherever we go, staying connected to our social networks and tapping into the same sources of news and entertainment that we would access at home. Even when visiting remote or exotic locales, we now need never go without the social chit-chat, political commentary, celebrity gossip, sports scores, and jokes that fill our everyday conversations. In the twentieth century, industrialization and mass culture, for all their blessings, greatly eroded local flavor and the particular character of places. Now, the 24/7 hum of electronic communication is having a similar effect, making our experience of every place like every other.

Mobility also continues to erode social institutions. As one writer for the Carnegie Council put it in summarizing the findings of a German research project, "Increased mobility goes hand in hand with increased economic uncertainty, especially among young professionals," which has led to delays in marriage and childrearing. "Not only are young people less economically able to start a family, but they also change locations more often than ever with the fluidity of labor markets. Spouses or couples are less likely to find appropriate work in the same place." What was at first the *freedom* that mobility newly granted us to move about is increasingly becoming an economic *necessity*.

Seen in this light, mobility is less appealing. When mobility becomes transience, ennui often follows. In Keith Gessen's 2008 novel *All the Sad Young Literary Men*, one character remarks, "If you walked around America and looked properly, what you saw was a group of wandering disaggregated people, torn apart and carrying with them, in their hands, like supplicants, the pieces of flesh they'd won from others in their time." They are probably also carrying their iPhones, thinking them a relief.

Losing Our Place

Perhaps it is time to reconsider "location awareness." Nearly forty million Americans change residences each year; our daily commutes to work are getting longer and longer. A genuine awareness of location or place might lead us to rethink mobility, to recognize that much of the ritual and happenstance of daily life—from the family meal to a passing conversation with a stranger on the bus— is necessarily tied to place. We outsource location awareness to mobile technology and exercise too little of it ourselves.

In a recent symposium about the Internet, architect Galia Solomonoff noted the way "our sense of orientation, space, and place has changed" because of the connectedness and mobility made possible by our new technologies. But she cautions: "The Internet at this point privileges what we can see and read over many other aspects of knowledge and sensation, such as how much something weighs, how it feels, how stable it is." And she wonders whether we are better able to navigate places now than we were before the advent of location awareness technology: "Do we have longer, better sojourns in faraway places or constant placelessness? How have image, space, place, and content been altered to give us a sense of here and now?"

These are good questions to grapple with as we think about the future of mobility and membership in particular communities. Serendipity is not, *contra*

Google's former CEO, something we can engineer; it is the ability to find something valuable when we are not even seeking it. Mobile technologies promise us access to just such a world whose vast riches we can explore, but in practice, Internet serendipity has come to resemble targeted advertising rather than exciting unexplored horizons.

The more fundamental question is whether, in inhabiting these virtual worlds, we lose sight of the importance of the real one—and our deeply felt human need for place, for community, and for the unpredictable pleasures of face-to-face interaction. Just as architects and urban planners can design buildings and city centers that encourage rather than discourage community, so technological designers and individual users can construct boundaries that make use of our tools without undermining the good life we originally devised them to better. ∎

—————————————————— AUTHOR PROFILE

Christine Rosen holds a Ph.D. in History from Emory University. Currently, she is an adjunct scholar at the American Enterprise Institute and a senior editor of *The New Atlantis*, where she writes about the social and cultural impact of technology, as well as bioethics and the history of genetics. Her essays and reviews have appeared in publications such as *The New York Times Magazine, The Wall Street Journal, The Washington Post, The New Republic, The Weekly Standard, Policy Review, The American Historical Review,* and *The New England Journal of Medicine.* Rosen's books include *Preaching Eugenics: Religious Leaders and the American Eugenics Movement* (2004), and *My Fundamentalist Education* (2005). She was recently a Future Tense Fellow at the New America Foundation, where she worked on her forthcoming book, *The Extinction of Experience.* "The New Meaning of Mobility" originally appeared in the April 2011 issue of *The New Atlantis.*

R

Invention, Memory, and Place

By Edward W. Said

Over the past decade, there has been a burgeoning interest in two overlapping areas of the humanities and social sciences: memory and geography or, more specifically, the study of human space. Both of them have spawned an extraordinary amount of interesting work, work that has in effect created new fields of study and inquiry. The concern with memory, for example, has branched out to include such increasingly prevalent forms of writing as personal memoirs and autobiography, which nearly every fiction writer of note has attempted, to say nothing of the outpourings of academics, scientists, public figures, and so forth. The national fixation on recollection, confession, and witness has run the whole gamut from public confession—as in the Clinton-Lewinsky scandal—various studies of the meaning of collective memory, extended reflection and analyses of instances of it, plus numerous chronicles embodying it. I shall have more to say about that later. In addition, and somewhat on the margins, has been a serious, sometimes bitter inquiry into the authenticity of certain memories, as well as, at the other, calmer end of the spectrum, a remarkable academic analysis of the role of invention in such matters as tradition and collective historical experience.

Some examples of intense and even anguished controversy are the following: Was Anne Frank's diary really hers, or was it so altered by publishers, members of her family, or others in its published form so as to conceal the disturbances in her domestic life? In Europe there has been a great and often acerbic debate over the meaning of the Holocaust, with a whole range of opinions as to what happened, why it happened, and what it tells us about the nature of Germany, France, and several other involved countries. The celebrated French classicist Pierre Vidal-Naquet wrote a powerful book some years back called *Assassins of Memory* about French deniers of the Holocaust, and more recently the Papon trial in Bordeaux raised uncomfortable questions related not just to memories of the Occupation but the centrality of French collaborators with the Nazis and what it said about French selective memories of the Vichy regime. In Germany of course debate on the testimonials of the death camps and their philosophical as well as political meaning periodically receives new infusions of controversy, fuelled most recently by the publication of the German translation of Daniel Goldhagen's book *Hitler's Willing Executioners*. In the United States consider the anger provoked by representatives of the official culture and members of the government by the Smithsonian Institution—seen correctly as a sort of embodier of official memory in the country—in its unsuccessful attempts to mount exhibitions, one about the *Enola Gay* and another on the African American experience. Earlier there was a furor over an impressive exhibition at the National Gallery of American Art, *America as West*, which set out to contrast representations of the land, the Indian natives, and the conditions of life in the Western U.S. during the 1860s with the way the land was being forcibly settled and the Indians destroyed, and the transformation of a once peaceful rural environment into a predatory urban one. Senator Ted Stevens of Alaska decried the whole thing as an attack on America even though he avowed that he himself had not seen the exhibit. In any event these controversies raise the question not only of what is remembered but how and in what form. It is an issue about the very fraught nature of representation, not just about content.

Memory and its representations touch very significantly upon questions of identity, of nationalism, of power and authority. Far from being a neutral exercise in facts and basic truths, the study of history, which of course is the underpinning of memory, both in school and university, is to some considerable extent a nationalist effort premised on the need to construct a desireable loyalty to and insider's understanding of one's country, tradition, and faith. As is well known, there's been a robust debate in the U.S. on the matter of national standards in history, in which issues such as whether George Washington or Abraham Lincoln should be allowed more time than they have at present in history curricula have generated very angry arguments. Similarly, as Howard Zinn has suggested in his work, there has been skepticism expressed as to why the study of American history should glorify only the big deeds of big people and neglect to mention what happened to the small ones, the people who built railroads, worked the farms, sweated as laborers in the enormous industrial companies that lie at the heart of this country's immense wealth and power. (He redresses this imbalance in his impressive *People's History of the United States*, which has already sold well over half a million copies.)[1] In a recent article he goes even further. Having been asked to participate in a symposium on the Boston Massacre, Zinn reflected to himself that he wanted

> to discuss other massacres because it seemed to me that concentrating attention on the Boston Massacre would be a painless exercise in patriotic fervor. There is no surer way to obscure the deep divisions of race and class in American history than by uniting us in support of the American Revolution and all its symbols (like Paul Revere's stark etching of the soldiers shooting into the crowd).

> I suggested to the people assembled at Faneuil Hall (the wall around us crowded with portraits of the Founding Fathers and the nation's military heroes) that there were other massacres, forgotten or dimly remembered, that deserved to be recalled. These ignored episodes could tell us much about racial hysteria and class struggle, about shameful moments in our continental and overseas expansion, so that we can see ourselves more clearly, more honestly.[2]

These remarks immediately transport us to the vexed issue of nationalism and national identity, of how memories of the past are shaped in accordance with a certain notion of what "we" or, for that matter, "they" really are. National identity always involves narratives—of the nation's past, its founding fathers and documents, seminal events, and so on. But these narratives are never undisputed or merely a matter of the neutral recital of facts. In the United States, for example,

---

[1] See Howard Zinn, *A People's History of the United States* (New York, 1980).

[2] Zinn, "The Massacres of History," *The Progressive* 62 (Aug. 1998): 17.

1492 was celebrated very differently by people who saw themselves as victims of Columbus's advent—people of color, minorities, members of the working class, people, in a word, who claimed they had a different collective memory of what in most schools was celebrated as a triumph of advancement and the collective march forward of humanity. Because the world has shrunk—for example, communications have been speeded up fantastically—and people find themselves undergoing the most rapid social transformations in history, ours has become an era of a search for roots, of people trying to discover in the collective memory of their race, religion, community, and family a past that is entirely their own, secure from the ravages of history and a turbulent time. But this too has provoked very sharp debate and even bloodshed. In the Islamic world, how one reads the orthodox tradition (*sunnah*) is being debated, as are the questions of how one interprets stories about the Prophet, which are, basically, memories reconstructed by disciples and friends, and how one can derive an image of contemporary Islamic codes of behavior and law that is consonant and in accordance with those precious, early, in fact aboriginal, memories. Similar questions arise in interpretations of the Christian Gospels, as well as the Judaic prophetic books; these questions have a direct impact on matters of community and politics in the present. Some of this lies behind the much-touted controversy over family values that have been vaunted by political candidates, moral philosophers, and public scolds.

To this whole matter of memory as a social, political, and historical enterprise has been added a complication, to which I referred above, namely, the role of invention. In 1983 two distinguished British historians Eric Hobsbawm and Terence Ranger edited a book of essays by various other well-known historians entitled *The Invention of Tradition*.[3] I won't try to summarize the ideas in this subtle and rich collection except to say that what was being studied was the way rulers—social and political authorities in the period since about 1850—set about creating such supposedly age-old rituals and objects as the Scottish kilt or, in India, the *durbar*, thereby providing a false, that is, invented memory of the past as a way of creating a new sense of identity for ruler and ruled. In India, for example, the *durbar*—whose status as "tradition" was a total fiction—was said to be a great ceremonial pageant designed to be implanted in the Indian memory though it served the British colonial authorities to compel Indians to believe in the age-old history of British imperial rule. "In Africa, too," writes Ranger, "whites drew on invented tradition in order to derive the authority and confidence that allowed them to act as agents of change. Moreover, insofar as they were consciously applied to Africans, the invented traditions [such as compelling Africans to work as laborers on European gentlemen's farms] of nineteenth-century Europe were seen precisely as agents of 'modernization.'"[4] In modern France, according to Hobsbawm, the demise of Napoleon III's empire and the emergence of a politicized working class as evidenced in the Paris Commune convinced the "moderate Republican bourgeoisie" that only it could head off the dangers of revolution by producing a new kind of citizen, "turning peasants into Frenchmen...[and] all Frenchmen into good Republicans." Thus the French revolution was institutionalized in education by developing "a secular equivalent of the church...imbued with

---

3   See *The Invention of Tradition*, ed. Eric Hobsbawm and Terence Ranger (Cambridge, 1983).

4   Ranger, "The Invention of Tradition in Colonial Africa," in *ibid.*, p. 220.

revolutionary and republican principles and content." In addition, there was "the invention of public ceremonies. The most important of these, Bastille Day, can be exactly dated in 1880." Thirdly, there "was the mass production of public monuments," of two main kinds—images of the Republic itself such as Marianne—and images of the "bearded civilian figures of whoever local patriotism chose to regard as its notables."[5]

In other words, the invention of tradition was a practice very much used by authorities as an instrument of rule in mass societies when the bonds of small social units like village and family were dissolving and authorities needed to find other ways of connecting a large number of people to each other. The invention of tradition is a method for using collective memory selectively by manipulating certain bits of the national past, suppressing others, elevating still others in an entirely functional way. Thus memory is not necessarily authentic, but rather useful. The Israeli journalist Tom Segev shows in his book *The Seventh Million* that the Holocaust was consciously used by the Israeli government as a way of consolidating Israeli national identity after years of not paying much attention to it.[6] Similarly, historian Peter Novick, in a recently published study of the image of the Holocaust amongst American Jews, shows that before the 1967 war and the Israeli victory against the Arab states, American Jews paid very little attention to that appallingly horrible episode (and in fact tried consciously to deemphasize it as a way of avoiding anti-Semitism).[7] It is a long way from those early attitudes to the construction of the Holocaust Museum in Washington. Similarly the controversy surrounding the memories of the Armenian genocide is fuelled by the Turkish government's denial of its role.

My point in citing all these cases is to underline the extent to which the art of memory for the modern world is both for historians as well as ordinary citizens and institutions very much something to be used, misused, and exploited, rather than something that sits inertly there for each person to possess and contain. Thus the study and concern with memory or a specifically desirable and recoverable past is a specially freighted late twentieth-century phenomenon that has arisen at a time of bewildering change, of unimaginably large and diffuse mass societies, competing nationalisms, and, most important perhaps, the decreasing efficacy of religious, familial, and dynastic bonds. People now look to this refashioned memory, especially in its collective forms, to give themselves a coherent identity, a national narrative, a place in the world, though, as I have indicated, the processes of memory are frequently, if not always, manipulated and intervened in for sometimes urgent purposes in the present. It's interesting to contrast this more modern and somehow loosely malleable form of memory with the codified, rigorous art of memory in classical antiquity described by Frances Yates.[8] Memory for Cicero was something organized and structured. If you wanted to remember something for a speech you were about to give, you imagined a building with all sorts of rooms and corners, and in your mind's eye you subdivided the parts of the memory you

---

5   Hobsbawm, "Mass-Producing Traditions: Europe, 1870–1914," pp. 271, 272.

6   See Tom Segev, *The Seventh Million: The Israelis and the Holocaust*, trans. Haim Watzman (New York, 1993).

7   See Peter Novick, *The Holocaust in American Life* (New York, 1999), pp. 146–203.

8   See Frances A. Yates, *The Art of Memory* (Chicago, 1966).

S

wished to recall and placed them in various sections of the building; as you spoke you walked through the building in your head, so to speak, noting the places and the objects and phrases as you went along. That way order was maintained in the memory. The modern art of memory is much more subject to inventive reordering and redeploying than that.

As for geography, or geography as I want to use the word, as a socially constructed and maintained sense of place, a great deal of attention has been paid by modern scholars and critics to the extraordinary constitutive role of space in human affairs. Consider, as an easy instance, the word *globalization*, which is an indispensable concept for modern economics. It is a spatial, geographical designation signifying the global reach of a powerful economic system. Think of geographical designations like Auschwitz, think of what power and resonance they have, over and above a particularly specifiable moment in history or a geographical locale like Poland or France. The same applies to Jerusalem, a city, an idea, an entire history, and of course a specifiable geographical locale often typified by a photograph of the Dome of the Rock, the city walls, and the surrounding houses seen from the Mount of Olives; it too is overdetermined when it comes to memory, as well as all sorts of invented histories and traditions, all of them emanating from it, but most of them in conflict with each other. This conflict is intensified by Jerusalem's mythological—as opposed to actual geographical—location, in which landscape, buildings, streets, and the like are overlain and, I would say, even covered entirely with symbolic associations totally obscuring the existential reality of what as a city and real place Jerusalem is. The same can be said for Palestine, whose landscape functions in the memories of Jews, Muslims, and Christians entirely differently. One of the strangest things for me to grasp is the powerful hold the locale must have had on European crusaders despite their enormous distance from the country. Scenes of the crucifixion and nativity, for instance, appear in European Renaissance paintings as taking place in a sort of denatured Palestine, since none of the artists had ever seen the place. An idealized landscape gradually took shape that sustained the European imagination for hundreds of years. That Bernard of Clairvaux standing in a church in Vezelay, in the heart of Burgundy, could announce a crusade to reclaim Palestine and the holy places from the Muslims never fails to astound me, and that after hundreds of years of living in Europe Zionist Jews could still feel that Palestine had stood still in time and was theirs, again despite millennia of history and the presence of actual inhabitants. This too is also an indication of how geography can be manipulated, invented, characterized quite apart from a site's merely physical reality.

Simon Schama's book *Landscape and Memory* chronicles the to-ing and fro-ing between specific geographical locales and the human imagination. Surely the most compelling aspect of Schama's book is that he shows in dozens of different ways that forests, villages, mountains, and rivers are never coterminous with some stable reality out there that identifies and gives them permanence. On the contrary, as in the example he gives of his family's original village in Lithuania, most of its traces disappeared; he finds instead through the poetry of Adam Mickiewicz how Jews and Poles "were snarled up.... in each other's fate" despite his contemporaries' belief that they were "necessarily alien to each other." Geography stimulates not only memory but dreams and fantasies, poetry and painting, philosophy (as in Heidegger's *Holzwege*), fiction (think of Walter Scott's Highland novels), and music (as in Sibelius's *Finlandia* or Copland's *Appalachian Spring*).[9]

But what specially interests me is the hold of both memory and geography on the desire for conquest and domination. Two of my books, *Orientalism* and *Culture and Imperialism*, are based not only on the notion of what I call imaginative geography—the invention and construction of a geographical space called the Orient, for instance, with scant attention paid to the actuality of the geography and its inhabitants—but also on the mapping, conquest, and annexation of territory both in what Conrad called the dark places of the earth and in its most densely inhabited and lived-in places, like India or Palestine. The great voyages of geographical discovery from da Gama to Captain Cook were motivated by curiosity and scientific fervor, but also by a spirit of domination, which becomes immediately evident when white men land in some distant and unknown place and the natives rebel against them. In the modern era Defoe's *Robinson Crusoe* is the essential parable of how geography and conquest go together, providing an almost eerie prefiguration of historical figures like Clive and Hastings in India, or scientific adventurers and explorers like Murchison in Africa decades and decades later. These experiences enable complicated memories for natives and (in the Indian case) Britishers alike; a similar dialectic of memory over territory animates the relationship of French and Algerian accounts of the 130 years of French rule in North Africa. We should never have left or given up India or Algeria, say some, using strange atavistic sentiments like the Raj revival—a spate of TV shows and films like *The Jewel in the Crown*, *A Passage to India*, *Gandhi*, and the fashion of wearing safari suits, helmets, desert boots—as a way of periodically provoking nostalgia for the good old days of British supremacy in Asia and Africa, whereas most Indians and Algerians would likely say that their liberation came as a result of being able after years of nationalist struggle to take hold of their own affairs, reestablish their identity, culture, and language, and, above all, reappropriate their territory from the colonial masters. Hence, to some extent, we witness the remarkable emergence of an Anglo-Indian literature by Anita Desai, Salman Rushdie, Arundhati Roy, and many others, reexcavating and recharting the past from a postcolonial point of view, thereby erecting a new postimperial space.

It is easy to see the fact of displacement in the colonial experience, which at bottom is the replacement of one geographical sovereignty, an imperialist one, by another, native force. More subtle and complex is the unending cultural struggle over territory, which necessarily involves overlapping memories, narratives, and physical structures. No one has studied this more powerfully than the late Raymond Williams in his classic book, *The Country and the City*. What he shows is that literary and cultural forms such as the ode, the political pamphlet, and different kinds of novels derive some of their aesthetic rationale from changes taking place in the geography or landscape as the result of a social contest. Let me explain this more concretely. The mid-seventeenth to eighteenth-century genre of the country-house poem, with its emphasis on the house's calm stateliness and classical proportions—"Heaven's Centre, Nature's Lap"— is not the same thing in Marvell, Ben Jonson, and, later, in Pope. Jonson draws attention to the way the house was won from disturbing, encroaching peasant populations; Marvell in

---

[9]   Simon Schama, *Landscape and Memory* (New York, 1995), p. 30.

a more complicated way understands the country house as the result of a union between money, property, and politics; in Pope the house has become a sort of moral center; and later in Jane Austen's *Mansfield Park* it is the very embodiment of all that is benign and actively good in England. Property in all four writers is being consolidated; what we watch is the gradual triumph of a social dialectic celebrating the virtues and necessities of a propertied class, which itself seems to stand for the nation at its best. In each case the writer remembers the past in his or her own way, seeing images that typify that past, preserving one past, sweeping away others. Later writers, say, urban novelists like Dickens and Thackeray, will look back to this period as a sort of rural paradise from which England has fallen; the beauties of the field are replaced by the grimy, dark, sooty, industrial city. Both the retrospective image and the contemporary one, says Williams, are historical constructs, myths of the social geography fashioned in different periods by different classes, different interests, different ideas about the national identity, the polity, the country as a whole, none of it without actual struggle and rhetorical dispute.[10]

All of what I have been discussing here—the interplay between geography, memory, and invention, in the sense that invention must occur if there is recollection—is particularly relevant to a twentieth-century example, that of Palestine, which instances an extraordinarily rich and intense conflict of at least two memories, two sorts of historical invention, two sorts of geographical imagination. I want to argue that we can go behind the headlines and the repetitively reductive media accounts of the Middle East conflict and discern there a much more interesting and subtle conflict than what is customarily talked about. Only by understanding that special mix of geography generally and landscape in particular with historical memory and, as I said, an arresting form of invention can we begin to grasp the persistence of conflict and the difficulty of resolving it, a difficulty that is far too complex and grand than the current peace process could possibly envisage, let alone resolve.

Let us juxtapose some relevant dates and events with each other. For Palestinians 1948 is remembered as the year of the *nakba*, or catastrophe, when 750,000 of us who were living there—two-thirds of the population—were driven out, our property taken, hundreds of villages destroyed, an entire society obliterated. For Israelis and many Jews throughout the world 1998 was the fiftieth anniversary of Israel's independence and establishment, a miraculous story of recovery after the Holocaust, of democracy, of making the desert bloom, and so on. Thus, two totally different characterizations of a recollected event have been constructed. What has long struck me about this radical irreconcilability at the origin of the Palestinian-Israeli conflict is that it is routinely excluded from considerations of related subjects concerning ethnic or collective memory, geographical analysis, and political reflection. This is most evident in studies of the German catastrophe as well as of ethnic conflicts in former Yugoslavia, Rwanda, Ireland, Sri Lanka, South Africa, and elsewhere.

Take Germany first. There is little doubt that it is important to prevent assassins of memory from denying or minimizing the Holocaust; but it is also important not to forget to show the link, well-established in contemporary Jewish

---

10 See Raymond Williams, *The Country and the City* (London, 1973).

consciousness, between the Holocaust and the founding of Israel as a haven for Jews. That this link also meant the disestablishing of the Palestinians from their homes and farms is practically never stated, although for Palestinians it increases the agony of their plight: why, they ask, are we made to pay for what happened to the Jews in Europe by what was in effect a Western Christian genocide? The question never emerges out of the debate in or about Germany, even though it is directly entailed by such facts as the enormous amount of money paid by Germany to Israel in Holocaust reparations and has surfaced again in the claims against Swiss banks. I have no hesitation in saying, yes, Germany and Switzerland ought to pay, but that also means that Palestinians over the past fifty years whose own losses are staggering deserve a hearing, too, especially since to us these payments to Israel go to consolidate Israel's hold not only on what we lost in 1948 but on the territories occupied in 1967. The Palestinians have never received even the slightest official acknowledgement of the massive injustice that was done to them, much less the possibility of staking material claims against Israel for the property taken, the people killed, the houses demolished, the water taken, the prisoners held, and so forth. There is also the complex, almost equally dense and far-reaching matter of Britain's responsibility. What strikes me as more significant is the refusal in the Israeli official narrative to take account of the state's complicity in and responsibility for the Palestinian dispossession. For years and years an assiduous campaign to maintain a frozen version of Israel's heroic narrative of repatriation and justice obliterated any possibility of a Palestinian narrative, in large part because certain key components of the Israeli story stressed certain geographical characteristics of Palestine itself. Take the key notion of liberation: so strong was the story of Jewish independence and reemergence after the Holocaust that it became virtually impossible to ask the question, Liberation and independence from whom? If the question was asked it was always answered as liberation from British imperialism. Or, as the story got elaborated, it was defense against invading Arab armies that wanted to crush the young state. The Palestinians thus faded into the encircling and menacing obscurity of "the Arabs," the fact that they were actual residents occluded and simultaneously denied.

Perhaps the greatest battle Palestinians have waged as a people has been over the right to a remembered presence and, with that presence, the right to possess and reclaim a collective historical reality, at least since the Zionist movement began its encroachments on the land. A similar battle has been fought by all colonized peoples whose past and present were dominated by outside powers who had first conquered the land and then rewrote history so as to appear in that history as the true owners of that land. Every independent state that emerged after the dismantling of the classical empires in the post–World War Two years felt it necessary to narrate its own history, as much as possible free of the biases and misrepresentations of that history by British, French, Portuguese, Dutch, or other colonial historians.

Yet the fate of Palestinian history has been a sad one, since not only was independence not gained, but there was little collective understanding of the importance of constructing a collective history as a part of trying to gain independence. To become a nation in the formal sense of the word, a people must make itself into something more than a collection of tribes, or political organizations of

the kind that since the 1967 war Palestinians have created and supported. With a competitor as formidable as the Zionist movement, the effort to rewrite the history of Palestine so as to exclude the land's peoples had a disastrous effect on the quest for Palestinian self-determination. What we never understood was the power of a narrative history to mobilize people around a common goal. In the case of Israel, the narrative's main point was that Zionism's goal was to restore, re-establish, repatriate, and reconnect a people with its original homeland. It was the genius of Herzl and Weizmann to draft thinkers like Einstein and Buber, as well as financiers like Lord Rothschild and Moses Montefiore, into giving their time and effort in support of so important and historically justified a scheme. This narrative of reestablishment and recovery served its purpose not only amongst Jews but also throughout the Western (and even in some parts of the Eastern) world. Because of the power and appeal of the Zionist narrative and idea (which depended on a special reading of the Bible) and because of the collective Palestinian inability as a people to produce a convincing narrative story with a beginning, middle, and end (we were always too disorganized, our leaders were always interested in main-taining their power, most of our intellectuals refused to commit themselves as a group to a common goal, and we too often changed our goals) Palestinians have remained scattered and politically ineffective victims of Zionism, as it continues to take more and more land and history.

Just how deliberate and sustained has been the assault on the history and con-sequently the dominant public memory of Palestine, and how much attention has been paid over the years to the reconstruction of Jewish history to suit the pur-poses of Zionism as a political movement, is made stunningly clear by the Scottish historian of the ancient Near East, Keith W. Whitelam, whose book *The Invention of Ancient Israel: The Silencing of Palestinian History* is of paramount importance. Not being myself a scholar of the ancient world generally, nor of ancient Palestine in particular, I cannot make a judgement about every one of the points that Whitelam makes; but I am able to judge what he says about modern scholarship on ancient Israel, and there I was very impressed with his careful, but nevertheless extremely audacious argument. In effect Whitelam is talking about two things: one, the politics of collective memory, and, two, the creation by Zionist scholars and historians of a geographical image of ancient Israel that is shaped by the ideo-logical needs and pressures of the modern Zionist movement.[11]

As I suggested above, collective memory is not an inert and passive thing, but a field of activity in which past events are selected, reconstructed, maintained, modified, and endowed with political meaning. In her 1995 book *Recovered Roots: Collective Memory and the Making of Israeli National Tradition*, the Israeli-American historian Yael Zerubavel shows how before the late nineteenth cen-tury the story of Masada was unknown to most Jews. Then in 1862 a Hebrew translation of the Roman sources of Masada in Josephus's *Wars of the Jews* was published, and in a short time the story was transformed by reconstruction into four important things: "a major turning point in Jewish history, a locus of modern pilgrimage, a famous archeological site, and a contemporary political metaphor."[12]

---

[11] See Keith W. Whitelam, *The Invention of Ancient Israel: The Silencing of Palestinian History* (New York, 1996); hereafter abbreviated *I*.

[12] Yael Zerubavel, *Recovered Roots: Collective Memory and the Making of Israeli National Tradition* (Chicago, 1995), p. 63.

When General Yigael Yadin excavated Masada after 1948 the expedition had two complementary aspects: an archeological investigation and "the fulfillment of a national mission."[13] In time the actual place was the site of Israeli army ceremonies, a commemoration of Jewish heroism, as well as a commitment to present and future military skill. Thus was a dim, relatively unknown incident in the past reformulated consciously as a major episode in the nationalist program of a modern state; Masada became a potent symbol of the Israeli national narrative of struggle and survival.

Whitelam presents a remarkably analogous picture of how the history of ancient Palestine was gradually replaced by a largely fabricated image of ancient Israel, a political entity that in reality played only a small role in the area of geographical Palestine. According to Whitelam, ancient Palestine was the home of many diverse peoples and histories; it was the place where Jebusites, Israelites, Canaanites, Moabites, Philistines, and others lived and flourished. Beginning in the late nineteenth century, however, this more complex and rich history was silenced, forced aside, in order that the history of invading Israelite tribes, who for a time suppressed and dispossessed the native peoples, became the only narrative worth considering. Thus the extinction of the indigenous population of Palestine in the late Bronze Age became an acceptable and gradually permanent feature of a sort of triumphalist *Jewish* history for scholars like W. F. Albright, the leading historian of ancient Palestine during the early twentieth century, and made it possible to silence native Palestinian history as it was supplanted by the history of the incoming Israelites. Albright goes so far as retrospectively to condone the destruction of the native inhabitants of ancient Palestine in favor of superior people: "From the impartial standpoint of a philosopher of history," he says, "it often seems necessary that a people of markedly inferior type [that is, the ancient Canaanite Palestinians] should vanish before a people of superior potentialities [the Israelites], since there is a point beyond which racial mixture cannot go without disaster" (quoted in *I*, p. 83).

In its remarkably frank expression of racist attitudes this statement by a supposedly objective scholar, who also happened to be the most influential figure in modern biblical archeology, is chilling. But it suggests how in its desire to overcome obstacles in its path, even to the point of retrospectively condoning dispossession and even genocide, modern Zionism also imposed a sort of teleology retrospectively. Whitelam proceeds to show how scholars like Albright and many others went on in their writing to construct "a large, powerful, sovereign and autonomous...state [which was] attributed to its founder David" (*I*, p. 124). Whitelam shows how this state was in effect an invention designed to accompany the Zionist attempt in the twentieth century to gain control over the land of Palestine; thus "biblical scholarship, in its construction of an ancient Israeli state, is implicated in contemporary struggles for the land" (*I*, p. 124). Whitelam argues that such a state was far less important than its champions in the present day say it was: The invented ancient Israel "has silenced Palestinian history and obstructed alternative claims to the past" (*I*, p. 124). By inventing an ancient Israeli kingdom that displaced Canaanite Palestinian history, modern scholars have made it nearly impossible for present-day Palestinians to say that their claims to Palestine

---

[13] *Ibid.*

have any long-term historical validity. Indeed such pro-Zionist scholars have gone on to assert that ancient Israel was qualitatively different from all other forms of government in Palestine, just as modern-day Zionists said that their coming to Palestine turned an "empty" desert land into a garden. The idea in both ancient and modern cases is identical and of course violently contradicts the far more complex, pluricultural identity of the place.

Whitelam is quite right to criticize my own work on the modern struggle for Palestine for not paying any attention to the discourse of biblical studies. This discourse, he says, was really a part of Orientalism, by which Europeans imagined and represented the timeless Orient as they wished to see it, not as it was, or as its natives believed. Thus biblical studies, which created an Israel that was set apart from its environment, and supposedly brought civilization and progress to the region, was reinforced by Zionist ideology and by Europe's interest in the roots of its own past. Yet, he concludes, "this discourse has excluded the vast majority of the population of the region." It is a discourse of power "which has dispossessed Palestinians of a land and a past" (*I*, p. 235).

Whitelam's subject is ancient history and how a purposeful political movement could invent a serviceable past that became a crucial aspect of Israel's modern collective memory. When the mayor of Jerusalem a few years ago proclaimed that the city represented 3,000 years of unbroken Jewish dominance, he was mobilizing an invented story for the political purposes of a modern state still trying to dispossess native Palestinians who are now seen only as barely tolerated aliens.

Along with the idea of Israel as liberation and independence couched in terms of a reestablishment of Jewish sovereignty went an equally basic motif, that of making the desert bloom, the inference being that Palestine was either empty (as in the Zionist slogan, "a land without people for a people without land") or neglected by the nomads and peasants who facelessly lived on it. The main idea was to not only deny the Palestinians a historical presence as a collectivity but also to imply that they were not a people who had a long-standing peoplehood. As late as 1984 a book by a relative unknown called Joan Peters appeared from a major commercial publishing house (Harper and Row) purporting to show that the Palestinians as a people were an ideological, propagandistic fiction; her book *From Time Immemorial* won all sorts of prizes and accolades from well-known personalities like Saul Bellow and Barbara Tuchman, who admired Peters's "success" in proving that Palestinians were "a fairy tale." Slowly, however, the book lost credibility despite its eight or nine printings, as various critics, Norman Finkelstein principal among them, methodically revealed that the book was a patchwork of lies, distortions, and fabrications, amounting to colossal fraud. The book's brief currency (it has since practically disappeared and is no longer cited) is an indication of how overwhelmingly the Zionist memory had succeeded in emptying Palestine of its inhabitants and history, turning its landscape instead into an empty space that, Peters alleged, was flooded in the middle 1940s with Arab refugees from neighboring countries attracted to the place by the hope of prosperity under Jewish settlers.[14] I remember my rage at reading a book that had

---

[14] See Edward W. Said, "Conspiracy of Praise" and Norman G. Finkelstein, "Disinformation and the Palestine Question: The Not-So-Strange Case of Joan Peters's *From Time Immemorial*," in *Blaming the Victims: Spurious Scholarship and the Palestinian Question*, ed. Said and Christopher Hitchens (New York, 1988), pp. 23–31, 33–69.

the effrontery to tell me that my house and birth in Jerusalem in 1935 (before Peters's flood of "Arab" refugees) to say nothing of the actual existence of my parents, uncles, aunts, grandparents, and my entire extended family in Palestine were in fact not there, had not lived there for generations, had therefore no title to the specific landscape of orange and olive groves that I remembered from my earliest glimmerings of consciousness. I recall also that in 1986 I purposefully published a book of photographs by Jean Mohr, *After the Last Sky: Palestinian Lives* for which I wrote an elaborate text whose effect with the interconnected pictures I hoped would be to dispel the myth of an empty landscape and an anonymous, nonexistent people.[15]

All along then the Israeli story, buttressed both subliminally and explicitly with memories of the horrors of an anti-Semitism that ironically took place in an entirely different landscape, crowded out the Palestinian history taking place in Palestine and out of it because of Israeli geographical and physical displacement of the people. The justified feeling of "never again," which became the watchword of Jewish consciousness as, for instance, the massively publicized Eichmann trial revealed the scope of the awfulness of the Holocaust, pushed away the deepening sense of the need for Palestinian assertion that was developing in that community. There is something almost tragically ironic about the way in which the 1967 war on the one hand intensified the assertiveness of a triumphal Israeli identity and, on the other, sharpened the need among Palestinians for organized resistance and counterassertion. Only this time Israel had occupied the rest of Palestine and acquired a population of almost two million people that it ruled as a military power (20 percent of Israel's citizens are Palestinians). Newly excavated memories from the Jewish past emerged—the Jew as warrior, militant, vigorous fighter—and replaced the image of the Jew as scholarly, wise, and slightly withdrawn. The change in iconography is brilliantly chronicled by Paul Breines in his book *Tough Jews*.[16]

With the rise of the PLO, first in Jordan, then after September 1970 in Beirut, a new Palestinian interest arose in the past, as embodied in such disparate activities as organized historical research and the production of poetry and fiction based upon a sense of recovered history, formerly blotted out but now reclaimed in the poetry of Zayyat, Darwish, Hussein, and al-Qassem, in the fiction of Kanafani and Jabra, as well as in painting, sculpture, and historical writing such as Abu Lughod's collection *The Transformation of Palestine*. Later work such as the compilations of Walid Khalidi—*Before Their Diaspora* and *All That Remains*— Rashid Khalidi's study *Palestinian Identity*, Sabry Jiryis's *The Arabs in Israel*, Bayan al Hout's study of the Palestinian elites, Elia Zureik's *The Palestinians in Israel*, and many others, all by Palestinian scholars, gradually established a line of dynastic descent, between the events of 1948 and before and after the catastrophe, that gave substance to the national memory of a Palestinian collective life that persisted, despite the ravages of physical dispossession, military occupation, and

---

[15] See Said and Jean Mohr, *After the Last Sky: Palestinian Lives* (New York, 1986).

[16] See Paul Breines, *Tough Jews: Political Fantasies and the Moral Dilemma of American Jewry* (New York, 1990).

Israeli official denials.[17] By the middle of the 1980s, a new direction had begun to appear in Israeli critical histories of the canonized official memories. In my opinion their genesis lay to some considerable extent in the aggravated, but close colonial encounter between Israelis and Palestinians in the occupied territories. Consider that with the accession to power of the right-wing Likud in 1977 these territories were renamed Judea and Samaria; they were onomastically transformed from "Palestinian" to "Jewish" territory, and settlements—whose object from the beginning had been nothing less than the transformation of the landscape by the forcible introduction of European-style mass housing with neither precedent nor basis in the local topography—gradually spread all over the Palestinian areas, starkly challenging the natural and human setting with rude Jewish-only segregations. In my opinion, these settlements, whose number included a huge ring of fortresslike housing projects around the city of Jerusalem, were intended visibly to illustrate Israeli power, additions to the gentle landscape that signified aggression, not accommodation and acculturation.

The new trend in Israeli critical history was inaugurated by the late Simha Flaphan, but then continued in controversial scholarly monographs and books by Bennie Morris, Avi Shlaim, Tom Segev, Ilan Pappe, and Beni Beit Halahmi. Much of this work I believe was fuelled by the Palestinian *intifada*, which laid to rest the idea of Palestinian silence and absence. For the first time a systematic critique of the official version programmatically revealed the crucial role played by invention in a collective memory that had ossified into unyielding, almost sacralized, and, with regard to Palestinians, dehumanized representation. Far from Palestinians having left or run away because they were told to do so by their leaders (this had been the prevalent argument for the suddenly depopulated landscape in 1948), these historians showed that according to Zionist military archives there had been a cold-blooded plan to disperse and exclude the native population, spiriting them away so that Palestinians would not clutter Israel with their non-Jewish presence. Far from the Jewish forces having been a small, outnumbered, and truly threatened population, it was shown that these forces were greater in number than the combined Arab armies, they were better armed, and they had a common set of objectives entirely lacking among their opponents. As for the Palestinians, they were effectively leaderless, unarmed, and in places like Jerusalem—which I recall vividly myself, since I was twelve at the time—completely at the mercy of the Hagganah and the Irgun, whose undeflected purpose was to clear them out unequivocally, as we were indeed. And far from there being a policy of "purity of arms," the stock-in-trade phrase for Israeli military policy, there was a series of massacres and atrocities designed specifically to terrorize the greatly disadvantaged Palestinians into flight and/or nonresistance.

More recently, the distinguished Israeli social historian Zeev Sternhell has revisited the official state archives to show with extraordinary force that what was

---

[17] See *The Transformation of Palestine: Essays on the Origin and Development of the Arab-Israeli Conflict*, ed. Abu Lughod (Evanston, Ill., 1971); Walid Khalidi, *Before Their Diaspora: A Photographic History of the Palestinians* (Washington, D.C., 1984); *All That Remains: The Palestinian Villages Occupied and Depopulated by Israel in 1948*, ed. Walid Khalidi (Washington, D.C., 1992); Rashid Khalidi, *Palestinian Identity: The Construction of Modern National Consciousness* (New York, 1997); Sabri Jiryis, *The Arabs in Israel*, trans. Inca Bushnag (New York, 1976); Bayan al Hout, *Political Leadership and Institutions in Palestine, 1917–48* [Arabic] (Beirut, 1984); and Elia Zureik, *The Palestinians in Israel: A Study in Internal Colonialism* (London, 1979).

presented to the world as a socialist democracy was not in fact that at all, but what he himself calls a nationalist socialism designed above all to create a new community of blood, to redeem the land by conquest, and to submit the Jewish individual to a collectivity of almost messianic fervency.[18] Thus in fact Israel was profoundly antisocialist and, rather than encouraging individual rights and an egalitarian concept of citizenship, in fact created a theocracy with a rigorous limit to what the individual was and could expect from the state. The Kibbutzim—long heralded as a unique social experiment in egalitarianism and innovative sharing—were, says Sternhell, window-dressing, extremely limited and circumscribed in their membership (no Arabs were ever allowed to be members). Israel is now the only state in the world that is not the state of its citizens but of the whole Jewish people wherever they may be. Not only has it never had until the present any international boundaries, Israel also has no constitution, but a set of Basic Laws, one of which, the Law of Return, entitles any Jew anywhere the right to immediate Israeli citizenship, whereas Palestinians whose families were driven out in 1948 are allowed no such right at all. Ninety-two percent of the land is held in trust by an agency for the Jewish people; this means that non-Jews, especially Palestinian citizens of Israel who constitute a population of one million people and are almost 20 percent of the state, are simply forbidden to buy, lease, or sell land. One can imagine the outcry in the United States if land was only permitted to Christian whites, for example, and not to Jews or nonwhites.

Thus the dominant pattern in thought about the geography of Palestine, for a millennium and a half inhabited by an overwhelming majority of non-Jews, has been the idea of return: to return to Israel for Jews who have never been there was to return to Zion and an earlier state from which Jews had been exiled. Carol Bardenstein notes in a sensitive study the way the same images of prickly pears, oranges, trees, and return thread their way into discourses of memory for both Jews and Palestinians. But the Jewish discourse eliminates from the landscape the former Palestinian presence:

> I had the opportunity to visit a number of sites of former Palestinian villages that have been variously reshaped through tree-planting and related JNF projects, in ways that would appear to promote "collective," if selective, forgetting. If one visits the site of the destroyed village of Ghabsiyah in the Galilee, for example, upon closer scrutiny the trees and landscape themselves yield two very different and contesting narratives converging on the same site. One has to rely on landscape readings, because little else remains. What is most readily visible to the first-time visitor are the JNF trees planted on the site—the recognizable combination of pine and other trees that have grown over the past four decades in a manner that makes it seem as if perhaps that is all that was ever there.[19]

---

[18] See Zeev Sternhell, *The Founding Myths of Israel: Nationalism, Socialism, and the Making of the Jewish State*, trans. David Maisel (Princeton, N.J., 1998).

[19] Carol Bardenstein, "Threads of Memory and Discourses of Rootedness: Of Trees, Oranges, and the Prickly Pear Cactus in Israel/Palestine," *Edebiyât* 8, no. 1 (1998): 9.

Let me note in a very brief conclusion what the interplay among memory, place, and invention can do if it is not to be used for the purposes of exclusion, that is, if it is to be used for liberation and coexistence between societies whose adjacency requires a tolerable form of sustained reconciliation. Again I want to use the Palestinian issue as my concrete example. Israelis and Palestinians are now so intertwined through history, geography, and political actuality that it seems to me absolute folly to try and plan the *future* of one without that of the other. The problem with the American-sponsored Oslo process was that it was premised on a notion of partition and separation, whereas everywhere one looks in the territory of historical Palestine, Jews and Palestinians live together. This notion of separation has also closed these two unequal communities of suffering to each other. Most Palestinians are indifferent to and often angered by stories of Jewish suffering since it seems to them that as subjects of Israeli military power anti-Semitism seems remote and irrelevant while their land is taken and homes are being bulldozed. Conversely most Israelis refuse to concede that Israel is built on the ruins of Palestinian society, and that for them the catastrophe of 1948 continues until the present. Yet there can be no possible reconciliation, no possible solution unless these two communities confront each's experience in the light of the other. It seems to me essential that there can be no hope of peace unless the stronger community, the Israeli Jews, acknowledges the most powerful memory for Palestinians, namely, the dispossession of an entire people. As the weaker party Palestinians must also face the fact that Israeli Jews see themselves as survivors of the Holocaust, even though that tragedy cannot be allowed to justify Palestinian dispossession. Perhaps in today's inflamed atmosphere of military occupation and injustice it is perhaps too much to expect these acknowledgements and recognitions to take place. But, as I have argued elsewhere, at some point they must. ■

AUTHOR PROFILE

Edward W. Said (1935–2003) was born in Jerusalem in what was then the British Mandate of Palestine. The Said family moved to Cairo in 1947 just before Israel's establishment, which resulted in the loss of the family's Jerusalem home as well as Said's lifelong intellectual and personal relationship with exile and displacement. Said attended Princeton as an undergraduate and received his Ph.D. from Harvard in 1964. He taught English and Comparative Literature at Columbia University until his death. Said is most famous for *Orientalism* (1978) and *Culture and Imperialism* (1993). Both books describe how Western cultural products create the "Orient," an imagined version of primarily Arab and Islamic countries that enables Western powers to invade, colonize, exploit, and control them. Said was a prolific writer, a passionate activist, and a talented pianist who envisioned music as a way of bridging divides between Israelis and Palestinians. "Invention, Memory, and Place" first appeared in the journal *Critical Inquiry* in 2000.

Riprap

By Gary Snyder

Lay down these words
Before your mind like rocks.
        placed solid, by hands
In choice of place, set
Before the body of the mind
        in space and time:
Solidity of bark, leaf, or wall
        riprap of things:
Cobble of milky way,
        straying planets,
These poems, people,
        lost ponies with
Dragging saddles
        and rocky sure-foot trails.
The worlds like an endless
        four-dimensional
Game of *Go*.
        ants and pebbles
In the thin loam, each rock a word
        a creek-washed stone
Granite: ingrained
        with torment of fire and weight
Crystal and sediment linked hot
        all change, in thoughts,
As well as things. ■

─────────────────────────── AUTHOR PROFILE

Gary Snyder (b. 1930) was born in San Francisco, California. Although he has written in several genres, he is best known for his poetry and often associated with the Beat Generation and the San Francisco Renaissance. His themes incorporate natural and spiritual beauty that resulted from his travels to the Far East and his immersion into Buddhism. His major awards include the American Book Award for *Axe Handles* (2008) and the Pulitzer Prize in Poetry for *Turtle Island* (1975). Snyder's poem "Riprap" is from his first collection of poems titled *Riprap and Cold Mountain Poems* (1959).

S

Detroit Arcadia

Exploring the Post-American Landscape

By Rebecca Solnit

Until recently there was a frieze around the lobby of the Hotel Pontchartrain in downtown Detroit, a naively charming painting of a forested lakefront landscape with Indians peeping out from behind the trees. The hotel was built on the site of Fort Pontchartrain du Détroit, the old French garrison that three hundred years ago held a hundred or so pioneer families inside its walls while several thousand Ottawas and Hurons and Potawatomis went about their business outside, but the frieze evoked an era before even that rude structure was built in the lush woodlands of the place that was not yet Michigan or the United States. Scraped clear by glaciers during the last ice age, the landscape the French invaded was young, soggy, and densely forested. The river frontage that would become Detroit was probably mostly sugar maple and beech forest, with black ash or mixed hardwood swamps, a few patches of conifers, and the occasional expanse of what naturalists like to call wet prairie—grasslands you might not want to walk on. The Indians killed the trees by girdling them and planted corn in the clearings, but the wild rice they gathered and the fish and game they hunted were also important parts of their diet. One pioneer counted badger, bear, fisher, fox, mink, muskrat, porcupine, rabbit, raccoon, weasel, wildcat, wolf, and woodchuck among the local species, and cougar and deer could have been added to the list. The French would later recruit the Indians to trap beaver, which were plentiful in those once-riverine territories—*détroit* means "strait" or "narrows," but in its thirty-two-mile journey from Lake St. Clair to Lake Erie, the Detroit River also had several tributaries, including Parent's Creek, which was later named Bloody Run after some newly arrived English soldiers managed to lose a fight they picked with the local Ottawas.

Fort Pontchartrain was never meant to be the center of a broad European settlement. It was a trading post, a garrison, and a strategic site in the scramble between the British and the French to dominate the North American interior. Cadillac, the ambitious Frenchman who established the fort in 1701, invited members of several Indian nations to surround the fort in order to facilitate more frequent trading, but this led to clashes not just between nations but also between races. Unknown Indians set fire to Fort Pontchartrain in 1703, and the Fox skirmished there in 1712. After the English took over in 1760, deteriorating relations with the local tribes culminated in the three-year-long, nearly successful Ottawa uprising known as Pontiac's Rebellion.

This is all ancient history, but it does foreshadow the racial conflicts that never went away in Detroit, though now white people constitute the majority who surround and resent the 83 percent black city. It's as if the fort had been turned inside out—and, in fact, in the 1940s a six-foot-tall concrete wall was built along Eight Mile Road, which traces Detroit's northern limits, to contain the growing African-American population. And this inversion exposes another paradox. North of Eight Mile, the mostly white suburbs seem conventional, and they may face the same doom as much of conventional suburban America if sprawl and auto-based civilization die off with oil shortages and economic decline. South of Eight Mile, though, Detroit is racing to a far less predictable future.

It is a remarkable city now, one in which the clock seems to be running backward as its buildings disappear and its population and economy decline. The second time I visited Detroit I tried to stay at the Pontchartrain, but the lobby was bisected by drywall, the mural seemed doomed, and the whole place was under some form of remodeling that resembled ruin, with puddles in the lobby and holes in the walls, few staff people, fewer guests, and strange grinding noises at odd hours. I checked out after one night because of the cold water coming out of the hot-water tap and the generally spooky feeling generated by trying to sleep in a 413-room high-rise hotel with almost no other guests. I was sad to see the frieze on its way out, but, still, as I have explored this city over the last few years, I have seen an oddly heartening new version of the landscape it portrays, a landscape that is not quite post-apocalyptic but that is strangely—and sometimes even beautifully—post-American.

This continent has not seen a transformation like Detroit's since the last days of the Maya. The city, once the fourth largest in the country, is now so depopulated that some stretches resemble the outlying farmland, and others are altogether wild. Downtown still looks like a downtown, and all of those high-rise buildings still make an impressive skyline, but when you look closely at some of them, you can see trees growing out of the ledges and crevices, an invasive species from China known variously as the ghetto palm and the tree of heaven. Local wisdom has it that whenever a new building goes up, an older one will simply be abandoned, and the same rule applies to the blocks of new condos that have been dropped here and there among the ruins: why they were built in the first place in a city full of handsome old houses going to ruin has everything to do with the momentary whims of the real estate trade and nothing to do with the long-term survival of cities.

The transformation of the residential neighborhoods is more dramatic. On so many streets in so many neighborhoods, you see a house, a little shabby but well built and beautiful. Then another house. Then a few houses are missing, so thoroughly missing that no trace of foundation remains. Grass grows lushly, as though nothing had ever disturbed the pastoral verdure. Then there's a house that's charred and shattered, then a beautiful house, with gables and dormers and a porch, the kind of house a lot of Americans fantasize about owning. Then more green. This irregular pattern occurs mile after mile, through much of Detroit. You could be traveling down Wabash Street on the west side of town or Pennsylvania or Fairview on the east side of town or around just about any part of the State Fair neighborhood on the city's northern border. Between the half-erased neighborhoods are ruined factories, boarded-up warehouses, rows of storefronts bearing the traces of failed enterprise, and occasional solid blocks of new town houses that look as though they had been dropped in by helicopter. In the bereft zones, solitary figures wander slowly, as though in no hurry to get from one abandoned zone to the next. Some areas have been stripped entirely, and a weedy version of nature is returning. Just about a third of Detroit, some forty square miles, has evolved past decrepitude into vacancy and prairie—an urban void nearly the size of San Francisco.

S

It was tales of these ruins that originally drew me to the city a few years ago. My first visit began somberly enough, as I contemplated the great neoclassical edifice of the train station, designed by the same architects and completed the same year as Grand Central station in Manhattan. Grand Central thrives; this broken building stands alone just beyond the grim silence of Michigan Avenue and only half a mile from the abandoned Tiger Stadium. Rings of cyclone fence forbid exploration. The last train left on January 5, 1988—the day before Epiphany. The building has been so thoroughly gutted that on sunny days the light seems to come through the upper stories as though through a cheese grater; there is little left but concrete and stone. All the windows are smashed out. The copper pipes and wires, I was told, were torn out by the scavengers who harvest material from abandoned buildings around the city and hasten their decay.

On another visit, I took a long walk down a sunken railroad spur that, in more prosperous times, had been used to move goods from one factory to another. A lot of effort had gone into making the long channel of brick and concrete about twenty feet below the gently undulating surface of Detroit, and it had been abandoned a long time. Lush greenery grew along the tracks and up the walls, which were like a museum of spray-can art from the 1980s and 1990s. The weeds and beer cans and strangely apposite graffiti decrying the 1993 passage of the North American Free Trade Agreement seemed to go on forever.

I took many pictures on my visits to Detroit, but back home they just looked like snapshots of abandoned Nebraska farmhouses or small towns farther west on the Great Plains. Sometimes a burned-out house would stand next to a carefully tended twin, a monument to random fate; sometimes the rectilinear nature of city planning was barely perceptible, just the slightest traces of a grid fading into grassy fields accented with the occasional fire hydrant. One day after a brief thunderstorm, when the rain had cleared away and chunky white clouds dotted the sky, I wandered into a neighborhood, or rather a former neighborhood, of at least a dozen square blocks where trees of heaven waved their branches in the balmy air. Approximately one tattered charred house still stood per block. I could hear the buzzing of crickets or cicadas, and I felt as if I had traveled a thousand years into the future.

To say that much of Detroit is ruins is, of course, to say that some of it isn't. There are stretches of Detroit that look like anywhere in the U.S.A.—blocks of town houses and new condos, a flush of gentility spreading around the Detroit Institute of Arts, a few older neighborhoods where everything is fine. If Detroit has become a fortress of urban poverty surrounded by suburban affluence, the city's waterfront downtown has become something of a fortress within a fortress, with a convention center, a new ballpark, a new headquarters for General Motors, and a handful of casinos that were supposed to be the city's economic salvation when they were built a decade ago. But that garrison will likely fend off time no better than Fort Detroit or the Hotel Pontchartrain.

Detroit is wildly outdated, but it is not very old. It was a medium-size city that boomed in the first quarter of the twentieth century, became the "arsenal of democracy" in the second, spent the third in increasingly less gentle decline, and by the last quarter was a byword for urban decay, having made a complete arc in a single century. In 1900, Detroit had a quarter of a million people. By midcentury the population had reached nearly 2 million. In recent years, though, it has fallen below 900,000. Detroit is a cautionary tale about one-industry towns: it shrank the way the old boomtowns of the gold and silver rushes did, as though it had been mining automobiles and the veins ran dry, but most of those mining towns were meant to be ephemeral. People thought Detroit would go on forever.

Coleman Young, Detroit's first African-American mayor, reigned from 1974 to 1993, the years that the change became irreversible and impossible to ignore, and in his autobiography he sounds like he is still in shock:

> It's mind-boggling to think that at mid-century Detroit was a city of close to two million and nearly everything beyond was covered with corn and cow patties. Forty years later, damn near every last white person in the city had moved to the old fields and pastures—1.4 frigging million of them. Think about that. There were 1,600,000 whites in Detroit after the war, and 1,400,000 of them left. By 1990, the city was just over a million, nearly eighty percent of it was black, and the suburbs had surpassed Detroit not only in population but in wealth, in commerce—even in basketball, for God's sake.

The Detroit Pistons are now based in Auburn Hills. According to the 2000 census, another 112,357 whites left the city in the 1990s, and 10,000 more people a year continue to leave. Even three hundred bodies a year are exhumed from the cemeteries and moved because some of the people who were once Detroiters or the children of Detroiters don't think the city is good enough for their dead. Ford and General Motors, or what remains of them—most of the jobs were dispatched to other towns and nations long ago—are in trouble, too. Interestingly, in this city whose name is synonymous with the auto industry, more than a fifth of households have no cars.

"Detroit's Future Is Looking Brighter," said a headline in the *Detroit Free Press*, not long after another article outlined the catastrophes afflicting the whole state. In recent years, Michigan's household income has dropped more than that of any other state, and more and more of its citizens are slipping below the poverty line. David Littmann, a senior economist for the Michigan think tank the Mackinac Center for Public Policy, told the paper, "As the economy slows nationally, we're going to sink much farther relative to the other states. We've only just begun. We're going to see Michigan sink to levels that no one has ever seen."

In another sense, the worst is over in Detroit. In the 1980s and 1990s, the city was falling apart, spectacularly and violently. Back then the annual pre-Halloween arson festival known as Devil's Night finished off a lot of the abandoned buildings; it peaked in 1984 with 810 fires in the last three days of October. Some of the arson, a daughter of Detroit's black bourgeoisie told me, was constructive—crack houses being burned down by the neighbors; her own respectable aunt had torched one. Between 1978 and 1998, the city issued 9,000 building permits for new homes and 108,000 demolition permits, and quite a lot of structures were annihilated without official sanction.

S

Even Ford's old Highland Park headquarters, where the Model T was born, is now just a shuttered series of dusty warehouses with tape on the windows and cyclone fences around the cracked pavement. Once upon a time, the plant was one of the wonders of the world—on a single day in 1925 it cranked out 9,000 cars, according to a sign I saw under a tree next to the empty buildings. Detroit once made most of the cars on earth; now the entire United States makes not even one in ten. The new Model T Ford Plaza next door struck my traveling companion—who, like so many white people born in Detroit after the war, had mostly been raised elsewhere—as auspicious. But the mall was fronted by a mostly empty parking lot and anchored by a Payless ShoeSource, which to my mind did not portend an especially bright future.

When I came back, a year after my first tour, I stopped at the Detroit Institute of Arts to see the Diego Rivera mural commissioned in 1932 by Henry Ford's son, Edsel. The museum is a vast Beaux-Arts warehouse—"the fifth-largest fine arts museum in the United States," according to its promotional literature—and the fresco covered all four walls of the museum's central courtyard. Rivera is said to have considered it his finest work.

It's an odd masterpiece, a celebration of the River Rouge auto plant, which had succeeded the Highland Park factory as Ford's industrial headquarters, painted by a Communist for the son of one of the richest capitalists in the world. The north and south walls are devoted to nearly life-size scenes in which the plant's gray gears, belts, racks, and workbenches surge and swarm like some vast intestinal apparatus. The workers within might be subsidiary organs or might be lunch, as the whole churns to excrete a stream of black Fords.

Rivera created this vision when the city was reveling in the newfound supremacy of its megafactories, but Detroit had already reached its apex. Indeed, the River Rouge plant—then the largest factory complex in the world, employing more than 100,000 workers on a site two and a half times the size of New York City's Central Park—was itself built in suburban Dearborn. In 1932, though, capitalists and Communists alike shared a belief that the most desirable form of human organization—indeed, the inevitable form—was not just industrial but this kind of industrial: a Fordist system of "rational" labor, of centralized production in blue-collar cities, of eternal prosperity in a stern gray land. Even the young Soviet Union looked up to Henry Ford.

But Detroit was building the machine that would help destroy not just this city but urban industrialism across the continent. Rivera painted, in a subsidiary all-gray panel in the lower right corner of the south wall, a line of slumped working men and women exiting the factory into what appears to be an endless parking lot full of Ford cars. It may not have looked that way in 1932, but a lot of the gray workers were going to buy those gray cars and drive right out of the gray city. The city-hating Ford said that he wanted every family in the world to have a Ford, and he priced them so that more and more families could. He also fantasized about a post-urban world in which workers would also farm, seasonally or part-time, but he did less to realize that vision. Private automobile ownership was a double blow against the density that is crucial to cities and urbanism and against the Fordist model of concentrated large-scale manufacture. Ford was sabotaging

Detroit and then Fordism almost from the beginning; the city had blown up rapidly and would spend the next several decades simply disintegrating.

Detroit was always a rough town. When Rivera painted his fresco, the Depression had hit Detroit as hard as or harder than anywhere, and the unemployed were famished and desperate, desperate enough to march on the Ford Motor Company in the spring of 1932. It's hard to say whether ferocity or desperation made the marchers fight their way through police with tear-gas guns and firemen with hoses going full bore the last stretch of the way to the River Rouge plant. Harry Bennett, the thug who ran Ford more or less the way Stalin was running the Soviet Union, arrived, and though he was immediately knocked out by a flying rock, the police began firing on the crowd, injuring dozens and killing five. The battle of the Hunger March or the huge public funeral afterward would've made a good mural.

It wasn't cars alone that ruined Detroit. It was the whole improbable equation of the city in the first place, the "inherent contradictions." The city was done in by deindustrialization, decentralization, the post-World War II spread of highways and freeways, government incentives to homeowners, and disinvestment in cities that aided and abetted large-scale white flight into the burgeoning suburbs of those years. Chunks of downtown Detroit were sacrificed early, in the postwar years, so that broad arterial freeways—the Edsel Freeway, the Chrysler Freeway—could bring commuters in from beyond city limits.

All of this was happening everywhere else too, of course. The manufacturing belt became the Rust Belt. Cleveland, Toledo, Buffalo, and other cities clustered around the Great Lakes were hit hard, and the shrinking stretched down to St. Louis and across to Pittsburgh, Philadelphia, and Newark. Now that it has entered a second gilded age, no one seems to remember that New York was a snowballing disaster forty or fifty years ago. The old textile district south of Houston Street had emptied out so completely that in 1962 the City Club of New York published a report on it and other former commercial areas titled "The Wastelands of New York City." San Francisco went the same way. It was a blue-collar port city until the waterfront dried up and the longshoremen faded away.

Then came the renaissance, but only for those cities reborn into more dematerialized economies. Vacant lots were filled in, old warehouses were turned into lofts or offices or replaced, downtowns became upscale chain outlets, janitors and cops became people who commuted in from downscale suburbs, and the children of that white flight came back to cities that were not exactly cities in the old sense. The new American cities trade in information, entertainment, tourism, software, finance. They are abstract. Even the souvenirs in these new economies often come from a sweatshop in China. The United States can be mapped as two zones now: a high-pressure zone of economic boom times and escalating real estate prices, and a low-pressure zone, where housing might be the only thing that's easy to come by.

This pattern will change, though. The forces that produced Detroit—the combination of bitter racism and single-industry failure—are anomalous, but the general recipe of deindustrialization, depopulation, and resource depletion will likely touch almost all the regions of the global north in the next century or two. Dresden was rebuilt, and so was Hiroshima, and so were the cities destroyed

S

309

by natural forces—San Francisco and Mexico City and Tangshan—but Detroit will never be rebuilt as it was. It will be the first of many cities forced to become altogether something else.

The Detroit Institute of Arts is in one of those flourishing parts of Detroit; it is expanding its 1927 building, and when I said goodbye to the Rivera mural and stepped outside into the autumn sunshine, workmen were installing slabs of marble on the building's new facade. I noticed an apparently homeless dog sleeping below the scaffolding, and as I walked past, three plump white women teetered up to me hastily, all attention focused on the dog. "Do you have a cell phone?" the one topped by a froth of yellow hair shrilled. "Call the Humane Society!" I suggested that the dog was breathing fine and therefore was probably okay, and she looked at me as though I were a total idiot. "This is downtown *Detroit*," she said, in a tone that made it clear the dog was in imminent peril from unspeakable forces, and that perhaps she was, I was, we all were.

I had been exploring an architectural-salvage shop near Rosa Parks Boulevard earlier that day, and when I asked the potbellied and weathered white man working there for his thoughts on the city, the tirade that followed was similarly vehement: Detroit, he insisted, had been wonderful—people used to dress up to go downtown, it had been the Paris of the Midwest!—and then it all went to hell. Those people destroyed it. My traveling companion suggested that maybe larger forces of deindustrialization might have had something to do with what happened to the city, but the man blankly rejected this analysis and continued on a tirade about "them" that wasn't very careful about not being racist.

On the Web you can find a site, Stormfront White Nationalist Community, that is even more comfortable with this version of what happened to the city and even less interested in macroeconomic forces like deindustrialization and globalization: "A huge non-White population, combined with annual arson attacks, bankruptcy, crime, and decay, have combined to make Detroit—once the USA's leading automotive industrial center—into a ruin comparable with those of the ancient civilizations—with the cause being identical: the replacement of the White population who built the city, with a new non-White population." It could have been different. "In more civilized environs, these facilities might have easily been transformed into a manufacturing and assembly center for any number of industrial enterprises," writes the anonymous author.

A few months before the diatribe in the salvage yard, I'd met a long-haired counterculture guy who also told me he was from Detroit, by which he, like so many others I've met, meant the suburbs of Detroit. When I asked him about the actual city, though, his face clenched like a fist. He recited the terrible things they would do to you if you ventured into the city, that they would tear you apart on the streets. He spoke not with the voice of a witness but with the authority of tradition handed down from an unknown and irrefutable source. The city was the infernal realm, the burning lands, the dragon's lair at the center of a vast and protective suburban sprawl.

The most prominent piece of public art in Detroit is the giant blackened bronze arm and fist that serve as a monument to heavyweight boxing champion Joe Louis, who grew up there. If it were vertical it would look like a Black Power fist, but it's slung from cables like some medieval battering ram waiting to be dragged up to the city walls.

Deindustrialization dealt Detroit a sucker punch, but the knockout may have been white flight—at least economically. Socially, it was a little more complex. One African-American woman who grew up there told me that white people seemed to think they were a great loss to the city they abandoned, "but we were glad to see them go and waved bye-bye." She lived in Ann Arbor—the departure of the black middle class being yet another wrinkle in the racial narrative—but she was thinking of moving back, she said. If she had kids, raising them in a city where they wouldn't be a minority had real appeal.

The fall of the paradise that was Detroit is often pinned on the riots of July 1967, what some there still refer to as the Detroit Uprising. But Detroit had a long history of race riots—there were vicious white-on-black riots in 1833, 1863, 1925, and 1943. And the idyll itself was unraveling long before 1967. Local 600 of the United Auto Workers broke with the union mainstream in 1951, sixteen years before the riots, to sue Ford over decentralization efforts already under way. They realized that their jobs were literally going south, to states and nations where labor wasn't so organized and wages weren't so high, back in the prehistoric era of "globalization."

The popular story wasn't about the caprices of capital, though; it was about the barbarism of blacks. In 1900, Detroit had an African-American population of 4,111. Then came the great migration, when masses of southern blacks traded Jim Crow for the industrialized promised land of the North. Conditions might have been better here than in the South, but Detroit was still a segregated city with a violently racist police department and a lot of white people ready to work hard to keep black people out of their neighborhoods. They failed in this attempt at segregation, and then they left. This is what created the blackest city in the United States, and figures from Joe Louis and Malcolm X to Rosa Parks and the bold left-wing Congressman John Conyers—who has represented much of the city since 1964—have made Detroit a center of activism and independent leadership for African Americans. It's a black city, but it's surrounded.

Surrounded, but inside that stockade of racial divide and urban decay are visionaries, and their visions are tender, hopeful, and green. Grace Lee Boggs, at ninety-one, has been politically active in the city for more than half a century. Born in Providence to Chinese immigrant parents, she got a Ph.D. in philosophy from Bryn Mawr in 1940 and was a classical Marxist when she married the labor organizer Jimmy Boggs, in 1953. That an Asian woman married to a black man could become a powerful force was just another wrinkle in the racial politics of Detroit. (They were together until Jimmy's death, in 1993.) Indeed, her think-ing evolved along with the radical politics of the city itself. During the 1960s, the Boggses were dismissive of Martin Luther King Jr. and ardent about Black Power, but as Grace acknowledged when we sat down together in her big shady house in the central city, "The Black Power movement, which was very power-ful here, concentrated only on power and had no concept of the challenges that would face a black-powered administration." When Coleman Young took over city hall, she said, he could start fixing racism in the police department and the

S

311

fire department, "but when it came time to do something about Henry Ford and General Motors, he was helpless. We thought that all we had to do was transform the system, that all the problems were on the other side."

As the years went by, the Boggses began to focus less on putting new people into existing power structures and more on redefining or dismantling the structures altogether. When she and Jimmy crusaded against Young's plans to rebuild the city around casinos, they realized they had to come up with real alternatives, and they began to think about what a local, sustainable economy would look like. They had already begun to realize that Detroit's lack of participation in the mainstream offered an opportunity to do everything differently—that instead of retreating back to a better relationship to capitalism, to industry, to the mainstream, the city could move forward, turn its liabilities into assets, and create an economy entirely apart from the transnational webs of corporations and petroleum. Jimmy Boggs described his alternative vision in a 1988 speech at the First Unitarian-Universalist Church of Detroit:

> We have to get rid of the myth that there is something sacred about large-scale production for the national and international market. We have to begin thinking of creating small enterprises which produce food, goods, and services for the local market, that is, for our communities and for our city.... In order to create these new enterprises, we need a view of our city which takes into consideration both the natural resources of our area and the existing and potential skills and talents of Detroiters.

That was the vision, and it is only just starting to become a reality. "Now a lot of what you see is vacant lots," Grace told me. "Most people see only disaster and the end of the world. On the other hand, artists in particular see the potential, the possibility of bringing the country back into the city, which is what we really need." After all, the city is rich in open space and—with an official unemployment rate in the mid-teens—people with time on their hands. The land is fertile, too, and the visionaries are there.

In traversing Detroit, I saw a lot of signs that a greening was well under way, a sort of urban husbandry of the city's already occurring return to nature. I heard the story of one old woman who had been the first African-American person on her block and is now, with her grandson, very nearly the last person of any race on that block. Having a city grow up around you is not an uncommon American experience, but having the countryside return is an eerier one. She made the best of it, though. The city sold her the surrounding lots for next to nothing, and she now raises much of her own food on them.

I also saw the lush three-acre Earth Works Garden, launched by Capuchin monks in 1999 and now growing organic produce for a local soup kitchen. I saw a 4-H garden in a fairly ravaged east-side neighborhood, and amid the utter abandonment of the west side, I saw the handsome tiled buildings of the Catherine Ferguson Academy for Young Women, a school for teenage mothers that opens on to a working farm, complete with apple orchard, horses, ducks, long rows of cauliflower and broccoli, and a red barn the girls built themselves. I met Ashley

Atkinson, the young project manager for The Greening of Detroit, and heard about the hundred community gardens they support and the thousands more food gardens that are not part of any network. The food they produce, Atkinson told me, provides food security for many Detroiters. "Urban farming, dollar for dollar, is the most effective change agent you can ever have in a community," she said. Everywhere I went, I saw the rich soil of Detroit and the hard work of the gardeners bringing forth an abundant harvest any organic farmer would envy.

Everyone talks about green cities now, but the concrete results in affluent cities mostly involve curbside composting and tacking solar panels onto rooftops while residents continue to drive, to shop, to eat organic pears flown in from Argentina, to be part of the big machine of consumption and climate change. The free-range chickens and Priuses are great, but they alone aren't adequate tools for creating a truly different society and ecology. The future, at least the sustainable one, the one in which we will survive, isn't going to be invented by people who are happily surrendering selective bits and pieces of environmentally unsound privilege. It's going to be made by those who had all that taken away from them or never had it in the first place.

After the Panic of 1893, Detroit's left-wing Republican mayor encouraged his hungry citizens to plant vegetables in the city's vacant lots and went down in history as Potato Patch Pingree. Something similar happened in Cuba when the Soviet Union collapsed and the island lost its subsidized oil and thereby its mechanized agriculture; through garden-scale semi-organic agriculture, Cubans clawed their way back to food security and got better food in the bargain. Nobody wants to live through a depression, and it is unfair, or at least deeply ironic, that black people in Detroit are being forced to undertake an experiment in utopian post-urbanism that appears to be uncomfortably similar to the sharecropping past their parents and grandparents sought to escape. There is no moral reason why they should do and be better than the rest of us—but there is a practical one. They have to. Detroit is where change is most urgent and therefore most viable. The rest of us will get there later, when necessity drives us too, and by that time Detroit may be the shining example we can look to, the post-industrial green city that was once the steel-gray capital of Fordist manufacturing.

Detroit is still beautiful, both in its stately decay and in its growing natural abundance. Indeed, one of the finest sights I saw on my walks around the city combined the two. It was a sudden flash on an already bright autumn day—a pair of wild pheasants, bursting from a lush row of vegetables and flying over a cyclone fence toward a burned-out building across the street. It was an improbable flight in many ways. Those pheasants, after all, were no more native to Detroit than are the trees of heaven growing in the skyscrapers downtown. And yet it is here, where European settlement began in the region, that we may be seeing the first signs of an unsettling of the very premises of colonial expansion, an unsettling that may bring a complex new human and natural ecology into being.

This is the most extreme and long-term hope Detroit offers us: the hope that we can reclaim what we paved over and poisoned, that nature will not punish us, that it will welcome us home—not with the landscape that was here when we arrived, perhaps, but with land that is alive, lush, and varied all the same. "Look on

S

313

my works, ye mighty, and despair!" was Shelley's pivotal command in his portrait of magnificent ruins, but Detroit is far from a "shattered visage." It is a harsh place of poverty, deprivation, and a fair amount of crime, but it is also a stronghold of possibility.

That Rivera mural, for instance. In 1932 the soil, the country, the wilderness, and agriculture represented the past; they should have appeared, if at all, below or behind the symbols of industry and urbanism, a prehistory from which the gleaming machine future emerged. But the big panels of workers inside the gray chasms of the River Rouge plant have above them huge nude figures—black, white, red, yellow, lounging on the bare earth. Rivera meant these figures to be emblematic of the North American races and meant their fistfuls of coal, sand, iron ore, and limestone to be the raw stuff of industrialism. To my eye, though, they look like deities waiting to reclaim the world, insistent on sensual contact with the land and confident of their triumph over and after the factory that lies below them like an inferno. ■

2007

AUTHOR PROFILE

Rebecca Solnit is an independent writer who explores a diverse range of topics through a variety of genres, but primarily creative nonfiction essays. Her most celebrated work includes *River of Shadows: Eadweard Muybridge and the Technological Wild West* (2004), *The Faraway Nearby* (2013) and most recently, *Men Explain Things to Me* (2014), which is credited with providing the background necessary to generate the term "mansplaining," though Solnit did not coin the term. Solnit's other books include atlases as well as essays that cover such diverse topics as gender, art, indigenous history, walking, and natural disaster. Solnit is currently a contributing editor at *Harper's Magazine*. "Detroit Arcadia" is part of the essay collection *The Encyclopedia of Trouble and Spaciousness* (2014).

Keeping Things Whole

By Mark Strand

In a field
I am the absence
of field.
This is
always the case.
Wherever I am
I am what is missing.

When I walk
I part the air
and always
the air moves in
to fill the spaces
where my body's been.

We all have reasons
for moving.
I move
to keep things whole. ■

——————————————— AUTHOR PROFILE

Mark Strand (1934–2014) was born in Canada and grew up in several cities in the United States, Colombia, Mexico, and Peru. He earned his B.A. at Antioch College in Ohio (1957), his B.F.A. at Yale University (1959), and his Master of Arts from the University of Iowa (1962). In 1981 Strand served as Poet Laureate Consultant in Poetry to the Library of Congress. He received numerous awards throughout his lifetime, including the MacArthur Fellowship in 1987 and the Pulitzer Prize for Poetry for *Blizzard of One* in 1999. From 2005 until his death, Strand taught Literature and Creative Writing at Columbia University in New York. "Keeping Things Whole" originally appeared in *Selected Poems* (2002).

S

Political and Legal Challenges in a Mars Colony

By Konrad Szocik, Kateryna Lysenko-Ryba,
Sylwia Banaś, and Sylwia Mazur

1. Introduction

The exploration and colonization of other cosmic places seems to be the next stage of human development. NASA is preparing for deep space missions to Mars.[1] The European Space Agency (ESA) mentions the opportunity to launch permanent bases on the Moon.[2] These expansions have various motives. One of them is outlined by Elon Musk, who suggests sending one million people to Mars because the future existence of humanity on the Earth is threatened.[3] In this context the idea of the colonization of outer space is interpreted as a unique possibility for the survival of the humanity. Expected future dangers on the Earth are perhaps a good reason to really think about moving human life to Mars.

Another reason is associated with the human ability to expand. Humans have settled in all ecological niches on the Earth despite very different and difficult conditions for life. This outer space expansion could be a good backdrop and provide a catalyst for highly advanced developments in the fields of technology and science. Deep space missions could be a good place for testing new solutions. Astronauts who will be sent on deep space missions will be under intensive selective pressure. This pressure theoretically could affect the path of future human evolution.

How to predict behaviors and reactions of human body and psyche on Mars? Now we can study it on The International Space Station. Its microgravitational environment enables testing of the human organism. However, we cannot predict the cultural evolution of Martian politics, society and its legal system. We have found some ethical and cultural issues[4] as well as the problematic nature of cooperation in such a difficult environment.[5] In this paper we will be focusing on some particular questions associated with the possible political, social and legal challenges faced by a future Mars colony.

The question of the long journey to Mars seems to be a very hard challenge for these astronauts. It is not clear how long this journey will take or how long the first mission will last.[6] The distance between these two planets is from 55 million to ca. 100 million km dependently on their orbital position.[7] Such a long journey could

[1]   NASA's Journey to Mars. Pioneering next steps in space exploration, NASA, Washington 2015.

[2]   http://www.esa.int/spaceinvideos/Videos/2016/02/ESA_Euronews_Moon_Village.

[3]   http://www.outerplaces.com/science/
item/9914-elon-musk-s-plans-for-sending-1-million-people-to-mars-for-500-000-each.

[4]   K. Szocik, *Unseen challenges in a Mars colony*, Spaceflight, January 2016, Vol 58, pp. 20–23.

[5]   K. Szocik, *Etyczne i polityczne problemy kolonizacji Marsa*, Astronomia, nr 45, marzec 2016, pp. 28–29.

[6]   http://www.mars-one.com/faq/mission-to-mars/how-long-does-it-take-to-travel-to-mars (15.02.16).

[7]   http://odkrywcy.pl/kat,111402,title,Na-Marsa-w-39-dni-a-nawet=krocej,wid,14386894,wiadomosc.
html?smg4sticaid=6167b5.

prove to be fatal, not only due to the high risk of technical breakdowns or malfunctions, but also due to physiological and psychological strength of our astronauts.

What will be the astronauts' behaviors during this long journey? We suggest that we cannot compare these future missions with current missions on International Space Station (ISS). We can study the human body after a one year space mission: Scott Kelly and Mikhail Kornienko completed their one year mission on the International Space on the 2nd March of 2016. However, the mental and emotional reactions will be more difficult to measure and compare. These first astronauts will be aware that after the almost one year journey they will have to live on Mars for at least several years or probably their entire lives due to the fact that their return will most likely be technologically impossible. Perhaps these first colonizers will know that their mission is a "one way ticket".

The MarsOne project is going to send the first astronauts to Mars in 2027. In the following two years crews will be sent to enlarge the Martian colony.[8] However, it is difficult to predict the impact of such a long journey on human health and the effects of long term exposure to the Martian microgravitational environment. Some researchers suggest placing the crew into a coma before the journey. Others suggest removing the appendix to avoid great dangers.[9] Another troublesome question is possibility of the death of a crew member during the journey. It seems that neither leaving the corpse in space nor its removal outside is a good solution.

We would also like to underline some ethical questions. It is not easy to predict the behaviors of astronauts confined in a small permanently sealed spacecraft during their journey and what problems or conflicts they will encounter and how they resolve them. We suggest that it will not be easy to find astronauts who are without any conflicts of interests such as politics, religion, or outlook. Is it possible that the small space of the spacecraft will increase probability of aggression among the astronauts? To avoid these dangers the environmental conditions should be similar to the Earth conditions. The first challenge is the optimal selection of astronauts, especially in the context of their social abilities.[10] In this context it is worth bearing in mind that these astronauts will be aware of the fact that they will be unable to return to the Earth at least a number of years. It is not clear how this awareness will affect their psyche and behavior. Will it cause aggression, defection or perhaps depression?

On the one side, the colonization of Mars will greatly effect technological and scientific progresses. On the other we can assume that this progress may require the death of astronauts that may not survive this journey. Another question is the justification of such a monumental financial commitment for this deep space mission program which has such a high risk of failure. What possible potential benefits could justify the high risk of the death and the great expense? Even in the case of the success of this mission, this human colony will consist of only a few people. Is it worth it to undertake this program for only this small group? If the further of life on the Earth is threatened, perhaps it would be better to focus on increasing the chances of survival on the Earth and for preventing the climate change.

---

[8] http://www.cnbc.com/2015/03/26/the-millionaire-offering-a-one-way-ticket-to-mars.html.

[9] http://www.astrotime.ru/mars_oneway.html.

[10] http://www.astrotime.ru/flight_mars.html.

Consider another question. What will be the legal status of the Mars colony? We can find in the 1967 "United Nations Treaty on Principles Governing the Activities of States in the Exploration and Use of Outer Space, Including the Moon and Other Celestial Bodies", that the outer space and all Solar System bodies are free for research for all countries without any discrimination. The outer space and its objects cannot be appropriated by any country. We can find also the idea of planetary protection which assumes that interplanetary missions should avoid the risk of "harmful contamination".[11] In this context it is worth bearing in mind "Mars Special Regions" which involves regions where theoretically some now unidentified forms of life could exist.[12] We mean not only the special protection of some parts of Mars but also the question of possible conflicts of interests between different countries which could be interested in Mars exploration. Could we look for analogy in the conquest of the North Pole?

The spacecraft will be the property of the country which will take a control over this spacecraft and its crew. Let's assume however, that this first spacecraft will have an international status. Which law will be obliged for the crew and consequently which legal system will be obliged for Martian colony? We can assume that there will be prepared a new legal system. However, what about the conflict of interests of some countries, their impact on the legal regulations? How to prepare a new legal system before preparing the colony in such particular ecological niche?

The legal system is the result of complex social process which is influenced by many various factors. Living on Mars will be characterized by high levels of stress and existential anxiety and uncertainty. It seems that the terrestrial legal systems cannot be applied into Martian environment. The next generations of colonizers can create specific legal norms which will be compatible with Martian limit situations. These legal systems will be easily applied at the level of small group. The more and complex the group, the more difficult the social and legal organization which can require an authority to create and to protect the law. Effective law is a regulator of human conflicts. In this context it is worth it to remember that the natural human feature is a tendency to take an advantage over others.[13]

We suppose that other theoretically troublesome question could be the relationship between the Earth metropolis and the Martian colony. We will find for the first time in the human history that the Earth will be the owner of an extraterrestrial colony. Is it possible that colonizers will want to achieve independence? What will the metropolis do in this case? Is it possible to cut off supplies? Can we predict or exclude the risk of conflict on Mars? In the case of a Martian rebellion is it possible and profitable to destroy colony? In the case of an independent

---

[11] Układ o zasadach działalności państw w zakresie badań i użytkowania przestrzeni kosmicznej łącznie z Księżycem i innymi ciałami niebieskimi, sporządzony w Moskwie, Londynie i Waszyngtonie dnia 27 stycznia 1967 r. (Dz.U. 1968 nr 14 poz. 82) Treaty on Principles Governing the Activities of States in the Exploration and Use of Outer Space, including the Moon and Other Celestial Bodies (RES 2222 (XXI)).

[12] Rettberg Petra, Anesio Alexandre M., Baker Victor R., Baross John A., Cady Sherry L., Detsis Emmanouil, Foreman Christine M., Hauber Ernst, Ori Gian Gabriele, Pearce David A., Renno Nilton O., Ruvkun Gary, Sattler Birgit, Saunders Mark P., Smith David H., Wagner Dirk, and Westall Frances. Planetary Protection and Mars Special Regions—A Suggestion for Updating the Definition, Astrobiology. February 2016, 16(2): 120. http://dx.doi.org/10.1089/ast.2016.1472.

[13] K. Szocik, *Roots of self-domestication*, Science, 28 November 2014, Vol 346 Issue 6213, pp. 1067.

colony what will be the relationship between The Earth and Mars? We assume that the future Martian law should also include these questions. For instance, in a conflict situation which part of conflict will be supported by the Earth? It will be possible to accept conflict migrants on the Earth?

We suppose that the Martian legal system will be one of the most important challenges because the new Martian environment and difficult living conditions can generate conflicts. Is it possible that the social evolution of the new Martian colony will repeat the same evolutionary patterns as human evolution of the Earth? Is it possible for the development of a social hierarchy on Mars? What about a struggle for power? What about the economical system? We suppose that natural stage of the evolution of the Martian colony will be exchange of goods and services. It seems that the most probable economical solution will be the barter system. However, in the context of the difficult conditions of life we can suppose that the Martian "struggle for existence" could have even greater brutal nature because everyone tends to survival, especially in such specific conditions. In the context of biological evolution through natural selection we can ask which traits will be the best adaptations and which kind of individuals will be more the fit? Which kinds of behavioral features will be favored in the Martian environment? Cooperation or defection? It is worth remembering that natural selection on the lower level of competition, in-group, favors rather defectors than cooperators. On the level of in-group selection favors egoists not altruists. The population of altruists is favored only on the level of inter-group relations. Of course, inter-group relations will not be possible in a Mars colony which will only include a small group. In this context we can predict that according to the nature of natural selection this small group will favor egoists rather than altruists.

We also find another important question: an attitude of colonizers towards the inhabitants of the Earth. It seems obvious that generations born on Mars can have other approach than first colonizers from the Earth. Generations born on Mars will require specific pedagogical model. We suppose that a good cultural tool could be a new Martian religion. We know what role was played by religious beliefs and religion on the Earth.[14] Such Martian religion should underline the sense and purpose of this mission, especially by the justification of the difficult conditions of life. The strategic role of this religion would be the strengthening of cooperation and the feeling of existential and social sense of life.

2. Conclusions

Living on Mars will be existentially limited situation. The new Martian colony will need not only the same cultural and social tools as in human evolution on the Earth. The new ecological niche will require specific solutions.

Of course, we dispose only our terrestrial experience. How much we can take from these experiences? It seems that we cannot find the strict analogy between human evolution on the Earth and the future evolution on Mars. Living on Mars will require the artificial support for life. The small group of the first colonizers will have highly advanced technologies and the awareness that their life is constantly threatened. How to organize the human life in such specific environmental conditions? Which values will be the most important and dominant? What will

---

[14] A. Norenzayan, Big Gods: How Religion Transformed Cooperation and Conflict, Princeton University [Press2013].

be the human behaviors in such crisis situations? As we mentioned above natural selection on the level of small group favors rather egoists than altruism. In this context, the Martian colonizers could overcome the biological processes associated with the relationship between the group size and tendency to altruism? First of all, we cannot predict the evolution of human psyche. Perhaps in these environments high levels of stress will cause fear, aggression and a tendency to conflict situations. In this context, how to design the law and social organization?

We claim that human beings are not evolutionarily adapted to colonize cosmic environments. Technological barriers between humans and their environment can be insufficient in the case of the Martian colony. Intensive selective pressure appropriate for the Martian environment probably rather causes the death of the crew than their fast adaptation. We suggest that the best solution could be the artificial acceleration of the biological evolution of the astronauts before they start their space deep mission. ■

Further Reading

1. Rettberg Petra, M. Anesio Alexandre, R. Baker Victor, A. Baross John, L. Cady Sherry, Detsis Emmanouil, M. Foreman Christine, Hauber Ernst, Ori Gian Gabriele, A. Pearce David, O. Renno Nilton, Ruvkun Gary, Sattler Birgit, P. Saunders Mark, H. Smith David, Wagner Dirk, Westall Frances, Planetary protection and Mars special regions—a suggestion for updating the definition, Astrobiology 16 (2) (February 2016) 119–125, http://dx.doi.org/10.1089/ast.2016.1472.

2. Szocik K., *Etyka kolonizatorów Marsa*, http://filozofiawpraktyce.pl/.

3. K. Szocik, Mars, Human nature and the evolution of the psyche, J. Br. Interplanet. Soc 68 (No. 12) (2015) 403–405.

AUTHOR PROFILE

"Political and Legal Challenges in a Mars Colony" is written by the following: **Konrad Szocik**—Department of Cognitive Science, University of Information Technology and Management in Rzeszow, Poland, **Kateryna Lysenko-Ryba**—Chair of Process Engineering, University of Information Technology and Management in Rzeszow, Poland, **Sylwia Banaś**—Chair of Administrative Law, University of Information Technology and Management in Rzeszow, Poland, and **Sylwia Mazur**—Institute for Research on Civilizations, University of Information Technology and Management in Rzeszow, Poland. The article was published in the May 2016 edition of the journal *Space Policy*, "an international, interdisciplinary journal which draws on the fields of international relations, economics, history, aerospace studies, security studies, development studies, political science and ethics to provide discussion and analysis of space activities in their political, economic, industrial, legal, cultural, and social contexts."

"Lovely Hula Hands": Corporate Tourism and the Prostitution of Hawaiian Culture

By Haunani-Kay Trask

I am certain that most, if not all, Americans have heard of Hawai`i and have wished, at some time in their lives, to visit my Native land. But I doubt that the history of how Hawai`i came to be territorially incorporated, and economically, politically, and culturally subordinated to the United States is known to most Americans. Nor is it common knowledge that Hawaiians have been struggling for over twenty years to achieve a land base and some form of political sovereignty on the same level as American Indians. Finally, I would imagine that most Americans could not place Hawai`i or any other Pacific island on a map of the Pacific. But despite all this appalling ignorance, five million Americans will vacation in my homeland this year *and* the next, and so on, into the foreseeable capitalist future. Such are the intended privileges of the so-called American standard of living: ignorance of and yet power over one's relations to Native peoples. Thanks to post-war American imperialism, the ideology that the United States has no overseas colonies and is, in fact, the champion of self-determination the world over holds no greater sway than in the United States itself. To most Americans, then, Hawai`i is *theirs*: to use, to take, and, above all, to fantasize about long after the experience.

Just five hours away by plane from California, Hawai`i is a thousand light years away in fantasy. Mostly a state of mind, Hawai`i is the image of escape from the rawness and violence of daily American life. Hawai`i—the word, the vision, the sound in the mind—is the fragrance and feel of soft kindness. Above all, Hawai`i is "she," the Western image of the Native "female" in her magical allure. And if luck prevails, some of "her" will rub off on you, the visitor.

This fictional Hawai`i comes out of the depths of Western sexual sickness that demands a dark, sin-free Native for instant gratification between imperialist wars. The attraction of Hawai`i is stimulated by slick Hollywood movies, saccharine Andy Williams music, and the constant psychological deprivations of maniacal American life. Tourists flock to my Native land for escape, but they are escaping into a state of mind while participating in the destruction of a host people in a Native place.

To Hawaiians, daily life is neither soft nor kind. In fact, the political, economic, and cultural reality for most Hawaiians is hard, ugly, and cruel.

In Hawai`i, the destruction of our land and the prostitution of our culture is planned and executed by multinational corporations (both foreign-based and Hawai`i-based), by huge landowners (such as the missionary-descended Castle & Cook of Dole Pineapple fame), and by collaborationist state and county governments. The ideological gloss that claims tourism to be our economic savior and the "natural" result of Hawaiian culture is manufactured by ad agencies (such as

321

the state-supported Hawai`i Visitors Bureau) and tour companies (many of which are owned by the airlines) and spewed out to the public through complicitous cultural engines such as film, television and radio, and the daily newspaper. As for the local labor unions, both rank and file and management clamor for more tourists, while the construction industry lobbies incessantly for larger resorts.

The major public educational institution, the University of Hawai`i, funnels millions of taxpayer dollars into a School of Travel Industry Management and a business school replete with a Real Estate Center and a Chair of Free Enterprise (renamed the Walker Chair to hide the crude reality of capitalism). As the propaganda arm of the tourist industry in Hawai`i, both schools churn out studies that purport to show why Hawai`i needs more golf courses, hotels, and tourist infrastructure and how Hawaiian culture is "naturally" one of giving and entertaining.

Of course, state-encouraged commodification and prostitution of Native cultures through tourism is not unique to Hawai`i. It is suffered by peoples in places as disparate as Goa, Australia, Tahiti, and the southwestern United States. Indeed, the problem is so commonplace that international organizations—for example, the Ecumenical Coalition on Third World Tourism out of Bangkok, the Center for Responsible Tourism in California, and the Third World European Network— have banded together to help give voice to Native peoples in daily resistance against corporate tourism. My focus on Hawai`i, although specific to my own culture, would likely transfer well when applied to most Native peoples.[1]

Despite our similarities with other major tourist destinations, the statistical picture of the effects of corporate tourism in Hawai`i is shocking:

Fact: Nearly forty years ago, at statehood, Hawai`i residents outnumbered tourists by more than 2 to 1. Today, tourists outnumber residents by 6 to 1; they outnumber Native Hawaiians by 30 to 1.[2]

Fact: According to independent economists and criminologists, "tourism has been the single most powerful factor in O`ahu's crime rate," including crimes against people and property.[3]

Fact: Independent demographers have been pointing out for years that "tourism is the major source of population growth in Hawai`i" and that "rapid growth of the tourist industry ensures the trend toward a rapidly expanded population that receives lower per capita income."[4]

Fact: The Bank of Hawai`i has reported that the average real incomes of Hawai`i residents grew only *one* percent during the period from the early seventies through the early eighties, when tourism was booming. The same held true throughout the nineties. The census bureau reports that personal income growth in Hawai`i during the same time was the lowest by far of any of the fifty American states.[5]

Fact: Groundwater supplies on O`ahu will be insufficient to meet the needs of residents and tourists by the year 2000.[6]

Fact: According to *The Honolulu Advertiser*, "Japanese investors have spent more than $7.1 billion on their acquisitions" since 1986 in Hawai`i. This kind of volume translates into huge alienations of land and properties. For example, nearly 2,000 acres of land on the Big Island of Hawai`i was purchased for $18.5 million and over 7,000 acres on Moloka`i went for $33 million. In 1989, over $1 billion was spent by the Japanese on land alone.[7]

Fact: More plants and animals from our Hawaiian Islands are now extinct or on the endangered species list than in the rest of the United States.[8]

Fact: More than 29,000 families are on the Hawaiian trust lands list, waiting for housing, pastoral, or agricultural lots.[9]

Fact: The median cost of a home on the most populated island of O`ahu is around $350,000.[10]

Fact: Hawai`i has by far the worst ratio of average family income to average housing costs in the country. This explains why families spend nearly 52 percent of their gross income for housing costs.[11]

Fact: Nearly one-fifth of Hawai`i's resident population is classified as *near-homeless*, that is, those for whom any mishap results in immediate on-the-street homelessness.[12]

These kinds of statistics render a very bleak picture, not at all what the posters and jingoistic tourist promoters would have you believe about Hawai`i.

My use of the word *tourism* in the Hawai`i context refers to a mass-based, corporately controlled industry that is both vertically and horizontally integrated such that one multinational corporation owns an airline and the tour buses that transport tourists to the corporation-owned hotel where they eat in a corporation-owned restaurant, play golf, and "experience" Hawai`i on corporation-owned recreation areas and eventually consider buying a second home built on corporation land. Profits, in this case, are mostly repatriated back to the home country. In Hawai`i, these "home" countries are Japan, Taiwan, Hong Kong, Canada, Australia, and the United States. In this sense, Hawai`i is very much like a Third World colony where the local elite—the Democratic Party in our state—collaborate in the rape of Native land and people.[13]

The mass nature of this kind of tourism results in megaresort complexes on thousands of acres with demands for water and services that far surpass the needs of Hawai`i residents. These complexes may boast several hotels, golf courses, restaurants, and other "necessaries" to complete the total tourist experience. Infrastructure is usually built by the developer in exchange for county approval of more hotel units. In Hawai`i, counties bid against each other to attract larger and larger complexes. "Rich" counties, then, are those with more resorts, since they will pay more of the tax base of the county. The richest of these is the City and County of Honolulu, which encompasses the entire island of O`ahu. This island is the site of four major tourist destinations, a major international airport, and 80 percent of the resident population of Hawai`i. The military also controls nearly 30 percent of the island, with bases and airports of their own. As you might imagine, the density of certain parts of Honolulu (e.g., Waikiki*) is among the highest in the world. At the present annual visitor count, more than five million tourists pour through O`ahu, an island of only 607 square miles.

With this as a background on tourism, I want to move now into the area of cultural prostitution. *Prostitution* in this context refers to the entire institution that defines a woman (and by extension the *female*) as an object of degraded and victimized sexual value for use and exchange through the medium of money. The *prostitute* is a woman who sells her sexual capacities and is seen, thereby, to possess and reproduce them at will, that is, by her very "nature." The prostitute and the institution that creates and maintains her are, of course, of patriarchal origin. The pimp is the conduit of exchange, managing the commodity that is the prostitute while acting as the guard at the entry and exit gates, making sure the prostitute behaves as a prostitute by fulfilling her sexual-economic functions. The victims participate in their victimization with enormous ranges of feeling, from resistance to complicity, but the force and continuity of the institution are shaped by men.

There is much more to prostitution than my sketch reveals but this must suffice, for I am interested in using the largest sense of this term as a metaphor in understanding what has happened to Hawaiian culture. My purpose is not to exact detail or fashion a model but to convey the utter degradation of our culture and our people under corporate tourism by employing *prostitution* as an analytic category.

Finally, I have chosen four areas of Hawaiian culture to examine: our homeland, our *one hanau** that is Hawai`i, our lands and fisheries, the outlying seas and the heavens; our language and dance; our familial relationships; and our women.

The *mo`olelo*, or history of Hawaiians, is to be found in our genealogies. From our great cosmogonic genealogy, the *kumulipo*, derives the Hawaiian identity. The "essential lesson" of this genealogy is "the interrelatedness of the Hawaiian world, and the inseparability of its constituents parts." Thus, "the genealogy of the land, the gods, chiefs, and people intertwine one with the other, and with all aspects of the universe.".[14]

In the *mo`olelo* of Papa and Wakea*, "earth mother" and "sky father," our islands were born: Hawai`i, Maui, O`ahu, Kaua`i, and Ni`ihau. From their human offspring came the *taro* plant and from the *taro* came the Hawaiian people. The lessons of our genealogy are that human beings have a familial relationship to land and to the *taro*, our elder siblings or *kua`ana*.

In Hawai`i, as in all of Polynesia, younger siblings must serve and honor elder siblings who, in turn, must feed and care for their younger siblings. Therefore, Hawaiians must cultivate and husband the land that will feed and provide for the Hawaiian people. This relationship of people to land is called *malama * aina** or *aloha `aina*, "care and love of the land."

When people and land work together harmoniously, the balance that results is called *pono*. In Hawaiian society, the *ali`i*, or "chiefs," were required to maintain order, an abundance of food, and good government. The *makaainana** or "common people," worked the land and fed the chiefs; the *ali`i* organized production and appeased the gods.

Today, *malama 'aina* is called *stewardship* by some, although that word does not convey spiritual and genealogical connections. Nevertheless, to love and make the land flourish is a Hawaiian value. *`Aina**, one of the words for "land," means "that which feeds." *Kamaaina**, a term for native-born people, means "child of the land." Thus is the Hawaiian relationship to land both familial and reciprocal.

Hawaiian deities also spring from the land: Pele is our volcano, Kane* and Lono our fertile valleys and plains, Kanaloa our ocean and all that lives within it, and so on with the numerous gods of Hawai`i. Our whole universe, physical and metaphysical, is divine.

Within this world, the older people, or *kupuna**, are to cherish those who are younger, the *mo`opuna*. Unstinting generosity is a prized value. Social connections between our people are through *aloha*, simply translated as "love" but carrying with it a profoundly Hawaiian sense that is, again, familial and genealogical. Hawaiians feel *aloha* for Hawai`i from whence they come and for their Hawaiian kin upon whom they depend. It is nearly impossible to feel or practice *aloha* for something that is not familial. This is why we extend familial relations to those few non-Natives whom we feel understand and can reciprocate our *aloha*. But *aloha* is freely given and freely returned; it is not and cannot be demanded or commanded. Above all, *aloha* is a cultural feeling and practice that works among the people and between the people and their land.

The significance and meaning of *aloha* underscores the centrality of the Hawaiian language or *olelo**, to the culture. *Olelo** means both "language" and "tongue"; *mo`olelo*, or "history," is that which comes from the tongue, that is, "a story." *Haole*, or white people, say that we have oral history, but what we have are stories, such as our creation story, passed on through the generations. This sense of history is different from the *haole* sense of history. To Hawaiians in traditional society, language had tremendous power, thus the phrase, *i ka `olelo ke ola; i ka `olelo ka make*—"in language is life, in language is death."

After nearly two thousand years of speaking Hawaiian, our people suffered the near extinction of our language through its banning by the American-imposed government in 1900, the year Hawai`i became a territory of the United States. All schools, government operations and official transactions were thereafter conducted in English, despite the fact that most people, including non-Natives, still spoke Hawaiian at the turn of the century.

Since 1970, *`olelo Hawai`i*, or the Hawaiian language, has undergone a tremendous revival, including the rise of language immersion schools. The state of Hawai`i now has two official languages, Hawaiian and English, and the call for Hawaiian language speakers and teachers is increasing every day.[15]

Along with the flowering of Hawaiian language has come a flowering of Hawaiian dance, especially in its ancient form, called *hula kahiko*. Dance academies, known as *halau**, have proliferated throughout Hawai`i, as have *kumu hula*, or dance masters, and formal competitions where all-night presentations continue for three or four days to throngs of appreciative listeners. Indeed, among Pacific Islanders, Hawaiian dance is considered one of the finest Polynesian art forms today.

Of course, the cultural revitalization that Hawaiians are now experiencing and transmitting to their children is as much a *repudiation* of colonization by

so-called Western civilization in its American form as it is a *reclamation* of our own past and our own ways of life. This is why cultural revitalization is often resisted and disparaged by anthropologists and others: they see very clearly that its political effect is decolonization of the mind. Thus our rejection of the nuclear family as the basic unit of society and of individualism as the best form of human expression infuriates social workers, the churches, the legal system, and educators to this day. Hawaiians continue to have allegedly "illegitimate" children, to *hanai**, or "adopt," both children and adults outside of sanctioned Western legal concepts, to hold and use land and water in a collective form rather than a private property form, and to proscribe the notion and the value that one person should strive to surpass and therefore outshine all others.

All these Hawaiian values can be grouped under the idea of `ohana*, loosely translated as "family," but more accurately imagined as a group of both closely and distantly related people who share nearly everything, from land and food to children and status. Sharing is central to this value, since it prevents individual decline. Of course, poverty is not thereby avoided; it is only shared with everyone in the unit. The `ohana* works effectively when the *kua`ana* relationship (elder sibling/younger sibling reciprocity) is practiced.

Finally, within the `ohana*, our women are considered the lifegivers of the nation and are accorded the respect and honor this status conveys. Our young women, like our young people in general, are the *pua*, or "flower" of our *lahui**, or our "nation." The renowned beauty of our women, especially their sexual beauty, is not considered a commodity to be hoarded by fathers and brothers but an attribute of our people. Culturally, Hawaiians are very open and free about sexual relationships, although Christianity and organized religion have done much to damage these traditional sexual values.

With this understanding of what it means to be Hawaiian, I want to move now to the prostitution of our culture by tourism.

Hawai`i itself is the female object of degraded and victimized sexual value. Our *aina**, or lands, are not any longer the source of food and shelter, but the source of money. Land is now called "real estate," rather than "our mother," Papa. The American relationship of people to land is that of exploiter to exploited. Beautiful areas, once sacred to my people, are now expensive resorts; shorelines where net fishing, seaweed gathering, and crabbing occurred are more and more the exclusive domain of recreational activities such as sunbathing, windsurfing, and jet skiing. Now, even access to beaches near hotels is strictly regulated or denied to the local public altogether.

The phrase, *malama** `aina*—"to care for the land"—is used by government officials to sell new projects and to convince the locals that hotels can be built with a concern for "ecology." Hotel historians, like hotel doctors, are stationed in-house to soothe the visitors' stay with the pablum of invented myths and tales of the "primitive."

High schools and hotels adopt each other and funnel teenagers through major resorts for guided tours from kitchens to gardens to honeymoon suites in preparation for post-secondary school jobs in the lowest paid industry in the state. In the meantime, tourist appreciation kits and movies are distributed through the state Department of Education to all elementary schools. One film, unashamedly titled *What's in It for Me?*, was devised to convince locals that tourism is, as the newspapers never tire of saying, "the only game in town."

Of course, all this hype is necessary to hide the truth about tourism, the awful exploitative truth that the industry is the major cause of environmental degradation, low wages, land dispossession, and the highest cost of living in the United States.

While this propaganda is churned out to local residents, the commercialization of Hawaiian culture proceeds with calls for more sensitive marketing of our Native values and practices. After all, a prostitute is only as good as her income-producing talents. These talents, in Hawaiian terms, are the *hula*; the generosity, or *aloha*, of our people; the *u`i*, or youthful beauty of our women and men; and the continuing allure of our lands and waters, that is, of our place, Hawai`i.

The selling of these talents must produce income. And the function of tourism and the State of Hawai`i is to convert these attributes into profit.

The first requirement is the transformation of the product, or the cultural attribute, much as a woman must be transformed to look like a prostitute—that is, someone who is complicitous in her own commodification. Thus *hula* dancers wear clownlike makeup, don costumes from a mix of Polynesian cultures, and behave in a manner that is smutty and salacious rather than powerfully erotic. The distance between the smutty and the erotic is precisely the distance between Western culture and Hawaiian culture. In the hotel version of the *hula*, the sacredness of the dance has completely evaporated, while the athleticism and sexual expression have been packaged like ornaments. The purpose is entertainment for profit rather than a joyful and truly Hawaiian celebration of human and divine nature.

The point, of course, is that everything in Hawai`i can be yours, that is, you the tourists', the non-Natives', the visitors'. The place, the people, the culture, even our identity as a "Native" people is for sale. Thus the word "Aloha" is employed as an aid in the constant hawking of things Hawaiian. In truth, this use of *aloha* is so far removed from any Hawaiian cultural context that it is, literally, meaningless.

Thus, Hawai`i, like a lovely woman, is there for the taking. Those with only a little money get a brief encounter, those with a lot of money, like the Japanese, get more. The state and counties will give tax breaks, build infrastructure, and have the governor personally welcome tourists to ensure that they keep coming. Just as the pimp regulates prices and guards the commodity of the prostitute, so the state bargains with developers for access to Hawaiian land and culture. Who builds the biggest resorts to attract the most affluent tourists gets the best deal: more hotel rooms, golf courses, and restaurants approved. Permits are fast-tracked, height and density limits are suspended, new groundwater sources are miraculously found.

Hawaiians, meanwhile, have little choice in all this. We can fill up the unemployment lines, enter the military, work in the tourist industry, or leave Hawai`i. Increasingly, Hawaiians are leaving, not by choice but out of economic necessity.

Our people who work in the industry—dancers, waiters, singers, valets, gardeners, housekeepers, bartenders, and even a few managers—make between

327

$10,000 and $25,000 a year, an impossible salary for a family in Hawai`i. Psychologically, our young people have begun to think of tourism as the only employment opportunity, trapped as they are by the lack of alternatives. For our young women, modeling is a "cleaner" job when compared to waiting on tables or dancing in a weekly revue, but modeling feeds on tourism and the commodification of Hawaiian women. In the end, the entire employment scene is shaped by tourism.

Despite their exploitation, Hawaiians' participation in tourism raises the problem of complicity. Because wages are so low and advancement so rare, whatever complicity exists is secondary to the economic hopelessness that drives Hawaiians into the industry. Refusing to contribute to the commercialization of one's culture becomes a peripheral concern when unemployment looms.

Of course, many Hawaiians do not see tourism as part of their colonization. Thus, tourism is viewed as providing jobs, not as a form of cultural prostitution. Even those who have some glimmer of critical consciousness do not generally agree that the tourist industry prostitutes Hawaiian culture. This is a measure of the depth of our mental oppression: we cannot understand our own cultural degradation because we are living it. As colonized people, we are colonized to the extent that we are unaware of our oppression. When awareness begins, then so, too, does decolonization. Judging by the growing resistance to new hotels, to geothermal energy and manganese nodule mining, which would supplement the tourist industry, and to increases in the sheer number of tourists, I would say that decolonization has begun, but we have many more stages to negotiate on our path to sovereignty.

My brief excursion into the prostitution of Hawaiian culture has done no more than give an overview. Now that you have read a Native view, let me just leave this thought with you. If you are thinking of visiting my homeland, please do not. We do not want or need any more tourists, and we certainly do not like them. If you want to help our cause, pass this message on to your friends. ■

Notes

1. The Center for Responsible Tourism and the Third World European Network were created out of the activism and organizing of the Ecumenical Coalition on Third World Tourism (ECTWT). This umbrella organization is composed of the following member bodies: All Africa Conference of Churches, Caribbean Conference of Churches, Christian Conference of Asia, Consejo Latinoamericano de Iglesias, Federation of Asian Bishops Conference/ Office of Human Development, Middle East Council of Churches, Pacific Conference of Churches. In addition, sister organizations, like the Hawai`i Ecumenical Coalition on Tourism, extend the network worldwide. The ECTWT publishes a quarterly magazine with articles on Third World tourism and its destructive effects from child prostitution to dispossession of Native peoples. The address for ECTWT is P.O. Box 24, Chorakhebua, Bangkok 10230, Thailand.
2. Eleanor C. Nordyke, *The Peopling of Hawai`i*, 2nd ed. (Honolulu: University of Hawai`i Press, 1989), pp. 134–172.

T

3. Meda Chesney-Lind, "Salient Factors in Hawai`i's Crime Rate," University of Hawai`i School of Social Work. Available from author.
4. Nordyke, *The Peopling of Hawai`i*, pp. 134–172.
5. Bank of Hawai`i Annual Economic Report, 1984.
6. Estimate of independent hydrologist Kate Vandemoer to community organizing group *Kupa`a * He`eia*, February 1990. Water quality and groundwater depletion are two problems much discussed by state and county officials in Hawai`i but ignored when resort permits are considered.
7. *The Honolulu Advertiser*, April 8, 1990.
8. David Stannard, Testimony against West Beach Estates. Land Use Commission, State of Hawai`i, January 10, 1985.
9. Department of Hawaiian Home Lands, phone interview, March 1998.
10. *Honolulu Star-Bulletin*, May 8, 1990.
11. Bank of Hawai`i Annual Economic Report, 1984. In 1992, families probably spent closer to 60 percent of their gross income for housing costs. Billion-dollar Japanese investments and other speculation since 1984 have caused rental and purchase prices to skyrocket.
12. This is the estimate of a state-contracted firm that surveyed the islands for homeless and near-homeless families. Testimony was delivered to the state legislature, 1990 session.
13. For an analysis of post-statehood Hawai`i and its turn to mass-based corporate tourism, see Noel Kent, *Hawai`i: Islands Under the Influence*. For an analysis of foreign investment in Hawai`i, see "*A Study of Foreign Investment and Its Impact on the State*," (Honolulu: Hawai`i Real Estate Center, University of Hawai`i, 1989).
14. Lilikala * Kame`eleihiwa, *Native Land and Foreign Desires* (Honolulu: Bishop Museum Press, 1992), p. 2.
15. See Larry Kimura, "Native Hawaiian Culture," *Native Hawaiians Study Commission Report*, vol. 1, pp. 173–197.

———————————————————————————— AUTHOR PROFILE

Haunani-Kay Trask is a Native Hawaiian rights activist, poet, and educator. She was born in California and grew up in Hawai'i; she is the former director of the Center for Hawaiian Studies at the University of Hawai'i at Mānoa and a founding member of Ka Lahui Hawai'i, the major Native Hawaiian sovereignty organization. Trask's awards include the National Endowment for the Arts Writer-in-Residence fellowship in Santa Fe, NM (1996) and the Pacific Basin Research Center fellowship at Harvard University (1998). She has written two poetry books, *Light in the Crevice Never Seen* (1994) and *Night Is a Sharkskin Drum* (2002) and co-produced and co-wrote the film *Act of War: the Overthrow of the Hawaiian Nation* (1993). "Lovely Hula Hands" is an excerpt from her acclaimed critical volume *From a Native Daughter: Colonialism and Sovereignty in Hawai'i* (1993).

Decision: 39 COM 7A.27, Old City of Jerusalem and Its Walls

By UNESCO

Decision: 39 COM 7A.27

The World Heritage Committee,

1. <u>Having examined</u> Document WHC-15/39.COM/7A.Add,

2. <u>Recalling</u> the relevant provisions on the protection of cultural heritage including the four Geneva Conventions (1949), the Hague Convention for the Protection of Cultural Property in the Event of Armed Conflict of 1954 and its related protocols, the Convention on the Means of Prohibiting and Preventing the Illicit Import, Export and Transfer of Ownership of Cultural Property (1970), the *Convention for the Protection of the World Cultural and Natural Heritage* of 1972, the Delhi UNESCO Recommendation of 1956 concerning excavations undertaken in occupied territories, the inscription of the Old City of Jerusalem and its Walls at the request of Jordan on the World Heritage List (1981) and on the List of World Heritage in Danger (1982) and related recommendations, resolutions and decisions of UNESCO,

3. <u>Reaffirming</u> that nothing in the present decision, which aims at the safe-guarding of the authenticity, integrity and cultural heritage of the Old City of Jerusalem on both sides of its Walls, shall in any way affect the relevant United Nations resolutions and decisions, in particular the relevant Security Council resolutions on the legal status of Jerusalem,

I

4. <u>Deeply concerned</u> by the persistence of the Israeli illegal excavations and works conducted by the Israeli Occupation authorities and the extreme settler groups in the Old City of Jerusalem and on both sides of its Walls and the failure of Israel to cease such harmful interventions, <u>requests</u> Israel to timely stop all such violations, in conformity with its obligations under the provi-sions of related UNESCO Conventions and recommendations,

5. <u>Regrets</u> the damage caused by the Israeli security forces on 30th October 2014 to the historic Gates and windows of the Qibli Mosque inside Al-Aqsa Mosque/ Al-Haram Al-Sharif, which is a Muslim holy site of worship and an integral part of a World Heritage Site;

6. <u>Expresses its deep concern</u> over the Israeli closure and ban of the renovation of Al-Rahma Gate building, one of Al-Aqsa Mosque/ Al-Haram Al-Sharif Gates, and <u>urges</u> Israel to stop obstruction of the necessary restoration works, in order to fix the damage caused by the weather conditions, especially the water leakage into the rooms of the building;

7. Deplores the damaging effect of the Jerusalem Light rail (tram line) at few meters from the Walls of the Old City of Jerusalem which severely affects the visual integrity and the authentic character of the site and requests Israel, the Occupying Power, to restore the original character of the site in conformity with its obligations under the provisions of related UNESCO Conventions and recommendations;

8. Calls on Israel, the Occupying Power, to stop the obstruction of the immediate execution of all the 19 Hashemite restoration projects in and around Al-Aqsa Mosque/ Al-Haram Al-Sharif;

9. Also deplores the Israeli decision to approve: the plan to build a two-line cable car system in East Jerusalem, the plan to construct of the so called "Liba House" project in the Old City of Jerusalem, the demolition and new construction of the so-called Strauss Building, and the project of the elevator in the Buraq Plaza (Western Wall), the digging of a Mamluk structure beneath the Buraq Plaza (Western Wall), the excavations and construction of new levels underneath the Buraq Plaza, and urges Israel, the Occupying Power, to renounce the above mentioned projects in conformity with its obligations under the provisions of related UNESCO Conventions and recommendations particularly the Hague Convention for the Protection of Cultural Property in the Event of Armed Conflict of 1954 and its related protocols, as well as UNESCO Decisions particularly the World Heritage Committee decisions **37COM7A.26** and **38COM7A.4**;

10. Expresses its deep concern regarding the plan for building of the so called "Kedem Center" a visitors centre near the southern wall of Al-Aqsa Mosque/ Al-Haram Al-Sharif, which severely affects the visual integrity and the authentic character of the site, in addition, its placement at the northern entrance to Silwan village will cut off the Palestinian residents' direct connection to Old City and the Palestinian neighbourhoods to the north and east of the village, furthermore, most of the remains resulted from the excavation therein have been completely removed without documentation;

11. Expresses its concern regarding the restricting obstacles imposed by Israel, the Occupying Power, on the freedom of access that shall be provided to the competent national authorities including the Jordanian Waqf experts to safeguard the Old City of Jerusalem and both sides of its Walls;

12. Welcomes the relative improvement of Muslim worshippers' access into Al-Aqsa Mosque/ Al-Haram Al-Sharif over the past seven months, regrets the Israeli extremist groups' continuous storming of Al-Aqsa Mosque/ Al-Haram Al-Sharif, and urges Israel, the Occupying Power, to take necessary measures to prevent such provocative abuses that violate the sanctity and integrity of the Al-Aqsa Mosque/ Al-Haram Al-Sharif and inflame tension on the ground;

13. Further regrets the damage by Israel, the Occupying Power, of the historic ceramics atop of the main gates of the Dome of the Rock and the damage of the historic gates and windows of the Qibli Mosque inside Al-Aqsa Mosque/

Al-Haram Al-Sharif and <u>reaffirms</u>, in this regard, the necessity to respect and safeguard the integrity, authenticity and cultural heritage of Al-Aqsa Mosque/ Al-Haram Al-Sharif, as reflected in the Status Quo, as a Muslim Holy Site of worship and as an integral part of a World Cultural Heritage site;

14. <u>Calls upon</u> Israel to return the remains and to provide the World Heritage Centre with the relevant documentation in particular concerning the re-moved and found historic remains, as well as to restore the original character of the sites of all the above mentioned projects;

15. <u>Requests</u> the World Heritage Centre to continue applying the Reinforced Monitoring Mechanism to the Old City of Jerusalem on both sides of its Walls, and <u>also requests</u> it to report every four months on this matter;

16. <u>Thanks</u> the Director-General of UNESCO and the World Heritage Centre for their efforts aimed at the Safeguarding of the Cultural Heritage of the Old City of Jerusalem on both sides of its walls and <u>invites</u> them to report on this matter at the 40th session of the World Heritage Committee in 2016;

II

17. <u>Recalling</u> 176 EX/Special Plenary Meeting Decision, and all UNESCO Executive Board Decisions relating to the Ascent to the Mughrabi Gate in the Old City of Jerusalem,

18. <u>Affirms</u> that the Mughrabi Ascent is an integral and inseparable part of Al-Aqsa Mosque/ Al-Haram Al-Sharif,

19. <u>Takes into consideration</u> all the previous Reinforced Monitoring Reports and their addenda prepared by the World Heritage Centre as well as the State of Conservation report submitted to the World Heritage Centre by the Hashemite Kingdom of Jordan and the State of Palestine,

20. <u>Expresses its growing concern</u> regarding the continuous, intrusive demolitions and illegal excavations in and around the Mughrabi Gate Ascent, and the latest excavation works conducted at the beginning of May 2015 at the Buraq Plaza (Western Wall) of Al-Aqsa Mosque/ Al-Haram Al-Sharif, and <u>calls on</u> Israel, the Occupying Power, to end such violations, respect the Status Quo, and enable the Jordanian Awaqf experts as a part of the competent national authorities to maintain and safeguard the site in accordance with the relevant provisions of the UNESCO Conventions and Recommendations in par-ticular the Hague Convention for the Protection of Cultural Property in the Event of Armed Conflict of 1954 and its related protocols;

21. <u>Commends</u> the Jordanian design for the restoration and preservation of the Mughrabi Ascent, submitted to the World Heritage Centre on 27 May 2011, and <u>thanks</u> Jordan for its cooperation in accordance with the provisions of the relevant UNESCO Conventions for the Protection of Cultural Heritage;

22. <u>Urges</u> Israel, the Occupying Power, to cooperate with Jordanian Awqaf Department, in conformity with its obligations under the provisions of the UNESCO related Conventions, to facilitate access of Jordanian Awqaf experts with their tools and material to the site in order to enable the execution of the Jordanian design of the Ascent to the Mughrabi Gate;

23. <u>Further expresses</u> its deep concern regarding demolitions of Ummayad, Ottoman and Mamluk remains at the site of the Mughrabi Gate Pathway, and <u>urges</u> Israel, the Occupying Power, to abide by its obligations in this regard;

24. <u>Thanks</u> the Director-General for her attention to the sensitive situation of the Ascent to the Mughrabi Gate and <u>asks</u> her to take the necessary measures in order to enable the execution of the Jordanian design of the Ascent to the Mughrabi Gate;

III

25. <u>Recalls</u> the Executive Board decisions concerning the reactive monitoring mission to the Old City of Jerusalem and its Walls particularly decision 196EX/Decision26.4 as well as the World Heritage Committee decisions particularly decision **34 COM 7A.20**;

26. <u>Deeply regrets</u> the continuous Israeli failure to implement the Reactive Monitoring Mission and <u>urges</u> Israel, the Occupying Power, to accept and facilitate the implementation of that Mission;

27. <u>Stresses</u> the need of the urgent implementation of the above-mentioned UNESCO mission and, in case of non-implementation according to the above mentioned Executive Board decision 196EX/Decision26.4, decides to consider, in conformity with the provisions of the *Convention Concerning the Protection of the World Cultural and Natural Heritage* 1972, adequate measures to have the concerned party implement it;

28. <u>Requests</u> that the report and recommendations of the mission be presented to the concerned parties prior to the next 197 EX Board session;

29. <u>Thanks</u> the Director-General for her continuous efforts to implement the above-mentioned UNESCO mission and all related UNESCO decisions and resolutions, and invites her to report on this matter at the next 40th World Heritage Committee session;

IV

30. **<u>Decides</u> to retain the Old City of Jerusalem and its Walls on the List of World Heritage in Danger.** ■

AUTHOR PROFILE

UNESCO stands for the United Nations Educational, Scientific, and Cultural Organization. UNESCO's Constitution was ratified by twenty UN nations in 1945. The agency describes its mission as "contribut[ing] to the building of peace, the eradication of poverty, sustainable development and intercultural dialogue through education, the sciences, culture, communication, and information." UNESCO is run by a Director-General (currently Audrey Azoulay). In 1972, it adopted the Convention concerning the Protection of World Cultural and Natural Heritage. The World Heritage Centre now maintains lists of global sites with major cultural or historical significance and identifies sites on the list that are endangered by natural disaster or conflict. Decision: 39 COM 7A.27, "Old City of Jerusalem and Its Walls," was released in 2015 during the 39th meeting of the World Heritage Committee.

Buried in the Unremissive Ground: Reading Richmond's Subterranean Signs

By Katherine D. Walker

Cities do not touch the ground directly; today's cities sit on the remains of yesterday's cities. Urban denizens rebuild their worlds, layer upon layer, burying the past beneath the needs of the present. Like the forgotten memories of seminal events that purportedly lurk in the mind's subconscious, the buried substrata of a city can contain unresolved pasts, forgotten incidents that have shaped the present. And like memories, these buried artifacts can be painful once unearthed. In this article, I explore how the public reaction to a city's buried past serves as a map to the social worth of its citizens. It is my argument that contemporary reactions to what is underground signal the relative status of contemporary groups; the treatment of the dead can be read as a code for contemporary race and class relations. A surface reading suggests that the forgotten bodies of the powerless are often seen as inconsequential and easily ignored, while buried elites and their subterranean ruins remain sacred. Beneath this surface reading, however, lies a semiotic inversion; popular folklore about the underground hints at an uneasiness with contemporary power relations, and disputes about ownership of "buried treasures" reveal disputes about ownership of the past.

My study examines Richmond, Virginia, a city first settled by Europeans in 1611 (the city proper was laid out much later in 1737)(Silver 1984). The data for this study arise from a multi-year ethnographic examination of Richmond's commemorative practices and memorial landscape, during which I studied monuments, holidays, and statues. Beneath the deliberately crafted interpretations of the past I saw a formation of signs that often contradicted the city's overt ideology of equality. This article is based on analysis of commemorative events, unstructured observation of physical spaces of the city, and a reading of newspaper accounts of the urban underground. I have examined how people use or ignore spaces, how they write about them in newspapers and tell stories about them, and how people codify their beliefs about places into official memorials.

While my primary purpose is to unpack the relationship between the underground and the Other, this study delves into several theoretical questions. First I wish to explore the idea of terrain—not just physical geography, but also the uses people make of the landscapes in which they find themselves. Fields (1990) has defined ideology as terrain, but the inverse is also true: terrain is ideology, insofar as, quite literally terrain provides a background, the field on which our knowledge of the world is grounded. People inscribe meanings on their surroundings; access is code for belonging or exclusion, and rituals of segregation and separation are signs signifying the lower status of restricted groups. We interpret the meanings of signs in part by considering where we find them. The landscape's meaning

changes over time, so exploring the terrain is also a means of considering semiotic shifts, and also a means of grounding the analysis of signs in the material world (Vannini 2007). Second, I wish to consider how counter-narratives survive and flourish beneath the accepted semiotic field. The most entrenched signs reify the existing social order and power structure, but new memorials and popular folklore embody a message subversive to the older order.

To understand buried Richmond and the discourse about it, this article examines: the sacredness of Hollywood Cemetery, final resting place of two US presidents and other notables, in the city's center on a bluff overlooking the James River; the city's old "Burial Ground for Negroes", which is near Lumpkin's "jail", which was used as a holding pen before slave auctions (both of which were recently rediscovered in time to block a planned baseball stadium); and a 1925 train tunnel collapse that left a train and at least one Black worker (possibly more) buried under the oldest part of the city.

Reading the codes hidden in the treatment of the buried requires a circular journey across Richmond's landscape and through its past. We can begin with Richmond's most respected and hallowed underground city: Hollywood Cemetery. When its first gravesite was sold in 1849, the cemetery lay comfortably to the west of the bustling downtown, seated high above the banks of the James River. The city crept forward and surrounded it; now the dead who rest there occupy some of the best real estate in the city limits. Designed as a "romantic and natural" cemetery (Tyler-McGraw 1994, 187), Hollywood sprawls, its roads winding up and down tree-covered hills, curving toward and away from the river. It is the final resting place of the fifth and tenth US presidents, James Monroe and John Tyler, as well as the president of the former Confederate States of America, Jefferson Davis, and various philanthropists, schoolteachers, industrialists, and politicians. It is the final home for the people who shaped the city and the state, those who owned the plantations that became the neighborhoods of Richmond and the factories that drew workers to the area, the iron-makers, flour-millers, historians, Pulitzer Prize winners, tobacco barons and a US Supreme Court Justice. Jefferson Davis is kept company by Confederate General JEB Stuart and 18,000 other Confederate soldiers, buried under a 90-foot tall pyramid made of rough granite stones. There are Union soldiers too, but the casual visitor could easily miss their presence, as they are scattered here and there, their smallish headstones overshadowed by the more impressive Confederate obelisks, angels, and pyramid—a benign neglect unsurprising in the former capital of the Confederacy. The cemetery is known for beautiful statuary and bas-reliefs; angels and crosses, obelisks and more unusual monuments—an iron dog here, a relief of a train there (Hollywood Cemetery n.d.).

This is a bastion of People Who Mattered, and in death, as in life, they are treated with respect. The cemetery is open every day from 8 am to 5 pm (6 pm during the longer days of summer). Its lawns are kept manicured and its paths are swept. There are still lots open, should anyone eventually wish to join these elite dead. Shorter-term visitors can always just walk or ride around, joining the legions of mourners, nature-lovers, and the art students who walk the eight blocks from Virginia Commonwealth University's campus to draw or photograph the monuments and mausoleums for class projects. Visitors can even buy postcards, a map, or a guide that gives the cemetery's history and shows the location of the most famous residents. The message of Hollywood Cemetery seems, on the surface, quite simple. Richmond's elites, those who occupied the inner social circles in life, are tended to and respected just as much after they are buried as they were in life. Death has not yet erased their influence or importance.

If Hollywood Cemetery is the extreme example of how people hallowed in life are also hallowed when they join the underground city, then what of the other extreme, people who are held as the lowest members of society during their lives? If presidents and industrialists and authors stand as the pinnacle of society, then in Richmond their antithesis—the denizens seen as the lowest—would have to be the African Americans held as slaves prior to the Civil War. The place of slaves in the underground city mirrors the place of the elites. Just as the hallowed in life are also hallowed in death, those held in contempt in life are treated with contempt in death. In fact, a few years ago this question—what happened to the slaves, where was their resting place—would have been unanswerable. Richmond's oldest African American burial ground—"the Burial Ground for Negroes" as it was officially known—lay forgotten from around 1806, when it closed, until 1992 when a local historian, Elizabeth Cann Kambourian, heard of its existence in an account of Richmond's slave insurrectionist Gabriel. Gabriel planned what was, in the opinion of many historians, the largest and best thought-out slave insurrection in US history; delayed for 24 hours by a freak rainstorm, his insurrection was betrayed by co-conspirators who lost courage during the delay. After he was captured, he was hung with his followers on the gallows at the Negro Burial Grounds. He is presumably buried on the site.

Reading this account, Kambourian realized she had never heard of these burial grounds and went looking for them. After poring over old maps she discovered that the plot where slaves were anonymously buried prior to 1806 had been located in the old warehouse district, Shockoe Bottom. In a low spot between the central business district and the city's oldest residential neighborhood, Church Hill, Shockoe Bottom was the site of a bustling dock and the center of the old slave trading district. These days it is full of just the sort of old, ramshackle warehouses that entrepreneurs love to convert into high-end lofts and nightclubs, hampered only by the area's tendency to flood. Interstate 95, the major east coast highway, carries a heavy load of traffic on bridges raised high above the area. According to the old maps, the old African American burial grounds are in this area, running under a parking lot and the interstate. Even after Kambourian's identification of the site, cars continued to park in the lot. Enslaved in life, consigned to oblivion in death, the slaves' remains were rescued from the realm of the forgotten only to enter the realm of the ill-treated.

This situation could be worse. After the burial ground was identified, the only plan for the site that seemed to gain momentum was a proposal to build a baseball diamond for Richmond's minor league team on it. Luckily, after a year of protests the ballpark project was scuttled, although that seemed to result more from the developers' refusal to offer firm schedules and costs, and less from concern over the historical site. While Richmond is a city that pays a fair amount of attention

to historical preservation, pleas to do something respectful to the African American Burial Ground went largely unnoticed by the surrounding neighborhoods, where the siren call of the ballpark seemed to drown out the fainter voice of the forgotten past. This is not completely incomprehensible. As part of their proposal, the ballpark developers promised to repair some of the damage caused by the flood of 2004, during which the aftermath of Hurricane Gaston destroyed many local businesses. In contrast to this tangible offer of economic development, the groups working to preserve the site had more inchoate plans and little funding to spread around the community; they just thought that the site should somehow be reclaimed and treated with respect. While the groups working for preservation were racially diverse, the preponderance of business owners who favored the stadium were white, and pro-stadium frontyard signs were more heavily clustered in the gentrified and mostly white areas of the surrounding neighborhoods.

After the ballpark idea was scuttled, the parking lot in question was purchased by Virginia Commonwealth University, which at first spoke of repaving it; after predictable protests, in 2008 the school's administration expressed surprise that members of the community were concerned about the fate of the site and commissioned a survey to try to determine the exact location and condition of the old burial grounds. The report that resulted claimed that the old burial ground was mainly located under Interstate 95, with a sliver under the parking lot, and also suggested that since the site was under a presumed six to ten feet of infill, it could be considered "protected" from present-day disturbance. Discussions on the fate of the site are likely to continue for some time (Komp 2005; Defenders for Freedom, Justice and Equality n.d.; Stevenson 2008; Walters 2006).

With these first two sites, we see a simple formula describing the relationship between the underground and Otherness in Richmond. To be elite in life is to be elite in death; to be seen as less than human in life translates to the same treatment in death. The treatment of the slaves' burial ground reveals hypocrisy in present-day Richmond's attempts to distance itself from a slave-owning past. Many white citizens (especially those who identify strongly with the city's Confederate past) claim that while slave-owning was a sordid chapter in the city's past, it is time to let resentment about this past go. This desire to avoid a discussion about slavery is voiced repeatedly whenever the issue of slavery returns to the forefront of public discussion. For example, the files at the Museum of the Confederacy contain letters from Sons of Confederate Veterans complaining about the proximity of a slave whip to an image of Robert E. Lee. In another example, former Governor Jim Gilmore's Confederate History Month proclamation drew fire for mentioning slavery, and finally, when in 2007 the Virginia General Assembly debated issuing an apology for slavery, many white citizens wrote letters to local papers opposing such a measure; one General Assembly delegate told a reporter that "black citizens should get over it" (Meola 2007, A1; Museum of the Confederacy Files n.d.; Walker 2008). A mixed message is sent, however, when at the same time as some people are declaring slavery's effects to be over, the abusive treatment of slaves begun centuries ago continues in the lack of respect shown to the slaves' remains. As the treatment of the buried elites of Hollywood Cemetery shows, the neglect of the slave cemetery does not arise from a belief on the part of Richmond's living that what is buried is no longer relevant. The history of Hollywood actually shows the opposite trend; whereas the slave cemetery is considered potentially less important than urban development, during the Civil War, respectful burial of war dead superseded the building of necessary infrastructure. The Confederate dead arrived so fast during the war that:

> the two acres set aside for the Confederate dead filled before the end of the Peninsular Campaign in the summer of 1862. Confederate Secretary of War George Wythe Randolph…grant[ed] the Hollywood Cemetery Company the right to bury on adjacent city land. The city protested that graves were about to occupy the best site for a needed new water reservoir. (Tyler-McGraw 1994, 145–146)

In the 1860s, the Confederate dead were deemed more important than the needs of the living citizens of the city; needed infrastructure and development lost out to the cemetery, which still occupies the same centrally-located, valuable and scenic parcel. Dead and buried elites outrank development, but development outranks dead and forgotten slaves.

While official public discourse in Richmond makes much of racial progress and points to the spread of the ideology of equality, many property-owners and city officials are still willing to treat slave remains poorly, to make a distinction with the dead that they do not dare to make with the living.

Unfortunately, even if activists turn the African American burial grounds into a memorial or a museum, nothing they do can bestow upon the people buried there the respect—fashioned through continuous remembrance—of the elites buried in Hollywood Cemetery. The slaves' identities, however tenuously sustained in bondage, were obliterated in death; their public remembrance creates social awkwardness. Modern-day citizens, sensitive about the wrongs done in the past, hesitate to dig up both the remains and the painful memories, to drag them into daylight for examination. The dead slaves that lie underground in the burial ground have been banished from the public memory for too long; they have not been kept alive by memorials or rituals. Their individuality is gone. Nameless and faceless, they will remain irretrievably Other. Even the people who would redeem them are at a bit of a loss about how to proceed.

The equation thus far is simple; people are treated in death as they are in life. Otherness above ground in life corresponds to Otherness in the underground in death. This is actually too simple. Life is not divided up this neatly and neither should be the reading of Richmond's underground.

Almost across the street from the African American burial ground is hidden the former site of Lumpkin's jail (known to some who passed through its doors as the Devil's Half Acre), which held slaves on their way to the auction block. This site marks an aspect of the past that many Richmonders would rather keep out of the city's public history—its involvement in the slave trade. Over one-third of a million slaves were sold out of Virginia, and Richmond, with its busy port, was the center of this trade in the decades before the Civil War. The building that housed Lumpkin's jail was knocked down long ago, although enough maps

and photographs of the site exist to keep its exact old location from fading into mystery. If the site lived on in public memory in Richmond, this is partly because after the Civil War ended, after its use as a slave holding-pen was obsolete, the jail evolved into something new and surprising. The Lumpkin who owned the jail at war's end—Robert Lumpkin—married an African American woman, Mary—his former slave and mother of his children. When Robert Lumpkin died, Mary Lumpkin inherited the site and eventually rented it out to a group that started a school for African Americans. After undergoing significant transformations, and changing locations a few times, the school evolved into Virginia Union University, a historically black college that still exists in Richmond. The story of Lumpkin's Jail reminds contemporary Richmonders that the complexities of the past are at times buried along with the ruins. No simple categories of Oppressor/Oppressed or Powerful/Powerless can explain how the reportedly cruel owner of the Devil's Half Acre could father children with a slave, and then send the much-beloved children North to protect them from the slave trade that helped support him (Williams 2005). The ease with which current storytellers assign guilt and neatly categorize villains and victims becomes suspect.

In April 2006, spurred on by the threat of the proposed ballpark, multiple preservation groups sponsored a preliminary dig to look for the remains of the jail. The dig turned up pottery, glass and nails. Another dig began in the summer of 2008. One of the organizations involved with the dig is the Richmond Slave Trail Commission, which has worked to preserve not only this site but also the old burial ground and the old docks central to the slave trade. During the annual celebration of Juneteenth,[1] a night-time walk of the trail recreates the path taken by slaves as they left Lumpkin's Jail for Richmond's Manchester docks where they began the journey further south. As it raises money, the Commission gradually adds markers and interpretive material to this path; it seeks to tell the story of the former slaves, to re-inscribe their buried story on the landscape. The narrative created by the Commission emphasizes the former slaves' role in building the city and shaping the nation; their works remain integrated into the fabric of society, even if they have vanished into the dust. This effort, combined with the intricate history of Lumpkin's Jail, is a reminder that reducing the stories of former slaves—powerless and oppressed as they were—to only a story of oppression is another form of obliteration (Alliance to Conserve Old Richmond Neighborhoods 2009; Jones 2008; Robertson 2006; Williams 2005, 2006; Yoder 2006).

With the threat of the ballpark averted, members of the Slave Trail Commission have begun to make plans for the site of Lumpkin's Jail. Some envision turning the site into what they call an Ellis Island for African Americans. Just as so many white Americans have traced their family trees back to ancestors who were processed into the United States through Ellis Island, so many African Americans could trace their lineage through Lumpkin's Jail and Richmond's Shockoe Bottom. Of course, the experience, while symmetrical, cannot evoke identical sentiments. No matter what hardships or hopes drove the ancestors of

---

[1] Juneteenth is a celebration of the day the last slaves were freed in Texas after the Civil War—19 June 1865, when federal troops arrived and enforced the Emancipation Proclamation, over two and a half years after it officially took effect. Celebrated for many years by African Americans, the holiday has now gained recognition from many US state and local governments.

white people through the gates of Ellis Island, they arrived as free people, unlike the ancestors who were processed through Lumpkin's jail.

Memorials and historical markers are constructed by the living to speak for the dead. For example, former Governor of Virginia and President of the United States James Monroe lies buried and silent in Hollywood Cemetery; the cemetery's website speaks for him, stating that:

> More popular than Jefferson, who fled town when the British approached, was Governor James Monroe. Monroe held more high offices than anyone else in American history and his Doctrine shaped nations of the Western hemisphere. Monroe opposed slavery, knew it must end, but as Governor of Virginia in 1800 he had the difficult task of keeping order when there was discovered a conspiracy by thousands of slaves to kill their masters. His calm and just response to Gabriel's Insurrection was his greatest legacy to Richmond. (Hollywood Cemetery n.d.)

The cemetery offers a justification for Monroe's failure to end slavery and for his execution of the rebel Gabriel, suggesting that these acts were necessary evils required by his times. The arrest and execution of Gabriel is described as the "calm and just" reaction of a man who understood the necessity of staving off rebellion. This explanation seems to enter into a dialogue with a roadside marker recently erected above the old Negro Burial Grounds, which states that:

> Near here is the early site of the Richmond gallows and "Burial Ground for Negroes." On 10 Oct. 1800, Gabriel, an enslaved blacksmith from Brookfield Plantation in Henrico County, was executed there for attempting to lead a mass uprising against slavery on 30 Aug. 1800. A fierce rainstorm delayed the insurrection, which was then betrayed by two slaves. Gabriel escaped and eluded capture until 23 Sept., when he was arrested in Norfolk. He was returned to Richmond on 23 Sept. and incarcerated in the Virginia State Penitentiary. On 6 Oct. he stood trial and was condemned. At least 25 of his supporters were also put to death there or in other jurisdictions.

This marker, erected in 2005, challenges the story about Gabriel offered by Hollywood Cemetery. Some historians who have studied Gabriel's life say he never intended his rebellion to be a complete bloodbath. Some claim that he planned to end his insurrection by dining with the merchants of the city on equal terms—a scenario that would have been impossible had he just slaughtered them by the thousands. Monroe's response might appear calm when compared with similar responses of his peers in contemporaneous situations; generally rumors of rebellions sparked horrific reprisals (Egerton 1993; Sidbury 1997). Even so, after entering into dialogue with the highway marker, the cemetery's epitaph seems to protest too much. By our lights, it hardly seems "just" to hang 25 men who

merely wanted to escape slavery. Such an inversion of the old hierarchy of belonging and heroism is one purpose of the new marker memorializing Gabriel. So in Richmond, as it turns out, the living use the underground as a metaphor, as a way to talk about justice, as a means to wipe away Otherness. The buried past can be used strategically to unsettle accepted hierarchies.

The cemetery and Lumpkin's jail are in the Bottom. Above this floodplain rise several hills—Church Hill, the original site of the city, Union Hill, Jefferson Hill, and others. Jefferson Hill's base is a short walk east from the site of the forgotten African American burial grounds. A casual walk up Jefferson Hill brings us to a different sort of underground treasure, one end of a train tunnel that caved in with a train inside it 81 years ago. The buried tunnel winds for 4407 feet under Church Hill; the other end, also boarded up, emerges below a battlefield park to the east. The boards are always falling off; a peek inside shows that the tunnel goes in for a few feet and stops, blocked off with concrete. Interest in the tunnel wanes and then waxes when new sections collapse, as happened in 1962 and 1996.

We can easily follow the story of the tunnel collapse in newspaper archives from 1925; on Saturday 3 October, oddly enough a day after the *Richmond Times Dispatch* was heralding the discovery of an "ancient subterranean prison" in town, a headline announced that the train tunnel had collapsed, killing two men and injuring at least two others. The details are harrowing even now. The tunnel had been closed for a decade for safety. C&O wished to reopen it, so workers were inside widening and strengthening the structure. A train pulling flatcars had just entered the tunnel. The flatcars were used to load dirt for removal; workers also stood on the flatcars to reach and repair the roof of the tunnel. The survivors said they had only a few seconds of warning before the ceiling caved in completely; some of them escaped by crawling under the flatcars as dirt crashed down on them (*Richmond Times Dispatch* 1925e, 1925f, 1925n). Details about the missing and the dead are unclear now, mainly because of the uncertainty and many rumors circulating at the time. For example, on the Monday after the collapse, the *Richmond Times Dispatch* reported that:

> A report was started about 4 o'clock yesterday afternoon by some speculative person in the crowd, that one negro workman had managed to crawl out from the death pit, and that he had said that other men were still alive in the tunnel. This created great excitement, especially among the hundreds of negroes who mingled with the thousands of white persons about the place. (1925g, 3)

This rumor was quickly quashed, although others constantly circulated, driven by the official uncertainty about how many workers were in the tunnel at the time of the disaster. It was certain that the train's white fireman, Benjamin Franklin Mosby, had crawled or staggered from the tunnel, largely scalded, asking that his rescuers take messages to his wife. He died fairly quickly. The train's white engineer, Tom Mason, was known to be missing, and the *Richmond Times Dispatch* reported that "two negro laborers" identified as R. Lewis and H. Smith, were also reported missing. Originally it was feared that 100 men were trapped; thousands of spectators thronged to the site and stood in the pouring rain to witness the spectacle, even after the numbers were revised significantly downward. Weeks passed as rescuers gave up hope of finding survivors and looked only for missing bodies; the papers trumpeted the modern technology used in the effort, and told the heart-wringing stories of Mosby's funeral and Mason's young son who insisted on sleeping at the site, hoping his father would be found (Richmond Public Library n.d.; *Richmond Times Dispatch* 1925b, 1925c, 1925d, 1925h, 1925i, 1925j, 1925k, 1925l, 1925m). The story gradually moved from the front pages as hope faded and the recovery work was finally abandoned.

Unlike the sacred, somber mood that prevails when the burial ground or the jail are discussed, the train tunnel is discussed like a treasure hunt, almost with glee. This happens despite the fact that this is also a story of Otherness. First, African American worker Richard Lewis, barely named in the *Richmond Times Dispatch* coverage, was never found; the story of his loss and its impact on his family was carried in African American newspapers, but not the main paper of the white community. It is rumored that more black workers lie buried at the site. The rumor—no latter-day urban legend, but a question unsettled at the time of the tragedy—was that new laborers had gone into the tunnel to apply for jobs, or alternately, had been hired on to work, but not yet recorded as workers. The missing, unknown and possibly non-existent workers have remained a prominent part of the train tunnel story, underlining the city's treatment of this category of the powerless: the nameless, faceless worker who sacrifices to build the city and then vanishes into the ground unknown to the historical narrative. The workers' sacrifice was great and also unnecessary in this case. While rescuers were still at the scene of the cave-in looking for bodies, a coroner's jury found that C&O's negligence caused Mason's death; the tunnel had not been shored with enough braces (*Richmond Times Dispatch* 1925a). That there is still a worker's body or potentially many bodies still buried at the site figures prominently in popular retellings of the accident, sometimes serving to underline the city's treatment of Others, at other times simply salving the disappointment of ghoulish citizens who find themselves oddly disappointed that the tunnel did not collapse on a passenger train.

The mid-1990s cave-in of part of the tunnel spurred enough curiosity about the fate of the train that, in the summer of 2006, a public/private partnership made plans to excavate the buried train. Preliminary shafts showed that the old tunnel was flooded; a week of pumping water showed that the problem would not be easily solved, and the ensuing publicity made city officials aware that the public/private partnership had not conducted feasibility studies to ensure that the neighborhoods on top of the tunnel would remain standing after the water was removed. In fact, no permits had been applied for at all. This neglect was upsetting to residents who remembered the previous cave-ins, which swallowed a tennis court and damaged two houses beyond repair. Again, the treatment of the underground says something about Otherness. The tunnel runs beneath old neighborhoods, a few of which are gentrified, most of which are inhabited by poor or working-class African Americans. In these neighborhoods, there was a perception that wealthy white people on a treasure hunt were showing a reckless disregard for the property and lives of non-elites (Holmberg 2000, 2006a, 2006b, 2006c; Hsu 2006a, 2006b, 2006c; Virginia Historical Society n.d.).

To understand how old categories of belonging and Otherness can be inverted by creative use of what lies buried under the city, it is necessary to circle back around to the Hollywood Cemetery. While generally mention of the cemetery evokes discussion about the beauty of the site and the importance of those who lie beneath, urban legends about the site reveal that even beauty and privilege can cause unease, can be read as sinister. The cemetery is supposed to be haunted. (What old cemetery is not?) Reports say that a vampire rises from the tomb marked W.W. Pool, and a statue of an iron dog that marks the grave of a young girl moves, barks, and even chases people. Other statues content themselves with crying, or turning their heads to watch passers-by. Most of the ghost stories are urban legends of the "my uncle Mike saw this" or "my boyfriend's roommate swears this is true" variety. The vampire story, which seems to be the most widespread of the supernatural tales, has deeper roots.

According to local urban legend expert Greg Maitland, the vampire story arose after the train tunnel collapse in 1925 scalded fireman Benjamin Mosby so badly than his skin was mostly burned off. Mosby crawled from the collapsed tunnel, was taken to the hospital, and later died. Cut to the current vampire story. In one version of the vampire story, the creature was first seen by Richmonders after the train tunnel collapse. After feeding on the workers trapped in the tunnel, it crawled out and ran away, although pursuers followed it to Hollywood Cemetery and the Pool tomb. Obviously, somehow the story of Mosby morphed into the story of the vampire. The description of the tragically burned Mosby matches the description of the horrific half-decomposed vampire, and both are described as crawling out of the collapsed tunnel. Maitland has a ready explanation; he says that "at the time, the saying 'going to Hollywood' meant that you were dying" (Curran 2003; see also Center for Paranormal Investigation and Research n.d.a, n.d.b). It is easy to see how the fireman's tragic end and gruesome appearance could remain a topic of conversation long enough for the phrase "he went to Hollywood" to lose its original meaning and connote something far more sinister. Yet it is interesting not just that Mosby has metamorphosed into a vampire, but that his identity has vanished. The creature who arises from the Pool tomb is now, in the more common versions of the tale, assumed to be Pool himself, one of the elite.[2] And so the eyewitness account of a worker mangled by the forces of progress has changed into a story about one of the elite who, not satisfied with the bounty that life gave him, still arises to suck the life-force from the ordinary citizens of the city.

The position of the elites of Hollywood is thus tenuous on the symbolic level; the hierarchy of power and privilege remain a source of unease, revealed in the metaphor of the undead predator. While their hold on the city's institutions remains secure, they do not triumph in the city's folklore; in the scary stories Richmonders tell each other, the elites morph into the Others.

In the semiotic field of Richmond's underground, then, things are not as they seem on the surface. Ostensibly, the treatment of the dead is a continuation of the treatment of the living; ostensibly that which is buried remains buried. In

---

2 Pool was reportedly a schoolteacher. The choice of his tomb as the vampire's lair would seem to have more to do with its particularly sinister appearance and less to do with Pool himself.

truth, forgotten remains are unearthed physically or metaphorically—or both—all the time, and excavation of the past invokes re-evaluation of the present. Formal burial practices, older memorials and restrictions on excavation reify the current power structure, but counter-narratives found in protests, new historical markers and folklore remind more privileged present-day inhabitants that privilege has a darker underside, that surface calm can hide unpleasant buried truths and smoldering resentments. ■

References

Alliance to Conserve Old Richmond Neighborhoods. n.d. Sellabration: Unearthing Richmond's slave history. Lumpkin's jail archaeological survey reveals significant artifacts. http://www.richmondneighborhoods.org/LumpkinJailSURVEYRESULTS6-06.html.

Center for Paranormal Investigation and Research. n.d.a. Hollywood cemetery in Richmond VA. http://virginiaghosts.com/hollywood_cemetery.php.

Center for Paranormal Investigation and Research. n.d.b. VGHRS: Strange creatures of the night: The Richmond Vampire. http://virginiaghosts.com/vampire_update.htm.

Curran, Colleen. 2003. Richmond's urban legends. http://www.richmond.com/news/output.aspx?Article_ID=2716539&Vertical_ID=155&tier=20&position=5 (accessed 31 October, 2003).

Defenders for Freedom, Justice and Equality. n.d. Sacred ground historical reclamation project. http://defendersfje.tripod.com/sacredgroundproject/.

Egerton, Douglas. 1993. *Gabriel's rebellion: The Virginia slave conspiracies of 1800 and 1802*. Chapel Hill: The University of North Carolina Press.

Fields, Barbara. 1990. Slavery, race, and ideology in the United States of America. *New Left Review* 181: 95–118.

Hollywood Cemetery. n.d. http://www.hollywoodcemetery.org/.

Holmberg, Mark. 2006a. Crawling into the belly of a Richmond legend. *Richmond Times Dispatch*, June 27. http://www.timesdispatch.com/servlet/Satellite?pagename=RTD/MGArticle/RTD_BasicArticle&c=MGArticle&cid=1149188762097.

Holmberg, Mark. 2006b. Mystique surrounds engine 231. *Richmond Times Dispatch*, June 28. http://www.timesdispatch.com/servlet/Satellite?pagename=RTD/MGArticle/RTD_BasicArticle&c=MGArticle&cid=1149188788849.

Holmberg, Mark. 2006c. A peek at a buried train, via scientific tunnel vision. *Richmond Times Dispatch*, August 9. http://www.timesdispatch.com/servlet/Satellite?pagename=RTD/MGArticle/RTD_BasicArticle&c=MGArticle&cid=1149189874719.

Holmberg, Mark. 2000. Legend gets some due. *Richmond Times Dispatch*, October 1, sec. B.

Hsu, Tiffany. 2006a. Camera finds flooded tunnel. *Richmond Times Dispatch*, July 14, sec. B.

Hsu, Tiffany. 2006b. Train stuck in time. *Richmond Times Dispatch*, June 27, sec. B.

Hsu, Tiffany. 2006c. Work halted on Church Hill Tunnel. *Richmond Times Dispatch*, July 18. http://www.timesdispatch.com/servlet/ Satellite?pagename=RTD/MGArticle/RTD_BasicArticle&c=MGArticle&c id=1149189216497.

Jones, Will. 2008. Experts aim to unearth slave jail site. *Richmond Times Dispatch*, June 4, sec. B.

Komp, Catherine. 2005. Stadium developers threaten historic slave-trade site. *New Standard News*, August 12. http://newstandardnews.net/content/index. cfm/items/2213.

Meola, Olympia. 2007. Local residents split over value of slavery apology. *Richmond Times Dispatch*, February 4, sec. A.

Museum of the Confederacy. n.d. Embattled emblem; Heritage violations August–September 1993; SCV resolution, slave whip. Richmond, VA: Museum of the Confederacy (Files accessed June–July 2001).

Richmond Public Library. n.d. The train in the tunnel. Newspaper clipping file. http://www.richmondpubliclibrary.org/rplresources/ncTrainTunnel.htm.

Richmond Times Dispatch. 1925a. Blames railway for mason death. October 17, sec. A.

Richmond Times Dispatch. 1925b. Continue digging in spite of rain. October 15, sec. A.

Richmond Times Dispatch. 1925c. Employ acetylene torch to release body of engineer. October 12, sec. A.

Richmond Times Dispatch. 1925d. Engineer's body recovered from C&O train. October 11, sec. A.

Richmond Times Dispatch. 1925e. Excavators find ancient subterranean prison here. October 2, sec. A.

Richmond Times Dispatch. 1925f. Fear additional slide of hill will halt rescue workers; Abandon hope of life in tunnel. October 4, sec. A.

Richmond Times Dispatch. 1925g. Fear of slide stops works of steam shovel. October 5, sec. A.

Richmond Times Dispatch. 1925h. Lateral tunnel work is started. October 9, sec. A.

Richmond Times Dispatch. 1925i. Many attend burial of fireman Mosby. October 6, sec. A.

Richmond Times Dispatch. 1925j. May reach bodies in tunnel tonight. October 10, sec. A.

Richmond Times Dispatch. 1925k. Rescuers near tragedy scene. October 8, sec. A.

Richmond Times Dispatch. 1925l. Son of engineer remains at tunnel which holds dad. October 6, sec. A.

Richmond Times Dispatch. 1925m. Take many hours to reach tunnel. October 7, sec A.

Richmond Times Dispatch. 1925n. Two men known to be dead; Two injured; Several others missing as tunnel caves in. October 3, sec. A.

Robertson, Gary. 2006. Archaeological survey set at former slave-sale site. *Richmond Times Dispatch*, April 1. http://www.timesdispatch.com/servlet/Sat ellite?pagename=RTD%2FMGArticle%2FRTD_BasicArticle&c=MGArticle &cid=1137835081866&path=!news&s=1045855934842.

Sidbury, James. 1997. *Ploughshares into swords: Race, rebellion, and identity in Gabriel's Virginia 1730–1810*. New York: Cambridge University Press.

Silver, Christopher. 1984. *Twentieth century Richmond*. Knoxville: The University of Tennessee Press.

Stevenson, Christopher M. 2008. Burial ground for negroes, Richmond, Virginia: Validation and assessment. http://www.news.vcu.edu/pdf/SlaveCemeteryReport.pdf.

Tyler-McGraw, Marie. 1994. *At the falls: Richmond, Virginia and its people*. Chapel Hill: The University of North Carolina Press.

Vannini, Phillip. 2007. Social semiotics and fieldwork: Method and analytics. *Qualitative Inquiry* 13: 113–40.

Virginia Historical Society. n.d. Richmond's buried train. http://www.vahistorical.org/news/richmondtunnel.htm.

Walker, Katherine. 2008. United, regardless, and a bit regretful: Confederate History Month, the slavery apology, and the failure of commemoration. *American Nineteenth Century History* 9: 315–38.

Walters, Brandon. 2006. Without a ballpark: What's next for Bottom? *Style Weekly*, February 8. http://styleweekly.com/article.asp?idarticle=11773.

Williams, Michael Paul. 2006. Excavators look for remnants of slave jail. *Richmond Times Dispatch*, April 4, sec. B.

Williams, Michael Paul. 2005. Mary Lumpkin. *Richmond Times Dispatch*, February 23, sec. B.

Yoder, Bruce. 2006. Into the Earth: From Lumpkin's Jail to a great harvest. http://www.richmond.com/religion/output.aspx?Article_ID=4199126&Vertical_ID=2&tier=1&position=3 (accessed April 7, 2006).

W

AUTHOR PROFILE

Katherine D. Walker earned a B.A. in Art History from the University of Virginia, an M.S. in sociology from Virginia Commonwealth University, and a Ph.D. in sociology from the University of Massachusetts, Amherst. She taught Focused Inquiry from 2007–2016. Currently, she is serving as the Director of Institutional Effectiveness and Research at Randolph-Macon College. "Buried in the Unremissive Ground" was originally published in *Social Semiotics* in December 2009.

Some Houses (Various Stages of Dissolve)

By Claire Vaye Watkins

Tecopa House

A miner's shack, expanded by our father before he was our father with whatever materials he could find. A Mojave valley, a wash, crumbly clay hills beyond. To the north a mound of ore with cacti and sage and horny toads all through it, so that it might be mistaken for a hill. Beyond the ore a plateau, a cemetery. At the pleat of plateau and ore, a spring: flaking iron water tank and a grove of bamboo. A garden, a parachute for shade, tented by a creosote-greased telephone pole. One planter box surrendered to any lizards or tortoises we caught, fed iceberg lettuce until they escaped. Horny toads we tagged with nail polish and cataloged in your diary that locked until our mom said they breathe through their skin and you're killing them. In fall Mom would open the front door and the back so randy tarantulas could migrate through. Green linoleum in the kitchen and once, a toddler, you practiced shaving with our dad's razor. I remember them holding you down, lots of red-black blood on the green floor. You remember me walking on a wall in front of the post office, playing Olympics. *Calif.* had just become *CA* but *–lif.* was still sun stamped on the block wall. I slipped and caught my chin. My blood red-orange in the noon sun. Later you watched them sew me up, nine black stitches ants along my jaw, makes my smile look sarcastic. A swamp cooler, Raggedy Ann and Andy bedding bought on layaway. You and me, naked, leaders of a small pack of dogs—Barry, Spike, and Garfield. A larger pack of coyotes beyond the near ridge, yipping, cackling, waiting. They got Garfield, then Barry, but not Spike and not us, not yet. Rattlesnakes came out at dawn and dusk, a bobcat in the bamboo up by the spring.

The Trailer School

A single-wide, grades K through six in one room, seven through twelve in the other. In between: two bathrooms and a drinking fountain. The only girl in my grade, but can that be true? Four of us, me, two white boys, and a Shoshone. Something had happened to one of the white boys as a baby and it made him slow, made his front top teeth four silver ingots, made his voice always hoarse. I had a bad singing voice too. For this reason he and I were put in a closet whenever the class sang. There, a seam of light allowed us to hear the music and me to stare privately at his teeth. I wanted them.

Fifth Wheel

The first boy I ever loved lived in a fifth wheel his father had parked on a friend's property. An accordion door, cupboards that latched. K's bed was also the dinner table. He wore poverty like a fashion statement: ripped jeans, wallet chains, boots with soles flapping open like laughter. He worked at KFC, his Dickies velvety with vegetable oil, smell of sweet batter when I pulled them down.

Malibu

Somersaults in a busted hot tub filled with water from a hose at a guesthouse in Trancas Canyon. Half-drained swimming pool a pit of frogs. A neighbor's house a giant barrel, another's a geodesic dome, flowers called birds of paradise that looked just like them, snails—their shells crunching, salt shrinking—the beach. Where our father went to die and did, while I was in the busted hot tub doing underwater somersaults and you were counting them.

Shoshone

In the back office at our mother's rock shop and museum, making banners from dot matrix printer paper, making bird's-nest crowns with the shred bin, coloring with highlighters, picking pomegranates from the tree outside, walking back into the wash, alkali soil crunch, a river that was sometimes there and sometimes not. Parents scolding their kids and our mother nicer to them than she often was to us, gave them TV rock or pyrite, which she never called fool's gold. It seemed we were alone forever, the three of us. Then suddenly we were not, you and I not allowed in her bed anymore, not allowed to drink the Mountain Dew not ours in the fridge, a hulking Igloo lunch box on top.

Ann Arbor

Now I live in a movie about college written by a high schooler. There are actual letter jackets, actual cheerleaders, actual frats. There is an actual quad flung with Frisbees and an actual grove strung with hammocks. In the fall the leaves are blown into actual piles, though I never jump in. All the things we grew up thinking were real only on TV are real in the Midwest: rain pouring down windows and making the house a submarine; leaves turning gold, maroon, purple; raccoons; mailmen strolling the sidewalk with satchels; snow enough for igloos. When you come to visit you point and say, Look! A squirrel!

Mom

She wasn't cruel but she made her decisions quickly. She said we three had the same hands, artist hands. She taught me painting and you photography. Even though we looked exactly alike she said you got her Dutch parts, her Indian parts. I got Dad's fun Irish, the mean English. She said we both got the crazy because it came from both sides. Confirmed, years later, when I told a psychiatrist a severely abridged version of our family history and he said "You're the reason they should do mental health screenings before marriage." Or years earlier, when you overheard your guidance counselor ask her colleague, "What kind of sixth-grader knows she is a lithium responder?"

Navajo House

Some rules: We could not call someone stupid. We could not say shut up. We could not answer the phone during dinner and never if the caller ID said UNKNOWN. If a person came to the door we were to sic the dogs on them.

Barney Road

In her trailer when they found her: dozens of try-me eyeglasses from Walmart, the antitheft sensors still on. A pack of six mail-order self-help cassettes

called *Depression and You*, tape number two missing, found later in the boom box in the bathroom. Books I had read in college and passed along, thinking they would heal her (*The House on Mango Street*, *Love Medicine*). Every episode of *Star Trek: The Next Generation* on VHS. Every episode of *The X-Files*. A coin stamped PAUL LOVES MARTHA, DISNEYLAND, 1989. An answering machine with neither of our voices on it.

Watkins Ranch

Now, years after both our parents are gone, a boy who'd been in the grade above us at the trailer school messages me online. No one is living in your house anymore, he says. E moved out. E, once our babysitter, had been paying our mother one hundred dollars a month to live in the Tecopa house, money Mom spent on cigarettes and ice cream and methadone. After Mom died, we said E could live in the Tecopa house for free, since you were in San Francisco and I was in the Midwest, moving every year, always in August, to another apartment or another college in another city or to live with a different man. Neither of us had much of an address. E herself had no phone, no Internet, no e-mail, so after Mom died we told someone to tell her that she could live in the Tecopa house as long as she liked, on the condition that we could come and visit the garden, where our pet tortoises had once lived, where our mother had scattered our father's ashes, and where we had scattered hers. But this messenger person was not very reliable, we knew even then, and there is a good chance that E never got the message and kept sending checks. But to where? And who would they be made out to? I wanted E to live in the Tecopa house for years and years, rent-free, until she died a peaceful, painless death, and we'd be some kind of filial for once, bring some sort of serenity to someone, if only when it was too late. (E's husband had already swallowed a shotgun in the shed, which had been our father's workshop.) I realize I want all this only when I receive my former classmate's message online. I'd never seen a deed or a mortgage or any other paperwork for the miner's shack, which my classmate generously called "the Watkins Ranch." Family yarns had my father squatting there, hiding from his past lives. My mother joined him, had us, we four trespassing on BLM land. Last summer I visited a friend of my parents and he told me this was more or less true. I tell the boy from the trailer school that the house does not belong to us, has never belonged to us, is *public land*, and that in my opinion my parents would have been honored to have it preserved and protected. "I think my parents would have been happy to see the property restored as public land and thereby contribute to the preservation of that beautiful desert." I say this despite that fact that my mother considered the Desert Protection Act a land grab, Diane Feinstein a carpetbagger. I say this though my former classmate needs a place to live and I could easily say, Go for it. I said this because at the time some rednecks were hunkered down at yet another a nature reserve, stroking their guns, trying to steal something that belongs to no one, and I thought maybe my former classmate sympathized with them, though I had no reason to believe this except that he'd stayed. In fact I knew nothing about him, had long ago erased him from my feed because the yowls from his difficult life interfered slightly with my enjoying my comfortable one. I never did get skeptical of the authority bestowed on me by being born first.

Tecopa House

It's possible that one day we will go back and it will have been bulldozed. Sometimes I wish for this. The shack or house or ranch, the screened porch, the parachute, the telephone pole and courtyard, all mangled, splintered in a dusty scrap pile. The spring run dry, the bamboo dead, the garden scraped away. Inevitably someone would come and throw tires and other garbage on the heap, maybe they'd spray-paint it, shoot it up, burn it. People do these things to desert ruins, you'll notice. Still, they tug us.

Lola Lane

Where we had, for a time, two pet donkeys. Mine was called Buckwheat, yours was called Spark. We kept them in the dog run, fed them sheaths of alfalfa from the farm at the end of the road. We got them one day when we were driving through the desert and we passed a house that Mom knew to be foreclosed, which she mentioned as we drove by. Behind the house we saw a pen, and in it two donkeys: one iconic brown, black cross of Bethlehem on its back, bristly Mohawk mane, the other entirely white. An albino. I didn't even know the word *foreclosed*, didn't even notice their ribs or the empty trough turned over in the pen, but you started howling and didn't stop until we brought them home. Then the brown one—Buckwheat—we took out for a ride. (The white one, not yet named, was skittish and mistrustful, would not tolerate mounting.) We walked Buckwheat into the desert and back again, a strange sound echoing over the hills as we walked. We returned and the sound had a source, the white donkey calling for her sister. When she saw Buckwheat, Spark leaped the fence. Atrophy and fear did not allow her grace—her hooves flinting the iron. And so she had her name. Everything of our childhood seems an allegory, you clamoring over an invisible fence after me, but it was also real. Real hooves, real sparks.

Navajo House

Each of us became immediately unhappy in that house and there were times when I considered it cursed. Everything seemed to change for the worse the moment we moved in. It was the first stick-built house we ever lived in, the first big house, a two-story, the style Mom described as Cape Cod. No insulation, instead a pigeon infestation. The sound of pigeons fucking day and night. Our stepfather an ex-felon, not permitted to have guns in the house, so Mom bought a pellet gun, sat in a lawn chair in the evenings, picked them off. You couldn't sleep there, had lava dreams, watched a lot of VH1. Our grandma bought you a porcelain doll and you were too gracious about it so she kept buying them, bought you more and more, one for every occasion, so your room filled with them—smooth glass heads, curls painted on, those drowsy eyelashes. I got into feng shui, broke the bad news: our front and back doors were perfectly aligned, inviting the worst kind of energy. The stairs were positioned in such a way that they shot all our blessings right out the front door. Open space upstairs but sound couldn't move through it. No one could hear anyone, ever, so by the time you got someone's attention you were already screaming.

Navajo House

Her hands began to shake there. One Christmas I waited for K to come pick me up (was it K?) and she said nonsense things to me, silly things she seemed to know were funny though not why, which amused me. I suppose she must have been in a great deal of pain—even now I cannot simply say: she was hurting. Cannot say: she was sick. She certainly was, but the question is with what? Addiction is one of those concepts I cannot recall learning. A notion I seem to have been born knowing. Others are depression, wife beating, molestation, the names for all the parts of my body. She taught us these because no one had taught them to her. She'd had to learn for herself, and told us when and where and how she'd learned, was learning. I knew addiction was a disease, cureless, though secretly I believed her cured, since she'd not had a drink—not even bananas flambéed in liqueur at the nice restaurant on Mother's Day—since I was maybe four years old. She was careful to never say she *used to be* an alcoholic. I always wanted her to—the present tense frightened me. I'd heard stories about when she drank, things she'd done to us when we were little, you protecting me, me protecting you, things neither of us remembered but which she confessed to anyway. For ten years she had cigarettes, coffee, work, gardening, petty fraud, making jewelry, making dinner. She was never still. She never played. I asked how come if people replaced one addiction with another like she said she couldn't just get addicted to playing with us? That's not how it works, she said. You can't get addicted to anything that's good for you.

Navajo House

Then suddenly she was very still. Hurting all over, she said, though no one could say why, meaning we waited too long. No one believed her, she said, and she was right. Lyme. Perhaps by then she was already her own doctor? (Most of it was out of pocket anyway.) She quit the museum or was fired, no one knew. The Navajo house filled with rocks, bared down on us, stick built with a brick-and-mortar mortgage. Our stepfather had been feeding his paychecks into slot machines, I learned when I asked him to fill out his portion of the FAFSA. The spring my classmates spent dropping out to have their babies and you spent raising our half sister I spent overexercising, baffled on the treadmill at how his tax returns said $100,000 per year and yet every day at lunch one of my girlfriends lent me two dollars so I could buy three Pizza Hut breadsticks or a seven-layer burrito. All the mail went into one massive drawer, unopened, envelopes white then yellow then pink. The phone rang and rang, we did not answer—the caller ID always said UNKNOWN. Soon there were morphine patches and a mortar and pestle so she could grind up her Oxy and snort it. Soon all the blankets and cushions had cigarette burns in them. She watched TV—*Star Trek: The Next Generation*, *The X-Files*, *Law & Order*—and we watched her fall asleep with a cigarette smoking between her fingers, caught the cigarette at the fabric's first singe but not before, for if she woke she'd accuse us of overreacting, of nagging, and we'd have no evidence to the contrary. Many mornings she did not wake up and on some of those she could not wake up. Often there were so many pills she still had some on her tongue in various stages of dissolve. We took turns waiting for the ambulance. We got to know the EMTs. One was a few years older than me, a friend of a friend, and did me the dignity of never acknowledging that we knew each other. I sometimes saw him at parties, sitting on old tires or tailgates, he and I the only ones not chugging Robitussin. He never let on that he'd carried my mother naked on a stretcher down our stairs on more than one occasion. And now I wonder and am often asked, how many occasions were there? So many that the emergency wore off. We called the ambulance and then argued who would wait for it, who had a test in first period, who had too many absences, whose teacher was more lenient and whose was a hardass. My first period was Drama 2. Yours was something hard, something you probably failed. Drama 2, Anatomy & Physiology, Civics, AP English. Volleyball and plays, answering the phones at Domino's pizza, lifeguarding and teaching swim lessons in the summer. She called her overdoses accidents. I believed her and you didn't, though you weren't unkind with your knowledge, allowed me some denial. So many years ago, when our father was dying, you'd been the one to tell me what dying meant. You'd explained permanence gently but exhaustively in the busted hot tub when I came up for air. So perhaps you thought you needn't explain it again. Still, it's a concept I struggle with.

Barney Road

One way to say all this is, Our mother was an addict and she overdosed.

Another way is, Our mother was suicidal and she killed herself.

Another way is, Our mother was poor and ignored and dismissed for years by doctors who put her on legal and extremely profitable heroin, which eventually killed her.

Another way is, Our mother needed help and no one, including us, gave it to her.

And yet you and I have loved each other and her and been loved by each other and by her in all these houses, through all these memories which were once moments, real and felt even if forgotten. We have loved and been loved despite the fissures and losses, violence, cruelty, smallness, timing, deficits in money and attention, despite the betrayals and indifferences, the distance and weather. Despite developing different definitions of certain words. *Death, expensive, cold.* Why, I wonder, or how? Because the little one was kind, pliant with forgiveness, because you absorbed my failings and defects, made them your grace. *There was not enough to go around.* Such a handy phrase to describe such mean circumstances.

Here is another:

I was born at a good time. ■

────────────────────────── AUTHOR PROFILE

Claire Vaye Watkins (b. 1984) grew up in the Mojave Desert and earned an MFA from Ohio State University. She is an assistant professor at the University of Michigan and runs the Mojave School, which provides Nevadan teenagers with free creative writing workshops. Watkins is the daughter of Paul Watkins, who was a member of the infamous Charles Manson "Family." Her prizewinning first collection of short stories, *Battleborn* (2012) deals in part with her father's legacy. *Battleborn* resulted in the National Book Foundation naming Watkins one of the 5 Best Writers Under 35 in 2012 and The New Yorker's heralding of a new genre: "Nevada Gothic." Watkins is also the author of 2015's *Gold Fame Citrus* and a Guggenheim Fellow. "Some Houses (Various Stages of Dissolve)" first appeared in John Freeman's edited volume, *Tales of Two Americas: Stories of Inequality in a Divided Nation* (2017).

Henrico Should Expand Mass Transit to Short Pump, and Here's Why

By Michael Paul Williams

Because civil rights and mass transit have historically been so intertwined, it's difficult to view any decision regarding the latter without considering race.

After all, the 1896 Plessy v. Ferguson ruling, in which the Supreme Court established the "separate but equal" doctrine, was about racially segregated passenger rail cars.

In Richmond—five decades before the Montgomery bus boycott made Rosa Parks and the Rev. Dr. Martin Luther King Jr. household names—John Mitchell Jr. led a boycott of Richmond's segregated electric trolley system.

Ultimately, in Richmond and elsewhere, the issue became not about where you sat on the bus but where it would take you—or wouldn't. When white residents and retail left our city for the suburbs, mass transit, for the most part, didn't follow.

In 1989, the Chesterfield County Board of Supervisors agreed to purchase half of what was then the Greater Richmond Transit Co., even though it has since demonstrated scant interest in expanding bus service into the county.

During a Q&A in 2007, Gerald P. McCarthy, then a member of the Commonwealth Transportation Board, told a Richmond Times-Dispatch reporter: "This is the largest metro area in the United States without a functioning regional transit system. We have a city transit system that has occasional buses going out beyond the city limits."

This is not a legacy to be proud of. But the Henrico County Board of Supervisors is taking steps to move forward.

During a weekend retreat, the board instructed county staff to include funding in the next budget to expand bus service to Short Pump.

This would not have happened if the board's composition had not switched from majority-Republican to majority-Democrat with the election of Courtney Lynch as the Brookland District supervisor.

County staff presented estimates showing that expanding GRTC's Route 19 to Short Pump—which now runs from downtown Richmond to the Costco at West Broad Street and Springfield Road—would cost about $800,000 annually.

That's not chump change. But it shouldn't be a deal breaker for a jurisdiction with an annual budget of nearly $1 billion.

It needs to be done.

Tyrone Nelson, supervisor for the Varina District, called Short Pump the county's "center of the universe." He sold it short. It's a retail hub of the entire region, with lots of jobs.

"The civil rights movement, the human rights movement, is always about fairness and looking at every human being as a whole being. When you look at it in the 21st century, what some of the challenges are, I think access is a challenge," Nelson said Monday. Greater access to Short Pump "could benefit thousands of people across the region and get them to what I call the service job epicenter."

John V. Moeser, emeritus professor of urban planning and studies at Virginia Commonwealth University, said "the civil rights movement, the post-World War II chapter of the civil rights movement, began with public transit."

He added: "Anyone who claims that the extension of public transit has no relationship whatsoever to race is living in a fantasy world."

In the wake of suburban growth in the Richmond region, he said, "there is no public transit going to the very area where the jobs are most plentiful. And it does become a civil rights issue when you have so many people of color kind of trapped in the central city, unable to get to the jobs, or when they do, it takes an enormous amount of time."

Ravi Perry, an associate professor of political science at VCU, said Virginia's legislative process and annexation policies, which effectively ended urban acquisition of the suburbs, enabled this inequity of mobility "and, we might say, sustained white flight." But the result has in some ways been self-defeating.

"You always want more access to your stores for both employees and consumers," said Perry, who added that it will be interesting to see whether companies with a stake in this decision "nod in some way their support of this (Henrico) changeover."

Perry said arguments that cite fiscal responsibility as a reason against bus service expansion should not exclude other variables.

In the limited reach of the region's mass transit, Perry likened the Richmond area to Detroit—a majority-black, economically challenged city surrounded by predominantly white, affluent suburbs. Such "economically disparate partners" can bring an entire region down, he said.

He also cited intangibles such as regional pride as an argument for more bus service.

"The city has a new changing identity every day with new students moving in every semester," he said. It has burgeoning residential and business development and a vibrant arts, culture and beer scene.

"We really have an opportunity to expand on that excitement," which is being fueled in part by people who live outside the city, he said.

Moeser echoed that, saying Richmond's resurgence—coupled with increasing diversity and poverty and more progressive shifts in the suburbs—has enhanced the climate for substantive regional efforts.

Perry also sees opportunity.

"Our history does not have boundaries, really," he said. Particularly on occasions like Martin Luther King Jr. Day, we should seize the opportunity to tear down boundaries in society, especially those "that have a real substantive effect on the lives of individuals."

King said the moral universe is long but bends toward justice. Let's hope there are fewer barriers and more mobility and opportunity around that curve. ■

──────────────────────────────── AUTHOR PROFILE

Michael Paul Williams is a columnist for the *Richmond Times-Dispatch*, the primary newspaper for Richmond and the state of Virginia. Williams is originally from Richmond; he graduated from Hermitage High School and attended Virginia Union University as an undergraduate. He received his Master's degree from Northwestern University. Since 1982, Williams has written for the *Richmond Times-Dispatch*, covering topics such as local politics, race, and culture. Williams has won awards such as the Will Rogers Humanitarian Award from the National Society of Newspaper Columnists, several Virginia Press Association Awards, and a Nieman Fellowship at Harvard University. This column, "Henrico Should Expand Mass Transit to Short Pump, and Here's Why" was originally published on January 15, 2018 in the *Richmond Times-Dispatch*.

W

STUDENT ESSAYS

A Bird Shouldn't Be Caged

By Yan Yun

1ST PLACE—NARRATIVE

2007: that was the start of my journey. I knew if I didn't leave then, I never would. Some say that a journey begins with a small step forward or a foot in the right direction. I didn't have either of those options. I had to take a huge leap, and it was now or never.

I lived 1,200 miles away from the prosperous east coast of China. I lived in northwest China, way west. My city, Lanzhou, was surrounded by miles and miles of mountains that were rugged and bare. Life there was very slow, and it was considered more of an underdeveloped area of China, when it came to economy. Growing up, I learned that the ideal job would be working for the government or a government-owned factory because it's stable and secure. We called these kinds of jobs "Iron Rice Bowls." During good times or bad times, like an iron bowl, your position with the company was stable and would never break. Most of these jobs themselves were monotonous, but once you got in, you would never need to worry about losing your position. That type of job was my mom's wish for me, too.

I finished high school that summer. I had never set a foot outside my city. I was so eager to get out that I felt like I wouldn't want to stop till I reached the other side of the earth. I decided to apply for a college on the east coast. I knew my mom wouldn't approve, but I was determined.

"Are you kidding me?! You don't know what's best for you!" Mom shouted, frustration visible all over her face. I told her I'd made my decision. She intently glared at me and continued, "It's gonna be quite inconvenient for you to come home. It's a twenty-four-hour train ride one-way!"

I tried to look away. I surveyed the room around me and my eyes caught the windows. I stared at those windows every night growing up, wishing one day I would have a different view when I went to bed. I gently said, "I wanna see what's going on out there, Mom. I need to go."

"Lili and Rong chose to stay! All the other neighbors I spoke with said their children decided to stay. They will have a strong support system here. They will be able to go home every weekend and all holidays, even the short ones."

"I know. But that's them; I am me."

Mom couldn't understand why I had to attend college half-way across China. Like most traditional Chinese parents, she wanted to keep her child by her side. Her generation went through the toughest times, The Great Chinese Famine and the Culture Revolution. Things had gotten much better since then, but she had never been able to feel secure and she hated to hear words like "risk" or "challenge."

A majority of children in my generation are the only child in their family under the "One Child Policy," and we are truly the apple in our parents' eyes.

They live for us. They don't feel a sense of "freedom, finally!" when the only child they have goes off to college or moves away for a new job. Instead, it's a feeling of complete hollowness, of being alone with no company. I've heard too many stories of children sacrificing their dreams and remaining at home with their parents because they felt bad leaving them all by themselves.

"Have I done something so wrong that you have to go to the other side of China just to avoid me? I gave you everything! And that's how you pay me back?! Tell me why, why?!" My mom's frustration turned into anger. "Have you thought about us? What are we gonna do when you are gone?"

"I don't want to stay here! This town is such a boring and hopeless place and I am counting down the days till I can get outta here and begin to see the world. I've lived here for twenty years and every day has been the same! I just don't wanna be stuck here for the rest of my life," I paused, "like you are."

As soon as I said it, I regretted those last words. I could taste the bitterness on my lips. I uneasily shifted my eyes and stared at the floor. But I didn't say sorry. I didn't say anything.

She froze and wearily turned away and gazed off into the distance.

As time went by, I drifted further and further away from home. Ten years later, I am on the other side of the earth, with a twelve-hour time difference and ten thousand miles between us. I'm glad that I am able to talk to her frequently, thanks to technology.

As I grew older, the guilt of my being absent finally caught up with me. I often wondered how she got through those first few years without me, day in and day out. Every time I went back home to visit, she was always in tears when she saw me.

I remember a book I came across a few years ago. It was titled *Kahlil Gibran's Poems*, and to this day I can still clearly remember those lines, "Your children are not your children, they are the sons and daughters of Life's longing for itself. They come through you but not from you, and though they are with you, yet they belong not to you." My eyes swell up and wet every time I read those words. I doubt that my mom would ever understand "love is in the letting go." Or maybe she did, but she just didn't want to lose her sweet, precious baby. I wonder if I will feel the same when I am a mom and when it's time for my children to leave home, to leave me, to end our journey together and begin their own. ■

STUDENT PROFILE

Yan Yun is a transfer student from China at VCU, currently majoring in Marketing. She wrote "A Bird Shouldn't Be Caged" for UNIV 111 in the 2017 fall semester. This essay is based on her own life experiences.

A Seat at the Table

By Myia Samuels

2ND PLACE—NARRATIVE

I stand in line behind a woman wearing a long, green dress. Glancing up at her, I can see she has on a large church hat that blocks me from seeing her entire face. She does not seem familiar. I look around at everyone in the room. Some of the people here I have never met before in my five years of life. Neither their voices nor their laughter are recognizable. It seems like there are new faces here every week. I hear an old woman singing melodically at her table as she waits for someone to bring her a plate of food. I notice a man with an unshaven face and worn out shoes. I do not know these people, yet there we are, sharing a meal together.

I look up and find a familiar face. My grandfather, dressed in his red and white striped candy cane suit, gives me a big smile and squeezes my tiny hand. The service has just finished, and everyone around us is talking and laughing. A few people are even singing along to the slow gospel music quietly playing in the background.

Stepping forward in the line, I scan the room again in search of another new face. This time, I see people that were not even here for the church service. Why are they here? Where are their fancy church clothes? My parents have always told me to dress nicely when we go to church, but if it were up to me, I would come in my princess PJ's. I quickly take note of their appearance, but I do not stare for too long because my mother tells me it is rude to do so.

An older woman, dressed in a weathered t-shirt and leggings, approaches my grandfather and me. She speaks with a shaky voice. "I just wanted to say thank you, Pastor, for your words today. I've never gone to church before now, but I really enjoyed the service." This happened quite often; people always approached my grandfather to "thank him for his words." At that age, I did not fully understand their importance. The woman looks down and smiles at me, then my grandfather. I notice she is missing some teeth.

My grandfather simply smiles back, thanks her, and then grabs her hands. "Did you get your food? Have you eaten yet?" he asks. He would always make sure that everyone around him was helped. She shakes her head no and joins the line.

I finally get my small plate of food and sit with my grandfather at a table. My parents are sitting further down, talking with other adults. I look again at the strangers in the room. They aren't wearing their best church clothes, don't have on fancy shoes, and some of them were not even here for the sermon. However, they are still sitting and eating with everyone else. Why are they here? And why does this seem to happen every week? Am I the only one that notices this?

At that time, I did not take into consideration that some of these unfamiliar people just didn't have nice church clothes. I did not realize this meal they received might be the only meal they have that day.

As lunch begins to end, I see people standing up to get another serving of food. I notice the same man with worn out shoes grabbing foil to cover his second meal before walking out of the church doors. He reminds me of another man I once saw outside of a small bodega; he was homeless and asking shoppers for spare change. I throw away my empty plate and sit back down next to my grandfather.

"Grandpa, why are people leaving with plates?" I ask him quietly, afraid that someone else will hear me.

"So they can eat it later," he plainly responds.

"Are we going to leave with plates?"

My grandfather softly laughs. "Of course not, silly. *You're* gonna cook dinner for us!" He taps me on my nose. I giggle loudly and move his hand away.

I watch as other people continue to leave the church with a plate in their hands. There is something similar about all of them. They don't have gaudy or lavish church outfits like the people still sitting down and talking.

I begin to think. We aren't taking plates home because my mom will be cooking dinner for my family and me. Do the people taking meals not have someone to cook for them? Are they homeless, like the man outside the bodega? They must be: why else would they be here?

I look at my grandfather and smile. Obviously, he knows they are homeless, and he wants to help them. Even if they are not here for religion, he makes sure they are taken care of and well fed. At such a young age, I learned that no matter who you are, whether you have nice clothes or not, you still deserve a seat at the table. ■

STUDENT PROFILE

Myia Samuels is currently a first-year student at VCU, majoring in Political Science with a concentration in International Relations. She composed "A Seat at the Table" for UNIV 111 in the fall of 2017. Her interests include volunteering and advocating for human rights.

Ignorance as a Theme in the Works of Butler, Bechdel, DeGhett, and Dillard

By Chloe Gardner

1ST PLACE—ANALYSIS/SYNTHESIS

The phrase "ignorance is bliss" is often used without much thought in day-to-day life. Looking closer into the saying, however, causes some intrigue. The word "ignorance" is most commonly used with a negative connotation, yet is associated with the undeniably positive word "bliss." Four different works all share varying themes within the topic of ignorance. When placed together, the passages provide more insight than they ever could alone. "Bloodchild" by Octavia Butler begins the conversation with two conflicting views about ignorance; Alison Bechdel's *Fun Home* weighs in specifically on how childhood innocence prefaces adult understanding; and "The War Photo No One Would Publish" by Torie Rose DeGhett criticizes the unawareness caused by censorship. Finally, "Living Like Weasels" by Annie Dillard ends the conversation with a twist by presenting an entirely different opinion. All in all, the interaction between these texts sheds light on how ignorance is treated by humanity as a whole.

The short story "Bloodchild" by Octavia Butler is a fascinating science fiction narrative that when delved into reveals a treasure trove of hidden meaning about rape culture and reproductive rights. The distress a woman may feel over not having control of her own body is shown, surprisingly, in a male character. The protagonist, Gan, expresses this distress to the alien parasite that will impregnate him with her eggs: "No one ever asks us.…You never asked me" (p. 121). Although the feminist undertones in the story are important, evidencing the passage's complexity is the fact that many more themes can be pulled from "Bloodchild." The story carries strong messages about ignorance, specifically two conflicting ideas: one, that people should be protected from disturbing truths for their own good, and the other, that people have the right to know these truths. These two beliefs are each embodied by a character. T'Gatoi, an alien also known as a Tlic, represents the former while Gan, her human host, represents the latter. Their conflicting views form an interesting duet within the story, culminating in the conversation they have as T'Gatoi is impregnating Gan with her eggs. On the topic of witnessing a Tlic birth, T'Gatoi says, "Terrans [humans] should be protected from seeing" (p. 124). In response, Gan expresses to T'Gatoi that humans should be educated about the Tlic birthing process. He thinks that ignorance leads only to more fear. He says, "Not protected … Shown. Shown when we're young kids, and shown more than once" (p. 124). Therefore, he asserts his belief that ignorance has an overall negative effect on a group of people. Ultimately, Butler's beliefs align with Gan, as evidenced by the fact that the text allows the reader to empathize with his situation more so than that of T'Gatoi.

Another text that deals with the topic of ignorance is a selection from *Fun Home* by Alison Bechdel. The autobiographical graphic novel discusses themes of family and sexuality as well as the nature of innocence giving way to understanding as a person grows up. In response to Butler's argument on ignorance, Bechdel takes a more ambiguous stance. One of the main instances of ignorance in the work is that of the Bechdel children in regard to their father's closeted homosexuality. At such a young age, the kids had no way of knowing that their father was gay. At the same time, however, Bechdel expresses that she had some awareness that he was different from most men. For example, she says, "I measured my father against the grimy deer hunters at the gas station uptown, with their yellow workboots and shorn-sheep haircuts" (p. 73). In this situation, Butler would have suggested educating young Alison on the topic. Perhaps, if their father had come out and explained his sexuality to her, a closer understanding would have developed between parent and child. This possibility is strengthened by the fact that even after his death, Alison Bechdel still feels a connection to her father over the fact that both are gay. She says, "Perhaps I identify too well with my father's illicit awe" (p. 77). This quote shows that, as a lesbian, Bechdel can relate to her father's feelings and experiences. However, Bechdel as a child may not have been able to form the same connection. A younger Alison would have had no "illicit awe," and furthermore would have been distressed at the discovery of her father's affairs. Therefore, Bechdel does not regret her childhood ignorance, although she does mourn the fact that her relationship with her father was strained by the lack of understanding between them. Overall, Bechdel's response to Butler is that natural ignorance in children does well to shield them, but at some point in life a person should learn to face the truths that a child would not understand.

"The War Photo No One Would Publish" by Torie Rose DeGhett takes a similar stance on the theme of ignorance. The central argument of the text is that the media should not censor graphic images of war. DeGhett believes that American citizens must take responsibility for the country's actions instead of remaining blissfully ignorant. In response to Bechdel's argument, DeGhett agrees that children have a right to be protected from difficult topics. Both *Life* and *Time* magazines, for example, are cited in the text as refusing to publish a disturbing photo due to their large child audiences. DeGhett quotes a managing editor reacting, "'*Time* is a family magazine,'" as photo directors pressured him to publish the picture (Muller, qtd. in DeGhett, p. 163). The problem, in DeGhett's eyes, starts when adults are ignorant—sometimes willfully so—of reality. Not only do grown people have the right to knowledge as Bechdel believes, they have a duty to be informed of the consequences of their country's actions. Furthermore, in comparing "The War Photo No One Would Publish" to "Bloodchild," a parallel can be drawn between two dominating forces capable of controlling the public's intake of information. The American media and T'Gatoi both wish to use ignorance to protect people from a gruesome reality. Both parties, however, are presented as morally questionable, and may even have ulterior motives. T'Gatoi wants the human population to remain docile for the benefit of her kind, and the media wants

1

to support the military's deceptively bloodless way of displaying the Gulf War to the public. Butler and DeGhett agree that this form of "protection" is immoral. For example, DeGhett says that "shielding the public from the messy, imprecise consequences of a war" can make the media coverage "incomplete, and even deceptive" (p. 157). In contrast to Butler's argument, though, DeGhett believes that the people share partial accountability for their own ignorance. In some cases, American citizens remain ignorant not only because of media bias, but because they do not want to face difficult truths. DeGhett calls for Americans to assume some responsibility for the actions of the military, and the argument culminates in the last line: "'If we're big enough to fight a war, we should be big enough to look at it'" (Jarecke, qtd. in DeGhett, p. 164).

Lastly, the reading "Living Like Weasels" by Annie Dillard presents a view that contradicts the other three. The main point of the narrative is that people should live more simply and yield to a singular purpose. Dillard finds a certain beauty in the single-mindedness and drive of the weasel, and longs to lead a similar life herself. Her view on ignorance, surprisingly, is a positive one, and an inverse to that of Bechdel. She says, "I might learn something of mindlessness, something of the purity of living in the physical sense and the dignity of living without bias or motive" (p. 170). While Bechdel believes in the natural shift from ignorance to understanding as a person grows, Dillard wishes to regress from human knowledge into an animal-like state. Although she and DeGhett share the idea that ignorance is easier on a person than knowledge, Dillard believes that being unaware of global happenings is actually beneficial. Here, their stances ultimately diverge. DeGhett thinks that being educated is the duty and right of the people whereas Dillard instead values the lack of thinking.

Finally, the themes of ignorance in "Living Like Weasels" relate uniquely to those in "Bloodchild." One character in particular stands out. Qui, Gan's brother, serves as his foil in the story. Just like Dillard, Qui yearns not for knowledge, but for oblivion. Because he knows that escape from the Tlic is futile, he focuses solely on self-preservation and ingests any of the intoxicating Tlic eggs he can get his hands on to help him forget. Qui's behavior, however, is portrayed as unhealthy. Gan even observes that Qui can never truly escape reality until he dies: "That's Qui's 'away.' I wonder if he knows" (p. 125). The natures in which Dillard and Qui strive for ignorance are two sides of the same coin. Where Dillard is driven, Qui is directionless. Where Dillard is searching for reality in its simplest form, Qui is only running away. Overall, even when compared with a character who shares similar ideas, the stance presented in "Living Like Weasels" remains unique.

Through all the twists and turns in the conversation between these texts, one thing becomes apparent. All of the authors, to some degree, wish for ignorance themselves. At the core of the argument is a deep yearning for something simpler. Do we not all, sometimes at least, wish to escape from reality? Humanity as a whole, despite searching constantly for meaning and understanding in life, seems to regard ignorance with some longing. Even those who frown upon ignorance use the phrase "ignorance is bliss." This deep dissatisfaction with the complexity of life is uniquely human. We cannot simply exist without thought and rely on instinct. We seek escape through drugs, alcohol, or anything else that may bring temporary relief. In Greek mythology, Prometheus is credited for bringing the gift of fire, and therefore knowledge, to mankind. But fire can burn, and all great gifts come with a price. ■

References

Bechdel, A. (2017). Selection from *Fun Home*. In *Focused Inquiry. True Stories: Narrative & Understanding* (pp. 66–84). Plymouth, MI: Hayden-McNeil. (Original work published 2006)

Butler, O. (2017). Bloodchild. In *Focused Inquiry. True Stories: Narrative & Understanding* (pp. 111–125). Plymouth, MI: Hayden-McNeil. (Original work published 1984)

DeGhett, T. (2017). The war photo no one would publish. In *Focused Inquiry. True Stories: Narrative & Understanding* (pp. 157–164). Plymouth, MI: Hayden-McNeil. (Original work published 2014)

Dillard, A. (2017). Living like weasels. In *Focused Inquiry. True Stories: Narrative & Understanding* (pp. 168–171). Plymouth, MI: Hayden-McNeil. (Original work published 1982)

STUDENT PROFILE

Chloe Gardner is currently a second-year art student at VCU, majoring in Craft and Material Studies. She enjoys knitting, collecting, participating in the LGBT community, and appreciating local flora and fauna.

It's a White Man's World: Institutional Racism Is Real

By Nana Afia Twumasi-Ankrah

2ND PLACE—ANALYSIS/SYNTHESIS

Despite its geographical prominence on most world maps, numerous conventional beliefs regarding Africa are rooted in negativity. In his article entitled "Africa's Tarnished Name," Chinua Achebe discusses the causes of these adverse viewpoints on the continent. African American author Ta-Nehisi Coates expounds on the topic in his article "Acting French" by explaining how said negative perceptions of Africa wrongfully influence social attitudes towards African Americans. Additionally, *New York Times* author Timothy Williams addresses the reality and frequency of institutional racism in America in his article "A Persistent Case in Ferguson Raises Doubts on Reform." In doing so, all three writers denounce the conventional belief that mental and physical incapability functions as the primary cause of black disadvantage. Rather, they argue that social practices such as institutional racism and overall negative attitudes towards black people bear the blame for current social divisions between black individuals and their white peers.

Many negative views regarding African Americans stem from pro-slavery movements that began several centuries ago. Chinua Achebe defines this dissemination of "derogatory images" portraying Africa in a negative light as the cause of unfavorable contemporary perceptions of blacks (13). During the imperialist period, proponents of the slave-trade began producing literary texts that painted Africa and its inhabitants as "gyrating and babbling savages" in desperate need of European intervention and ideology (Achebe 18). The modern products of these efforts take form in the existence of numerous false stereotypes crediting black misfortune to an intrinsic lack of intelligence and motivation. Ta-Nehisi Coates rejects this notion by emphasizing the negative influence that false stereotypes can have on academic and economic advancement amongst blacks (128). In his article, Coates argues that the presence of various social constraints such as institutional racism and blatant racial inequality obstruct the ability for African Americans to advance further in society.

While institutional racism makes one leg of the issue, black disadvantage makes up the other. Coates implicitly defines black disadvantage as societally imposed obstacles that people of color must overcome to match their white counterparts in status. To illustrate the social divide between black and white Americans, Coates writes: "a white family born into the lower middle class can expect to live around a critical mass of people who are more affluent or worldly… [while a] black family with a middle-class salary can expect to live around a critical mass of poor people" (128). Through their respective articles, Achebe and Coates define the extensive influence the white majority possesses in both building and enforcing its social constructs upon the colored minority. This obvious emphasis on the white majority gives way to the social exclusion of minorities who feel neglected in a world that caters so heavily to those of European descent. Consequently, the pervasiveness of institutional racism occurs.

The Oxford Living Dictionary defines systematic or "institutionalized racism" as "racial discrimination that has become established as normal behavior within a society or organization." Regardless of growing public awareness of systematic or institutional racism, many continue to regard the issue as a rather latent concept—lacking legitimate evidence supporting its consistent practice. Timothy Williams provides conclusive evidence of the practice of systematic racism within the town of Ferguson, Mississippi. Ferguson gained a lot of media attention in 2014 upon the death of Michael Brown, an African American youth, at the hands of a white police officer. The death of Brown launched numerous discussions concerning race and discrimination. Williams summarizes the town's long history of "routine civil rights violations" against African Americans in his article. The story of Ferguson clearly illustrates the permanence of not just institutional racism, but racial injustice as well. Ferguson functions as a distillation of race issues in America today.

Acts of institutional racism and discrimination dominate numerous parts of America. The decision by Ferguson's white police officers to target African Americans as victims of their prejudice illustrates the survival of outdated racist ideals in modern society. Coates, too, captures the prevalence of institutional racism by defining the numerous inequalities that exist between black and white Americans. He states that the great difference in lifestyles between working-class white and black Americans, translates also into education (Coates, 127–128). Coates explains his belief by stating that the idea of educating black children under the primary intention of "impressing" their white counterparts, is a habit rooted in the belief of white supremacy (128). Achebe explains the origin of this practice when he writes "the alleged tendency of [blacks] to offer worship to any European who comes along is another favorite theme in European writing about Africa" (17). The notion that African Americans must stay in their marginalized lanes and simply cater to the sensibilities of their white peers continues to plague entire towns and populations in present day America. Despite describing many of the reforms taking place in Mississippi, Williams closes with a reflection from a former member of the Ferguson Commission: "It is a reminder of how slow the pace of freedom can be, and ultimately, how deeply entrenched the systems [the people of Ferguson] are fighting are" (Packnett, qtd. in Williams, par. 48). Coates concludes that to restrict the spread of racism, a bipartisan effort must take place. Not only must the African American community stop subscribing to deprecating ideals of subservience, but white Americans must begin growing cognizant of the racial inequalities that continue to exist today (132).

To gain awareness of various racially questionable issues, one must grow socially and racially aware. While Williams' article illustrates a relatively extreme example of institutional racism, the practice takes numerous forms that yield both minor and major consequences if not recognized and quickly acted against. Towards the end of his article, Achebe discusses a PBS documentary where cameras film a black woman giving birth in an unnecessarily graphic manner. Achebe explains that the choice of a black subject in the filming of the documentary exemplifies the prevalence of indeliberate racism. He writes, "[while] Race is no longer a visible presence in the boardroom…it may lie, unseen, in our subconscious" (21). Achebe's subsequent request for people to become more conscious of race to avoid "committing grave injustices absentmindedly" brings direct light to the subject of institutionalized racism (21). In citing the story of the pregnant woman, Achebe attacks the relative ease the show's producers possess in exposing the woman in such an undignified manner. In the writer's viewpoint, the objectification of the woman—while for scientific reasons—enforces racist ideals that may trigger images of black subjugation and dehumanization within a race-conscious individual. Using the example of the black mother, Achebe demonstrates the importance of racial sensitivity in identifying even the most understated acts of racism.

For years, the stereotypes that were used to characterize and denigrate African American males centered around violent acts, criminal behavior, lack of intelligence, and drug use, among many others. The proliferation and continuing endurance of these slanted views of African Americans function as the causes of racial discrimination today. While many debates continue to arise regarding the validity of institutional racism, the facts show evidence of severe injustices occurring in modern American society rooted in racism. While many of these beliefs hold some historical origin for their existence, no viable reasons exist for their perpetuation. Achebe, Williams, and Coates all recognized this fact and as a result sought to amend these beliefs by questioning the purpose for their existence through their texts. Conventional axioms may seem rather trivial, but people must realize the role they play in shaping the society they live in. The process of bringing change requires transforming public opinion. However lengthy or difficult the process, the quality of life for future generations hangs in the balance. ■

Works Cited

Achebe, Chinua. "Africa's Tarnished Name." *Focused Inquiry True Stories: Narrative & Understanding*, Hayden-McNeil, 2017, pp. 12–21.

Coates, Ta-Nehesi. "Acting French." *Focused Inquiry True Stories: Narrative & Understanding*, Hayden-McNeil, 2017, pp. 126–132.

"Institutional Racism." *Oxford Living Dictionaries*, 2018, oxforddictionaries.com/definition/institutional_racism. Accessed 16 Oct. 2017.

Williams, Timothy. "A Persistent Case in Ferguson Raises Doubts About Reform." *The New York Times*, 4 September 2017, nytimes.com/2017/09/04/us/ferguson-watson-brown.html. Accessed 16 Oct. 2017.

STUDENT PROFILE

Nana Afia Twumasi-Ankrah is a first-year student at VCU. She is a Bioinformatics major with a concentration in biology and genomics. She wrote "It's a White Man's World: Institutional Racism Is Real" for her UNIV 112 class last fall (2017). She likes spending time with her family and her research interests are based in public health, genomics, and epidemiology.

Philanthropy Catastrophe: An Ethical Discussion of Philanthropy in the Virginia Museum of Fine Arts

By Theresa Castellucci

1ST PLACE—RESEARCHED ARGUMENT

Tucked away from North Boulevard's traffic and bustle, behind the gleaming silver building that is the Virginia Museum of Fine Arts (VMFA), the E. Claiborne Robins sculpture garden exists as a little wonderland. Red glass reeds stand tall in a pond of colorful koi. A head sculpture larger than life towers over the garden, like a giant with a soft disposition whose expression changes as you move. They call her Chloe. Inside the museum, a glowing fireball hovers above the spacious atrium. Through the corridors and gallery spaces lie wondrous works from Andy Warhol to the Terracotta Army of the Qin dynasty. On any given day, an amalgamation of museum-goers finds a place of refuge and discovery within the cool atmosphere of the galleries.

The museum has always been free to the public. Special exhibition tickets can cost around ten dollars, but almost the whole museum is accessible to everyone. Littered throughout these galleries are various names of generous benefactors that keep the museum open with no admission fee. The Robins sculpture garden, McGlothlin Gallery, and Gans Gallery are a few examples of philanthropic contributions to the museum. However, the stories behind these names run deeper than their engravement on gallery walls.

E. Claiborne Robins, Jr. was president of the A. H. Robins Company, a pharmaceutical company located in Richmond, Virginia. Initially, the company was called A. H. Robins Apothecary, started by E. Claiborne's grandfather in 1866, and passed down through many generations. In the 1970s, when Robins was vice president of the pharmaceutical division, the company acquired a product from the Dalkon Corporation called the Dalkon Shield. The Robins company marketed this contraceptive intrauterine device as a safer alternative to birth control pills (Stoner, 2008). More than 300,000 lawsuits were filed against the company and almost 200,000 women reported injuries from this device, which caused severe pelvic infections resulting in infertility and even death. A survey by the Center for Disease Control (CDC) reported five device-related fatalities from pelvic infections. However, the CDC also estimates that about one million women a year develop a pelvic inflammatory disease. Although the claims against the Robins company are staggering, several other factors can lead to such a disease besides the Dalkon Shield itself (Kolata, 1987).

The Robins Gallery is not the only gallery at the VMFA funded by questionable means. The McGlothlin Gallery's benefactor, James W. McGlothlin, served as the Chairman/CEO and is now the sole owner of The United Company, a company which operates in oil and gas development as well as coal mining and supply ("About the McGlothlins," 2017). The Gans Gallery is funded by Rita and Jerome Gans: Mr. Gans works to build power plants (Moonan, 2007). Both families' businesses capitalize on practices that are threatening the health of our planet; coal mining and emissions from power plants release harmful carbon dioxide gas, rising levels of which are responsible for climate change (Shapley, 2010).

These factors are cause for alarm and, consequently, they raise an ethical dilemma. The beautiful gallery spaces in the VMFA are made possible only by some of the ugliest money-making practices that the museum is not blind to. In fact, there is a suggestion that the VMFA is attempting to address this dilemma: the museum is considering introducing a new admission policy. Instead of taking money from philanthropists, the museum would instill a twenty-five dollar general admission fee. However, this exacerbates the ethical dilemma presented by philanthropy. The addition of an entry fee would significantly lower the number of children, seniors on fixed incomes, and lower-income families that could enjoy the museum. This is where an opportunity for the discussion of the ethics of philanthropy arises. According to "A Framework for Ethical Decision Making," an article by the Markkula Center for Applied Ethics (2009), a situation can be analyzed by means of five ethical standards. The predicament at the VMFA is cause for a discussion including three prominent ethical standards.

The first of these standards is the utilitarian approach, which emphasizes that the most ethical choice is the one that produces the greatest balance of good over harm. Many of the grievances caused by Robins, Gans, and McGlothin happened in the past. Due to this, ceasing philanthropic donations would only ease the minds of museum curators, not amend any actual wrongs of the benefactors. An entry fee would significantly limit the educational benefits the museum provides, ultimately causing more harm than good. However, supporting such galleries delegitimizes those individuals who were negatively affected by these philanthropists' actions, as supporting a gallery indirectly supports the benefactor. Thus, from a utilitarian perspective, it seems that having no entry fee does more harm than good. In applying these standards for ethical reasoning, it is clear that each standard presents its own complications.

The fairness or justice approach emphasizes that all equals should be treated equally. Through this perspective, charging an entry fee treats lower-income individuals unfairly. If all are equal then anyone who wants to go to the museum should be able to, regardless of their financial status. On the contrary, it is not fair to glorify philanthropists for their donations when their wealth was built immorally.

The virtue approach furthers this ethical controversy. This approach makes recommendations according to the highest standard of human character. In this situation, charging an entry fee for the VMFA would seem most logical. By not supporting philanthropists who have wronged thousands of people, we, in turn, cleanse ourselves of their injustices. However, alienating low-income individuals from the museum is also unjust, as restricting public services based on financial status is fundamentally unfair.

As of late, philanthropy is a popular topic of controversy. *The New Yorker* recently published an article titled "The Family that Built an Empire of Pain" by Patrick Keefe (2017). Keefe discusses the Sackler family, who are almost solely responsible for the opioid crisis sweeping America. Their privately owned pharmaceutical company, Purdue Pharma, facilitated the manufacture and sale of Oxycontin, a severely addictive opioid. Millions of Americans suffer from addiction because of the aggressive marketing campaign that promoted sales and prescription of Oxycontin. The family also donates lavishly to numerous museums and universities such as The Metropolitan Museum of Art, The Guggenheim, The Louvre, and The Sackler Center for Arts Education at Harvard. Although their contributions have increased opportunities for art education, their wealth was built on a deception that has wrecked a multitude of lives.

Although philanthropists at the VMFA have not committed crimes on this scale, *The New Yorker* article makes evident that many philanthropists go unpunished and are glorified no matter how monstrous their practices were. Should the VMFA continue this trend of ignorance? If the residents of Richmond refuse to acknowledge these grievances, does that mean they will continue to overlook other evils?

Not all philanthropy is rooted in corruption. An article published by Sean Parnell, "In Defense of Philanthropic Freedom" (2017), gives examples of how philanthropy has made unparalleled positive impacts on society. The NAACP wouldn't exist if it weren't for a few generous philanthropists who helped jumpstart the agency. Parnell argues that philanthropists give the public a greater voice in society, as their contributions often reflect the priorities and perspectives of what Americans value. Although Parnell isn't wrong in his claims, he fails to mention the fact that many public institutions are funded through corrupt or immoral means. This alone does not diminish the value of what the public can gain from these privately funded institutions, but it does significantly change the context in which we view them.

As a resident in the Richmond area, I have come to love the VMFA and all it provides. I have never seen a museum more cherished or well loved. Many museums in big cities feel impersonal and crowded, but the intimate galleries and sculpture garden fit perfectly in this city. In learning the background of the galleries, albeit one of corruption and faults, I have found there is a price to everything we love. It is often a hard truth we have to surpass in order to hold true to our beliefs. I have never seen anything affect an individual the way art does. There is nothing as personal or inspiring as seeing an artwork that leaves you breathless. It can change the way we view the world, and how we interact with people in it.

Through the ethical dilemmas I have studied, I considered these issues of philanthropy in a new light. Initially, it seemed as though the misconduct and crimes that the museum was made of were too heinous to ignore. Charging an entry fee would rid the museum of the stain these philanthropists have left, and it seemed that each of the ethical standards could be viewed in a light that made this the best ethical choice. But I recognize the huge impact art has on the Richmond

community. There are many low-income workers and families here, especially in the areas nearby the museum. The VMFA serves as a place of refuge for them, for kids, and for anyone looking to find a little peace. Taking this away or limiting access would only negatively impact the community, ultimately signifying that art is for the elite. There are less damaging ways to mend the lives these philanthropists put in danger, ones that do not involve alienating an entire group from something that only benefits them. Fire cannot be fought with fire. Perhaps if members of the community became more educated about the philanthropists of the VMFA, a united effort to right the wrongs they have done could begin. ■

References

Keefe, P. (2017, October 30). The family that built an empire of pain. *The New Yorker*. [Website]. Retrieved from https://www.newyorker.com/

Kolata, G. (1987, December). The sad legacy of the Dalkon Shield. *The New York Times*. [Website]. Retrieved from http://www.nytimes.com

Markkula Center for Applied Ethics. (2009). A framework for ethical decision making. *Markkula Center for Applied Ethics*. [Website]. Retrieved from https://www.scu.edu/ethics/ethics-resources/ethical-decision-making/a-framework-for-ethical-decision-making/

Moonan, W. (2007, February 3). Collections of noble silver in three U.S. exhibitions. *The New York Times*. [Website]. Retrieved from https://www.nytimes.com

Parnell, S. (2017). In defense of philanthropic freedom." *Alliance for Charitable Reform*. [Website]. Retrieved from http://acreform.org/charitable-deduction/indefenseofphilanthropicfreedom/

Raymond A. Mason School of Business. (2017). About the McGlothlins. *Raymond A. Mason School of Business*. [Website]. Retrieved from http://mason.wm.edu/mcglothlin_forum/james_mcglothlin/index.php

Shapley, P. (2010). Pollution from power plants. *Sources and Effects of Air Pollution in the U.S.* [Website]. Retrieved from http://butane.chem.uiuc.edu/pshapley/environmental/l17/1.html

Stoner, L. (2008). A guide to the A. H. Robins Company records, 1885–2004. [Website]. Retrieved from http://www.vahistorical.org/collections-and-resources/how-we-can-help-your-research/re searcher-resources/finding-aids/ah-robins

──────────────────────**STUDENT PROFILE**

Theresa Castellucci is currently a second-year student at VCU, majoring in Kinetic Imaging with a minor in Computer Science. She wrote "Philanthropy Catastrophe: An Ethical Discussion of Philanthropy in the Virginia Museum of Fine Arts" for UNIV 111 last winter (2017). In her spare time, she enjoys writing, reading, and playing music.

Ethical Reasoning in the Workplace

By Kelsy Boyle

2ND PLACE—RESEARCHED ARGUMENT

2

As a kid, I had always looked up to and valued the National Parks Service (NPS), so naturally, I was pretty excited for my summer job as part of the maintenance crew at a local park. Unfortunately, my enthusiasm slowly died away when I was placed with employees that did everything in their power to avoid working. After spending forty hours a week with these people, I came to develop a unique friendship with them, but I was always bothered by their behavior on the job. They'd constantly waste time cruising around in our truck, people watching, and always stretched our breaks as long as possible. Our workday started at 7 a.m., but they'd often sit around chatting with their morning coffee for at least an hour before making any moves to get out into the field. We were also told not to go anywhere outside of the park grounds, especially not while in the government vehicle, but they would occasionally sneak off to buy themselves a hamburger in town. I wasn't necessarily excited about working either, but I couldn't help feeling a sense of responsibility to work efficiently when I was on the clock. I found it frustrating that the NPS was being represented by lousy employees such as these, and worried when the condition of facilities suffered due to our inattention. I wanted to help change the situation, but wasn't sure what to do or say. The last thing I wanted to do was ruin the friendship between us or damage the work environment. Being the newest and lowest ranking employee, I was afraid to do anything that might upset the workplace.

There are several important stakeholders to consider in this situation. The first is myself because depending on how I choose to act, I could lose the friendship with my co-workers and become isolated from the work community. My co-workers are also at stake for losing their jobs if I choose to expose their behavior to a higher authority. This could even occur if I stay silent because they could receive complaints from others due to their unproductivity. They are also harming themselves by failing to perform to their fullest potential, thus damaging the chance for advancement in their career. Another stakeholder is our supervisor, who may be harmed by being perceived a poor representative of the NPS. The general public's ability to enjoy NPS land in its best state is at stake here as well. Visitor dissatisfaction due to poor conditions of the park's grounds and facilities could potentially harm the reputation of the NPS itself, making it another major stakeholder in this situation. Finally, taxpayers and donors to the NPS are affected because their contributions are helping to pay the salaries of indolent employees such as my co-workers.

In this situation, I have several options for approaching the problem: do nothing, confront my co-workers, tell my supervisor about the situation, or lead by example and work hard myself. Staying silent is certainly the most tempting option to follow, considering that it won't result in any harm that I would be responsible for. Although I wouldn't see any direct damage from my passive action, I would be violating the Virtues approach to ethical reasoning by not being the best version of myself. This would entail having the courage to actively seek a solution to this issue as well as striving to be the best employee I can be. Additionally, by choosing to do nothing, my unproductive co-workers will continue to inhibit the NPS' ability to serve society at its fullest potential. This directly goes against the Common Good approach, which aims to support the good of the community.

This approach of prioritizing the NPS' full benefits to the world would call for the action of directly confronting my co-workers, even if it means an end to the friendship between us. There is no way to predict what their response may be, but it is plausible that they'll empathize with my thoughts and begin to work harder on the job. Assuming this is the result, their increased productivity will further empower the NPS to fulfil their promise to "protect and restore ecosystems, preserve and conserve cultural resources, provide visitors with venues for physical activity and natural experiences, and assist states and local communities in developing recreational sites and facilities and preserve historic assets" (Fiscal 1). These actions are extremely valuable to the common good and come at a very small cost. According to a taxpayer receipt, "A typical American shells out more for one movie than their annual income taxes contribute to the NPS" (Repanshek). Due to such low funding received from Congress, they've suffered budget shortfalls forcing them to delay $11.5 billion in maintenance (Josephson). At times like these, the NPS depends on productive employees to help make their goals a reality. In the interest of society as a whole, it is best for me to speak directly to my co-workers in an attempt to improve their performance on the job.

This goal could also possibly be achieved by talking to my boss instead, which would be supported by the Justice approach. The current situation is unfair considering my co-workers are being paid sufficiently for their lousy work, while others work harder and more efficiently for a lower compensation. According to a study by the Heritage Foundation, "federal employees receive 22 percent higher wages than similar workers in the private sector" (Grezler and Sherk). By talking to a higher authority, there would be a greater chance of eliminating this injustice in America's workforce. This option for action, however, may not be as effective as one may think: "Just 0.5% of federal civilian workers a year get fired for any reason, including poor performance and misconduct. That rate is just one-sixth of the private-sector firing rate" (Edwards). If I were to expose my coworker's behavior to my boss, it is unlikely that any direct action would result. Instead, it may backfire and damage work relations. *The Federal Viewpoint Survey* showed that in 2016, only 41% of employees believed their senior leaders generated high levels of motivation and commitment in the workforce, and just 53% had a high level of respect for their organization's senior leaders (*Federal*, 6, 21). That said, involving our boss in the situation would likely deepen existing disrespect and conflict. The relationship between myself and my co-workers would also likely be damaged because I would be seen as a "tattletale" or "traitor" for turning them in. This may cause deeper consequences because respectful coworker relationships are vital in the workplace and prove to have a positive correlation to an employee's overall quality of work life and wellbeing (Nilgün 577). Considering these sources, choosing to involve my boss may fight existing injustices in the workforce as a whole but will risk negatively impacting our immediate work environment.

Looking through the lens of other methods in ethical reasoning, the option to lead by example aligns with the Virtues, Utilitarian, and Moral Rights approaches. Rather than doing nothing, I would be acting as my best self by possessing the courage to act against the behavior of my co-workers, whatever the result may be. I would also be challenging myself and earning a more rewarding job during my time with the NPS. The Utilitarian approach would apply here as well since this action is peaceful, indirect, and unassertive. No one is likely to take offense, and no group or individual will be harmed by my behavior. Overall, this action causes more good than harm. Following the Moral Rights approach, my co-workers would be provided with the right to decide for themselves what kind of life to lead. Additionally, I'm claiming my right to freedom of thought and expression. In other words, I may say and act as I like, regardless of my coworker's behavior. This action presents several benefits, but it fails to guarantee an instantaneous change in the situation.

After considering all of the options for action, the last, to lead by example, is what I would choose in response to the situation. This strategy aligns with three of the five ethical approaches and is shown to be successful in many other cases in the past. For example, a scholarly study found that "Regardless of whether leadership is exogenous or endogenous, leading by example outperforms leading by words. Groups are best off if there is a leader who leads by example, and they should strive to impose one" (Dannenberg 83). The benefits of this option are also reiterated in the article "How to Handle a Slacker Colleague" when the author states, "The best possible strategy for any workplace challenge is to treat a crisis as an opportunity. Where others might see an underperforming team forcing you to stay late and grind hard, you should see a chance to show your superiors that you are reliable, hardworking and a natural leader" (Kress). Kress warns against giving in to the poor behavior of colleagues, and advises us to "[b]e polite and not judgmental in your refusal so that you don't create enemies, but don't be afraid to pave your own route to success, even though it may look like more fun to hang out with everyone else." ■

Works Cited

Avci, Nilgün. "The Relationship between Coworker Supports, Quality of Work Life and Wellbeing: An Empirical Study of Hotel Employees." *International Journal of Management Economics & Business*, vol. 13, no. 3, July 2017, pp. 577–589. *EBSCOhost*, doi:10.17130/ijmeb.2017331328.

Dannenberg, Astrid. "Leading by Example Versus Leading by Words in Voluntary Contribution Experiments." *Social Choice & Welfare*, vol. 44, no. 1, Jan. 2015, pp. 71–85. *EBSCOhost*, doi:10.1007/s00355-014-0817-8.

Edwards, Chris. "Reforming Federal Worker Pay and Benefits." *Downsizing the Federal Government*, 20 Sept. 2017, downsizinggovernment.org/federal-worker-pay. Accessed 1 Dec. 2017.

Federal Employee Viewpoint Survey. United States Office of Personnel Management, fedview.opm.gov/2017FILES/2017_FEVS_Gwide_Final_Report.PDF. Accessed 2 Dec. 2017.

Fiscal Year 2016 Budget Justifications. National Parks Service, Department of Interior, United States. nps.gov/aboutus/upload/FY-2016-Greenbook.pdf. Accessed 2 Dec. 2017.

Greszler, Rachel, and James Sherk. "Why It Is Time to Reform Compensation for Federal Employees." *The Heritage Foundation*, 27 July 2016, downsizinggovernment.org/federal-worker-pay. Accessed 1 Dec. 2017.

Josephson, Amelia. "The Economics of National Parks." *SmartAsset*, 1 Jan. 2016, smartasset.com/taxes/the-economics-of-national-parks. Accessed 2 Dec. 2017.

Kress, R. "How to Handle a Slacker Colleague." *Ivy Exec Blog*, 24 July 2016, ivyexec.com/executive-insights/2016/handle-slacker-colleague/. Accessed 1 Dec. 2017.

Repanshek, Kurt. "A Typical American's Income Tax Contribution Towards National Parks Is Little More Than The Cost of A Latte." *National Parks Traveller*, 22 Nov. 2010, nationalparkstraveler.org/2010/11/typical-americans-income-tax-contribution-towards-national-parks-little-more-cost-latte7254. Accessed 1 Dec. 2017.

STUDENT PROFILE

Kelsy Boyle is currently an Art Foundation student entering the Graphic Design program. She is originally from the mountains of North Carolina, where she enjoys backpacking, mountain biking, and skiing.

AUTHOR AND
TITLE INDEX

Acknowledgements

(Continued from page ii)

American Press Insitute—"'Who Shared It?': How Americans Decide What News to Trust on Social Media." https://www.americanpressinstitute.org/publications/reports/survey-research/trust-social-media/. Reprinted by permission of the publisher.

Darran Anderson—"Story of Cities #future: What Will Our Growing Megacities Really Look Like?" *The Guardian.* Reprinted by permission of the The Guardian.

Lesley Nneka Arimah—"What It Means When a Man Falls from the Sky." *What It Means When a Man Falls from the Sky.* Reprinted by permission of Penguin Random House. Any third party use of this material, outside of this publication, is prohibited. Interested parties must apply directly to Penguin Random House LLC for permission.

Davarian L. Baldwin—"When Universities Swallow Cities." *The Chronicle of Higher Education*, Vol. 63, No. 42. Reprinted by permission of © 2017; permission conveyed through Copyright Clearance Center, Inc.

Laurel Johnson Black—"Stupid Rich Bastards." *This Fine Place So Far From Home: Voices of Academics from the Working Class*, edited by C. L. Barney Dews and Carolyn Leste Law. Used by permission of Temple University Press. © 1995 by Temple University. All rights reserved.

Roger Bonair-Agard—"In defense of the code-switch or why you talk like that or why you gotta always be cussing." *The Breakbeat Poets: New American Poetry in the Age of Hip-Hop*, eds. Kevin Coval, Quraysh Ali Lansana, and Nate Marshall. Used by permission of the author.

William Booth and Sufian Taha—"A Palestinian's Daily Commute through an Israeli Checkpoint." From *The Washington Post*, May 25, 2017. © 2017 The Washington Post. All rights reserved. Used by permission and protected by the Copyright Laws of the United States. The printing, copying, redistribution, or retransmission of this Content without express permission is prohibited.

Garnette Cadogan——"Black and Blue." from *Freeman's Arrival.* Copyright © 2015. Reprinted from *The Fire This Time: A New Generation Speaks about Race*, edited by Jesmyn Ward (Scribner 2016), by permission of the author.

Rachel Carson—Excerpts from *Silent Spring.* Copyright © 1962 by Rachel L. Carson, renewed 1990 by Roger Christie. Reprinted by permission of Houghton Mifflin Harcourt Publishing Company. All rights reserved.

Tiana Clark—"Nashville." *I Can't Talk About the Trees Without the Blood*, © 2018. Reprinted by permission of the University of Pittsburgh Press.

Conference on College Composition and Communication—"Students' Right to Their Own Language." Appeared as a special issue of *College Composition and Communication*, Fall, 1974, Vol. XXV.

William Cronon—"The Trouble with Wilderness; or, Getting Back to the Wrong Nature." From *Uncommon Ground*, edited by William Cronon. Copyright © 1995 by William Cronon. Used by permission of W. W. Norton & Company, Inc.

Delegates to FNPCELS—"Principles of Environmental Justice." Reprinted, by permission, from *Proceedings: The First National People of Color Environmental Leadership Summit, Principles of Environmental Justice*, October 1991, Charles Lee, ed., 1992. Copyright 1991 by United Church of Christ Commission for Racial Justice: New York (now Justice and Witness Ministries, a Covenanted Ministry of the United Church of Christ, Cleveland, Ohio).

Ceridwen Dovey—"The Mapping of Massacres." *The New Yorker*. © 2015 by Condé Nast.

Patricia Engel—"La Ciudad Mágica." *Tales of Two Americas: Stories of Inequality in a Divided Nation*. Copyright © 2017 by Patricia Engel. Reprinted by permission of the author.

Claude S. Fischer—"The Great Settling Down." *Aeon*. https://aeon.co/essays/the-increasingly-mobile-us-is-a-myth-that-needs-to-move-on. Reprinted by permission of Aeon Media Group Limited © 2016.

Max Fisher—"The Dividing of a Continent: Africa's Separatist Problem." *The Atlantic*. https://www.theatlantic.com/international/archive/2012/09/the-dividing-of-a-continent-africas-separatist-problem/262171/. Reprinted with permission from the publisher.

Carolyn Forché—"Photograph of My Room." *The Country Between Us*. Copyright © 1981 by Carolyn Forche. Reprinted by permission of HarperCollins Publishers.

William Gibson—"Life in the Meta City." *Scientific American*, Vol. 305, Issue 3, pp. 88–89. Reprinted by permission of Scientific American, a division of Nature America, Inc. Copyright © 2011. All rights reserved.

Tom Gjelten—"Should Immigration Require Assimilation?" *The Atlantic*. https://www.theatlantic.com/politics/archive/2015/10/should-immigration-require-assimilation/406759/. Reprinted with permission from the publisher.

bell hooks—"Coming to Class Consciousness." *Where We Stand: Class Matters*. Reprinted by permission of Taylor & Francis LLC Books © 2000, www.tandfonline.com; permission conveyed through Copyright Clearance Center, Inc.

Carlo Invernizzi-Accetti—"A Small Italian Town Can Teach the World How to Defuse Controversial Monuments." *The Guardian*. Reprinted by permission of the The Guardian.

Kate Jeffery—"Maps in the Head." *Aeon.* https://aeon.co/essays/how-cognitive-maps-help-animals-navigate-the-world. Reprinted by permission of Aeon Media Group Limited © 2017.

Josée Johnston, Alexandra Rodney, and Michelle Szabo—"Place, Ethics, and Everyday Eating: A Tale of Two Neighbourhoods." *Sociology*, Vol. 46, No. 6 (December 2012), pp. 1091–1108. Reprinted by permission of Sage Publications Ltd. © 2012; permission conveyed through Copyright Clearance Center, Inc.

Jocelyn Kaiser—"The Dirt on Ocean Garbage Patches." *Science*, Vol. 328, No. 5985 (June 2010), p. 1506. Reprinted by permission of the American Association for the Advancement of Science © 2010; permission conveyed through Copyright Clearance Center, Inc.

Gwyn Kirk and Margo Okazawa-Rey—"Who Am I? Who Are My People?" *Women's Lives: Multicultural Perspectives.* Reprinted by permission of McGraw-Hill Education © 2001.

Yusef Komunyakaa—"Facing It." *Pleasure Dome: New and Collected Poems.* Copyright © 2001 by Yusef Komunyakaa. Published by Wesleyan University Press. Used by permission of the publisher.

Ursula K. Le Guin—"The Ones Who Walk Away from Omelas." Copyright © by Ursula K. Le Guin. First appeared in *New Dimensions 3* in 1973, and then in *The Wind's Twelve Quarters.* Published by HarperCollins in 1975. Reprinted by permission of Curtis Brown, Ltd.

Bill Lohmann—"New Monuments Honor People Forced from Their Homes to Make Way for Shenandoah National Park." *Richmond-Times Dispatch.* Reprinted by permission of the publisher.

Andrew Marantz—"When an App Is Called Racist." *The New Yorker.* © 2015 by Condé Nast.

Michael N. Mautner—"Life-Centered Ethics, and the Human Future in Space." *Bioethics*, Vol. 23, No. 8 (2009), pp. 433–440. Reprinted by permission of John Wiley & Sons Inc. © 2009; permission conveyed through Copyright Clearance Center, Inc.

Ted V. McAllister—"Making American Places: Civic Engagement Rightly Understood." *Why Place Matters*, editors Wilfred McClay and Ted V. McAllister. Encounter Books. Reprinted by permission of The New Atlantis © 2014.

Wilfred M. McClay—"Introduction." *Why Place Matters*, editors Wilfred McClay and Ted V. McAllister. Encounter Books. Reprinted by permission of The New Atlantis © 2014.

Richard McGuire—"Here." *Raw,* Vol. 2., No. 1. (1989). Reprinted by permission of the author on behalf of Wylie Agency.

China Miéville—"The Limits of Utopia." Originally published in *Salvage*. http://salvage.zone/mieville_all.html. Used by permission of the publisher.

NASA—"Outer Space Treaty of 1967." Found at https://history.nasa.gov/1967treaty.html. In the public domain.

The New York City Council—Res 1723-2008: "Resolution Declaring a Symbolic Ban on the Negative Use of the Word 'Ghetto.'" Found at http://legistar.council.nyc.gov/ViewReport.ashx?M=R&N=Text&GID=61&ID=485836&GUID=5E1F E8E2-E214-4555-8AF9-C3E435E4052E&Title=Legislation+Text

Katie Nodjimbadem—"The Racial Segregation of American Cities Was Anything But Accidental." *Smithsonianmag.com*. Copyright 2017 Smithsonian Institution. Reprinted with permission from Smithsonian Enterprises. All rights reserved. Reproduction in any medium is strictly prohibited without permission from Smithsonian Institution.

Sharon Olds—"Alcatraz." *Strike Sparks*. Reprinted by permission of Penguin Random House. Any third party use of this material, outside of this publication, is prohibited. Interested parties must apply directly to Penguin Random House LLC for permission.

Brian Palmer—"For the Forgotten African-American Dead." from *The New York Times*, Jan. 8 © 2017 by The New York Times. All rights reserved. Used by permission and protected by the Copyright Laws of the United States. The printing, copying, redistribution, or retransmission of this Content without express permission is prohibited.

William Rathje and Cullen Murphy—Excerpt from "Yes, Wonderful Things." *Rubbish! The Archaeology of Garbage*. Reprinted by permission of University of Arizona Press © 2001; permission conveyed through Copyright Clearance Center, Inc.

Ben Rawlence—"Story of Cities #44: Will Dadaab, the World's Largest Refugee Camp, Really Close?" *The Guardian*. Reprinted by permission of the The Guardian.

Christine Rosen—"The New Meaning of Mobility." *The New Atlantis*, April 2011, issue 31, pp. 40–46. Reprinted by permission of The New Atlantis © 2011.

Edward W. Said—"Invention, Memory, and Place." *Critical Inquiry*, Vol. 26, No. 2. Reprinted by permission of University of Chicago Press Journals © 2000; permission conveyed through Copyright Clearance Center, Inc.

Gary Snyder—"Riprap." *Riprap and Cold Mountain Poems*. Copyright © 1958, 1959, 1965 by Gary Snyder. Reprinted by permission of Counterpoint Press.

Rebecca Solnit—"Detroit Arcadia." *The Encyclopedia of Trouble and Spaciousness*. Reprinted by permission of Trinity University Press © 2014; permission conveyed through Copyright Clearance Center, Inc.

Mark Strand—"Keeping Things Whole." *Selected Poems*. Copyright © 1979, 1980 by Mark Strand. Reprinted by permission of Penguin Random House. Any third party use of this material, outside of this publication, is prohibited. Interested parties must apply directly to Penguin Random House LLC for permission.

Konrad Szocik, et al.—"Political and Legal Challenges in a Mars Colony." *Space Policy*, Vol. 38. Reprinted by permission of Elsevier © 2016; permission conveyed through Copyright Clearance Center, Inc.

Haunani-Kay Trask—"'Lovely Hula Hands': Corporate Tourism and the Prostitution of Hawaiian Culture." *From a Native Daughter: Colonialism and Sovereignty in Hawaii*. Copyright © 1999 University of Hawaii Press. Used by permission of University of Hawaii Press.

UNESCO—Decision: 39 COM 7A.27, "Old City of Jerusalem and Its Walls." From https://whc.unesco.org/en/decisions/6243.

Katherine D. Walker—"Buried in the Unremissive Ground." *Social Semiotics*, Vol. 19, No. 4. Reprinted by permission of Taylor & Francis Ltd © 2009, www.tandfonline.com; permission conveyed through Copyright Clearance Center, Inc.

Claire Vaye Watkins—"Some Houses (Various Stages of Dissolve)." From *Tales of Two Americas: Stories of Inequality in a Divided Nation*, ed. John Freeman, New York: Penguin, 2017, pp. 79–88. Reprinted with permission from the author and Aragi, Inc.

Michael Paul Williams—"Henrico Should Expand Mass Transit to Short Pump, and Here's Why." *Richmond-Times Dispatch*. Reprinted by permission of the publisher.